CRIMINAL LITIGATION

CRIMINAL LITIGATION

Craig Osborne BA, MA (Econ), Solicitor

BLACKSTONE
PRESS LIMITED

First published in Great Britain 1993 by Blackstone Press Limited, Aldine Place, London W12 8AA. Telephone: 0181-740 2277

First edition 1993
Reprinted 1993
Second edition 1994
Third edition 1995
Fourth edition 1996
Fifth edition 1997

ISBN: 1 85431 648 6

British Library Cataloguing in Publication Data
A CIP catalogue record for this book is available from the British Library.

Typeset by Montage Studios Limited, Tonbridge, Kent
Printed by Ashford Colour Press, Gosport, Hampshire

CONTENTS

PREFACE

PREFACE

This book is intended to be a 'legal resource book' for the Legal Practice Course in Criminal Litigation. It deals with all aspects of the written standards produced by the Law Society for that course but it is my intention to go well beyond them. It is intended to be a legal resource book in the fullest sense, being a full and self-contained treatment of the relevant aspects of mainstream criminal practice. It includes not merely details of criminal procedure but also the law of evidence and practical and tactical considerations in dealing with clients and the criminal courts. Students will of course derive advantage from referring from time to time to other texts, in particular, the statutes or cases referred to in this text.

The content of a book on criminal litigation is perhaps rather less contentious than one on civil litigation, where strong differences of opinion may arise about what should or should not be included at a certain level. In the present text I have included a chapter on the European Convention on Human Rights and Fundamental Freedoms which the Law Society, rightly, stresses as being a vital part of the armoury of all litigation practitioners. Notwithstanding that at present the contribution of cases under the Convention to the annual fee income of the average practitioner is minimal, the Convention's importance as a weapon of last resort and a means of righting injustices, especially for those caught up in the criminal justice system, cannot be overemphasised. That is the justification for the rather lengthy discussion of the origins and practice and procedure of the organs of the Council of Europe which implement the European Convention.

This edition has been written on the basis that the provisions of the Criminal Procedure and Investigations Act 1996, all the most important of which came into force in April 1997, are effective in relation to current criminal prosecutions. In fact this is not entirely accurate because the procedural and other provisions of the Act only apply to 'criminal investigations' which commenced after 1 April 1997. For a long time therefore, in reality, there will be two procedural systems running alongside — one in relation to those offences whose investigation began before 1 April 1997 and the other to those after that date. It seemed preferable, rather than risk causing confusion by the description of different systems, to concentrate on the one which will overwhelmingly be that applicable for the students reading this book as and when they first become involved in criminal practice. There is the briefest mention of 'full' committal proceedings in their pre-April 1997 format and also sufficient introduction to the previous case law on prosecution disclosure of unused material to give at least some indication of the preceding practice.

A greater difficulty was caused by the Crime (Sentences) Act 1997 passed late in the life of the last government. Whilst most of the provisions in this Act did not lead to any great opposition objection, the issue of the various parties' postures on law and order perhaps being relevant at the time, certain of the provisions, in particular those relating to mandatory and minimum custodial sentences, have evoked a great deal of judicial criticism and anxiety. At the time of writing none of the provisions of the 1997 Act has been brought into force. Some of its provisions may well be duplicated or amended by legislation which the Labour government is intending to bring in during the autumn, particularly relating to juvenile offenders in what at present appears likely to be called the Crime and Public Disorder Bill. It remains to be seen whether the Crime (Sentences) Act 1997 will be brought into force at all and, if so, when. For that reason, although it will affect the practice of the courts substantially, an outline only is given at the end of **Chapter 10**.

I have been grateful throughout for the enthusiasm, commitment and professionalism of the publishers and particularly to Paula Doolan, the managing editor of this series.

I am very grateful to the Magistrates' Association for permission to reproduce the two examples of sentencing guidelines.

Craig Osborne
July 1997

TABLE OF CASES

TABLE OF STATUTES

PART I
CRIMINAL PROCEDURE

ONE

AN OUTLINE OF CRIMINAL PROCEDURE: EARLY STAGES

1.1 The Course of Criminal Proceedings

In order to show in simple form the course of criminal proceedings, a very brief preliminary outline of the progress of a criminal prosecution will be given here.

1.1.1 POLICE INVESTIGATIONS

After a crime has been committed it will be investigated by the police and unless the offender has been apprehended at the scene of the crime, detection work of various kinds may occur until the police have a suspect. They have powers of arrest and search and the right to interrogate. They may also, for example, hold an identity parade, obtain fingerprints, and so on. We will then assume that they consider they know who committed the offence.

1.1.2 PROSECUTING THE SUSPECT

The police then have an option to proceed against the suspect in one of two ways:

(a) causing a *summons* to be issued against the suspect; or

(b) *charging* the suspect.

The first option would be more likely in the case of routine or trivial crime such as driving offences. In such situations the accused may well have been apprehended at the scene of the crime. He will usually be released there and then and told that he may later be prosecuted. Subsequently, the police will adopt a procedure known as *laying an information* before a magistrates' court and a summons will be issued against the suspect. The prosecution will then be taken over by the Crown Prosecution Service (CPS) and will come before the courts where it may be dealt with on the first occasion or adjourned for a variety of reasons depending on which course the case takes.

Alternatively, the accused may have been arrested by the police and actually *charged* at the police station. In this case the charge sheet which notifies the charge will specify the date on which the accused is to appear before the magistrates' court. The decision on whether or not to charge is normally that of the arresting and investigating officers, sometimes after consultation with the CPS. A charge is the appropriate form of prosecution for more serious offences. At the time of charging, the police will also have to make the decision about whether to allow the suspect bail pending his or her first appearance in court or whether to keep the suspect in custody until that time. If the police keep a suspect in custody then they have a duty to produce him or her to a court as soon as reasonably practicable, which usually means at the start of the next working day's business so that the court may consider questions of bail. If a suspect is released pending first appearance then the date of the first appearance is likely to be in some weeks' time.

1.1.3 PROCEDURE IN THE MAGISTRATES' COURT

With very few exceptions, not relevant at present, all prosecutions commence in the magistrates' court. Offences may broadly be classified into three types for procedural purposes:

(a) Those that are triable *purely summarily*, i.e. those of relative triviality where only a magistrates' court has jurisdiction (e.g., careless driving).

(b) Those triable only *on indictment* in the Crown Court before a judge and jury, i.e. those offences too serious to be tried by magistrates (e.g., murder, rape).

(c) Those offences which may be more or less serious depending on a variety of circumstances including inter alia the degree of violence (e.g., assaults) or the amount involved (e.g., theft). These offences are known as *'either way'* offences.

In the case of these latter offences there needs to be a decision as to which court, magistrates' court or Crown Court, will try the case.

In the case of purely summary offences, when the accused person appears before the magistrates' court it is unlikely that the case will be dealt with at the first appearance if the accused is pleading not guilty. This is because of the expense of calling witnesses and preparing the case fully which can be avoided if the accused pleads guilty. Thus if he pleads guilty he will be dealt with then and there, if he pleads not guilty the case will be adjourned for trial at some later date. In the case of some offences (mainly motoring offences) the accused may be offered the opportunity to plead guilty by post without attending court.

In the case of an offence triable either way the court has to decide on the *mode of trial*. It will hear representations about what factors relevant to the offence make it more suitable that the accused should be tried in either the magistrates' court or the Crown Court, and the magistrates' court will then decide. However, whilst the magistrates' court may decide to send the case to the Crown Court for trial, if it decides that it is willing to try it then, in the case of 'either way' offences, the accused always has the power to overrule the court and insist on the right to jury trial.

In the case of offences which are triable purely on indictment or those triable either way which are being taken to the Crown Court, there is a preliminary stage known as 'committal for trial'. This involves a magistrates' court examining the prosecution case to see whether it discloses a prima facie case for trial in the Crown Court. Until recently this might well involve witnesses attending court, giving evidence and being cross-examined about the facts, but following changes introduced by the Criminal Procedure and Investigations Act 1996 there is now merely an examination by the magistrates of documentary evidence tendered by the prosecution only and witnesses are not called to give oral evidence (see **8.1**).

At any stage of this procedure, questions of bail, legal aid and adjournment may arise. The magistrates' court has the power to adjourn a case at any time and when it does so it will sometimes be required to consider how to deal with the accused during the adjournment, for example, whether or not to allow him bail. The magistrates' court will also often have to decide whether an accused is entitled to legal aid.

The accused will be tried in the magistrates' court or committed for trial to the Crown Court. At the end of his trial in either court, if he is convicted, matters of sentencing and mitigation will arise.

In this book we shall be describing the usual procedures in English criminal courts. However, it should be noted that to some degree procedures may vary locally. For example, magistrates' clerks may take certain decisions under delegated powers without ever referring the matter to the magistrates. These decisions largely concern issues on which there are no disputes such as aspects of bail or whether an adjournment is to be granted. Likewise some magistrates' courts have been keener than others to address particular procedural problems, e.g., the way in which cases are listed. Efforts to devise a listing system which works efficiently have hitherto been hampered by uncertainty as to how long a case may take since its duration may depend on last minute decisions by the defendant. Consequently, there have been inherent difficulties in fixing how many cases should be allocated to a given day's list. For one or other reason, magistrates may sometimes be left with nothing to do by mid-morning while on other days the list will be so heavy with cases involving substantial areas of dispute that it is impossible to deal with every case listed. Some magistrates' courts have now taken the initiative to address this problem by putting in place local arrangements to assist their clerks to get better information as to the course which proceedings may take. Other magistrates' courts have instituted systems for 'pre-trial reviews' so that where it is clear that a case is to be contested before the magistrates, there is a chance for the parties to disclose their intentions to each other and attempt to agree how long the case is likely to last and what form it may take. Where these arrangements apply they are entirely informal and can only exist with the consent of all parties because there is no mechanism for the magistrates' court to insist upon this kind of cooperation. Often courts have made these arrangements after lengthy consultations with local criminal practitioners through their local Law Society.

To the extent therefore that these kind of features exist, the standard course which criminal proceedings take may have local variations.

1.2 Professional Ethics

1.2.1 DUTIES OF THE PROSECUTOR

In principle a prosecutor has a duty to act as a minister of justice and to see that all relevant facts and law are before the courts. He should not strive for a conviction at any price and should indeed even present matters favourable to the defendant. Other aspects of this principle are that the prosecution generally play no part at the sentencing stage and do not as in other countries press for any particular sentence or for the defendant to be dealt with severely; nor do they present facts in emotive language.

The prosecution have a specific duty to make available to the defence by way of 'primary disclosure' material which has not previously been disclosed and which in the prosecutor's opinion might assist the defendant in various ways. This was formerly a common law duty originating in case law and then subsequently under guidelines issued by the Attorney-General which appeared at [1982] 1 All ER 734. Case law in the early part of this decade, particularly *R v Ward* [1993] 1 WLR 619 and *R v Keane* [1994] 1 WLR 746, further refined the prosecution's duties. Those common law requirements have now been superseded by the Criminal Procedure and Investigations Act 1996 and Codes of Practice issued under s. 23 of that Act, which came into force in April 1997. The 1996 Act applies in both magistrates' courts and the Crown Court. For fuller discussion see **9.6**. In addition there is a Code for Crown Prosecutors published by the CPS which sets out various considerations appropriate for a Crown Prosecutor in respect of the commencement and course of a prosecution including evidential and ethical matters.

1.2.2   DUTIES OF THE DEFENCE SOLICITOR

The defence solicitor has a basic duty to do what is best for his client but in addition has an overriding duty not to mislead the court. Within these confines however he must act as vigorously as possible in his client's interests even if he privately believes him to be guilty.

It is appropriate here to consider a number of aspects of the defence solicitor's duties.

1.2.2.1   Confidentiality

A solicitor may not reveal anything which the client has told him while the solicitor–client relationship exists, without the client's proper authority. One aspect of this is that in the magistrates' court a solicitor is under no obligation to give the prosecution any advance warning of the nature of his client's defence to a charge. He is entitled to maintain the secrecy of this, in principle until the defence case opens, although usually it will be necessary to indicate the nature of the defence case when cross-examining prosecution witnesses. However, the accused's general 'right to silence' has now been affected by the fact that under the Criminal Justice and Public Order Act 1994 a suspect who does not answer reasonable questions from the police about certain matters at the outset, or who chooses not to go into the witness box at his trial, may be subject to adverse comment by the judge and prosecuting counsel during his trial, and to that extent the principle that a defendant may keep silent throughout has been infringed. It nevertheless remains the case that it does not amount to any separate offence for a suspect to maintain silence. There are also three instances where the prosecution are entitled to some notice of matters relevant to the defence case.

(a)   Under s. 81, Police and Criminal Evidence Act 1984, a person who proposes to rely on *expert evidence* in a criminal trial must give advance disclosure of this to the opposition.

(b)   Following the coming into force of s. 5 of the Criminal Procedure and Investigations Act 1996, there is a requirement for the accused, in a Crown Court trial, to give a 'defence statement' to the court and the prosecutor, setting out in general terms the nature of his defence and indicating the matters on which he takes issue with the prosecution and why. If the defence statement involves an alibi, then he must give appropriate particulars of that alibi. Failure to give this disclosure, for example by an accused not putting forward any defence statement or at trial embarking on a completely different line of defence to that which was in his statement, will lead to the prosecution, with the leave of the court, being able to make adverse comment and is likely to lead to the judge inviting the jury to draw appropriate inferences from the failure of the accused to put forward his defence at the appropriate time.

In the magistrates' court by virtue of s. 6 of the 1996 Act the giving of a 'defence statement' is voluntary and may not lead to adverse inferences, but it may still be tactically desirable for the reasons discussed in 7.6.

(c)   *Matters of law.* As is common throughout the criminal and civil processes, authorities to which a party intends to refer ought in principle to be disclosed to the opponent before trial.

Finally, it will be noted that unlike in the case of civil legal aid there is no requirement as such to report to the legal aid authorities, e.g., if one considers one's client is behaving unreasonably. It may be a prudent step to obtain prior authority for the incurring of major items of expenditure but even where a solicitor personally feels that his client's case is hopeless, if the latter persists in pleading not guilty there is no duty to report the matter and the solicitor may continue to represent him and do his best for him.

1.2.2.2   **A client who admits his guilt**

Where a client admits his guilt a solicitor may continue to act for him even on a not guilty plea to a limited extent. A solicitor may permit the client to plead not guilty and thereafter may do everything possible during the prosecution case, e.g., cross-examine their witnesses as vigorously as possible (provided this does not involve advancing any untruthful version of events), argue to have identification evidence excluded, and in particular, if the prosecution case depends on a confession, he may make every appropriate attempt to have the confession ruled inadmissible. Thereafter he may make a submission of no case to answer.

If however the case is not dismissed at that stage then a solicitor may not permit his client to go into the witness box or call perjured evidence. Accordingly if a client does admit his guilt it is vital for the solicitor to point out to the client that he may continue to act for the client even if he pleads not guilty, but only if he agrees not to testify or call evidence.

This aspect of acting for a client who has admitted his guilt will now be made much more difficult in a Crown Court trial by the requirement to put forward a 'defence statement' indicating the nature of the defence. A solicitor must not be party to drafting a statement which he knows to be untruthful and therefore in such a case no defence statement can be put forward and the defence will have to take the form simply of attacking the prosecution evidence in the hope of having the case dismissed by way of no case to answer. In the magistrates' court the giving of a 'defence statement' remains voluntary and therefore no equivalent problem arises at that stage.

1.2.2.3   **Knowledge of a client's previous convictions**

What if a client has previous convictions and the solicitor is aware of this but the court is not? As indicated previously a solicitor would not be permitted to let his client assert in the witness box that he was a person of good character, nor could the solicitor's conduct of the case take that path. More commonly the problem will arise after a guilty plea or conviction. When mitigating for such a client, if the prosecution have not got proper details of his criminal record or think that he has no offences recorded against him, then whilst his solicitor may not positively stress his good character he can do everything possible otherwise by way of mitigation. The solicitor can therefore leave the court to conclude that his client is of good character from the absence of criminal record but must not positively state that this is so. If on the other hand the client has adopted a false name, address or date of birth in order to deceive the court by making it difficult to link his criminal record to him, the solicitor must advise his client to give his identity properly and if there is a refusal he must withdraw from the case.

1.2.2.4   **A client who gives inconsistent instructions**

Clients often change their instructions. They may significantly change their version of much that has occurred. Here the solicitor is essentially in no different a position from when acting for a party in a civil case who gives different versions of events. So long as he is not absolutely sure that the client is positively trying to invent some version, he can still continue to act although it may be appropriate to give the client advice with regard to his plea and the risk of conviction for perjury. It is of course perfectly proper to attempt to argue that some aspect of the facts provides a defence for the client. What the solicitor must never do however, is to suggest to the client what facts might constitute a defence and thus to encourage a change of story by the client which accords with those more favourable facts.

1.2.2.5   **Interviewing prosecution witnesses**

There is no property in a witness and it is perfectly proper to interview prosecution witnesses. In the course of interviewing them no attempt should be made to put words into their mouths nor should one misrepresent whom one is, for example, by giving the person the impression that one might be a prosecution solicitor. Apart from this however, no court is likely to conclude that a respectable solicitor is trying to pervert the course of justice. It is sometimes thought appropriate to warn the prosecution of one's desire to interview their witnesses. It is doubtful whether there is any rule positively requiring this. Certainly in the converse cases when the police are checking on defence alibis they do not trouble to give the defence solicitor a chance to be present.

1.2.2.6   Conflicts of interest

It is very important when acting in a criminal case to ensure that there is no conflict of interest between co-accused. This is particularly so because in most courts where legal aid is granted to the accused there is an attempt to assign the same solicitor to each of the accused in the interest of saving time and costs. Sometimes if there is only a slight possibility of conflict of interest in such a situation and the matter is proceeding to the Crown Court, matters may be satisfactorily resolved by briefing separate counsel for each of the accused.

In criminal cases however, you should always be aware of the possibility of a conflict of interest suddenly arising. If, having taken on two clients, a conflict of interest does arise then generally it will be impossible to continue to act for either. This is because you will have received confidential information and will wish to use it in the conduct of client A's case against former client B. This might particularly be so where one of two clients changes his plea and pleads guilty, perhaps even subsequently testifying for the prosecution. In such a situation, if you would have wished to cross-examine former client B in a very vigorous manner, you would be unable to do so without breaching the duty of confidentiality and you would be hopelessly hamstrung in the conduct of client A's defence.

It should also be borne in mind that a conflict of interest may arise at the mitigation stage although there was nothing apparent at the stage when guilt was still being contested. Thus, for example, if faced with two clients who are aged say 18 and 28 and the latter has a bad criminal record, then when mitigating for the younger should they both be convicted, it might well be appropriate to suggest that he has been corrupted and led astray. This is clearly not possible if you are also acting for the elder.

Therefore, great care should always be taken to beware of a conflict of interest in a criminal case and to act appropriately where such arises. If assigned to act on legal aid for two or more co-accused you should always interview them separately. If it is then apparent after seeing the first accused that there is a possibility of conflict arising you can decline to act for the other accused then and there. If there is no such apparent conflict then you can interview the second accused. If it transpires from *his* version of events that there is a conflict, confidential information will now have been obtained from both and you cannot act for either.

Finally, you should not overlook the possibility that you may have acted for both of two co-accused on previous occasions. If there now seems to be any possibility of a conflict arising then everything will depend upon the nature of the confidential information which was obtained on those previous occasions. If the information could in any sense be used against B to A's benefit you cannot act for either.

1.3   Preliminary Considerations

In this section, we shall consider the matters which are likely to arise in the course of routine criminal proceedings. In the case of civil proceedings, there is generally no particular urgency about the issue of the writ. If the limitation period has not yet expired, then you would generally be well advised first to collect all the information relevant to liability, and possibly information relevant to quantum. In the case of civil proceedings, it may of course be possible to obtain a negotiated settlement at a very early stage, or even without the issue of proceedings at all. There is nothing that corresponds to those features in criminal practice. In criminal practice, the solicitor will usually only be consulted after proceedings have been instituted, and he has no control over when the client is likely to be brought before the court.

The one obvious exception to this is the case of a client who is suspected of an offence and may already have been interrogated at a police station but has not yet been charged. He might require advice about, say, the nature of police bail, about whether, if he returns to the police station as he has been requested to or bailed to do in a few days' time, he should consent to having his fingerprints taken or to taking part in an identification parade, and so on. More experienced criminal clients who, before the Criminal Justice and Public Order Act 1994 were well aware of their right of silence, may wish to discuss whether they should continue to maintain silence in the face of police questioning, or whether the giving of some carefully prepared exculpatory statement or even the giving of some limited assistance to the police in enquiries, might result in their not being charged at all. In this sense, therefore, you might act for a client to help him achieve the best outcome without there needing to be any court proceedings as such. (For further consideration of this see **1.3.2** below.)

In the mainstream of cases, however, the prosecution will already have been instituted and the solicitor's duty is to do the best for his client as defendant. We shall therefore consider steps to take in the conduct of a normal case, although some individual tactical considerations, e.g., whether to opt for summary trial or Crown Court trial where that choice arises, will be dealt with separately under the relevant aspects of procedure.

There are two essential preliminary matters which are likely to need consideration. The first is bail and the second is legal aid.

If, when the client comes into your office, having been charged, he has already been granted police bail, then you can generally anticipate that there will be no objection to his having continued bail from the court. This is the usual position in reality although it would be wrong to say that it can be relied on in every single case. The courts are given a broad mandate to enquire into the question of bail and the absence of a prosecution objection may not always be treated as conclusive, although cases where it is not are rare.

Exceptionally even where the police have released someone on bail, they may find, after having done so, good reason to object to bail at the first hearing. Such a case might well be where the alleged victim expresses terror at the continued freedom of the accused, or the police become suspicious that the accused may have committed offences other than the one which they were initially investigating. So bail must always be considered. However, where an accused has been released on bail, then the date of the preliminary hearing might well not be for some time.

It ought to be mentioned here that one common trait of persons charged with criminal offences is that they are not always as well organised, or systematic, as they might be, and despite the fact that they may well have been charged weeks ago they may only get around to making an appointment with a solicitor the day before the first hearing. There may thus be very little time to take preliminary steps before that hearing. This is a well-known facet of criminal litigation with which all practitioners learn to cope. It may be appropriate in cases where there seems any possible doubt to telephone the prosecution to get confirmation that no objection to bail will be raised.

The second matter that needs to be considered is legal aid. The initial interview can be given under the Green Form Scheme if the client qualifies, and a full legal aid application will need to be completed and sent to the magistrates' court, or perhaps taken round by hand if the case is to be heard in the immediate future. If the case is, for example, to be heard the next day, then it is for the solicitor to decide whether he is prepared to risk legal aid being refused, or not dealt with in time, and to continue with the case.

An option might be to send the client down to court to ask for an adjournment for the purpose of obtaining legal aid but many consider it unwise to do this. First, there is always the fear of the policeman involved in the case 'persuading' the unrepresented accused to see sense and plead guilty for his own good, and secondly, there is always the risk that the court might insist on dealing with the case, particularly if there has already been one adjournment, and might instruct the accused to seek the assistance of the duty solicitor, or some other solicitor who is within the precincts of the court, and therefore the client will be lost.

Of course, many busy criminal solicitors who practise most of the time at the same court may well be in that court the next day in connection with other matters and therefore there will be no great risk of lost costs if one agrees to see the client there to pursue his legal aid application orally if need be. Normally, if one can get the legal aid application down to the court at least a day before, that will be long enough for it to be dealt with in most urban courts.

We now turn to the other important aspects of preparing the case.

1.3.1 THE FIRST INTERVIEW

If it takes place in a police station or in custody just before a first appearance, it will inevitably be rather hurried. All one may have time to do is to find out matters relevant to a bail application. But whatever the outcome of that first meeting, subsequently there will be an opportunity to interview the client in complete privacy and at greater length. If the bail application has been successful, or no objection to bail has ever arisen, this will be in one's own office; if the bail application has been unsuccessful, it will be in the remand centre or prison. There are a number of important matters which need to be discussed with the client. These are as follows.

1.3.1.1 An objection to bail

If it is clear that there is to be an objection to bail, then the first issue, and certainly the one uppermost in the client's mind, will be this question. One must have regard to the grounds for refusing bail and the factors to be considered in assessing those grounds. (For further details see in particular 6.5.) The client's first proof of evidence therefore, whilst dealing with the background to the alleged offence in as much detail as seems appropriate, should concentrate on matters relevant to bail. If it is anticipated that the main objection is on the basis that the client is likely to abscond then details of his current address, length of residence there, other ties in the area, present work record, family ties, financial position and the like will be relevant. If the objection is that he will commit further offences, then his previous record when on bail, the nature of his previous criminal record generally, together with other factors to do with his family and work situation will be relevant. If the objection is that he will interfere with witnesses, then one must concentrate on the precise nature of the allegation that will be made and see what matters can be brought up to deal with it, in particular in this case the suggestion of bail conditions. The client should in such a case be asked what he knows about the suggestion of potential interference and what conditions he would be willing to submit to in order to avoid being remanded in custody.

Relevant to any objection to do with bail are more general details of his personal life and history. These must be obtained together with telephone contact numbers for persons who might assist with bail, e.g., friends, relatives or his employer.

Having dealt with obtaining the preliminary information for a bail application, it is then appropriate to deal with the charges brought against the client and the question of how, if he were unfortunately to be convicted, the court might deal with him. This is equally relevant whether or not the client has been given bail by the police.

1.3.1.2   The precise charges

If the client has come in to see you in your office it is commonly the case that he will have forgotten or lost his charge sheet, in which case a duplicate will need to be obtained. In such a situation you should never rely on a client's recollection of what offence has been charged. 'Theft' will all too often prove to mean 'robbery' in such circumstances. The charge sheet ought also to reveal whether he has been charged with other people, which it is vital to know.

1.3.1.3   Details of the charge

Personal details should be taken from the client and then he should be invited to give his account of the incident resulting in the charge. This is as important in the case of a criminal client as it is with a client in a civil case, or a witness in either case. The more fresh the events are in the mind of the accused, the better the statement will be. This is particularly so where some fast moving or interlinked series of events is what needs to be described, for example, precisely how a fight started, or the precise course of events at work which led to the accused being charged with theft of the employer's property. It may be that something will be thrown up which can immediately be investigated to good effect.

Many clients in criminal cases give vague or apparently unconvincing accounts of incidents. This may be because of lack of intelligence or natural diffidence. Every attempt should be made to draw the client out about his case. In some instances, kindness and sympathy may be needed for this, in others it may perhaps be better to attempt to put the client through a vigorous cross-examination about the vaguer or apparently more improbable features of his version. Everything will depend upon the circumstances and the personality of the client.

1.3.1.4   Details of the plea

All the foregoing assumes that the client is intending to plead not guilty. If he is pleading guilty, then circumstances and details relevant to a plea in mitigation need to be considered. Indeed details of these matters must also be taken from a client who denies the charge, although the collection of evidence relevant to mitigation is often left until somewhat later in the case. It must be remembered however that the likely sentence to be imposed is an important factor in a bail application. In the case of a client pleading not guilty, which is what we are primarily concerned with, once the solicitor has tested the client's own story and looked for possible leads to further avenues of enquiry (e.g., other witnesses who could be contacted), this is perhaps as much as can be done at this stage. The client should be asked to give any account he can of his own criminal record, if he has one, but as we shall see below it is most unwise to rely on this.

There will inevitably need to be another full interview with the client to discuss matters in the light of what you subsequently manage to find out about the prosecution evidence, or about lines of investigation that you have yourself pursued. If the client requires advice about how to plead it may be possible to give this at this stage or it may need to be postponed until a later stage.

1.3.1.5   Writing to the prosecution

In contrast to the position in a civil case, in a criminal case one is entitled to a certain amount of assistance from one's opponent. The prosecution is supposed not to press for conviction at any price in the full adversarial manner, but rather the Crown Prosecutor, whether solicitor or counsel, is supposed to act as 'a minister of justice' presenting facts and law impartially and fairly to the court. In the heat of the action it may be sometimes difficult for the accused or his advocate to discern this in the manner in which the Crown Prosecutor seems to be conducting the case, and one may feel that on occasions a somewhat indecent enthusiasm for the fray for its own sake may colour the Crown Prosecutor's attitude. However, at this stage anyway, the prosecution are obliged to assist the defence solicitor and a letter should be written requesting the following:

(a) A copy of the client's criminal record, if any.

(b) A copy of any written records required to be kept under the Police and Criminal Evidence Act 1984, e.g., custody records.

(c) A copy of any statement made by the client under caution.

(d) The criminal record of any co-defendant.

(e) The criminal record of any prosecution witnesses.

(f) The material which the prosecution is obliged to disclose under 'primary disclosure' by virtue of the Criminal Procedure and Investigations Act 1996 (see **9.6**).

(g) If the client has been interviewed on tape then one should ask for a copy of the tape. Many police forces prefer to supply a so-called 'balanced summary' but experience shows that these are often not an accurate reflection of the whole course of the interview and it is best to insist upon having the tape to listen to oneself.

Some of the above, especially items (e) and (f), may not be made available until much later, but there is no harm in making the formal request at this stage. If the case is proceeding to the Crown Court for trial there will be committal proceedings by which stage a set of documents containing the evidence upon which the charges are based, must be sent to the defendant's solicitors.

Furthermore, if the matter is proceeding as a summary trial and concerns an offence such as theft (i.e., an 'either way' offence — for definition see **5.3.3**), then advance information as to the facts and matters on which the prosecution propose to rely must be given to the accused, in accordance with the Magistrates' Court (Advance Information) Rules 1985. This must include a copy of the statements of the witnesses who are going to be called by the prosecution, or a summary of the evidence in those statements.

Moreover, even in the case of summary offences, then, depending upon the defending solicitor's relationship with the prosecution, the Crown Prosecutor may well be willing to let the solicitor look at copies of his witness statements in advance, no doubt in the hope that, when seeing the overwhelming nature of the case against the accused, the accused can be persuaded to plead guilty.

1.3.2 'NEGOTIATIONS'

When reasonably full information about an alleged offence and offender has been obtained, it may be appropriate to approach the prosecution to see whether they might be willing to reconsider the decision to prosecute. The Code for Crown Prosecutors to which we have already referred sets out some of the criteria on which a prosecution should be based. Thus the following factors may be relevant:

(a) *Triviality* of the offence such that, even if there is a successful conviction, the offender is bound to be dealt with leniently so that the cost of the proceedings is hardly worth the time and trouble.

(b) *Staleness*, e.g., if the offence occurred a considerable time ago then a prosecution may be oppressive.

(c) The loss or harm can be described as *minor* and was the result of a single incident, particularly if it was caused by misjudgment.

(d) The prosecution is likely to have a very bad effect on the *victim's* physical or mental *health* (always bearing in mind the seriousness of the offence).

(e) The defendant has *put right* the loss or harm that was caused (but defendants must not avoid prosecution simply because they can pay compensation).

(f) The defendant is *elderly* or is or was at the time of the offence suffering from significant mental or physical *ill health* (unless the offence is serious or there is a real possibility that it may be repeated).

(g) The offence was committed as a result of a *genuine mistake or misunderstanding* (these factors must be balanced against the seriousness of the offence).

In addition to these factors you may attempt to argue that there is insufficient evidence or that the public interest, for some other reason, does not require a prosecution. You can then concentrate on the above factors suggesting perhaps that the accused is a young adult who could be dealt with by caution rather than prosecution, that the client is elderly or infirm or that the strain of criminal proceedings may lead to a considerable worsening in the accused's mental health.

It may be that you will be able to supply the prosecution with information to support your argument, e.g., information that, say, a middle-aged defendant who appears to have acted significantly out of character was suffering a serious illness, or had experienced recent bereavement. If all or any of these things can be advanced it may be possible to persuade the prosecution to reconsider.

It may also be possible, although this is usually left until later in the procedure, to argue that a certain charge should be reduced to one of less seriousness (e.g., that what is presently charged as a robbery really only constituted theft even on the prosecution's version).

1.3.3 REINTERVIEWING THE CLIENT AND ADVISING ON PLEA

Thus in all cases you should have found out the substance of the prosecution evidence. It is then necessary to see the client again to get his comments on this evidence. At this time, it may be appropriate, in the light of all that is known about the prosecution case, to suggest to the client lines of questioning which will be put to him in cross-examination, so that he can consider how he might deal with them. This is not in any sense with a view to inviting him to think up glib answers well in advance, but genuinely to see whether he does have answers to the points that will be raised.

It may be that when the full weight of the prosecution evidence is known, the case will appear overwhelming against the client. In such a situation, the client should be questioned carefully to see whether he might not wish to plead guilty. An advocate has a difficult and delicate task here. A client ought to be given the advantage of having explained to him that a plea of guilty might, in a borderline case, make the difference between going to prison and not going to prison, especially if the nature of his defence involves a frontal attack on the truthfulness or integrity of prosecution witnesses, e.g., policemen. Such advice, however, to a client who is at the moment maintaining a not guilty plea must be tempered with the very strongest affirmation that he should not consider pleading guilty unless he actually is guilty. In other words, no attempt should be made to bully a person into pleading guilty but this must be combined with the realistic advice on sentence previously referred to.

It is at this stage, where the whole of the evidence is being reviewed, that the client should be taken through any previous convictions and be asked to explain something of the background to each of the offences, or those which are most recent. We will return to this in the section on sentencing and mitigation later, but the point is that it may well be that something can be said to make an apparently bad criminal record look at least a little better. For example, some of the offences may have occurred at a time when the accused had a drug addiction, since cured, and stole to finance the habit. This is obviously a matter which might, in the eyes of some courts, present some explanation for an apparently consistent course of criminal conduct.

The client should also be told in general terms about the need for there to be a 'defence statement' if the case is likely to go to the Crown Court for trial and preliminary steps should be taken with a view to preparing it (see **9.6.4**).

1.3.4   OTHER STEPS

In the light of all the information obtained from the accused, one will need to consider other steps — it is very much a matter of 'feel' whether one does this immediately after the first interview or somewhat later in the light of having seen some of the prosecution evidence steps. These may briefly be summarised as follows:

(a)   Consider interviewing other witnesses as soon as possible. If these are prosecution witnesses already, as previously indicated, it is normally considered courteous to inform the prosecution that you propose to do this, although there is in fact no property in a witness and it ought not to be considered an attempt to interfere with the course of justice to want to interview a witness.

(b)   Consider whether expert evidence (e.g., a psychiatrist's report on the accused) is needed. This is unlikely in a routine case.

(c)   If the location where an event happened is material, visit it so that you can gain a clear picture. It may even be desirable to take photographs or make a plan. For example, if a fight broke out in the confines of a crowded public house, then a plan of the layout of the public house might assist. If the matter is a driving offence, just as in the case of a civil action involving a road accident, it may be appropriate to make plans, or take photographs of the scene, to enable the court to get a full picture of the layout of the road junction etc. In this connection also, you should ask the accused to show you his driving licence to ensure that actual endorsements correspond to his criminal record.

1.3.5   CALLING WITNESSES

It is perhaps useful here to summarise the ways in which witnesses may be called before magistrates' courts and the Crown Court.

(a)   In the magistrates' court, a *witness summons* is obtained from the clerk to the justices. This is done by attending in person, or writing a letter requesting the issue of the summons. A summons can, in principle, only be issued if the clerk (or a magistrate) is satisfied that a witness at a summary trial or committal proceedings will not attend voluntarily. This requirement is contained in s. 97 of the Magistrates' Courts Act 1980.

Individual courts and clerks vary in the enthusiasm with which they require this condition to be fulfilled. Many will issue a witness summons simply on a request from a solicitor and his assurance that it seems in all the circumstances likely to be required. Others, more pedantically, require some positive assertion that the witness will not attend voluntarily. Indeed, they may require there to be a first attempt to have the witness attend voluntarily, and only if he does not will a summons be issued. This can be highly inconvenient and is arguably very foolish in view of the difficulties in efficiently arranging the listing of criminal cases. The time of many people may be wasted if the trial cannot go ahead because a clerk has insisted that there be some evidence that the witness will not attend voluntarily before a summons can be issued. It is a fact of life that even witnesses who have given an assurance of attending voluntarily often fail to do so because they wish to avoid the inconvenience, possible expense and loss of earnings of attending court proceedings. It is for this reason that it is prudent in every case in *civil proceedings* to subpoena witnesses.

A new provision in section 97 of the Magistrates' Courts Act 1980, inserted by the Criminal Procedure and Investigation Act 1996, gives a magistrate a discretion to refuse to issue a witness summons 'if he is not satisfied that an application for the summons was made by a party to the case as soon as is reasonably practical after the accused pleaded not guilty'. Therefore the need for a witness summons must be considered very early on in the case and should not be left until shortly before a magistrates' court trial.

(b) In the case of Crown Court proceedings, there will have been previous committal proceedings in the magistrates' court. The 1996 Act repeals the power of magistrates' courts to make witness orders in respect of Crown Court proceedings and provides a new s. 2 to the Criminal Procedure (Attendance of Witnesses) Act 1965. It is a simple administrative procedure of the Crown Court, to be made under new Crown Court rules and provides that if the Crown Court is satisfied that a person is likely to be able to give material evidence and will not voluntarily attend, then a witness summons may be issued which is directed to that person requiring him to attend and, if necessary, to produce any document or thing in his possession.

(c) Finally, consideration ought to be given in the case of the evidence of apparently uncontroversial witnesses to the serving of the evidence in the form of a statement prepared under s. 9 of the Criminal Justice Act 1967. The use of this section will be considered in due course in the section on evidence (see **16.10.1**).

TWO

FINANCING CRIMINAL LITIGATION

2.1   Introduction

The need to ensure that the financial basis of the relationship between the litigation client and the solicitor is clearly established applies as much in criminal as in civil litigation. Thus, subject to obvious individual exceptions (e.g., a wealthy regular client on a driving charge), it is prudent, indeed essential, to obtain payment in advance for work done in criminal litigation. Whilst the criminal case will not run for as long as the average civil case, there are, for obvious reasons, even greater risks of non-payment by the clientele.

Privately paying clients are, however, considerably rarer than in civil litigation. We shall now therefore consider the question of legal aid. As we shall see, there are important differences from civil legal aid in the manner of application, criteria for eligibility and other ancillary matters.

We will then briefly examine the principles for the award of costs in criminal proceedings.

2.2   Legal Aid and Advice

2.2.1   THE GREEN FORM SCHEME

The Green Form Scheme can be used just as in legal aid in civil proceedings. Legal advice and assistance on any matter of English law can be given to a person who qualifies on a financial eligibility test. Financial eligibility is worked out with the aid of a 'key card' and if, after taking into account certain permissible deductions, the client is left with a disposable income of no more than £77 per week, Green Form assistance can be given. Naturally, criminal matters come within the scope of this scheme. Work up to a total value of two hours' fees can be done by a solicitor for a client and this would cover such things as taking the first statement, filling in application forms for legal aid proper and perhaps some preliminary collection of evidence.

2.2.2   ADVICE AT THE POLICE STATION

If a client is at the police station, and this applies whether he is in custody or attending voluntarily in connection with assisting the police with their enquiries into an offence, a person is entitled to free legal advice and assistance from either his own solicitor or the duty solicitor (see **2.2.4**) up to an initial limit of £90 worth of work. Unlike the Green Form Scheme, this scheme is not means tested in any way so even the wealthy are entitled to assistance under it. The claim for fees is made to the Legal Aid Area Office on a prescribed form.

2.2.3 ASSISTANCE BY WAY OF REPRESENTATION (ABWOR)

Neither the Green Form Scheme nor the police station scheme referred to above cover actually taking a step in proceedings (i.e., representing the client in court). For this, in general, full legal aid is required. However there is an exception, namely under reg. 7 of the Legal Advice and Assistance (Scope) Regulations 1989, which provides for assistance by way of representation (ABWOR) in the criminal courts in certain circumstances. This scheme is means tested in a similar way to the Green Form Scheme. Unlike the Green Form Scheme however, where if one has an income of more than £77 per week assistance cannot be given, there is a sliding scale of contributions above that figure. Between the figures of £69 and £166 net income assistance can be given but the client must pay a contribution of one-third of his net disposable income above £69. The scheme is available to cover representation for a defendant who does not have full legal aid but has not been refused legal aid where the magistrates' court:

(a) is satisfied that the hearing should proceed on the same day;

(b) is satisfied that the party would not otherwise be represented; and

(c) requests a solicitor who is within the precincts of the court to represent that party.

This might come about if a person, newly taken into custody or otherwise, happened to be before the court without legal representation and it appeared that a solicitor was available and the matter seemed relatively straightforward and brief (e.g., a plea in mitigation after a guilty plea). If a solicitor was present in the precincts of the court for the purpose of representing somebody else and was able to come to represent this client then the court can authorise such representation under the ABWOR scheme. In fact many courts deal with applications for legal aid proper very swiftly, and in such cases there would be no advantage in granting assistance by way of ABWOR as opposed to considering a full legal aid application, except the saving of such time as it takes to fill in a full legal aid application form. The use of the ABWOR scheme therefore varies considerably from court to court.

2.2.4 DUTY SOLICITOR SCHEMES

Duty solicitor schemes originated more than 20 years ago in schemes run in some parts of the country on a voluntary basis, whereby solicitors experienced in criminal work would attend on a rota system, either at a police station or in magistrates' court cells in the early morning before the day's sittings, to give advice and assistance and to represent persons in custody (or in some cases also persons not in custody who came to court and were in need of assistance and were unrepresented) on such matters as a preliminary bail application or a plea in mitigation.

The method of remuneration was sometimes by the Green Form or in some cases by the prompt grant of legal aid, and the persons attending as duty solicitors were, if the client wished, entitled to act for the client for further stages of the proceedings. These voluntary schemes have now been replaced by a formal duty solicitor scheme under the Legal Aid Board Duty Solicitor Arrangements 1989. The duty solicitor scheme has two principal aspects.

2.2.4.1 At the police station

Under this scheme persons who are at a police station, whether under arrest or voluntarily, are entitled to free legal advice and assistance up to an initial limit of £90 from a duty solicitor or, if they prefer, from their own solicitor. The main point of duty solicitor schemes however is that they operate throughout the night and therefore there ought in principle always to be a duty solicitor available whereas the client's own solicitor may well not be willing to come out, even if the client knows his home telephone number.

The remuneration for duty solicitors under this scheme is by a combination of fees for various elements of the duty, e.g., for being 'on duty' overnight, and a fixed fee per telephone call to persons in custody where the duty solicitor does not attend at the police station, together with various other fees calculated on a time basis for actual work at police stations. Duty solicitors in this scheme are volunteers in ordinary private practice with experience of criminal cases, who participate on a rota basis.

2.2.4.2 At court

The court duty solicitor will see persons before they go before the court for the first time and may represent them at that stage. Many courts now deal only with bail applications on the first occasion where the duty solicitor is acting, though others may deal with pleas in mitigation after a guilty plea. If the case goes past that first hearing then the defendant must apply for legal aid proper.

2.3 Legal Aid Proper

The Legal Aid Act 1988 allows application for legal aid at any stage in criminal proceedings. The most important and significant differences from civil legal aid are:

(a) Application is made not to the Legal Aid Board but to the court before whom the accused is to appear, whether it is a magistrates' court or the Crown Court; and

(b) There is no time for an exhaustive and thorough investigation of means as occurs in civil proceedings. Often the accused is in custody and the case ought for that reason to proceed very swiftly, but in any event the delays of some weeks which are common in deciding on financial eligibility in civil legal aid applications would clearly be out of the question in criminal cases. Accordingly, the courts both assess the applicant's means and decide whether or not the person should receive legal aid in principle.

2.3.1 CRITERIA FOR THE GRANT OF LEGAL AID

There are two criteria for the grant of legal aid in a criminal matter. By s. 21 of the Legal Aid Act 1988 legal aid must be granted when:

(a) it appears that the applicant's *financial resources* are such that he requires assistance in meeting the costs of the proceedings; and

(b) it is *desirable* to do so *in the interests of justice*.

2.3.1.1 Applicant's financial resources

A person applying for legal aid, as we shall see below in a moment, has to provide some evidence as to his means. This is done by filling in a legal aid application form giving details of income and capital. The court will then assess his means. This will be done very swiftly indeed, often on the same day on which the legal aid application is received by the court, or indeed, if application is made at the court in the course of proceedings, there and then.

The accused's financial eligibility is worked out on a sliding scale in a somewhat similar way to the computation in civil proceedings. An individual who is in work will be expected to produce recent wage slips to the court together with any appropriate evidence of capital. However, he is not subject to cross-examination or interview about these matters. In case law in 1992 and 1993 some uncertainty was shown about whether legal aid could be granted at all where there was insufficient evidence of means. This has been resolved by the Legal Aid in Criminal and Care Proceedings (General) (Amendment) (No. 2) Regulations 1993 which are now in force. The purpose of these regulations is to ensure that there is proper documentation to support means statements without the need for this causing unnecessary delay in criminal proceedings. Legal aid may be granted without supporting documentation if it is reasonable to grant it but such legal aid may be withdrawn if the documents are not subsequently produced.

As in the case of civil legal aid, a person whose disposable income or capital are below a certain amount will receive legal aid without contribution; those above certain prescribed maxima will have legal aid refused on financial grounds; and between the two a legal aid contribution order will be made on a sliding scale which will require the person to make some contribution toward the cost of his legal representation. The contribution may either be required in one lump sum, if it is from capital, or in instalments over the life of the case if it is from income.

The court is required to assess the approximate likely cost of the case, which is naturally somewhat difficult in view of the fact that the case may take several different courses, e.g., the costs may be multiplied many times by the defence electing Crown Court trial. The recent introduction of 'standard fees' for many cases will make this assessment somewhat easier.

Legal aid may be reassessed throughout the course of the case should the client's means change.

If a legally-aided person subject to a contribution order fails to pay any instalment of contribution, the court may revoke the grant of legal aid (s. 24(2), 1988 Act). An accused must be given the opportunity to make representations on the matter.

2.3.1.2 'In the interests of justice'

We turn now to the second criterion that of 'desirable in the interests of justice'. This naturally confers a discretion on the court, and regard must be had to s. 22 of the 1988 Act in deciding on whether the interests of justice make it desirable for an accused to have legal aid. This section lays down that legal aid should be granted in particular whenever one of the following factors applies:

(a) the offence is such that if proved it is likely that the court would impose a sentence which would deprive the accused of his liberty, or lead to loss of his livelihood or serious damage to his reputation;

(b) the charge may involve consideration of a substantial question of law;

(c) the defendant has inadequate knowledge of English, or suffers from mental illness or physical disability;

(d) the defence will involve the tracing and interviewing of witnesses or the expert cross-examination of a prosecution witness;

(e) legal representation is desirable in the interests of someone other than the defendant.

It is now appropriate to consider these matters.

(a) *The offence is such as might lead to the defendant losing his liberty, livelihood, or suffering serious damage to his reputation*

A client's liberty will obviously be at risk if the charge is serious in itself; if there are serious aggravating circumstances, e.g., breach of trust of some kind; if the accused already has a bad criminal record, especially if the accused is already under a suspended sentence; and possibly if the accused will be in breach of a probation order if convicted.

Loss of livelihood might be particularly relevant in the case of a driving offence which might lead to the loss of a driving licence in the case of someone who needs it for his job. Thus, an offence which is disqualifiable in itself, or disqualifiable under the 'totting-up' procedure, would be an example of an offence which might lead to loss of livelihood, and this might be so even where the actual offence charged is not a particularly serious one, e.g., speeding, if the points allotted for the offence might lead to the defendant being disqualified and the loss of his job. This would also be applicable in the case of other offences which are not sufficiently serious to merit a custodial sentence. For example, in the case of someone whose job requires them to handle money and of whom utter financial probity is required, e.g., a bank clerk or a cashier, any conviction for an offence of dishonesty may be sufficiently serious to lead to dismissal.

Finally, there is a separate ground where an offence would cause serious damage to reputation but is not in itself serious enough to be likely to lead to a custodial sentence; an example would be where the person accused had a certain standing in the community such that a conviction would cause grave embarrassment, e.g., a vicar charged with shoplifting some trivial item.

The suggestion of risk of loss of reputation can sometimes be prayed in aid even for a client who has a criminal record if the kind of offence with which he is now charged is significantly different, e.g., where previous convictions were for, say, trivial public order offences but the present charge involves some element of dishonesty.

With the introduction of the Criminal Justice Act 1991, which provides a strong presumption in favour of offenders being sentenced only to 'community orders' which do not in themselves involve loss of liberty, a number of magistrates' courts declined to grant legal aid even in respect of relatively serious offences. That basis for a decision to refuse legal aid was considered improper by the Divisional Court in *R v Liverpool City Magistrates ex parte McGhee* (1993) 158 JP 275. The court held that although the likelihood of a community order was not specified in the Legal Aid Act 1988 as one of the grounds for grant of legal aid, s. 22 of the Act is not exhaustive and the likelihood of a community order was a further ground upon which legal aid could be granted.

(b) *The charge raises a substantial question of law*

If the facts of the offence are such as to raise a difficult matter of law, e.g., there is a conflict of authority on some relevant matter, then this ground may apply. The defendant clearly will need the assistance of a solicitor in saying whether or not this is the case.

(c) *Inadequate knowledge of English or suffers from mental illness or physical disability*

This ground needs little explanation. If legal aid would otherwise normally be refused on the basis that the particular case was sufficiently minor or straightforward for the person to be able to represent himself, then this might be appropriate.

(d) *The defence involves the tracing and interviewing of witnesses or expert cross-examination of a prosecution witness*

In other words, the case needs a lawyer's special skills and laypersons could not do these things for themselves.

21

(e) *Legal representation is desirable in the interests of someone other than the defendant*

> An example commonly given is the case of a sexual offence against a young child where it is undesirable that the defendant should personally conduct the cross-examination of the child which might distress the latter. This example would, of course, be covered also by the first of the criteria.

It must be noted that these criteria are not in themselves exhaustive. Moreover, there is specific provision that, where a doubt exists about the granting of legal aid, the doubt should be resolved in favour of the applicant.

In addition to the more general criteria for the grant of legal aid in s. 22 of the 1988 Act, there are four separate situations where a legal aid order *must* be made subject to means. These are:

(a) where an accused is committed for trial on a charge of murder;

(b) where an unrepresented accused who wishes to be represented appears before magistrates following an earlier remand in custody by them, was unrepresented on the earlier occasion and is at risk of a further remand in custody or of being committed to the Crown Court in custody;

(c) where an offender is remanded in custody by a magistrates' court or the Crown Court with a view to reports being prepared on him prior to passing sentence;

(d) to a successful appellant in the Court of Appeal whose case has been taken to the House of Lords by the prosecution.

2.3.1.3 Legal aid and the apparently wealthy

In view of public criticism of the receipt of legal aid by apparently wealthy persons, the Lord Chancellor made regulations effective from 1 June 1996, the most important of which concerns the treatment of an assisted person's dwelling house which previously was wholly exempt for assessing financial eligibility. Now the market value of the property will be taken into account insofar as it exceeds £100,000 and moreover, mortgage debt will not be offset against this insofar as it exceeds £100,000. Thus the court will need to look at the value of an assisted person's home and reduce that by the amount of the mortgage or by £100,000, whichever is the less, to produce a net equity figure. If that net equity figure exceeds £100,000 the excess over £100,000 is taken into account as the capital of the assisted person. In addition there is a discretionary power to allow the assessment officer to take into account the assets of persons other than the applicant himself. This is designed to catch those who have access to substantial income or capital assets which are held in the name of other people or companies.

2.3.2 METHOD OF APPLICATION

A legal aid application is made in writing to the magistrates' court on Form 1, together with a prescribed form of information about means and resources (Form 5). In principle, legal aid cannot be granted until Form 5 has been lodged duly completed. The application should be taken or sent to the magistrates' court as soon as possible. Generally it will be dealt with very swiftly, perhaps even the same day, and the result telephoned through to the solicitor's office. The solicitor will then be sent a legal aid order together with a form of 'Report on Case' on which the eventual application for fees must be made. The application forms when received are dealt with by a magistrates' clerk, or referred to the magistrates.

It will be observed that the 'interests of justice' criteria do not require as such that the accused is likely to *win* the case, which is (roughly speaking) the criterion for the grant of *civil* legal aid. Indeed, one may obtain legal aid even though the accused always intends to plead guilty.

If the magistrates' court refuses to grant legal aid, then a further application can be made and this will be referred to a different magistrate or bench of magistrates, and therefore there will in effect be fresh minds considering the application. In principle, this can be done any number of times. Moreover, even if previously refused, a further oral application can be made to the magistrates at the start of the hearing to which the application relates. It may be possible then to amplify the grounds upon which the application is made.

In fact refusal of legal aid is often because the solicitor has not given sufficient information as to why legal aid is required in the interests of justice. For example, in the case of a person with a bad criminal record who might be under a suspended sentence at present, the solicitor might merely have put 'accused may receive custodial sentence' on the application form without giving details. If the application is refused, it is likely to be because the magistrates are unable to see that there is a real possibility of a custodial sentence. It goes without saying that, since in the application form it may often be appropriate to disclose a client's past criminal record, the same magistrates who consider the written legal aid application form, or hear an oral application, will not then go on to deal with the trial of the accused if he is pleading not guilty.

Magistrates' courts making a legal aid order may make one just for the magistrates' court proceedings, or in the case of an indictable offence may make a so-called 'through' order which will cover the accused for the proceedings when they reach the Crown Court. In fact, it makes very little difference which is granted because, at the end of committal proceedings, if one has not obtained a 'through' order, one simply applies to the court to extend the legal aid to cover the Crown Court proceedings. Moreover, if, for any reason that was not done, application may be made to the Crown Court itself in writing on a prescribed form.

2.3.3 WHAT IF LEGAL AID IS REFUSED?

First, as has previously been stated, a person who is refused legal aid can always make another application to the court, either in writing or at the hearing itself. Secondly, under regs 15 to 17 of the Legal Aid in Criminal and Care Proceedings (General) Regulations 1989 (SI 1989 No. 344), a person who has been refused legal aid in the case of an indictable offence, including an offence triable either way (that is triable either in the magistrates' court or the Crown Court), may apply to the Legal Aid Area Committee. This Committee is a body composed of practising solicitors and barristers who sit part-time on a rota basis. Application, on a prescribed form, may be made as follows:

(a) in the case of offences which are purely indictable or triable either way;

(b) where the refusal has not been on the grounds of means alone;

(c) where application is made within 14 days of receiving notification of refusal;

(d) where the original application for legal aid was made at least 21 days before the proposed hearing date of the case, whether committal or summary trial, assuming that such a date had been fixed at the relevant time (which is unlikely). The relevant information must be sent on Form CRIM 9. The Area Committee will then review the case and may grant legal aid.

2.3.4 LEGAL AID BOARD GUIDELINES FOR THE GRANT OF LEGAL AID

The Legal Aid Board has issued guidelines in an effort to regularise the practice of magistrates' courts, many of which have remarkably different rates of grant for legal aid in respect of similar offences. The guidelines are intended merely to be starting points after which each case must be considered on its particular merits by reference to the proper criteria.

The guidelines indicate that offences which are triable only on indictment always merit legal aid; and they give a list of the more common 'either way' and summary offences where legal aid may be appropriate. In addition they give a number of offences for which legal aid should normally be refused unless there are exceptional circumstances. Examples of the latter include drunk and disorderly conduct; prostitution; television licence offences; urinating in the street; and most road traffic cases, including driving with excess alcohol, unless such cases fall within the statutory criteria (e.g., where loss of livelihood might result from conviction and disqualification).

2.3.5 WHAT DOES LEGAL AID COVER?

(a) Legal aid covers preparation for and the conduct of proceedings in the court that grants it, whether magistrates' court or Crown Court. As explained in 2.3.2, in the magistrates' court a 'through' order may be made which will also cover proceedings in the Crown Court. Once legal aid is granted, then usually the conduct of the case is not reviewed in the same way as might be the case for civil legal aid. A solicitor who bona fide chooses a particular course of action which may be considerably more expensive than its alternative will not be subject to criticism or refusal of fees. For example, it is always an important question to decide how many witnesses are going to be called. Suppose it is contended that there is an alibi because an accused was in a room with eight other people present at the time. It would be perfectly legitimate for a solicitor to decide to call all eight as witnesses, with the consequent increase in length of trial and expense. Similarly, a solicitor may opt to attempt to raise oral arguments at the stage of committal for trial which will materially increase the fees of the case. Although 'standard fees' are currently in force (see below) these will not be expected to cover the conduct of oral applications at committal for trial.

(b) Legal aid orders in the magistrates' court do not usually cover representation by counsel, unless specific approval has been given by the clerk to the justices. Legal aid may be specifically granted for representation in the magistrates' court by both solicitor and counsel only where the offence is indictable and the court considers it to be unusually grave and difficult. If such an application is refused, the solicitor concerned may apply again to the court or to the Legal Aid Area Committee. It should be understood that this does not mean that in those cases where barristers are seen in the magistrates' court acting for legally-aided defendants that each is concerned with an indictable offence which is unusually grave or difficult. The individual advocacy resources of any given firm may mean that the firm is unable to cover all the criminal cases which are coming up on any given day. In such a case it is always open to the firm to instruct counsel on any particular case, but the allocation of fees payable will be affected in that the maximum fee to be paid would be that which would be appropriate if a solicitor had conducted the case. Consequently the fees to the barrister and the solicitor will be apportioned in accordance with what is reasonable.

(c) Legal aid in the Crown Court usually consists of representation by solicitor and counsel. Exceptionally, if the person is before the court and unrepresented, legal aid may be ordered to be by counsel alone, e.g., for a plea in mitigation. Counsel will take instructions direct from the client in such a case.

(d) There is one other vital difference between legal aid in civil and in criminal proceedings. Legal aid certificates are never retrospective in civil cases. Any work done for the person before legal aid is actually granted cannot be paid under the legal aid certificate. In *criminal cases* however, practice has recognised that it is often necessary for a solicitor, not only in his client's interest, but also in the interests of the smooth running of the court itself, to take instructions and take some action before the legal aid application can be considered. For example, suppose that an accused person came into your office the day before a charge was to be heard. You would use the Green Form to complete a legal aid application and for a preliminary interview with the client, but suppose that some further work was done in the way of contacting witnesses and trying to get them to court for the next day. All this would be done in expectation of legal aid eventually being granted. In such a case, if legal aid is in fact granted, then work done in urgent circumstances can be paid for even though the work was done before the grant of legal aid (reg. 44(7), Legal Aid in Criminal and Care Proceedings (General) Regulations 1989).

(e) Legal aid orders also cover preliminary advice on the giving of notice of appeal from the magistrates' court to the Crown Court, but further steps in connection with the appeal will not be covered and you will be required to apply to the Crown Court itself for legal aid for the conduct of the appeal. Legal aid orders granted by a magistrates' court do however cover the conduct of one application for bail to a Crown Court judge in chambers where the magistrates have refused bail.

2.3.6   PAYMENT OF FEES UNDER LEGAL AID

The question of payment of legal aid fees is at present in a state of some uncertainty. In Crown Court cases a bill on the prescribed form must be lodged with the taxing officer of the Crown Court and the costs will in that case be paid direct from the Crown Court itself. There are standard fees for most kinds of work done in Crown Court cases, which do not directly relate to time expended on the matters. There is a discretion to allow fees in excess of the standard fee where appropriate.

Until June 1993 payment in criminal cases in the magistrates' court, which is made by the Legal Aid Board, was by submitting a claim to the Legal Aid Board on the prescribed form of 'report on case', indicating the amount of time spent on preparatory work, travelling, waiting and advocacy. Payment was then allowed at certain hourly rates. Under provisions currently in force the Lord Chancellor has replaced that with a system of standard fees somewhat similar to those which apply in the Crown Court. The standard fees are meant to be an incentive to practitioners to conduct criminal litigation in a well-organised and efficient way and so, it is said by the Lord Chancellor, reasonable profits can be made for firms which are properly organised. The lawfulness of these provisions has been unsuccessfully challenged in the Divisional Court, it being contended that the basic requirement under the Legal Aid Act 1988 to offer fair and reasonable remuneration is breached by a system which must inevitably involve a 'swings and roundabouts' approach whereby solicitors will inevitably run some cases which are more difficult or time-consuming at a loss to be made up by those that can be processed more efficiently.

Many practitioners consider that the rates provided do not allow fair remuneration even on a 'swings and roundabouts' basis and indeed that all criminal work can now only be done at a loss, or at least in such a way that serious risks are taken with clients' interests by cutting corners. In particular it is suggested that a good deal of the preparatory and other crucial work on cases may need to be carried out by low paid and unqualified staff in order for a solicitor's firm to make reasonable profits on such work.

The standard fee scheme set by the Lord Chancellor's Department provides for standard fees for guilty pleas and not guilty plea cases. Other more complex possibilities, including cases where there has been a change in the venue from summary trial to Crown Court trial and cases involving a barrister being assigned, are outside the scheme. If a trial is listed as a not guilty plea but in fact the client decides to plead guilty at the start, then the solicitor is paid as if it were a not guilty case because the level of preparation will have had to be much the same.

In each category there are two levels of standard fee: a lower fee covering an estimated 70 per cent of all cases and a higher fee covering the next 20 per cent of cases, with the most expensive 10 per cent of cases outside the scheme. Those cases remain subject to the full legal aid assessment on an hourly basis as formerly. The fees claimable are different for London cases than for those outside London.

2.3.7 WHAT HAPPENS WHEN A LEGALLY-AIDED PERSON IS ACQUITTED?

In such a case, whether in magistrates' courts or the Crown Court, it is usually inappropriate for there to be any order for costs between the parties or from central funds. The normal order is that, if the legally-aided person has not had to pay any contribution, then no order for costs will be made; if he has had to pay a contribution, then the order will be that the contribution be returned to him and any unpaid parts of his contribution be remitted. This is the usual practice, although it is not invariably the case (e.g., if it appears to the court of trial that the accused has been acquitted on some unmeritorious technicality).

2.3.8 LEGAL AID FOR APPEALS BY WAY OF CASE STATED

This is considered to be within the civil jurisdiction of the High Court and consequently application is for civil legal aid to the Legal Aid Board.

2.4 Orders for Costs

2.4.1 ON CONVICTION

If an accused is convicted the court has a discretion to order that he pay all or some part of the prosecution's costs in addition to any penalty it imposes (s. 18(1), Prosecution of Offences Act 1985). This applies both in the magistrates' court and in the Crown Court and the amount to be paid must be specified in the order.

2.4.2 ON ACQUITTAL

If an accused who is not legally aided is acquitted then the matter is governed by ss. 16-21 of the Prosecution of Offences Act 1985 and by a Practice Direction entitled *Practice Direction (Crime: Costs)* [1991] WLR 498. This indicates that the normal consequences of an acquittal on indictment should be the making of an order for defendant's costs, that is costs out of *central funds*, which are funds established for this purpose by the government. Such an order should only be refused if:

(a) the defendant was at fault in bringing suspicion on himself and misleading the prosecution into thinking the case against him was stronger than it actually was; or

(b) he was acquitted on a technicality but there was ample evidence to support a conviction.

Similar principles should be applied in the magistrates' court. Where an accused is entitled to costs then he is also entitled to an allowance for travel and subsistence just as if he were a witness (reg. 23, Costs in Criminal Cases (General) Regulations) 1986).

2.4.3 UNNECESSARY OR IMPROPER ACTS OR OMISSIONS

The court may make an order that costs incurred by one party as a result of 'any unnecessary or improper act or omission' by another party shall be paid by that other party (s. 19(1), Prosecution of Offences Act 1985). This would only be appropriate as a final order in the case of a prosecution which has been unreasonably brought. It may however be appropriate as a means of obtaining the costs of a given part of the hearing, e.g., where an adjournment has been occasioned because the prosecution were not ready, then the costs of that day's adjournment may be ordered to be paid to the accused, and this applies even if he is ultimately convicted. However, magistrates' courts are particularly reluctant to make orders for costs against the prosecution believing that this implies criticism of the conduct of the CPS or the police in bringing the prosecution.

2.4.4 IMPROPER CONDUCT

The Courts and Legal Services Act 1990 inserted a new s. 19A into the Prosecution of Offences Act 1985. This gives the court power to order a solicitor or barrister to meet the whole or part of costs wasted 'as a result of any improper, unreasonable or negligent act or omission' by the representative or his staff. It is well established in the case law from the same words in civil cases that oppressive or improper conduct is not required and all that is needed is simple negligence. Thus if a trial is prolonged by the arguing of hopeless points of law, by the calling of unnecessary witnesses or by proceedings being brought in an improper form, a wasted costs order may be made against either prosecution or defence legal representatives.

It is obvious that this sanction is more likely to be applied in respect of improper conduct by the defence. Improper conduct by the prosecution is more susceptible to control during the course of the trial (e.g., a judge may be reluctant to interfere with the defence's right to call as many superfluous witnesses as it wishes because of the risk of appeal, but the same consideration does not apply to the prosecution). In any event if the prosecutor is sufficiently guilty as to be culpable within the section, such an order may be made, and this is especially likely to be the case if the accused is not legally aided.

THREE

MANAGING A CRIMINAL LITIGATION PRACTICE

3.1 Introduction

In this chapter we shall be considering some important features of managing a criminal litigation case load including office administration and organisation, file management and some practical considerations about the building up and organisation of a criminal law practice.

3.2 Keeping Time Records

It is essential for the efficient management of all legal work that a proper time recording system exists so that fee earners can identify what work they have done and for which clients. The extreme importance of this in civil litigation is stressed in the corresponding **LPC Guide: Civil Litigation** at 3.3.

In civil litigation one will need to know how much time has been expended on a client's business in order to be able to charge that client a fair and reasonable sum. The eventual charge reflects not merely the time expended, although that is an essential preliminary ingredient in the computation, but also factors such as the importance of the matter to the client, the urgency of the matter, the amount of work involved, the number of documents written or perused, and so on. In civil litigation it is necessary to have accurate information not merely for the purpose of charging the client but, in the event of success in the litigation, in order to be able to justify the fees to the court at the taxation of costs and obtain as much as possible from the losing opponent. In civil litigation moreover it makes no difference whether the client is or is not legally aided when considering the importance of keeping time records.

In criminal litigation a very much higher proportion of work will inevitably be for legally-aided clients, save in all but the most specialist practices dealing with substantial 'white collar' crime. With the growing importance of standard fees it may at first sight appear that it is unnecessary to keep proper time records since more or less the same fee will be obtained however fast or slowly a case is processed. This would however, be a bad misjudgement for a number of reasons. In particular:

(a) Only by having efficient office systems can a full criminal litigation case load be properly managed, and time recording is an essential part of this, quite apart from its use to justify the fees charged.

(b) There will still be many cases, in the average busy criminal practitioners' case load, where standard fees are not appropriate and the habit of proper time recording must therefore become ingrained.

(c) Some cases which arise in a criminal context may go to the Divisional Court of the Queen's Bench Division which, in matters of taxation of costs, applies civil procedures so that bills in a civil format under RSC Ord. 62 will be required. The practice of the Supreme Court Taxing Masters is to require full itemised bills together with time-based attendance records.

Time recording is therefore essential, and proper information must be retained on dedicated forms rather than odd scraps of paper. In particular, accurate records are essential to indicate:

(i) telephone calls and letters, ingoing and outgoing;

(ii) attendances with the client, witnesses and others;

(iii) conferences with counsel and time spent in drafting the brief to counsel;

(iv) other preparation time on the case;

(v) travelling time to and from court or to interview witnesses;

(vi) waiting time at court;

(vii) actual advocacy on one's feet in court both at trial and at every preliminary stage.

Only by keeping scrupulously accurate records can each case be charged for as appropriate.

3.3 Other Aspects of Office Management

The extreme importance of keeping accurate records and updating diaries in civil litigation is obvious. Missing key dates may mean the end of the client's case and will involve professional negligence, if not professional misconduct. See **LPC Guide: Civil Litigation** at **4.5.3.**

By contrast, initially at least, in criminal litigation, since the readers to whom this guide is addressed are likely to be acting for the defendant, it is possible to take a passive approach.

Although, as indicated above, the initial pace of proceedings is likely to be dictated largely by the prosecution or the court, one cannot leave things until the last moment. The earlier that witnesses are interviewed and an attempt is made to collect evidence, the better it will be for the defendant. Indeed, if the client has not yet been charged, there is nothing to stop one from collecting evidence in his favour and submitting it to the Crown Prosecution Service to assist them with their initial decision since the best possible outcome for any client is obviously not to be charged at all. The possibility therefore of taking the initiative and provoking action from the police or Crown Prosecution Service in appropriate cases should not be overlooked.

It is initially up to the police and prosecution to decide whether to charge at all and in what format to proceed and the first appointment at court will be fixed by a procedure over which the defendant has no control. As to subsequent hearings, when dates for major events such as a mode of trial hearing or summary trial are being canvassed at a first hearing, your own diary commitments can be taken into account by the justices' clerk. Thereafter it is vital to keep a proper diary both in relation to court appointments and in relation to key dates for specific preparatory steps, in particular:

(a) Under s. 5 of the Criminal Procedure and Investigations Act 1996, the date for disclosing the nature of the defence (see **21.4.1**), including particulars of alibi.

(b) Following up the client's proof of evidence and obtaining witness statements.

(c) Ensuring replies to letters written to the prosecution seeking the information described at **1.3.1.5** (i.e. witness statements, criminal record, custody record, copy of tape-recorded interview, etc.).

(d) Custody time limits. Under s. 22 of the Prosecution of Offences Act 1985, as amended by s. 71 of the Criminal Procedure and Investigations Act 1996, there are regulations which lay down custody time limits for trials on indictment. In particular the following are the maximum periods for which an accused can be held in custody:

(i) 70 days between first appearance in the magistrates' court and committal;

(ii) 70 days between first appearance and summary trial for an offence triable either way;

(iii) 112 days between committal for trial and the start of the trial in the Crown Court. A trial is deemed to start, generally speaking, when the jury is sworn in.

If these times are exceeded, the accused has an absolute right to bail no matter how serious the offence with which he is charged. The prosecution may however, apply for an extension of the time limit.

(e) After the final outcome in any case the appropriate date for appeal and delivery of bill.

3.4 File Management

Files are likely to run for a good deal less time and be less bulky than in civil cases. They may well therefore take less management. This is of course subject to major exceptions. In substantial cases, in particular in cases of commercial fraud, there may be several trolleys full of relevant documents; very bulky documentation will be sent to you by the prosecution quite apart from the documents which your own case has generated. The same aspects of case and file management then become necessary as in civil cases.

Even in factually more simple crimes such as serious cases of violence, the number of depositions collected by the police, irrelevant or marginally relevant though most of them are likely to be, may involve cupboards full of documents. There must be adequate accommodation in order to deal with such cases.

With regard to other documents which will constitute your own file, it is vital to keep proper receipts for disbursements and other material relevant to your own bill separate from such things as correspondence, witness statements and the like.

3.5 Office Personnel

The relatively small number of firms which handle large commercial fraud and 'white collar' criminal cases are so organised as to be able to devote considerable personnel resources to such cases. Relatively large teams are put together, often involving one or more partners, a number of assistant solicitors and other fee earners, and sometimes, if appropriate, specialists from outside the criminal law, e.g., company lawyers, accountants and the like. If these cases are for private-paying clients then substantial sums should be taken on account and interim bills delivered, the sums held on account being topped up so that one is always ahead just as in the case of civil clients. If such cases are run on legal aid there are provisions for obtaining interim payments as the case goes along, both for substantial disbursements (such as for accountants' reports) and for profit costs. Such cases would not of course be remunerated on a 'standard fees' basis.

Many of the bigger firms of solicitors employ their own enquiry agents, often ex-policemen, for purposes including finding witnesses and taking witness statements. Where more delicate enquiries are concerned it is probably better for a solicitor to employ an outside enquiry agent so as to keep his firm at one remove from the sometimes unorthodox tactics adopted by such persons to obtain useful information.

No matter how a team might be constituted, whether for a big case or a more modest one, it is vital that someone be designated to supervise the whole process and that the client should know with whom he has to deal.

3.6   Relations with the Client

A client on a criminal charge is entitled to every bit as much consideration and courtesy as any other client (and indeed arguably more so, given that he is likely to be under greater strain than most other clients). In particular you should remember that:

(a) It is unprofessional conduct not to discuss legal aid with a client even if it seems obvious on the face of it that he is unlikely to qualify. If he is a private-paying client, then where possible a fixed fee or a best estimate must be given for the work together with a quotation of the hourly rate. In such cases the estimate must be regularly reviewed and the client must be made aware of other factors that might increase costs which are outside the solicitor's control (e.g., that the prosecution might press for trial in the Crown Court). An appropriate 'client care' letter must be written to the client explaining the charging basis and confirming the hourly rates. Payments on account will be obtained and interim bills delivered as discussed above.

(b) Practice Rule 15 applies to criminal clients as much as to any others and clients must be informed whom to approach in the event of any problem and what the firm's complaints handling procedure is. This involves letting the client know, preferably in writing, the name and status of the person responsible for the day-to-day conduct of the case and the person responsible for its overall supervision (if different).

(c) The client should be kept fully informed in writing of each material development and of each stage of the case and reminded about key dates. Merely because a client has a criminal record one should not assume total familiarity with the criminal justice process. Despite the client's apparent knowledge of the various options available at every stage, in many cases you should bear in mind the possibility that much of what is said, and the 'underworld slang' in which it is expressed, is often mere bravado. The story is probably apocryphal of the client who on being charged said 'I am saying nothing until you get me my copy of Archbold!'. (Now such a client would obviously instead demand his copy of *Blackstone's Criminal Practice* ('A snip at £99 — a goldmine of information for the busy criminal' — per 'Nosher' Thribb, Cell 231, E Wing, Durham Prison)).

3.7   File Keeping

Within the file a full record should be kept of all relevant material. It is dangerous to keep material facts in one's head because of the possibility of urgent situations arising whilst one is away or unavailable. The files should be interchangeable within the office as far as possible; this is of course the virtue of having more than one person employed on a given file, although clearly run-of-the-mill matters will not merit such duplication of effort.

In particular, in practices which cover a number of courts, it may well be that the requirements of sensible management mean files, at least for preliminary stages such as initial applications, mode of trial hearings and the like, have to be exchanged between members of staff so that, for example, the advocate who is attending Barchester Magistrates' Court that day will deal with all matters there whilst his colleague at Middlemarch Magistrates' Court will deal with all matters there. If this is not done and each one deals with every aspect of his own file no matter where the cases are, there will be a remarkable amount of effort in duplicated travelling time hurtling between courts.

Moreover, the indulgence of the magistrates or their clerk in holding back cases for the convenience of late arrivals can never be guaranteed. Sensible practice management therefore usually means that all work in a given court is given to the same advocate. For that reason there should be a pro forma usually pinned to the inside of the file giving details of important aspects of the case; in particular the client's name, address, telephone number and contact address in the daytime if possible, any police or CPS reference number with telephone number, a box to be completed with details of the next hearing date, and the nature of that hearing. These are key things which need to be picked up at a moment's notice.

Other important but more basic information, in particular to do with costs, disbursements and the like, should also be kept somewhere in the file.

In firms with a substantial criminal litigation department, there must be a supervising partner of the whole advocacy resources of the firm so as to ensure that fee earners are efficiently used between several courts. It will be up to such a person to consider the requirements for advocacy in the week ahead in deciding whether it will be necessary to use counsel or solicitor agents to supplement the in-firm advocates where the latter are stretched over too many cases or too many courts.

3.8   Managing the Practice

It is important that the firm should be flexible enough to cope with slumps and peaks in workload since this may ebb and flow in criminal litigation. Having said that, it is notoriously difficult to combine a criminal litigation practice with any other field of work. This does not of course mean that a firm which deals with criminal litigation cannot deal with any other areas of work, simply that individuals or departments dealing with criminal litigation will find it hard to fit in much else; the calls on one's time are often unpredictable given the fact there is no fixed listing system in magistrates' courts. The problem with listing in the magistrates' court is that all defendants are instructed to attend at 9.45 a.m. for the morning's list. At the time of writing attempts are being made in larger courts to introduce some form of fixed listing so that at least for routine applications advocates are told that they need not attend before a certain given time, e.g., 11.30 a.m. on the day. The informal system of 'pre-trial reviews' which some courts use will often assist if all parties are willing to cooperate (see 1.1.3).

Unfortunately the nature of clients in the criminal litigation process makes it difficult for criminal courts to run even as efficiently as civil courts, fallible though the listing procedures in the latter may be. Criminal clients are often uncertain about how they will plead or as to their decisions about matters which may influence the course which a case may take. It is self-evident that the client who suddenly decides to plead guilty is likely to be dealt with in only four or five minutes because the case will then be adjourned for reports to be prepared before sentence. Had he, instead, indicated a not guilty plea then in principle a summary trial would have gone on which might have lasted all day, or even longer. The desire to keep the magistrates fully occupied throughout the day leads often to considerable 'over listing' so that if everyone to be dealt with in a given court does in fact plead not guilty, there will be no possibility of dealing fully with each case.

Some large urban courts may have 20 criminal courts in action at the same time and it is possible for them to be flexible so as to take cases from one court to another to be dealt with expeditiously. However, in much smaller courts in rural locations there may only be two courts sitting simultaneously in the same building. Although no courts are so capricious as to take full contested summary trials before shorter matters such as guilty pleas, bail, mode of trial hearings and the like, it is not unknown to arrive at 9.30 a.m. and not have one's case dealt with, short though the point may be, before mid-afternoon.

Sadly, in some locations the clerks, who, sometimes in conjunction with the CPS, choose the order of cases, may well play 'favourites', with local solicitors who often appear before them having priority in getting their cases dealt with. Thus if one is appearing in a strange location one may be left until towards the end of the list. For this reason one can never be entirely sure when one will be back in the office even if one only has one or two simple matters to deal with in court. It is thus usually unsafe for criminal advocates to book in any appointments much before mid-afternoon.

It may therefore be that preliminary action on new cases, such as completing legal aid applications and taking statements, is left to other fee earners within the department, and that those solicitors who wish to do so virtually specialise in advocacy. With magistrates' court advocacy it may even be difficult to combine it with other aspects of criminal practice, such as the time-consuming preparation of major trials for the Crown Court, and some specialist criminal practices have quite separate sections dealing with Crown Court cases.

3.9   Use of Counsel

There is nothing in the magistrates' court which should be beyond the scope of a competent solicitor advocate, even in the conduct of cases where the consequences for the client may be very serious such as where a charge of dishonesty may end the client's career or lead to very adverse publicity. Thus one should rapidly become perfectly competent to conduct bail applications before magistrates, a Crown Court judge or indeed a High Court judge in chambers; all aspects of other preliminary hearings such as adjournment requests or mode of trial hearings, committal proceedings and summary trial. In addition there are at present limited rights of audience in the Crown Court on appeals from magistrates' courts where one has acted in the court below. A good solicitor will want to take every opportunity early on to polish and improve his advocacy technique in all or any of these forums. In Crown Court trials on indictment hitherto solicitors have had no general rights of audience and therefore counsel would inevitably have been involved. Now solicitors may obtain the Higher Courts Advocacy Qualification entitling them to take Crown Court trials after they have achieved a certain level of experience and have attended an appropriate course and passed examinations in evidence and procedure. If the firm's advocacy resources do not include any qualified advocates then it will still be necessary to employ counsel. In such cases it may be that a conference with counsel of your choice is desirable quite soon after you obtain instructions, so as to plan your tactics and consider, for example, matters of oral evidence, documentary evidence received from the prosecution, and the like. In cases which involve expert evidence, rare though these are by comparison with civil cases, counsel may be able to advise on the appropriate expert to use in terms, for example, of psychiatrists, other doctors, document analysts, forensic accountants, etc.

It is important to establish that one is in funds to instruct counsel at the outset, or to ensure that legal aid is available.

In principle one will wish to select competent and experienced counsel of appropriate seniority for the case in hand. The much vaunted 'cab rank' principle of the Bar provides that a barrister is obliged to accept any brief in a court in which he usually practises for a form of work which he usually does, provided that he is available to do the case and the fee is reasonable. The Bar's Code of Conduct insists that, by definition, a legal aid fee is always reasonable and therefore counsel may not refuse a legal aid case.

One does not have to be an extreme cynic however to appreciate that much of the expertise of a barristers' clerk lies in ensuring that barristers who can be more profitably employed elsewhere are often 'unavailable' for run-of-the-mill legal aid Crown Court cases. There is, nonetheless, a large number of highly competent specialist barristers in all major trial centres whose practices are mainly built around criminal work, in the main out of personal preference notwithstanding that it is not the most remunerative of fields, and who are satisfied to be remunerated at legal aid rates for a great deal of the time. Such barristers generally alternate defence with prosecution work and the CPS generally pay standard fees similar to the going rate for legal aid cases.

3.9.1 INSTRUCTING COUNSEL

When preparing instructions to counsel, which are likely to be either to advise on plea or evidence or on some practical or tactical matter, it is important to give the matter your full professional attention and deal with it in as thorough and comprehensive a way as possible. All relevant documents should be included, namely relevant prosecution statements and other evidence received, where necessary the tape of the recorded interview, and proofs of evidence of the defendant and his witnesses.

The brief should contain full and detailed information and should be more than a mere recital of the statements. It should contain the solicitor's own analysis of the situation and, where appropriate, the result of his own researches or knowledge on matters of law, practice and evidence. It is always worthwhile for the solicitor to bring his or her own intelligence to bear on a case so that two minds can be working to the client's advantage rather than one.

3.9.2 CONFERENCES WITH COUNSEL

In substantial cases a conference with counsel is often desirable. If the client is on bail this will be at counsel's chambers or if he is in custody it will be at the remand centre or prison. Counsel may well wish to take the client through his proof of evidence and test him on possible inconsistencies or implausibilities in it. This is not with a view to suggesting a better story, which would be quite unprofessional; it is with a view to highlighting difficulties so that counsel may know how best tactically to approach the case.

It may be that specific advice needs to be given to the client about his plea if his version is transparently untruthful and counsel feels that there may be significant advantages to the client in pleading guilty (e.g., an indication of contrition may mean the difference between a custodial and a non-custodial sentence). The work of both barrister and solicitor in advising the client in such a situation is extremely onerous and delicate and must be undertaken with great care so that the client is not, in any sense, bullied into pleading guilty when he insists he is not.

The advantages of having a conference with the barrister include the fact that it makes the client feel more part of the team and should increase his confidence. Unfortunately, due to the unpredictability of the length of criminal trials, the listing system in the Crown Court is also somewhat haphazard and it is very common for the barrister of one's choice not to be available on the day. Moreover, this may even be the case if the barrister has actually represented the client in court before. For example, in the Crown Court most cases are listed for a 'plea and directions' hearing first, and a plea is taken so that the Crown Court can know roughly how long a case will take. The case may then be adjourned for some days, or weeks. It may therefore be that a client has seen his own barrister on one or several occasions and naturally he will be very disappointed if his own barrister is unable to attend the trial itself. Learning to cope with a disgruntled client in that situation, especially if at the trial the client is convicted, when he may attribute his conviction to the change of barrister, is an important part of a solicitor's skills.

3.9.3 BRIEFING COUNSEL FOR THE TRIAL

The subject of preparation for the trial is dealt with more specifically in **9.8**.

3.10 Building a Criminal Litigation Practice

Criminal litigation is one of the fields where it is perhaps easiest to build a practice from scratch. Even a new sole practitioner opening an office in the High Street may attract a reasonable number of clients, especially if he is qualified to get on the police station and court duty solicitor rotas. The onerous nature of being available throughout the night, especially when one's turn arrives at a weekend, makes the police station rota relatively unattractive to many solicitors. Such work usually falls to the most dedicated, which often means relatively young solicitors who still have their early enthusiasm. In some areas of the country there are so few solicitors on these rotas that one's turn may come round once a fortnight or indeed more often. The remuneration, whilst hardly adequate for those in large firms with substantial overheads, can be attractive for small firms, including sole practitioners of the kind previously mentioned.

If one is already a competent advocate, having worked for two or three years for some other firm, then one may well build a good clientele on the basis of enthusiasm, personality, and personal recommendations. There will undoubtedly be larger well established firms in the area with whom one is competing for clients. Such firms often have apparently unfair advantages and one will often find in the early stages that one mysteriously loses clients to such firms. Sometimes, and disappointingly, this even happens where one has, against the odds, secured bail for a client in the face of strenuous CPS opposition. Often these changes of solicitor come about for bizarre reasons. Sometimes it is claimed that the police or prison officers actually recommend persons in custody to take a particular solicitor. In most walks of life such a recommendation from people who are, in effect, the opposition, would be viewed strangely, but a surprising number of criminal clients seem to accept such 'advice' seriously. If the client is in custody he may well mix with other prisoners and ask them for their recommendation. There are also some bizarre beliefs commonly held by criminal clients some of which have been much discussed in the legal press. It is, for example, commonly believed by many criminal clients that legal aid fees include an element, often believed to be £5 or £10 per week, which the solicitor is obliged to spend for the client's comfort and particularly for the purpose of bringing him gifts while he is in custody on remand. To the writer's knowledge in a recent instance a criminal client informed his solicitor that he did not wish for any tobacco but wanted his allowance to be saved for seven weeks and for the solicitor to bring him a new pair of expensive training shoes instead. Where solicitors refuse to bring their clients treats in these forms, many use it as the pretext for transferring their legal aid order to another solicitor on a recommendation from other inmates of the remand centre. There has been some evidence that some solicitors do indeed offer financial inducements to clients to persuade others to transfer their legal aid to them. Matters have in some locations come to such a head that local Law Societies have had to devise additional Codes of Practice for criminal practitioners in their area. Many criminal clients do remain faithful to the solicitor of their choice and thus may be prepared to recommend him to others, to the detriment of the client's present solicitor who may be relatively unknown in the field. This appears to be so no matter how deplorable the performance of the other solicitor often is, criminal clients being particularly prone to adopt a 'better the devil you know' approach in these matters. Some solicitors retain their popularity with their clients by the regrettable expedient of taking them small presents such as smarties, jelly babies, or books of poetry (Sylvia Plath is a particular favourite in Wandsworth) whilst they are on remand. Nonetheless, despite these difficulties, competence and enthusiasm will eventually acquire a criminal practice for those who are so inclined.

FOUR

POLICE POWERS AND ADVISING THE CLIENT IN THE POLICE STATION

4.1   Introduction

In this chapter we shall be considering the early stages of the investigation of an offence and the powers of the police in relation to:

(a)   Arrest

(b)   Search

(c)   Taking fingerprints and photographs

(d)   The detention of a suspect

(e)   Interrogation of a suspect

(f)   Identification procedures

(g)   Bail.

In legal theory the police have no greater powers than the ordinary citizen save where such powers are expressly conferred by statute or have been deemed to exist at common law. The law has constantly striven to strike an appropriate balance between the liberty of the citizen to come and go as he pleases without being impeded by officers of the state and the realistic need to confer upon police and other investigative agencies limited powers to interfere with the freedom of citizens for good cause in the general interest of the suppression of crime.

The law at present is largely contained in the Police and Criminal Evidence Act 1984 (the '1984 Act') and in Codes of Practice issued under s. 66 of that Act, the latest versions of which are effective from 10 April 1995. We shall now go on to consider the various stages of the investigation process and police powers in relation to it.

4.2   Arrest

4.2.1   ARREST WITH A WARRANT

If the police know the identity of a suspect whom they wish to arrest they will lay an information in writing on oath before a magistrate. This is commonly done orally. The warrant of arrest then obtained may be endorsed for bail which would authorise the police to release the suspect once having arrested him and after they have made the decision whether to charge him. Alternatively the warrant may not be endorsed for bail, in which case the suspect must be brought before the court. Such warrants may only be issued where:

(a) the offence is triable on indictment or punishable with imprisonment; or

(b) the defendant's address is not sufficiently established for him to be subject to the alternative procedure of a summons being sent to him (s. 1(4), Magistrates' Courts Act 1980).

Arrest with a warrant is now somewhat unusual. As we shall see shortly, the police have such wide powers to arrest without a warrant that it will only be exceptionally that a warrant is required. We turn now to the more common procedure for arrest, namely arrest without warrant.

4.2.2 ARREST WITHOUT A WARRANT

The power to arrest without warrant is now contained in s. 24 of the 1984 Act which broadly restates the law previously contained in s. 2 of the Criminal Law Act 1967 with some refinements. It provides a power of summary arrest, that is immediate arrest without prior formalities, for the police in the case of arrestable offences. 'Arrestable offences' means:

(a) Offences for which the sentence is fixed by law (e.g., murder).

(b) Offences for which a first offender of 21 years or over may receive a prison sentence of five years or more. This therefore means that certain offences are always arrestable offences. Thus theft is one such offence since it carries a maximum penalty of seven years. It is irrelevant that for the purposes of the offence with which one is concerned there is no prospect whatsoever of the arrestee receiving a prison sentence of five years. Thus for example a person suspected of shoplifting some small item may still be arrested under these powers notwithstanding that there is little prospect of him going to prison at all, still less for five years.

(c) Sundry other offences listed in sch. 2 to the 1984 Act which are expressly made arrestable offences notwithstanding that they do not carry a maximum penalty of as long as five years, e.g., offences of indecent assault on a woman.

(d) Certain other offences which the statute creating the offence expressly made arrestable notwithstanding that they did not carry a penalty as long as five years, e.g., the offence of taking a vehicle without the owner's consent under s. 12 of the Theft Act 1968.

By s. 24(6) and (7) of the 1984 Act a constable has the following powers:

(a) if he has reasonable grounds for suspecting that an arrestable offence has been committed he may arrest without a warrant anyone whom he has reasonable grounds for suspecting to be guilty of the offence;

(b) to arrest without a warrant anyone who is about to commit an arrestable offence or anyone whom he has reasonable grounds for suspecting is about to commit an arrestable offence;

(c) to arrest without a warrant anyone who is in the act of, or whom he has reasonable grounds for suspecting to be in the act of, committing an arrestable offence.

In addition, by s. 25 of the 1984 Act, where a constable has reasonable grounds for suspecting that any offence which is *not* an arrestable offence (e.g., careless driving) has been committed or attempted or is being committed or attempted, he may arrest the relevant person if it appears to him that service of a summons is impracticable or inappropriate for any of the reasons specified in s. 25(3) of the 1984 Act, for example:

(a) that the name of the relevant person is unknown to and cannot be readily ascertained by the constable; or

(b) the constable has reasonable grounds for doubting whether a name furnished by the relevant person as his name is his real name; or

(c) the relevant person fails to furnish a satisfactory address.

In these latter cases, therefore, a policeman who stops someone whom he believes to be committing a driving offence which is not arrestable would be entitled to arrest the person concerned if he felt that he was not being given a true name and address so that criminal proceedings could be instituted through the summons procedure which, as we shall see shortly, does not usually involve the preliminary arrest of the suspect.

Quite apart from this, certain other statutory powers of arrest are expressly preserved, for example, that in s. 7 of the Bail Act 1976 for the offence of absconding.

4.2.3 PROCEDURE ON ARREST

On arrest a person is to be cautioned in the following words: 'You do not have to say anything. But it may harm your defence if you do not mention, when questioned, something which you later rely on in court. Anything you do say may be given in evidence.' Minor deviations from these words do not constitute a breach of the requirement to caution. In addition, under s. 28 of the 1984 Act an arrest is unlawful unless at the time, or as soon as is practicable thereafter, the person is informed of the ground for the arrest and this applies whether or not it is obvious what the ground for the arrest is. This does not mean that a suspect must be told in technical language what the offence is, still less need reference be made to the section of the statute under which he may eventually be charged, but the circumstances said to constitute the offence must be clearly indicated to him.

4.3 Search

4.3.1 STOP AND SEARCH

By s. 1 of the 1984 Act a policeman has the power to detain and search any person or vehicle for stolen or prohibited articles. 'Prohibited articles' are:

(a) offensive weapons;

(b) articles made or adapted for use in, or intended for use in:

(i) burglary;

(ii) theft;

(iii) offences of taking away a motor vehicle under s. 12 of the Theft Act 1968;

(iv) obtaining property by deception under s. 15 of the Theft Act 1968.

These provisions are supplemented by two additional powers contained in s. 81(1) and s. 60 of the Criminal Justice and Public Order Act 1994. Both are in turn supplemented by provisions in the Code of Practice A issued under the Police and Criminal Evidence Act 1984, effective from April 1995.

(a) Section 81 of the 1994 Act provides for an authorisation to be made by a senior policeman above the rank of commander or assistant chief constable for powers to stop and search persons, vehicles, ships and aircraft within a specified locality for a period not exceeding 28 days, where to do so is expedient to prevent acts of terrorism.

(b) Section 60 of the 1994 Act is more general and provides that a policeman of the rank of superintendent or above (or exceptionally an inspector if no more senior officer is available) may issue a written and signed authorisation which will permit all uniformed policemen in a particular locality to stop any pedestrian or vehicle driver and to search him or her or anything carried or the vehicle or any passenger in the vehicle, for offensive weapons or dangerous instruments. Such authorisation should only be given if the officer reasonably believes that incidents involving serious violence may take place in the locality.

Section 60(5) of the 1994 Act actually provides that any given constable may make such a search 'whether or not he has any grounds for suspecting that the person or vehicle is carrying weapons or articles of that kind'. These powers may be exercised at any place within the locality for a period not exceeding 24 hours, unless extended by a senior policeman.

It will be observed that these are very wide powers. Constables must only use the powers if they have reasonable grounds for suspecting that they will find stolen or prohibited articles subject to the express provision referred to above in s. 60(5) of the 1994 Act.

Those powers which require 'reasonable suspicions', as most of them do, must be properly exercised. As paragraph 1.7 of Code A indicates, reasonable suspicion can never be supported on the basis of personal factors alone, for example a person's colour, age, hairstyle or manner of dress or even previous convictions. There must be a specific reason for suspecting the individual concerned. The policeman may have reasonable grounds to suspect that a person is carrying such items even if that person's possession would be innocent.

4.3.2 POWERS TO ENTER AND SEARCH PREMISES

The police have the following powers:

(a) To enter and search any premises with the written permission of the occupier.

(b) To enter and search any premises to (inter alia):

(i) execute a warrant of arrest or commitment to prison;

(ii) arrest a person for an arrestable offence;

(iii) save life or limb or prevent serious damage to property (s. 17, 1984 Act).

(c) To search premises where an arrest took place for evidence relating to the offence for which the person has been arrested, but only to the extent that the power to search is reasonably required for the purpose of discovering any such evidence (s. 32).

(d) In the case of arrestable offences only, to search premises occupied or controlled by the person arrested for evidence relating to that offence or connected or similar arrestable offences.

Thus in this latter case a general fishing expedition is not permitted but no doubt a search will be easy enough to justify unless all the stolen property has been recovered and there can be no conceivable grounds for thinking that the individual was involved in other similar offences. A full record of any searches made under this provision must be made and entered on the individual's custody record (see below).

(e) Finally, a search may be executed under a search warrant which may be issued on application to the magistrates in certain circumstances.

In none of these cases do the police have powers to seize items subject to *legal privilege*. Such items include the contents of a solicitor's files or solicitor/client communications unless they could be regarded as coming into existence with the intention of furthering a criminal purpose (e.g., communications between a solicitor and a client constituting a conspiracy).

4.3.3 SEARCH OF PERSONS AFTER ARREST

4.3.3.1 Away from a police station

This is governed by s. 32 of the 1984 Act.

An arrested person may be searched upon arrest away from a police station if the constable has reasonable grounds for believing that the arrested person may present a danger to himself or others, or has reasonable grounds for believing that a person might have concealed on him anything which might:

(a) be used to assist him to escape from lawful custody; or

(b) be evidence relating to an offence.

However, the search may only take place to the extent that it is reasonably required for the purpose of discovering such things and in any event the constable may not require a person to remove any of his clothing in public other than an outer coat, a jacket or gloves.

4.3.3.2 At the police station

Under s. 54 of the 1984 Act a custody officer may order the search of an arrested person if he considers it necessary to ascertain or record property that that person has in his possession when he is brought to the station.

4.3.4 FINGERPRINTING

Previously the police had no power to take a person's fingerprints before he was charged with an offence unless he consented. However, now, under s. 61 of the 1984 Act, a person who gives his consent must give it in writing but if he does not consent an officer of at least superintendent rank may authorise the taking of fingerprints:

(a) before the individual has been charged where it is believed that fingerprints will tend to confirm or disprove his involvement in the commission of a particular offence; or

(b) after he has been charged or informed that he will be prosecuted for any recordable offence (that is an offence which, on conviction, will be recorded in national police records).

4.3.5 OBTAINING SAMPLES

The police have the power to obtain samples from a suspect in the case of 'recordable offences' which includes offences of any seriousness including assaults and burglaries. This power is under ss. 62–65 of the Police and Criminal Evidence Act 1984, as amended and inserted (s. 63A) by the Criminal Justice and Public Order Act 1994. For these purposes samples are divided into 'intimate' and 'non-intimate' samples.

(a) An intimate sample includes samples of blood, semen or other tissue, fluid, urine or pubic hair; a dental impression; and swabs taken from a bodily orifice other than the mouth.

Intimate samples can only be taken from persons in police detention if a superintendent authorises it, having reasonable grounds for suspecting the person to be involved in a recordable offence, and the superintendent has reasonable grounds for believing that the sample would confirm or disprove that person's involvement and that person has given his written consent.

If a consent is refused, then an intimate sample cannot be taken. However, in such a case by virtue of s. 62(10) inferences can be drawn in court from a refusal to consent without good cause. If an intimate sample is to be taken, it must be taken by a medical practitioner.

(b) Non-intimate samples include samples of hair other than pubic hair, nail scrapings, swabs from the mouth; saliva; and footprints. These may be taken either with the suspect's consent or, if he or she does not consent, they may still be taken provided an officer of at least superintendent rank authorises it and that officer has reasonable grounds for suspecting the involvement of the suspect in a recordable offence and that the giving of the sample will tend to confirm or disprove the suspect's involvement in that offence, or if the suspect has already been charged with a recordable offence. By virtue of new provisions in the Criminal Evidence (Amendment) Act 1997 non-intimate samples may also be taken without the suspect's consent where a person is imprisoned by virtue of previous convictions for certain sexual offences and offences of violence. Thus where the police suspect that someone already in custody may have been responsible for other offences it allows them to obtain samples to help them decide whether the person in custody is guilty of those offences, or to eliminate that person from their enquiries.

If eventually a suspect is acquitted, all samples should be destroyed.

4.3.6 PHOTOGRAPHING

A person's consent in writing must be provided for the taking of photographs before charging, but after he has been charged with a recordable offence he may be photographed without his consent.

4.3.7 MISUSE OF POLICE POWERS

So far we have considered in very brief outline police powers in relation to the preliminary conduct of an investigation. The description given is hardly adequate as a full treatment of the law and practice. There is, however, a reason for this which is that the nature of this text is essentially practical. We are only concerned with police powers and conduct in the context of the criminal process. In any of the cases previously described, breach of the law or misuse of powers may be a police disciplinary offence. Moreover, in many cases misconduct would also give rise to liability in tort, e.g., an arrest that was unlawful would be false imprisonment; entry of premises in improper circumstances would be trespass to land; and taking fingerprints forcibly in situations where it was not appropriate would be battery. We are not, however, for present purposes concerned with the consequences to the individual policemen or the police force of complaints or actions in tort. We are concerned with the effect of any abuse of process on the criminal prosecution. What then is the effect of any such misuse of police powers? The answer is likely to be that so far as the criminal prosecution is concerned, misconduct by the police, at least in relation to search and entry will have very little effect.

As we shall see later when dealing with the law of evidence, on the basis of the case law before the 1984 Act there was no power for the court to exclude such evidence; it could merely indicate disapproval of the way in which it was obtained. Therefore if a prosecution were commenced by an unlawful arrest and involved obtaining evidence by unlawful entry and seizure and the wrongful obtaining of fingerprints, these things would have had no effect whatsoever on the criminal process. Whatever the consequences (if any) in terms of disciplinary action against the police or action in tort, misconduct would not have given grounds for excluding the evidence thus unfairly or illegally obtained.

The present law is now contained in s. 78(1) of the Police and Criminal Evidence Act 1984 which provides:

> *In any proceedings the court may refuse to allow evidence on which the prosecution proposes to rely to be given if it appears to the court that, having regard to all the circumstances, **including the circumstances in which the evidence was obtained**, the admission of the evidence would have such an adverse effect on the fairness of the proceedings that the court ought not to admit it.* (Emphasis added.)

Despite a wealth of case law generally about s. 78, over a decade after the section came into force, its overall effect remains uncertain, but in the context of search and entry anyway, it is widely considered to have made little change to the previous law. It will be noted that the trial judge has to have regard to whether or not the conduct will have an effect on the fairness of the proceedings. 'Fairness' relates to the question of whether the jury will be adversely affected not by the item of evidence concerned but by the circumstances in which it was obtained. It is suggested that the way in which evidence is obtained by search or seizure will not in itself usually affect the fairness of the proceedings, however 'unfair' in general terms police conduct may have been. If evidence is relevant it will still be admissible. Accordingly it is suggested that for the purposes of the criminal prosecution, misconduct by the police in arrest, search, fingerprinting etc. will not have a great effect.

4.3.8   CONFESSIONS

It ought to be stressed, however, that if the police are relying on a *confession* then by virtue of s. 76 of the 1984 Act the court needs to investigate the circumstances in which the confession was obtained to see whether it is admissible, that is whether it was obtained by *oppression* or whether there is anything in all the surrounding circumstances which might render it *unreliable*. Therefore it could well be that the conduct of the police generally, which might include unlawful search, seizure or arrest, might have had such an effect on the mind of the person that it could be said to contribute to the unreliability of his confession. These matters will be discussed subsequently in the section on confessions (see **17.1**).

Under s. 78 of the 1984 Act a confession may be excluded even if it is not *unreliable* if the circumstances in which it was obtained lead to the conclusion that the admission of the evidence would have an adverse effect on the fairness of the proceedings. The occasions when ss. 76 and 78 together have most frequently led to the exclusion of confessions have mainly been connected with police misconduct or omission in the course of detention and interrogation, a stage of procedure at which the suspect is clearly vulnerable to improper pressures with direct consequences for the outcome of his trial.

We shall now discuss the rules in relation to detention and interrogation.

4.4   Detention

4.4.1   THE CUSTODY OFFICER

Part IV of the 1984 Act creates the post of custody officer, who is a policeman of at least sergeant rank who has various responsibilities at 'designated police stations'. Designated police stations are those which have sufficient accommodation and facilities for the purpose of detaining arrested persons.

In principle the custody officer takes formal charge of arrested persons on the premises and has the duty of supervising the detention and interrogation of such persons. He must also keep a 'custody record' which records details of the course of a suspect's detention and interrogation.

When a person is brought to the police station after arrest he must be brought before the custody officer who will at that stage decide whether there is sufficient evidence to charge him with the offence for which he was arrested. If there is he should be charged forthwith. He may then be released on bail, see **4.7**.

If the individual is not released on bail he must be brought before a magistrates' court as soon as practical and in any event not later than the first sitting of the court after he has been charged with an offence.

What however if the custody officer decides that there is as yet insufficient evidence to charge? The suspect must then be released unless detention is necessary to secure or preserve evidence relating to an offence for which he is under arrest or to obtain such evidence by questioning him (s. 37 of the 1984 Act). A written record of the grounds for detention must be made in the presence of the person arrested and the grounds must be conveyed to the person.

There are further limits on detention before charging namely:

(a)   There is an overriding duty on the police to charge an individual as soon as there is sufficient evidence to justify a charge.

(b)   No person may be detained for more than 24 hours from the time at which the arrested person is brought to the police station save where the offence being investigated is a *serious arrestable offence*.

Serious arrestable offences are a special category of offences. Where a serious arrestable offence is concerned the police have greater powers than they have in the case of other offences. Serious arrestable offences comprise:

(a)   Certain offences which are always serious, e.g., murder, manslaughter, rape, kidnapping, certain other sexual offences and various Firearms Act offences.

(b)   Any other arrestable offence if its commission has led or is intended or likely to lead to certain serious consequences as defined in s. 116 of the 1984 Act. The serious consequences are:

        (i)   serious harm to the security of the state or public order;

        (ii)   serious interference with the administration of justice or the investigation of offences;

        (iii) the death of any person;

    (iv) serious injury to any person;

    (v) substantial financial gain to any person; or

    (vi) serious financial loss to any person.

In relation to the last of these, it should be noted that there is a subjective criterion for establishing whether the offence involves 'serious loss'. By s. 116(7) 'serious' means 'serious for the person who suffers it'. Thus theft, e.g., of a person's welfare benefit Giro cheque might well qualify even though the amount involved is modest.

In the case of serious arrestable offences the police have the right to detain the suspect for longer than the basic 24 hours. However, even in such cases the total period of detention must not exceed 36 hours and requires authority of an officer of at least superintendent rank. This officer should have reasonable grounds for believing that it is necessary to detain that person without charge in order to secure or preserve evidence or to obtain such evidence by questioning him, and that the investigation is being conducted diligently and expeditiously.

The concept of the serious arrestable offence allows the police other greater powers. If the police do require to detain a person beyond 36 hours they must apply on oath by way of information to a magistrates' court for a *warrant of further detention* and the person must be present at the hearing and has the right to be legally represented. Detention may then be authorised until up to 96 hours from the 'relevant time', i.e. from the time at which the person first came to the police station.

In every case where a person is detained reviews must be made of his detention (whether he has been charged or not) no later than six hours after the detention was first authorised by the custody officer and thereafter every nine hours to ensure that the reasons justifying detention still exist. The review officer is an officer of inspector rank who must not have been directly involved in the investigation (in cases where the arrested person has not been charged) or the custody officer if he has. If the criteria for continued detention are not satisfied then the arrested person must be released.

4.5   The Conduct of Interrogation

Interrogation is now governed by Code of Practice C, issued under s. 66 of the 1984 Act and revised on 10 April 1995, concerning the detention, treatment and questioning of persons by the police. We shall consider this shortly, but meanwhile it is important to note two specific powers provided in the statute itself, namely:

    (a) By s. 58 of the 1984 Act a person arrested and held in custody in a police station is entitled to consult a solicitor privately at any time if he so requests. Any such request must be recorded in the custody record. The consultation may be in person or by telephone and may be with his own solicitor, if he has one, or with a duty solicitor. A delay in compliance is permitted only where the detainee is being held for a serious arrestable offence and an officer of at least superintendent rank has authorised the delay, and delay is in any event only permitted if the officer has reasonable grounds for believing that receiving such legal advice would:

        (i) lead to interference with evidence of an offence or to interference with, or physical injury to, some third person;

        (ii) lead to persons suspected of an offence being warned that the police are looking for them; or

(iii) hinder the recovery of the proceeds of an offence.

(b) Under s. 56 of the 1984 Act a person has the right not to be held incommunicado. Section 56 of the 1984 Act provides that a person under arrest at a police station shall be entitled on request to have one friend, relative or other person likely to take an interest in his welfare informed of his arrest and of the station where he is being held. Delay in permitting the person to exercise this right is only permitted in the circumstances where the right to legal advice may be delayed or refused.

Finally, an individual held in custody has the right to read the relevant Codes of Practice. However, a person arrested is not entitled to cause unreasonable delay to the investigation while he reads the Codes.

4.5.1 CODE OF PRACTICE C

Unfortunately the full text of this Code of Practice runs to over 50 pages and it is not practical to set it out here. The most important parts are ss. 10–12 and these appear in full towards the end of this chapter (see **4.9**) for ease of reference. It is only possible here to summarise some of the most important provisions. The Code in particular provides that:

(a) There is a basic duty to inform a person arrested of certain rights.

(b) Where there are grounds to suspect a person of an offence he must be cautioned in the same terms as those of the caution upon arrest. Further, where there is any break in questioning, the suspect should be recautioned when it resumes or he should be reminded that he is still under caution. Moreover, a detailed record must be made of the conduct of the interrogation; of meals and refreshment breaks; of complaints; and of any reasons for delaying a break in the interview.

A person must be charged as soon as an officer considers that there is sufficient evidence to prosecute him successfully and that the person has said all that he wishes to say about the offence. In other words the prosecution having already obtained such evidence may not delay charging merely because they wish to collect further information from the suspect. Having charged the suspect he may not be further questioned with regard to the offence except:

(a) where necessary for the purpose of preventing or minimising harm or loss to some other person or the public; or

(b) in order to clear up an ambiguity in a previous answer; or

(c) where it is in the interests of justice that he should have put to him, and have an opportunity to comment on, information concerning the offence which has come to light since he was charged.

In the latter case he should be cautioned again before questioning is resumed. He should not be referred to any written statement made by another person or to the contents of any interview with such person without first being cautioned and then shown the statement or interview record without any further comment being invited by the officer who tenders the statement etc. to him.

The temptation for the police to delay charging, so as to be able to continue interrogating, is therefore considerable but is in part alleviated by the provisions referred to above. As indicated at the outset, breach of these provisions is likely to be considerably more relevant to the criminal process in terms of the admissibility of evidence than breach of the provisions with regard to arrest and search.

A suspect will now be in the confines of a police station and unless he is already well used to custody he may have little idea of his rights (and the average suspect is unlikely perhaps to obtain much benefit from reading the 1984 Act and the Codes with which he may be supplied). He may have no idea about how long the police can keep him, what their powers are whilst he is there, or what they may be doing at his home or with his family meanwhile. He is therefore in a very vulnerable situation. The provisions requiring the keeping of exhaustive custody records are meant in part to ensure that the police thoroughly rationalise and justify each of the steps they propose to take with regard to the way in which they treat the suspect or the reasons why they are keeping him in custody or prolonging his custody. They also ensure that the police themselves keep their actions under review in the light of the fact that the custody record may come up for examination in court and they may be asked then to justify exactly why they behaved in the way in which they did.

Thus, for example, suppose that a suspect was arrested on a Saturday night and put in a cell before questioning started some hours later. It would be easy enough at the trial for the police to say that due to the volume of activity in the police station on the Saturday night it was impossible to question the suspect immediately. In fact they may very well have left him in the cell for a few hours as part of a well recognised softening-up process so as to make him more amenable to questioning later. Whilst the keeping of records does not prevent this kind of practice, the police will need to be very sure that they can justify it at the time they are writing up the custody record.

Interrogation procedures now involve a careful review of the case not by the investigating officer but by the custody officer, and in some cases by a review officer who also is not connected with the case. In both cases it is intended that the officers concerned will be sufficiently aware of the need to preserve their personal reputations and integrity to ensure that they do their job efficiently and do not merely succumb to the enthusiasm of their colleagues involved in the investigations who may wish to conduct matters in a certain way. It will be noted that both the custody officer and the review officer may well be of inferior rank to the investigating officers whose procedures they may be charged with supervising.

The process of interrogation may be vital for the success of the eventual prosecution. No matter what evidence the police already have, they are likely to try to obtain a confession from a suspect if at all possible, thinking it will then be harder for him to plead not guilty and a great deal of time and cost may well be saved. Breaches of the Codes or of the substantive sections of the 1984 Act, e.g., ss. 56 and 58, are not in themselves matters which invalidate a confession. They will, however, be seriously taken into account in considering whether in all the circumstances the confession is *unreliable*.

4.5.2 TAPE RECORDING OF INTERVIEWS

The tape recording of interviews is now dealt with as Code of Practice E, issued under the authority of s. 66 of the 1984 Act. The Code is too lengthy to set out in full. Interviews at a police station should now be tape recorded in the case of indictable offences, including those triable either way. If for any reason an officer decides not to tape record an interview there may be comment in court (and indeed consequences in respect of any confession allegedly obtained). The officer concerned should therefore be prepared to justify his decision in each case.

In principle the consent of the suspect is required though the police may carry on with tape recording even in the event of objection if they think it appropriate. To do so, however, might involve them in adverse comment in court. The following are the main features of the tape-recording process:

(a) The tape recording must be done openly and not without the knowledge of the suspect.

(b) Two tapes must be used on a twin deck machine; one of these will be the 'master tape' which is sealed at the end of the interview and will not be opened until the court proceedings.

(c) A balanced summary of the relevant parts of the interview will be prepared from the 'working' copy of the tape and this balanced summary will be sent to the defence. If the defence require it they may insist on listening to the whole tape.

(d) A transcript of the tape may be prepared for use in court to avoid the time needed to set up the recording and playing equipment. Naturally the tape may in some situations be played in court in order to resolve difficulties; to indicate authenticity; or so that the full picture can be conveyed to the court in terms of pauses, breaks, tone of voice, etc.

(e) Any interview which is not tape recorded must be contemporaneously recorded in note form whether or not the interview takes place at the police station. At the end of the interview an arrested person must be given the opportunity to read the interview record and to sign it as correct or to indicate in which respects he considers it inaccurate.

(f) The tape or interview record must indicate where the interview took place, where it began and ended, any breaks in it, and the persons present. This will usually be done by the interrogating officer giving details at the start and end of the interview.

This tape will be an essential tool for challenging the admissibility of any confession on the grounds of unreliability or unfairness. For further discussion of these aspects see **17.1.8.2** and **17.1.8.3**.

4.6 Identification Procedures

The Court of Appeal in *R* v *Turnbull* [1977] QB 224 laid down important guidelines as to the need for a jury or magistrates to exercise caution in convicting in a case depending wholly or substantially on disputed identification evidence. The normal case will be where an eye-witness at the scene of some incident believes he can recognise the perpetrator who is not apprehended at that time, and subsequently a suspect is found.

At one time the suspect might have been tried and the identifying witness would have seen him for the first time since the crime sitting in the dock and would purport to identify him then and there. There are clearly grave dangers in this course. The witness may feel sure that the police will have the right man and even if he entertains doubts may identify the man in the dock simply because he is there. Accordingly for a very long time now 'dock identifications' have been disapproved and identification parades have been used.

An identification parade is an opportunity for a witness to see the suspect as soon as possible after the crime and to test the witness's ability to pick the suspect out of a group of people of similar appearance. The guidelines for the conduct of identification parades are now contained in Code of Practice D, issued under s. 66 of the 1984 Act.

Where the police have a suspect and the evidence on which they base their case is wholly or substantially that of identification they should hold an identification parade. They must give the suspect the right to refuse to take part. If, however, he does refuse there are two important points to note and these will generally mean that it is prudent for a suspect to consent. If he refuses:

(a) The refusal may be referred to in evidence at any subsequent trial and may be subject to comment.

(b) Some less satisfactory method of identification, such as group identification or identification by video of the suspect and others, or even confrontation (that is one to one with the witness), or allowing the witness to see the suspect and a few other prisoners in the cell, may be adopted. Generally speaking a properly conducted identification parade gives the suspect a better chance. Parts of Code of Practice D are set out at the end of this chapter, including: Annex A which deals with the conduct of identification parades; Annex B which deals with video identification; Annex C which deals with confrontation; Annex D which deals with showing photographs; Annex E which deals with group identification, including the relatively new area of 'moving group' procedures which are increasingly common in some types of urban crime.

4.6.1   CONDUCT OF AN IDENTIFICATION PARADE

The following conditions must be complied with when conducting an identification parade:

(a) Certain information must be given to the suspect in a written 'notice to suspect'.

(b) The suspect may have a solicitor or friend present at the parade unless the parade officer reasonably considers that this cannot be arranged without causing unreasonable delay having regard to the lawful period of detention.

(c) The parade must be conducted by a uniformed officer of at least inspector rank who is not personally involved in the investigation. The point of this is to ensure that the procedure is scrupulously carried out and that the officer charged with organising the parade has no personal interest in the case which might lead him to shortcut any procedures.

(d) The parade must consist of at least eight persons other than the suspect who are so far as possible of the same age, height, general appearance and position in life as the suspect. The suspect may choose his own position in the line, and may change positions if he wishes in between inspections by identifying witnesses if there are more than one.

(e) It is vital to ensure that the witnesses are segregated from the parade so that they do not see any member of the parade beforehand, and are not prompted by any photograph or description of the suspect or given any clues, or communicate with each other or with any witness who has already seen the parade.

The procedure on the parade is that the witness is brought into the room where the members of the parade are and walks past them. Alternatively the parade may take place in a room equipped with a screen which permits witnesses to see members of the parade without being seen. The procedures are however, essentially the same in both cases, save that a parade involving a screen may take place only when the suspect's solicitor, friend, or appropriate adult is present, or the parade is recorded on video. Immediately before the witness inspects the parade, the identification officer (i.e., the officer organising the parade) shall tell the witness that the person he saw may or may not be in the parade and if he cannot make a positive identification he should say so, but that he should not make a decision before looking at each member of the parade at least twice. Once the witness has looked properly at the whole parade the identification officer asks him whether the person he saw on the earlier relevant occasion is on the parade, and the witness should then make the identification by indicating the number of the person concerned. The form of the warning to the witness is to indicate to him that he should not feel under pressure to pick someone out since he will no doubt be aware that the police have gone to a lot of time and trouble in organising the parade and looking for vital evidence.

The witness may ask, if he wishes, for any member of the parade to speak, move, or adopt any posture. If this suggestion comes from the witness then the officer in charge of organising the parade is required to remind the witness that the parade has been selected on the basis of physical appearance not, for example, similarity of voice and the officer must specifically ask the witness whether he is capable of identifying any person on the basis of appearance alone. However, thereafter the witness's request may be met.

4.6.2 THE USE OF PHOTOGRAPHS

Annex D to Code D sets out rules for the use of photographs. This Annex is set out for reference at the end of this chapter (see **4.13**) but it is convenient to summarise it and indicate some of the more important considerations here:

(a) Photographs should not be used where there is a suspect already available. At this stage one should go straight to an identification parade. Clearly an identification parade is preferable to photographs and moreover if photographs have been used they substantially detract from the value of any subsequent identification parade so far as that witness is concerned. This is because the witness who may have seen an incident for some few seconds and is able to pick out a photograph on the basis of his recollection of that incident will obviously clearly remember the features in the photograph should any subsequent identification parade be held. There is thus one vital further remove between the crime and the parade and a witness who has an opportunity of studying a photograph at leisure is unlikely to fail to pick out that person at the parade. Nonetheless the requirements of the Code are that if a witness has identified a suspect from a photograph he should still go on to confirm this at an identification parade.

(b) A witness must be shown at least 12 photographs at a time and, as far as possible, they should be of a similar type and with a resemblance to the suspect.

(c) If one witness makes a positive identification then there should be no further showing of photographs, and an identification parade should be held for other witnesses involved.

In the exceptional case where a witness attending an identification parade has previously been shown a photograph or photofit picture, the suspect and his legal representative must be informed of this fact before committal proceedings or summary trial.

To summarise therefore one can say that photographs should only be used where there is no suspect at all. Thus if for example some offence is committed in a large city and the police have little idea who might have committed it they will first look in criminal records for persons who have a propensity to that type of crime and who live locally. They will then show photographs of such suspects to one eye-witness in the hope that a lead can be obtained. If the eye-witness then identifies someone, an identification parade will be held with that suspect (if he is willing) for the first witness and subsequently any other eye-witnesses involved.

4.6.3 IRREGULARITY IN IDENTIFICATION PROCEDURE

What if there is irregularity in the showing of photographs or conduct of identification parades? The answer depends on the degree of the irregularity:

(a) Any deliberate leading of a witness, e.g., by showing only one photograph, or indicating which is the suspect in a parade, ought to invalidate the whole of the identification evidence thus obtained from the witness concerned.

(b) If there is some lesser breach of the rules, for example, if a parade had two individuals in it who did not look very much like the suspect, or was one person short of the required number, then that would be a matter within the discretion of the trial judge. He might very well rebuke the prosecution for these deficiencies but it is most unlikely that he would rule the evidence out entirely, although he ought to comment that because of the defects in procedure the evidence might be less reliable.

The problems of defects in the holding of an identification parade and the subsequent exclusion of identification evidence are discussed at 19.5.4.

Occasionally if a suspect has a very unusual appearance, for example in terms of height, hairstyle, etc., it may be impossible to organise a proper parade. In these circumstances there may be no alternative to group identification or simple confrontation, i.e., letting the witness see the suspect at the police station. It should be noted however that if a suspect wishes there to be an identification parade he generally has the right to one, and failure to accord him this right is likely to be fatal to the evidence (see 19.5.3).

Finally, it is important to note that, unless exceptionally the defence wish them to do so (e.g., to explore the procedure involved so as to point to impropriety), the prosecution must not lead any evidence before the jury of the use of photographs. This is because the reference to police photographs is tantamount to telling the jury that the accused has a criminal record.

4.7 Police Bail

Bail in the course of criminal proceedings is governed by the Bail Act 1976 (see **Chapter 6**). However, that Act applies only to bail granted by a *court*. The question of bail also arises where a custody officer is deciding on how to deal with a suspect. If an arrested person has been charged at the police station otherwise than on a warrant which is already 'backed for bail', the custody officer must decide whether:

(a) to keep the arrested person in custody at the police station until he or she can be brought before a magistrates' court at its next sitting, or

(b) to release the arrested person, and, if the decision is to release, whether to do so unconditionally or on bail (s. 38(1), Police and Criminal Evidence Act 1984).

Under s. 38(1), as amended by s. 28 of the Criminal Justice and Public Order Act 1994, a custody officer must order the release of a person charged with an offence unless he has a belief, based on reasonable grounds that one or other of the matters listed in the section apply. Section 28(2) of the 1994 Act brings the criteria which the police must have regard to more closely into line with the criteria which a court applies in its decision to refuse bail under the Bail Act 1976. Those criteria are discussed in **Chapter 6**. The conditions under which the custody officer need not order the release of the person charged are as follows, where either:

(a) the name or address of the person arrested cannot be ascertained or the custody officer has reasonable grounds for doubting whether a name or address furnished by him is his real name or address; or

(b) the custody officer has reasonable grounds for believing that the person arrested will fail to appear in court to answer bail; or

(c) in the case of a person arrested for an imprisonable offence, the custody officer has reasonable grounds for believing that the detention of the person arrested is necessary to prevent him from committing an offence; or

(d)   in the case of a person arrested for an offence which is not an imprisonable offence, the custody officer has reasonable grounds for believing that the detention of the person arrested is necessary to prevent him from causing physical injury to any other person or from causing loss or damage to property; or

(e)   the custody officer has reasonable grounds for believing that the detention of the person arrested is necessary to prevent him from interfering with the investigation of offences or of a particular offence; or

(f)   the custody officer has reasonable grounds for believing that the detention of the person is necessary for his own protection.

Thus where a person has been charged, the custody officer must consider bail.

We have so far dealt with the situation where a suspect has been charged. If a custody officer is not satisfied that there is sufficient evidence to charge a suspect and is not willing to authorise detention for questioning, then the suspect must be released either unconditionally or on bail (s. 37(2), Police and Criminal Evidence Act 1984). If the custody officer grants bail the condition of bail will be to return to the station on a specified future date for further enquiries (e.g., for putting on an identification parade or further questioning).

4.7.1   THE POLICE'S POWER TO IMPOSE CONDITIONS ON POLICE BAIL

Until s. 27 of the Criminal Justice and Public Order Act 1994 came into force in February 1995, the police could only grant bail either unconditionally or by requiring a surety or sureties. It was considered that this was inconvenient for several reasons and that there was no reason why the police should not have the power to impose conditions on bail in much the same way as a court could do. Section 27 of the 1994 Act, now in effect, applies s. 3 of the Bail Act 1976 to police bail with slight modifications. Thus a person now released by the police under s. 38 of the 1984 Act may be required to comply with such requirements as appear to the custody officer to be necessary to secure that he surrenders to custody, does not commit further offences, and does not interfere with witnesses or obstruct the course of justice.

Once the custody officer is satisfied that conditions are necessary, they may be imposed. They do not include the power to require a person to live in a bail hostel, but otherwise there would seem to be no limit on them except such limit as the courts would strike down as unreasonable. Thus custody officers must be prepared to justify their decisions, inform the person bailed of their reasons for imposing conditions and record them in the custody records. Such conditions may now include conditions of residence, notification of change of address, reporting at intervals to a police station, curfew and the like.

4.8   Advising a Suspect at the Police Station

We shall now consider some general aspects of assisting a suspect at the police station. Recent research has demonstrated the poor quality of legal advice and assistance often given to suspects at police stations. Some firms of solicitors send unqualified and inexperienced staff for this work partly because it is not well paid and partly because it is often required at inconvenient or unsocial hours or on very short notice and disrupts the working day. Clearly if a telephone call is received to say that a client is in custody within office hours and that the police are intending to interview him shortly, a difficult decision has to be made as to whether to drop everything, including possibly cancelling appointments with other clients, to attend the police station or to decline to assist thus losing the client. If the telephone call indicating that a client is in custody comes outside office hours, the disruption to personal life may be equally extreme. Nonetheless a firm which holds itself out as undertaking a substantial amount of criminal work ought to have the resources to send competent lawyers to assist at what, as recent case law shows, is often the most vital stage of all in the criminal justice process, where things may go seriously wrong for a defendant.

4.8.1 OBTAINING INSTRUCTIONS

You could be called out through the duty solicitor service, by the client direct if the police have permitted him to telephone, by the police themselves, or, quite often, by a third party such as the suspect's spouse who indicates that he has just been arrested. In the latter case you may have to ring around to see which police station he has been taken to. If it is possible that he may have been taken to one of several police stations it is important to ensure a record is made of the telephone call to each police station. The level of cooperation that can be expected may vary greatly. Sending a fax message is excellent evidence of any communications which are made and of the relevant times.

On arrival at the police station you should insist on a private interview with the client. In principle, by s. 58 of the 1984 Act, a suspect is entitled to consult his solicitor privately unless access may properly be delayed in the case of a serious arrestable offence and such delay is authorised by a superintendent. That delay may only be exercised on appropriate grounds set out in s. 58(8) of the 1984 Act and a solicitor should ask at the time what the grounds are and record the answer given to him. Section 58(8) provides as follows:

An officer may only authorise delay where he has reasonable grounds for believing that the exercise of the right conferred by subsection (1) above at the time when the person detained desires to exercise it—

    (a) *will lead to interference with or harm to evidence connected with a serious arrestable offence or interference with or physical injury to other persons; or*

    (b) *will lead to the alerting of other persons suspected of having committed such an offence but not yet arrested for it; or*

    (c) *will hinder the recovery of any property obtained as a result of such an offence.*

Very commonly the ground chosen is that access to a solicitor 'will lead to the alerting of other persons suspected of having committed a serious arrestable offence, but not yet arrested'. The real reason is often that the solicitor might advise the suspect not to cooperate or answer questions.

It may be possible in the course of discussion to reassure the policemen concerned or even to convince them that they are wrong in believing the alleged crime to be a serious arrestable offence. Where a refusal is maintained despite any argument that one can put forward, one should note the name and rank of the officer making the decision and check that a record of the refusal is made in the custody record.

4.8.2 FURTHER PRACTICAL MATTERS

On the assumption that one has been able to speak to the client, the following matters are worthy of attention.

    (a) Full records should be made of everything that happens at the police station. These can be useful for comparing with or challenging the custody record. The timing of arrival and departure and all relevant incidents within that time, especially the more formal ones such as participation in interviews or identification parades, should be noted. One must insist that the interview is in private and well out of hearing of others; it should take place in a closed room and not in a corridor or some area to which the public or other police have general access. As much information as there is time to obtain from the suspect should be gathered. At this stage one would have an eye to the possibility or probability of either an interrogation and/or identification and therefore the background facts to the alleged incident are what is material. Bail of course will need to be considered shortly but for the time being it is important to get the facts of the case.

(b) The Code of Practice provides that a solicitor must be permitted to consult the custody record of a person detained as soon as practicable after arrival at the police station. This should always be an important preliminary step which the police do not have the right to refuse.

(c) If one is advising a suspect before he is going to be interviewed, then the advice will vary with the circumstances. By far the best course probably remains, as previously, that one should advise the suspect to say nothing whatsoever during interview until one has a thorough picture and can give informed advice. Despite the changes to the 'right to silence' brought about by the new form of caution and ss. 34–37 of the Criminal Justice and Public Order Act 1994, at this stage, this should still usually be the correct approach. Once one has obtained all the background then, at least with a suspect of some intelligence, one may form the view that he will have little to lose by giving his version, for example if he has an apparently complete defence such as an alibi and you are confident that he is telling the truth and thus is not giving hostages to fortune by advancing it at this stage.

(d) The suspect's criminal record, if you do not already know it, should be checked so far as possible. This may be relevant to the likelihood of him having committed the offence itself, to the way in which the police will be inclined to treat him and, at a very early stage, to the possibility of bail. One should never however rely on the version of his criminal record given by one's client. Criminal clients have a strange tendency to tell their solicitor what they think the solicitor wants to hear, i.e. that they are of previous good character even though this will very shortly be exposed as totally untrue.

(e) If, having considered everything, it seems inappropriate to put forward the suspect's case at this stage, then firm advice to remain silent should be given and the suspect should be told the reasons for this and why answering questions may be undesirable. It is unfortunately true that many habitual criminals are not very intelligent. They are often also not aware of their limitations and may feel confident of their ability to exchange badinage with interrogating officers and talk themselves out of their predicament. Clients should be discouraged from this. The interview will be tape recorded and any smart answer or throwaway remark given by the suspect may sound much less impressive when played back to a jury at trial in six months' time. It can always be forcefully pointed out to the suspect that if the police had a cast-iron case against him they would hardly be bothering to ask him questions to improve it. This is not in fact entirely true, or logical, but it often strikes a chord with clients.

(f) It is of course always important to remember that what the client is really interested in is obtaining the best possible outcome. If he admits guilt to you it does not follow that you are obliged to advise him to plead guilty. It may be that the prosecution will have an extremely hard time proving their case especially in the face of his silence and you are entitled to give him that advice.

As indicated earlier (see 1.2.2), you must not be a party to him putting forward any untruthful version in court nor in interview, and therefore you must advise him to remain silent at all stages, leaving the police to decide whether they have sufficient evidence on which to charge. One should bear in mind however that obtaining the overall best result for a client may involve looking ahead to sentence as well as issues of guilt and innocence. There is no doubt that a prompt admission, especially one showing contrition, and cooperation with the police, especially to the point of assisting in the recovery of stolen goods, or even, if he is so inclined, assisting in the apprehension of his accomplices, will be powerful factors in mitigation. In this connection it is also important to discuss one other matter namely the possibility of a caution.

4.8.3   CAUTIONING

Cautioning is an important way of keeping minor offenders out of the courts and in some cases reducing the risk of them reoffending. A Home Office Circular No. 59/1990 provides police with guidance on cautioning offenders as an alternative to prosecution.

The caution may be given in the case of any criminal offence, including road traffic offences. A caution is a serious and formal matter which is recorded by the police and it is likely to influence the police in any decision about whether to prosecute if the person concerned should offend again. Evidence of the caution may be given in subsequent court proceedings. A caution is appropriate where:

(a)   The offender has admitted the offence.

(b)   The offender consents to be cautioned rather than charged (though very few are likely to refuse).

(c)   The public interest has been considered, in particular the nature of the offence, the likely penalty if the case was taken to court, the offender's age, state of health and previous criminal history, and the offender's attitude towards the offence.

(d)   There is a presumption in favour of a caution particularly in the case of juveniles and the elderly or infirm. The Home Office Circular stresses however that there is no presumption that a caution is inappropriate for other groups, e.g., adults in good health.

(e)   The views of the victim ought usually to be obtained and his or her consent to a caution asked for, although it is not fatal to cautioning that consent is refused.

It is therefore obvious that there may be an opportunity for what one might describe as 'negotiations' with the police on a suspect's behalf. The question of the procedure to be followed, a release on bail pending further investigations, the precise charge, the nature of the interview, and the possibility of caution might all arise. The negotiating skills necessary in civil litigation may be equally appropriate here.

4.8.4   THE CONDUCT OF THE INTERVIEW

Following the case of *R* v *Chandler* [1976] 1 WLR 585 (confirmed more recently in *R* v *Dunn* [1990] Crim LR 572) your presence during the interview may lead to adverse inferences being drawn from the exercise of the right to silence. It is possible also that the presence of a solicitor can rectify defects in an interview which might otherwise have been fatal to its admission as evidence. One must also bear in mind that it is usually tactically unwise for the suspect to reply to some questions and not others, and it is better either to attempt full cooperation or to remain silent throughout.

The investigating officer must be allowed to conduct the interview at his own pace and in his own way. You are allowed to intervene, for example where the officer is not asking questions but making statements or where the questions are offensive, oppressive or impossible to answer (e.g., they contain several muddled questions all rolled into one). You should remember throughout that by virtue of paragraph 6D of Code of Practice C, a solicitor is *not* guilty of any misconduct if he seeks to challenge improper questions to his client or the manner in which questions are put, if he advises his client during the course of an interview not to reply to particular questions or if he wishes for an adjournment to give his client further legal advice. A solicitor should not be asked to leave an interview unless his interference with its conduct goes beyond what is proper. Misconducts may include such things as answering questions on the client's behalf, prompting the client orally or giving him written replies to read out. If at any stage a solicitor feels that an interview is getting out of hand he should ask for it to be interrupted so that he may give further advice in private. That advice will usually be to say nothing more.

It is important that a solicitor maintains his own records of the times and events of the interview. You may think that it is pointless to try and make a transcript because the tape will eventually be available but you may not obtain access to that tape until some months later and it may be that the note is required earlier than that, e.g., to consider the facts fully or for a bail application.

At the end of the interview the police should be asked what the position is with regard to continued detention, further interviews and the like. If it is apparent that they are likely to reinterview and perhaps the hour is already late and you are very tired, then you should see whether other resources are available within your firm to ensure that the client has representation at the subsequent interview. This will not be as satisfactory as remaining or coming back yourself, because the element of continuity will be lost but it is certainly better than nothing.

4.8.5 THE RIGHT TO SILENCE

Sections 34–37 of the Criminal Justice and Public Order Act 1994 and the key consequent differences in the wording of the caution given are aimed at preventing defendants obtaining tactical advantage by keeping their defences secret until trial and then attempting to 'ambush' the prosecution. Clearly, how to advise one's client at the police station in connection with answering questions may be of paramount importance to the outcome of the trial. All aspects of the 'right to silence', both during interrogation and at trial, are discussed later (see **17.3**). In addition, now that the Criminal Procedure and Investigations Act 1996 is in force there will be a general duty to serve a notice, where cases are to be tried on indictment giving the prosecution certain information about the nature of the defence (see **9.6**).

4.8.6 IDENTIFICATION CASES

You must be prepared to give the client full advice about identification parades. In principle the decision is the client's but it is usual to attempt to cajole him towards the best tactical view which is that an identification parade gives him the best chance. In a case of disputed identification, a suspect has the basic right to a parade except where the identification officer (that is the officer in charge of the identification procedures) considers that, for example, by reason of the unusual appearance of the suspect or for some other reason, it would not be practicable to assemble sufficient people who resembled him to make a parade fair; or where the identification officer considers because of fear on the part of a witness or for some other reason that a group identification is more satisfactory than a parade, or where the identification officer considers for some other reason that a video film identification would be a more satisfactory course of action (Code of Practice D, paragraphs 2.3, 2.4, 2.7). The case law shows that the police must extend reasonable cooperation here so that a delay even of some weeks may be appropriate in order for the solicitor to attempt to obtain similar looking members of the public to participate in the parade (e.g., as in *R v Britton and Richards* [1989] Crim LR 144, where the suspect had dreadlocks and his solicitor felt that the cooperation of members of the West Indian community could be obtained to help the police put on a parade).

You should of course check the details of the parade to ensure that Code D is respected. It may be necessary to inspect the physical layout of the area where the parade is to take place to ensure that witnesses are brought in properly and by a route which will not involve them speaking to each other. Likewise you should ensure that the suspect and witnesses do not arrive at the police station at the same time. If your client has a unique feature, e.g., a scar, everyone in the parade should wear a sticking plaster over the place of the scar; if he wears glasses so should everyone else in the parade or he should take them off. Your client should be advised to remain silent at all times during the parade so as not to assist unnecessarily in any form of voice identification — this being notoriously suspect. Although a witness may ask for a voice identification there is no obligation on a suspect to cooperate.

If less satisfactory forms of identification are to be used, for example a group identification, perhaps in the street, then you should closely observe all aspects of it. It may for example be possible, if, as is increasingly common, the suspect is invited to walk down the street past the witness, to make a video of the event in case of any unfair procedure, for example where the client was the only black person walking down the street at the time.

For the same reason as with interrogations, records should be made showing precise dates, times and significant events.

Eventually the client will either be charged, released without charge, released on police bail pending further enquiries or asked to return at a given time to participate in other interviews or identification parades.

4.9   Code of Practice C, ss. 10–12

10.   *Cautions*

(a)   *When a caution must be given*

10.1   A person whom there are grounds to suspect of an offence must be cautioned before any questions about it (or further questions if it is his answers to previous questions which provide the grounds for suspicion) are put to him regarding his involvement or suspected involvement in that offence if his answers or his silence (i.e., failure or refusal to answer a question or to answer satisfactorily) may be given in evidence to a court in a prosecution. He therefore need not be cautioned if questions are put for other purposes, for example, solely to establish his identity or his ownership of any vehicle or to obtain information in accordance with any relevant statutory requirement (see paragraph 10.5C) or in furtherance of the proper and effective conduct of a search (for example to determine the need to search in the exercise of powers of stop and search or to seek cooperation while carrying out a search) or to seek verification of a written record in accordance with paragraph 11.13.

10.2   Whenever a person who is not under arrest is initially cautioned or is reminded that he is under caution (see paragraph 10.5) he must at the same time be told that he is not under arrest and is not obliged to remain with the officer (see paragraph 3.15).

10.3   A person must be cautioned upon arrest for an offence unless:

(a)   it is impracticable to do so by reason of his condition or behaviour at the time; or

(b)   he has already been cautioned immediately prior to arrest in accordance with paragraph 10.1 above.

(b)   *Action: general*

10.4   The caution shall be in the following terms:

> *You do not have to say anything. But it may harm your defence if you do not mention when questioned something which you later rely on in court. Anything you do say may be given in evidence.*

Minor deviations do not constitute a breach of this requirement provided that the sense of the caution is preserved. [See Note 10C]

10.5 When there is a break in questioning under caution the interviewing officer must ensure that the person being questioned is aware that he remains under caution. If there is any doubt the caution shall be given again in full when the interview resumes. [See Note 10A]

Special warnings under sections 36 and 37 of the Criminal Justice and Public Order Act 1994

10.5A When a suspect who is interviewed after arrest fails or refuses to answer certain questions, or to answer them satisfactorily, after due warning, a court or jury may draw such inferences as appear proper under sections 36 and 37 of the Criminal Justice and Public Order Act 1994. This applies when:

(a) a suspect is arrested by a constable and there is found on his person, or in or on his clothing or footwear, or otherwise in his possession, or in the place where he was arrested, any objects, marks or substances, or marks on such objects, and the person fails or refuses to account for the objects, marks or substances found; or

(b) an arrested person was found by a constable at a place at or about the time the offence for which he was arrested, is alleged to have been committed, and the person fails or refuses to account for his presence at that place.

10.5B For an inference to be drawn from a suspect's failure or refusal to answer a question about one of these matters or to answer it satisfactorily, the interviewing officer must first tell him in ordinary language:

(a) what offence he is investigating;

(b) what fact he is asking the suspect to account for;

(c) that he believes this fact may be due to the suspect's taking part in the commission of the offence in question;

(d) that a court may draw a proper inference if he fails or refuses to account for the fact about which he is being questioned;

(e) that a record is being made of the interview and that it may be given in evidence if he is brought to trial.

10.5C Where, despite the fact that a person has been cautioned, failure to cooperate may have an effect on his immediate treatment, he should be informed of any relevant consequences and that they are not affected by the caution. Examples are when his refusal to provide his name and address when charged may render him liable to detention, or when his refusal to provide particulars and information in accordance with a statutory requirement, for example, under the Road Traffic Act 1988, may amount to an offence or may make him liable to arrest.

(c) Juveniles, the mentally disordered and the mentally handicapped

10.6 If a juvenile or a person who is mentally disordered or mentally handicapped is cautioned in the absence of the appropriate adult, the caution must be repeated in the adult's presence.

(d) Documentation

10.7 A record shall be made when a caution is given under this section, either in the officer's pocket book or in the interview record as appropriate.

Notes for guidance

10A   In considering whether or not to caution again after a break, the officer should bear in mind that he may have to satisfy a court that the person understood that he was still under caution when the interview resumed.

10B   [Not used]

10C   If it appears that a person does not understand what the caution means, the officer who has given it should go on to explain it in his own words.

10D   [Not used]

11   Interviews: general

(a)   Action

11.1A   An interview is the questioning of a person regarding his involvement or suspected involvement in a criminal offence or offences which, by virtue of paragraph 10.1 of Code C, is required to be carried out under caution. Procedures undertaken under section 7 of the Road Traffic Act 1988 do not constitute interviewing for the purpose of this code.

11.1   Following a decision to arrest a suspect he must not be interviewed about the relevant offence except at a police station or other authorised place of detention unless the consequent delay would be likely:

(a)   to lead to interference with or harm to evidence connected with an offence or interference with or physical harm to other people; or

(b)   to lead to the alerting of other people suspected of having committed an offence but not yet arrested for it; or

(c)   to hinder the recovery of property obtained in consequence of the commission of an offence.

Interviewing in any of these circumstances shall cease once the relevant risk has been averted or the necessary questions have been put in order to attempt to avert that risk.

11.2   Immediately prior to the commencement or re-commencement of any interview at a police station or other authorised place of detention, the interviewing officer shall remind the suspect of his entitlement to free legal advice and that the interview can be delayed for him to obtain legal advice (unless the exceptions in paragraph 6.6 or Annex C apply). It is the responsibility of the interviewing officer to ensure that all such reminders are noted in the record of interview.

11.2A   At the beginning of an interview carried out in a police station, the interviewing officer, after cautioning the suspect, shall put to him any significant statement or silence which occurred before his arrival at the police station, and shall ask him whether he confirms or denies that earlier statement or silence and whether he wishes to add anything. A 'significant' statement or silence is one which appears capable of being used in evidence against the suspect, in particular a direct admission of guilt, or failure or refusal to answer a question or to answer it satisfactorily, which might give rise to an inference under Part III of the Criminal Justice and Public Order Act 1994.

11.3   No policeman may try to obtain answers to questions or to elicit a statement by the use of oppression. Except as provided for in paragraph 10.5C, no policeman shall indicate, except in answer to a direct question, what action will be taken on the part of the police if the person being interviewed answers questions, makes a statement or refuses to do either. If the person asks the officer directly what action will be taken in the event of his answering questions, making a statement or refusing to do either, then the officer may inform the person what action the police propose to take in that event provided that action is itself proper and warranted.

11.4   As soon as a policeman who is making enquiries of any person about an offence believes that a prosecution should be brought against him and that there is sufficient evidence for it to succeed, he shall ask the person if he has anything further to say. If the person indicates that he has nothing more to say the officer shall without delay cease to question him about that offence. This should not, however, be taken to prevent officers in revenue cases or acting under the confiscation provisions of the Criminal Justice Act 1988 or the Drug Trafficking Offences Act 1986 from inviting suspects to complete a formal question and answer record after the interview is concluded.

(b)   Interview records

11.5   (a)   An accurate record must be made of each interview with a person suspected of an offence, whether or not the interview takes place at a police station.

(b)   The record must state the place of the interview, the time it begins and ends, the time the record is made (if different), any breaks in the interview and the names of all those present; and must be made on the forms provided for this purpose or in the officer's pocket book or in accordance with the code of practice for the tape-recording of police interviews with suspects (Code E).

(c)   The record must be made during the course of the interview, unless in the investigating officer's view this would not be practicable or would interfere with conduct of the interview, and must constitute either a verbatim record of what has been said or, failing this, an account of the interview which adequately and accurately summarises it.

11.6   The requirement to record the names of all those present at any interview does not apply to policemen interviewing people detained under the Prevention of Terrorism (Temporary Provisions) Act 1989. Instead the record shall state the warrant or other identification number and duty station of such officers.

11.7   If an interview record is not made during the course of the interview it must be made as soon as practicable after its completion.

11.8   Written interview records must be timed and signed by the maker.

11.9   If an interview record is not completed in the course of the interview the reason must be recorded in the officer's pocket book.

11.10   Unless it is impracticable the person interviewed shall be given the opportunity to read the interview record and to sign it as correct or to indicate the respects in which he considers it inaccurate. If the interview is tape-recorded the arrangements set out in Code E apply. If the person concerned cannot read or refuses to read the record or to sign it, the senior policeman present shall read it to him and ask him whether he would like to sign it as correct (or make his mark) or to indicate the respects in which he considers it inaccurate. The policeman shall then certify on the interview record itself what has occurred. [See Note 11D]

11.11   If the appropriate adult or the person's solicitor is present during the interview, he shall also be given an opportunity to read and sign the interview record (or any written statement taken down by a policeman).

11.12   Any refusal by a person to sign an interview record when asked to do so in accordance with the provisions of the code must itself be recorded.

11.13   A written record shall also be made of any comments made by a suspected person, including unsolicited comments, which are outside the context of an interview but which might be relevant to the offence. Any such record must be timed and signed by the maker. Where practicable the person shall be given the opportunity to read that record and to sign it as correct or to indicate the respects in which he considers it inaccurate. Any refusal to sign shall be recorded. [See Note 11D]

(c)   Juveniles, mentally disordered people and mentally handicapped people

11.14   A juvenile or a person who is mentally disordered or mentally handicapped, whether suspected or not, must not be interviewed or asked to provide or sign a written statement in the absence of the appropriate adult unless paragraph 11.1 or Annex C applies.

11.15   Juveniles may only be interviewed at their places of education in exceptional circumstances and then only where the principal or his nominee agrees. Every effort should be made to notify both the parent(s) or other person responsible for the juvenile's welfare and the appropriate adult (if this is a different person) that the police want to interview the juvenile and reasonable time should be allowed to enable the appropriate adult to be present at the interview. Where awaiting the appropriate adult would cause unreasonable delay and unless the interviewee is suspected of an offence against the educational establishment, the principal or his nominee can act as the appropriate adult for the purposes of the interview.

11.16   Where the appropriate adult is present at an interview, he shall be informed that he is not expected to act simply as an observer; and also that the purposes of his presence are, first, to advise the person being questioned and to observe whether or not the interview is being conducted properly and fairly, and secondly, to facilitate communication with the person being interviewed.

Notes for guidance

11A   [Not used]

11B   It is important to bear in mind that, although juveniles or people who are mentally disordered or mentally handicapped are often capable of providing reliable evidence, they may, without knowing or wishing to do so, be particularly prone in certain circumstances to provide information which is unreliable, misleading or self-incriminating. Special care should therefore always be exercised in questioning such a person, and the appropriate adult should be involved, if there is any doubt about a person's age, mental state or capacity. Because of the risk of unreliable evidence it is also important to obtain corroboration of any facts admitted whenever possible.

11C   It is preferable that a juvenile is not arrested at his place of education unless this is unavoidable. Where a juvenile is arrested at his place of education, the principal or his nominee must be informed.

11D   When a suspect agrees to read records of interviews and of other comments and to sign them as correct, he should be asked to endorse the record with words such as 'I agree that this is a correct record of what was said' and add his signature. Where the suspect does not agree with the record, the officer should record the details of any disagreement and then ask the suspect to read these details and then sign them to the effect that they accurately reflect his disagreement. Any refusal to sign when asked to do so shall be recorded.

12   Interviews in police stations

(a)   Action

12.1   If a policeman wishes to interview, or conduct enquiries which require the presence of a detained person, the custody officer is responsible for deciding whether to deliver him into his custody.

12.2 In any period of 24 hours a detained person must be allowed a continuous period of at least 8 hours for rest, free from questioning, travel or any interruption by policemen in connection with the investigation concerned. This period should normally be at night. The period of rest may not be interrupted or delayed, except at the request of the person, his appropriate adult or his legal representative, unless there are reasonable grounds for believing that it would:

(i) involve a risk of harm to people or serious loss of, or damage to, property; or

(ii) delay unnecessarily the person's release from custody; or

(iii) otherwise prejudice the outcome of the investigation.

If a person is arrested at a police station after going there voluntarily, the period of 24 hours runs from the time of his arrest and not the time of arrival at the police station. Any action which is required to be taken in accordance with section 8 of this code, or in accordance with medical advice or at the request of the detained person, his appropriate adult or his legal representative, does not constitute an interruption to the rest period such that a fresh period must be allowed.

12.3 A detained person may not be supplied with intoxicating liquor except on medical directions. No person, who is unfit through drink or drugs to the extent that he is unable to appreciate the significance of questions put to him and his answers, may be questioned about an alleged offence in that condition except in accordance with Annex C. [See Note 12B]

12.4 As far as practicable interviews shall take place in interview rooms which must be adequately heated, lit and ventilated.

12.5 People being questioned or making statements shall not be required to stand.

12.6 Before the commencement of an interview each interviewing officer shall identify himself and any other officers present by name and rank to the person being interviewed, except in the case of people detained under the Prevention of Terrorism (Temporary Provisions) Act 1989 when each officer shall identify himself by his warrant or other identification number and rank rather than his name.

12.7 Breaks from interviewing shall be made at recognised meal times. Short breaks for refreshment shall also be provided at intervals of approximately two hours, subject to the interviewing officer's discretion to delay a break if there are reasonable grounds for believing that it would:

(i) involve a risk of harm to people or serious loss of, or damage to property;

(ii) delay unnecessarily the person's release from custody; or

(iii) otherwise prejudice the outcome of the investigation.

[See Note 12C]

12.8 If in the course of the interview a complaint is made by the person being questioned or on his behalf concerning the provisions of this code then the interviewing officer shall:

(i) record it in the interview record; and

(ii) inform the custody officer, who is then responsible for dealing with it in accordance with section 9 of this code.

(b) Documentation

12.9 A record must be made of the time at which a detained person is not in the custody of the custody officer, and why; and of the reason for any refusal to deliver him out of that custody.

12.10   A record must be made of any intoxicating liquor supplied to a detained person, in accordance with paragraph 12.3 above.

12.11   Any decision to delay a break in an interview must be recorded, with grounds, in the interview record.

12.12   All written statements made at police stations under caution shall be written on the forms provided for the purpose.

12.13   All written statements made under caution shall be taken in accordance with Annex D to this code.

Notes for guidance

12A   If the interview has been contemporaneously recorded and the record signed by the person interviewed in accordance with paragraph 11.10 above, or has been tape recorded, it is normally unnecessary to ask for a written statement. Statements under caution should normally be taken in these circumstances only at the person's express wish. An officer may, however, ask him whether or not he wants to make such a statement.

12B   The police surgeon can give advice about whether or not a person is fit to be interviewed in accordance with paragraph 12.3 above.

12C   Meal breaks should normally last at least 45 minutes and shorter breaks after two hours should last at least 15 minutes. If the interviewing officer delays a break in accordance with paragraph 12.7 of this code and prolongs the interview, a longer break should then be provided. If there is a short interview, and a subsequent short interview is contemplated, the length of the break may be reduced if there are reasonable grounds to believe that this is necessary to avoid any of the consequences in paragraph 12.7 (i) to (iii).

4.10   Code of Practice D, s. 2 and Annex A

SECTION 2: IDENTIFICATION BY WITNESSES

2.0   A record shall be made of the description of the suspect as first given by a potential witness. This must be done before the witness takes part in the forms of identification listed in paragraph 2.1 or Annex D of this code. The record may be made or kept in any form provided that details of the description as first given by the witness can accurately be produced from it in a written form which can be provided to the suspect or his solicitor in accordance with this code. A copy shall be provided to the suspect or his solicitor before any procedures under paragraph 2.1 of this code are carried out. [See Note 2D]

(a)   Cases where the suspect is known

2.1   In a case which involves disputed identification evidence, and where the identity of the suspect is known to the police and he is available (see Note 2E), the methods of identification by witnesses which may be used are:

(i)   a parade;

(ii)   a group identification;

(iii)   a video film;

(iv)   a confrontation.

2.2   The arrangements for, and conduct of, these types of identification shall be the responsibility of an officer in uniform not below the rank of inspector who is not involved with the investigation ('the identification officer'). No officer involved with the investigation of the case against the suspect may take any part in these procedures.

Identification parade

2.3   Whenever a suspect disputes an identification, an identification parade shall be held if the suspect consents unless paragraphs 2.4 or 2.7 or 2.10 apply. A parade may also be held if the officer in charge of the investigation considers that it would be useful, and the suspect consents.

2.4   A parade need not be held if the identification officer considers that, whether by reason of the unusual appearance of the suspect or for some other reason, it would not be practicable to assemble sufficient people who resembled him to make a parade fair.

2.5   Any parade must be carried out in accordance with Annex A. A video recording or colour photograph shall be taken of the parade.

2.6   If a suspect refuses or, having agreed, fails to attend an identification parade or the holding of a parade is impracticable, arrangements must if practicable be made to allow the witnesses an opportunity of seeing him in a group identification, a video identification, or a confrontation (see below).

Group identification

2.7   A group identification takes place where the suspect is viewed by a witness amongst an informal group of people. The procedure may take place with the consent and cooperation of a suspect or covertly where a suspect has refused to cooperate with an identification parade or a group identification or has failed to attend. A group identification may also be arranged if the officer in charge of the investigation considers, whether because of fear on the part of the witness or for some other reason, that it is, in the circumstances, more satisfactory than a parade.

2.8   The suspect should be asked for his consent to a group identification and advised in accordance with paragraphs 2.15 and 2.16 of this code. However, where consent is refused the identification officer has the discretion to proceed with a group identification if it is practicable to do so.

2.9   A group identification shall be carried out in accordance with Annex E. A video recording or colour photograph shall be taken of the group identification in accordance with Annex E.

Video film identification

2.10   The identification officer may show a witness a video film of a suspect if the investigating officer considers, whether because of the refusal of the suspect to take part in an identification parade or group identification or other reasons, that this would in the circumstances be the most satisfactory course of action.

2.11   The suspect should be asked for his consent to a video identification and advised in accordance with paragraphs 2.15 and 2.16. However, where such consent is refused the identification officer has the discretion to proceed with a video identification if it is practicable to do so.

2.12   A video identification must be carried out in accordance with Annex B.

Confrontation

2.13   If neither a parade, a group identification nor a video identification procedure is arranged, the suspect may be confronted by the witness. Such a confrontation does not require the suspect's consent, but may not take place unless none of the other procedures are practicable.

2.14   A confrontation must be carried out in accordance with Annex C.

ANNEX A: IDENTIFICATION PARADES

(a) General

1. *A suspect must be given a reasonable opportunity to have a solicitor or friend present, and the identification officer shall ask him to indicate on a second copy of the notice whether or not he so wishes.*

2. *A parade may take place either in a normal room or in one equipped with a screen permitting witnesses to see members of the parade without being seen. The procedures for the composition and conduct of the parade are the same in both cases, subject to paragraph 7 below (except that a parade involving a screen may take place only when the suspect's solicitor, friend or appropriate adult is present or the parade is recorded on video).*

2A. *Before the parade takes place the suspect or his solicitor shall be provided with details of the first description of the suspect by any witnesses who are to attend the parade. The suspect or his solicitor should also be allowed to view any material released to the media by the police for the purpose of recognising or tracing the suspect, provided it is practicable to do so and would not unreasonably delay the investigation.*

(b) Parades involving prison inmates

3. *If an inmate is required for identification, and there are no security problems about his leaving the establishment, he may be asked to participate in a parade or video identification.*

4. *A parade may be held in a Prison Department establishment, but shall be conducted as far as practicable under normal parade rules. Members of the public shall make up the parade unless there are serious security or control objections to their admission to the establishment. In such cases, or if a group or video identification is arranged within the establishment, other inmates may participate. If an inmate is the suspect, he shall not be required to wear prison uniform for the parade unless the other people taking part are other inmates in uniform or are members of the public who are prepared to wear prison uniform for the occasion.*

(c) Conduct of the parade

5. *Immediately before the parade, the identification officer must remind the suspect of the procedures governing its conduct and caution him in the terms of paragraph 10.4 of Code C.*

6. *All unauthorised people must be excluded from the place where the parade is held.*

7. *Once the parade has been formed, everything afterwards in respect of it shall take place in the presence and hearing of the suspect and of any interpreter, solicitor, friend or appropriate adult who is present (unless the parade involves a screen, in which case everything said to or by any witness at the place where the parade is held must be said in the hearing and presence of the suspect's solicitor, friend or appropriate adult or be recorded on video).*

8. *The parade shall consist of at least eight people (in addition to the suspect) who so far as possible resemble the suspect in age, height, general appearance and position in life. One suspect only shall be included in a parade unless there are two suspects of roughly similar appearance in which case they may be paraded together with at least twelve other people. In no circumstances shall more than two suspects be included in one parade and where there are separate parades they shall be made up of different people.*

9. *Where all members of a similar group are possible suspects, separate parades shall be held for each member of the group unless there are two suspects of similar appearance when they may appear on the same parade with at least twelve other members of the group who are not suspects. Where*

policemen in uniform form an identification parade, any numerals or other identifying badges shall be concealed.

10. *When the suspect is brought to the place where the parade is to be held, he shall be asked by the identification officer whether he has any objection to the arrangements for the parade or to any of the other participants in it. The suspect may obtain advice from his solicitor or friend, if present, before the parade proceeds. Where practicable, steps shall be taken to remove the grounds for objection. Where it is not practicable to do so, the officer shall explain to the suspect why his objections cannot be met.*

11. *The suspect may select his own position in the line. Where there is more than one witness, the identification officer must tell the suspect, after each witness has left the room, that he can if he wishes change position in the line. Each position in the line must be clearly numbered, whether by means of a numeral laid on the floor in front of each parade member or by other means.*

12. *The identification officer is responsible for ensuring that, before they attend the parade, witnesses are not able to:*

(i) *communicate with each other about the case or overhear a witness who has already seen the parade;*

(ii) *see any member of the parade;*

(iii) *on that occasion see or be reminded of any photograph or description of the suspect or be given any other indication of his identity; or*

(iv) *on that occasion, see the suspect either before or after the parade.*

13. *The officer conducting a witness to a parade must not discuss with him the composition of the parade, and in particular he must not disclose whether a previous witness has made any identification.*

14. *Witnesses shall be brought in one at a time. Immediately before the witness inspects the parade, the identification officer shall tell him that the person he saw may or may not be on the parade and if he cannot make a positive identification he should say so but that he should not make a decision before looking at each member of the parade at least twice. The officer shall then ask him to look at each member of the parade at least twice, taking as much care and time as he wishes. When the officer is satisfied that the witness has properly looked at each member of the parade, he shall ask him whether the person he himself saw on an earlier relevant occasion is on the parade.*

15. *The witness should make an identification by indicating the number of the person concerned.*

16. *If the witness makes an identification after the parade has ended, the suspect and, if present, his solicitor, interpreter or friend shall be informed. Where this occurs, consideration should be given to allowing the witness a second opportunity to identify the suspect.*

17. *If a witness wishes to hear any parade member speak, adopt any specified posture or see him move, the identification officer shall first ask whether he can identify any persons on the parade on the basis of appearance only. When the request is to hear members of the parade speak, the witness shall be reminded that the participants in the parade have been chosen on the basis of physical appearance only. Members of the parade may then be asked to comply with the witness's request to hear them speak, to see them move or to adopt any specified posture.*

17A. *Where video films or photographs have been released to the media by the police for the purpose of recognising or tracing the suspect, the investigating officer shall ask each witness after the parade whether he has seen any broadcast or published films or photographs relating to the offence and shall record his reply.*

18.   *When the last witness has left, the identification officer shall ask the suspect whether he wishes to make any comments on the conduct of the parade.*

(d)   Documentation

19.   *A colour photograph or a video film of the parade shall be taken. A copy of the photograph or video film shall be supplied on request to the suspect or his solicitor within a reasonable time.*

20.   *The photograph or video film taken in accordance with paragraph 19 and held by the police shall be destroyed or wiped clean at the conclusion of the proceedings unless the person concerned is convicted or admits the offence and is cautioned for it.*

21.   *If the identification officer asks any person to leave a parade because he is interfering with its conduct the circumstances shall be recorded.*

22.   *A record must be made of all those present at a parade whose names are known to the police.*

23.   *If prison inmates make up a parade the circumstances must be recorded.*

24.   *A record of the conduct of any parade must be made on the forms provided.*

4.11   Code of Practice D, Annex B: Video Identification

(a)   General

1.   *Where a video parade is to be arranged the following procedures must be followed.*

2.   *Arranging, supervising and directing the making and showing of a video film to be used in a video identification must be the responsibility of an identification officer or identification officers who have no direct involvement with the relevant case.*

3.   *The film must include the suspect and at least eight other people who so far as possible resemble the suspect in age, height, general appearance and position in life. Only one suspect shall appear on any film unless there are two suspects of roughly similar appearance in which case they may be shown together with at least twelve other people.*

4.   *The suspect and other people shall as far as possible be filmed in the same positions or carrying out the same activity and under identical conditions.*

5.   *Provisions must be made for each person filmed to be identified by number.*

6.   *If policemen are filmed, any numerals or other identifying badges must be concealed. If a prison inmate is filmed either as a suspect or not, then either all or none of the people filmed should be in prison uniform.*

7.   *The suspect and his solicitor, friend, or appropriate adult must be given a reasonable opportunity to see the complete film before it is shown to witnesses. If he has a reasonable objection to the video film or any of its participants, steps shall, if practicable be taken to remove the grounds for objection. If this is not practicable the identification officer shall explain to the suspect and/or his representative why his objections cannot be met and record both the objection and the reason on the forms provided.*

8.   The suspect's solicitor, or where one is not instructed the suspect himself, where practicable shall be given reasonable notification of the time and place that it is intended to conduct the video identification in order that a representative may attend on behalf of the suspect. The suspect himself may not be present when the film is shown to the witness(es). In the absence of a person representing the suspect the viewing itself shall be recorded on video. No unauthorised people may be present.

8A.   Before the video identification takes place the suspect or his solicitor shall be provided with details of the first description of the suspect by any witnesses who are to attend the parade. The suspect or his solicitor should also be allowed to view any material released to the media by the police for the purpose of recognising or tracing the suspect, provided it is practicable to do so and would not unreasonably delay the investigation.

(b)   Conducting the video identification

9.   The identification officer is responsible for ensuring that, before they see the film, witnesses are not able to communicate with each other about the case or overhear a witness who has seen the film. He must not discuss with the witness the composition of the film and must not disclose whether a previous witness has made any identification.

10.   Only one witness may see the film at a time. Immediately before the video identification takes place the identification officer shall tell the witness that the person he saw may or may not be on the video film. The witness shall be advised that at any point he may ask to see a particular part of the tape again or to have a particular picture frozen for him to study. Furthermore, it should be pointed out that there is no limit on how many times he can view the whole tape or any part of it. However, he should be asked to refrain from making a positive identification or saying that he cannot make a positive identification until he has seen the entire film at least twice.

11.   Once the witness has seen the whole film at least twice and has indicated that he does not want to view it or any part of it again, the identification officer shall ask the witness to say whether the individual he saw in person on an earlier occasion has been shown on the film and, if so, to identify him by number. The identification officer will then show the film of the person identified again to confirm the identification with the witness.

12.   The identification officer must take care not to direct the witness's attention to any one individual on the video film, or give any other indication of the suspect's identity. Where a witness has previously made an identification by photographs, or a photofit, identikit or similar picture has been made, the witness must not be reminded of such a photograph or picture once a suspect is available for identification by other means in accordance with this code. Neither must he be reminded of any description of the suspect.

12A.   Where video films or photographs have been released to the media by the police for the purpose of recognising or tracing the suspect, the investigating officer shall ask each witness after the parade whether he has seen any broadcast or published films or photographs relating to the offence and shall record his reply.

(c)   Tape security and destruction

13.   It shall be the responsibility of the identification officer to ensure that all relevant tapes are kept securely and their movements accounted for. In particular, no officer involved in the investigation against the suspect shall be permitted to view the video film prior to it being shown to any witness.

14.   Where a video film has been made in accordance with this section all copies of it held by the police must be destroyed if the suspect:

(a)   is prosecuted for the offence and cleared; or

(b)   is not prosecuted (unless he admits the offence and is cautioned for it).

An opportunity of witnessing the destruction must be given to him if he so requests within five days of being cleared or informed that he will not be prosecuted.

(d)   Documentation

15.   A record must be made of all those participating in or seeing the video whose names are known to the police.

16.   A record of the conduct of the video identification must be made on the forms provided.

4.12   Code of Practice D, Annex C: Confrontation by a Witness

1.   The identification officer is responsible for the conduct of any confrontation of a suspect by a witness.

2.   Before the confrontation takes place, the identification officer must tell the witness that the person he saw may or may not be the person he is to confront and that if he cannot make a positive identification he should say so.

2A.   Before the confrontation takes place, the suspect or his solicitor shall be provided with details of the first description of the suspect given by any witness who is to attend the confrontation. The suspect or his solicitor should also be allowed to view any material released by the police to the media for the purposes of recognising or tracing the suspect provided that it is practicable to do so and would not unreasonably delay the investigation.

3.   The suspect shall be confronted independently by each witness, who shall be asked 'Is this the person?' Confrontation must take place in the presence of the suspect's solicitor, interpreter or friend, unless this would cause unreasonable delay.

4.   The confrontation should normally take place in the police station, either in a normal room or in one equipped with a screen permitting a witness to see the suspect without being seen. In both cases the procedures are the same except that a room equipped with a screen may be used only when the suspect's solicitor, friend or appropriate adult is present or the confrontation is recorded on video.

5.   Where video films or photographs have been released to the media by the police for the purposes of recognising or tracing the suspect, the investigating officer shall ask each witness after the procedure whether he has seen any broadcast or published films or photographs relating to the offence and shall record his reply.

4.13   Code of Practice D, Annex D: Showing of Photographs

(a)   Action

1.   An officer of the rank of sergeant or above shall be responsible for supervising and directing the showing of photographs. The actual showing may be done by a constable or a civilian police employee.

1A.   The officer must confirm that the first description of the suspect given by the witness has been recorded before the witness is shown the photographs. If he is unable to confirm that the description has been recorded, he shall postpone the showing.

2.   Only one witness shall be shown photographs at any one time. He shall be given as much privacy as practicable and shall not be allowed to communicate with any other witness in the case.

3. *The witness shall be shown not less than twelve photographs at a time, which shall, as far as possible, all be of a similar type.*

4. *When the witness is shown the photographs, he shall be told that the photograph of the person he saw may or may not be amongst them. He shall not be prompted or guided in any way but shall be left to make any selection without help.*

5. *If a witness makes a positive identification from photographs, then, unless the person identified is otherwise eliminated from enquiries, other witnesses shall not be shown photographs. But both they and the witness who has made the identification shall be asked to attend an identification parade or group or video identification if practicable unless there is no dispute about the identification of the suspect.*

6. *Where the use of a photofit, identikit or similar picture has led to there being a suspect available who can be asked to appear on a parade, or participate in a group or video identification, the picture shall not be shown to other potential witnesses.*

7. *Where a witness attending an identification parade has previously been shown photographs or photofit, identikit or similar pictures (and it is the responsibility of the officer in charge of the investigation to make the identification officer aware that this is the case) then the suspect and his solicitor must be informed of this fact before the identity parade takes place.*

8. *None of the photographs used shall be destroyed, whether or not an identification is made, since they may be required for production in court. The photographs shall be numbered and a separate photograph taken of the frame or part of the album from which the witness made an identification as an aid to reconstituting it.*

(b)   Documentation

9. *Whether or not an identification is made, a record shall be kept of the showing of photographs and of any comment made by the witness.*

4.14   Code of Practice D, Annex E: Group Identification

(a)   General

1. *The purpose of the provisions of this Annex is to ensure that as far as possible, group identifications follow the principles and procedures for identification parades so that the conditions are fair to the suspect in the way they test the witness's ability to make an identification.*

2. *Group identifications may take place either with the suspect's consent and cooperation or covertly without his consent.*

3. *The location of the group identification is a matter for the identification officer, although he may take into account any representations made by the suspect, appropriate adult, his solicitor or friend. The place where the group identification is held should be one where other people are either passing by, or waiting around informally, in groups such that the suspect is able to join them and be capable of being seen by the witness at the same time as others in the group. Examples include people leaving an escalator, pedestrians walking through a shopping centre, passengers on railway and bus stations waiting in queues or groups or where people are standing or sitting in groups in other public places.*

4. *If the group identification is to be held covertly, the choice of locations will be limited by the places where the suspect can be found and the number of other people present at that time. In these cases, suitable locations might be along regular routes travelled by the suspect, including buses or trains, or public places he frequents.*

5.   Although the number, age, sex, race and general description and style of clothing of other people present at the location cannot be controlled by the identification officer, in selecting the location he must consider the general appearance and numbers of people likely to be present. In particular, he must reasonably expect that over the period the witness observes the group, he will be able to see, from time to time, a number of others (in addition to the suspect) whose appearance is broadly similar to that of the suspect.

6.   A group identification need not be held if the identification officer believes that because of the unusual appearance of the suspect, none of the locations which it would be practicable to use satisfy the requirements of paragraph 5 necessary to make the identification fair.

7.   Immediately after a group identification procedure has taken place (with or without the suspect's consent), a colour photograph or a video should be taken of the general scene, where this is practicable, so as to give a general impression of the scene and the number of people present. Alternatively, if it is practicable, the group identification may be video recorded.

8.   If it is not practicable to take the photograph or video film in accordance with paragraph 7, a photograph or film of the scene should be taken later at a time determined by the identification officer, if he considers that it is practicable to do so.

9.   An identification carried out in accordance with this code remains a group identification notwithstanding that at the time of being seen by the witness the suspect was on his own rather than in a group.

10.   The identification officer need not be in uniform when conducting a group identification.

11.   Before the group identification takes place the suspect or his solicitor should be provided with details of the first description of the suspect by any witnesses who are to attend the identification. The suspect or his solicitor should also be allowed to view any material released by the police to the media for the purposes of recognising or tracing the suspect provided that it is practicable to do so and would not unreasonably delay the investigation.

12.   Where video films or photographs have been released to the media by the police for the purposes of recognising or tracing the suspect, the investigating officer shall ask each witness after the procedure whether he has seen any broadcast or published films or photographs relating to the offence and shall record his reply.

(b)   Identification with the consent of the suspect

13.   A suspect must be given a reasonable opportunity to have a solicitor or friend present. The identification officer shall ask him to indicate on a second copy of the notice whether or not he so wishes.

14.   The witness, identification officer and suspect's solicitor, appropriate adult, friend or any interpreter for the witness, if present may be concealed from the sight of the persons in the group which they are observing if the identification officer considers that this facilitates the conduct of the identification.

15.   The officer conducting a witness to a group identification must not discuss with the witness the forthcoming group identification and in particular he must not disclose whether a previous witness has made any identification.

16.   Anything said to or by the witness during the procedure regarding the identification should be said in the presence and hearing of the identification officer and, if present, the suspect's solicitor, appropriate adult, friend or any interpreter for the witness.

17.   *The identification officer is responsible for ensuring that before they attend the group identification witnesses are not able to:*

  (i)   *communicate with each other about the case or overhear a witness who has already been given an opportunity to see the suspect in the group;*

  (ii)   *on that occasion see the suspect; or*

  (iii) *on that occasion see or be reminded of any photographs or description of the suspect or be given any other indication of his identity.*

18.   *Witnesses shall be brought to the place where they are to observe the group one at a time. Immediately before the witness is asked to look at the group, the identification officer shall tell him that the person he saw may or may not be in the group and if he cannot make a positive identification he should say so. The witness shall then be asked to observe the group in which the suspect is to appear. The way in which the witness should do this will depend on whether the group is moving or stationary.*

Moving group

19.   *When the group in which the suspect is to appear is moving, for example, leaving an escalator, the provisions of paragraphs 20 to 23 below should be followed.*

20.   *If two or more suspects consent to a group identification, each should be the subject of separate identification procedures. These may however be conducted consecutively on the same occasion.*

21.   *The identification officer shall tell the witness to observe the group and ask him to point out any person he thinks he saw on the earlier relevant occasion. When the witness makes such an indication the officer shall, if it is practicable, arrange for the witness to take a closer look at the person he has indicated and ask him whether he can make a positive identification. If this is not practicable, the officer shall ask the witness how sure he is that the person he has indicated is the relevant person.*

22.   *The witness should continue to observe the group for the period which the identification officer reasonably believes is necessary in the circumstances for the witness to be able to make comparisons between the suspect and other persons of broadly similar appearance to the suspect in accordance with paragraph 5.*

23.   *Once the identification officer has informed the witness in accordance with paragraph 21, the suspect should be allowed to take any position in the group he wishes.*

Stationary groups

24.   *When the group in which the suspect is to appear is stationary, for example, people waiting in a queue, the provisions of paragraphs 25 to 28 below should be followed.*

25.   *If two or more suspects consent to a group identification, each should be the subject of separate identification procedures unless they are of broadly similar appearance when they may appear in the same group. Where separate group identifications are held, the groups must be made up of different persons.*

26.   *The suspect may take any position in the group he wishes. Where there is more than one witness, the identification officer must tell the suspect, out of the sight and hearing of any witness, that he can if he wishes change his position in the group.*

27.   *The identification officer shall ask the witness to pass along or amongst the group and to look at each person in the group at least twice, taking as much care and time as is possible according to*

the circumstances, before making an identification. When he has done this, the officer shall ask him whether the person he saw on an earlier relevant occasion is in the group and to indicate any such person by whatever means the identification officer considers appropriate in the circumstances. If this is not practicable, the officer shall ask the witness to point out any person he thinks he saw on the earlier relevant occasion.

28.   *When the witness makes an indication in accordance with paragraph 27, the officer shall, if it is practicable, arrange for the witness to take a closer look at the person he has indicated and ask him whether he can make a positive identification. If this is not practicable, the officer shall ask the witness how sure he is that the person he has indicated is the relevant person.*

All cases

29.   *If the suspect unreasonably delays joining the group, or having joined the group, deliberately conceals himself from the sight of the witness, the identification officer may treat this as a refusal to cooperate in a group identification.*

30.   *If the witness identifies a person other than the suspect, an officer should inform that person what has happened and ask if they are prepared to give their name and address. There is no obligation upon any member of the public to give these details. There shall be no duty to record any details of any other member of the public present in the group or at the place where the procedure is conducted.*

31.   *When the group identification has been completed, the identification officer shall ask the suspect whether he wishes to make any comments on the conduct of the procedure.*

32.   *If he has not been previously informed the identification officer shall tell the suspect of any identifications made by the witnesses.*

(c)   Identification without suspect's consent

33.   *Group identifications held covertly without the suspect's consent should so far as is practicable follow the rules for conduct of group identification by consent.*

34.   *A suspect has no right to have a solicitor, appropriate adult or friend present as the identification will, of necessity, take place without the knowledge of the suspect.*

35.   *Any number of suspects may be identified at the same time.*

(d)   Identifications in police stations

36.   *Group identifications should only take place in police stations for reasons of safety, security, or because it is impracticable to hold them elsewhere.*

37.   *The group identification may take place either in a room equipped with a screen permitting witnesses to see members of the group without being seen, or anywhere else in the police station that the identification officer considers appropriate.*

38.   *Any of the additional safeguards applicable to identification parades should be followed if the identification officer considers it is practicable to do so in the circumstances.*

(e)   Identifications involving prison inmates

39.   *A group identification involving a prison inmate may only be arranged in the prison or at a police station.*

40.   Where a group identification takes place involving a prison inmate, whether in a prison or in a police station, the arrangements should follow those in paragraphs 36 to 38 of this Annex. If a group identification takes place within a prison other inmates may participate. If an inmate is the suspect he should not be required to wear prison uniform for the group identification unless the other persons taking part are wearing the same uniform.

(f)   Documentation

41.   Where a photograph or video film is taken in accordance with paragraph 7 or 8, a copy of the photograph or video film shall be supplied on request to the suspect or his solicitor within a reasonable time.

42.   If the photograph or film includes the suspect, it and all copies held by the police shall be destroyed or wiped clean at the conclusion of the proceedings unless the person is convicted or admits the offence and is cautioned for it.

43.   A record of the conduct of any group identification must be made on the forms provided. This shall include anything said by the witness or the suspect about any identifications or the conduct of the procedure and any reasons why it was not practicable to comply with any of the provisions of this code governing the conduct of group identifications.

FIVE

COMMENCEMENT OF PROCEEDINGS AND MODE OF TRIAL

5.1 Introduction

With very few exceptions, not relevant for our purposes, all prosecutions are commenced in a magistrates' court. They may be commenced by one of two methods, namely, the laying of an information which leads to the issue of a summons by the court, and by charging. We shall shortly consider these two methods but before doing so it is necessary to say a few words about some preliminary matters.

5.1.1 TIME LIMITS

In criminal cases there is in principle no statute of limitation comparable to that which applies in civil proceedings. There is thus no time limit within which a prosecution must be commenced. However, in the case of purely summary offences, that is those triable only before a magistrates' court, there is a provision that an information must be laid within six months of the date of commission of the offence. This provision is not applicable to an 'either way' offence, however the statute creating such an offence may itself lay down a time limit for prosecution (although this is rare). An information is laid for these purposes when it is received by the clerk to the justices of the magistrates' court concerned.

By s. 1 of the Road Traffic Offenders Act 1988, in the case of certain driving offences, including dangerous driving, careless driving and driving in excess of the speed limit, there is an additional provision. In these cases a defendant may not be prosecuted unless he was given notice of intended prosecution either orally at the time of the alleged offence or in writing within 14 days of the offence. However, where an accident occurs at the same time as, or immediately after the offence, provided the defendant was aware that the accident occurred there is no requirement to give him notice of intended prosecution.

5.1.2 GEOGRAPHICAL RESTRICTIONS

Magistrates' courts have jurisdiction to try *summary offences* committed within their respective counties. Additionally, a magistrates' court has jurisdiction over offences committed outside its county:

(a) Under s. 2(6) of the Magistrates' Courts Act 1980 where in addition to an offence (either summary or triable either way) which is alleged to have been committed in the court's county the accused is charged with any other summary offence wherever committed.

(b) Under s. 2(2) of the 1980 Act where it is 'necessary or expedient' that a person is charged or tried 'jointly or in the same place as' another person.

(c) Under s. 3 of the 1980 Act offences committed within 500 yards of the county border and continuing offences begun in one county and completed in another may be treated as having been committed in either of the relevant counties. A similar rule applies in the case of offences against persons or property committed in a moving vehicle which at the time crossed a county boundary.

These provisions are common sense. They allow the convenient joinder of offences and offenders and save difficulty in cases where it is not entirely clear where a substantive offence occurred because of closeness to boundaries (county boundaries are in any event often notoriously hard to define).

However, these rules as to jurisdiction apply only in the case of purely summary offences. In the case of an offence *triable either way* (e.g., theft), the magistrates' court does not have this limit on its jurisdiction. In effect therefore the prosecution have the choice of courts in the case of an offence triable either way and may seek to commence proceedings in the court most convenient to them.

5.2 Commencing Proceedings

5.2.1 PROCEDURE BY INFORMATION

The laying of an information fulfils two distinct purposes:

(a) it is the charge to which the accused must plead at the commencement of a summary trial, and

(b) it is the procedural device which leads to the issue of a summons in those instances where the accused's first appearance before the court is secured by summons.

An information may therefore come about in three ways:

(a) By the prosecutor delivering a signed written allegation against the accused to the court. The information must describe only one offence in ordinary language and must cite any relevant statutory provision. It may however allege, in the alternative, different ways of committing the same offence. Reasonable particulars must be disclosed but it is not essential that every legal element of the alleged defence be described. An information may be laid against more than one person. If it is required to bring more than one charge against an accused, separate informations must be delivered to the court.

(b) As an alternative to the above, an applicant may appear in person before a magistrate or magistrate's clerk who then reduces an oral allegation to writing. Following the laying of an information in this manner the court decides whether or not to issue a summons requiring the accused to attend the court. Although often a relatively automatic process, this procedure is nevertheless judicial in nature and case law provides that the question whether or not to issue a summons must be considered judicially by the court concerned. If the summons is issued it is then served on the accused and the contents of the information are embodied in the summons. A single summons may cover more than one information, i.e. may contain several different charges. A summons may be served personally or by post on the accused.

(c)   An alternative to the above procedures applies where a defendant is not in custody at the time of laying the information, the police may proceed by arrest without warrant and charge. In these cases the police will have arrested the defendant and charged him at the police station. They will subsequently either release him on bail until the date specified in the charge for his appearance at court or bring him before the magistrates' court in custody, normally within 24 hours of charging. In these cases the charge sheet serves as the information and no separate summons is issued.

The charge sheet will be read over to the accused and he will be given a copy, whether he is released on bail or kept in custody by the police pending his first appearance. In the case of a release on bail the charge sheet will specify when he is to surrender to his bail at court.

Cases therefore commence in one of the ways previously described. The question of defects in, and amendments of, a *summons* will shortly be described. In the cases of *charges* these may similarly be amended, however, it should be noted that if the case is going to be dealt with in the Crown Court, the form of the *indictment* which will constitute the final charges which an accused has to face at his Crown Court trial will not be drafted until the end of the committal proceedings. This is because it is open to the magistrates to commit on different charges from those originally brought by the prosecution and on any charge disclosed by the material they have considered. In a case of complexity the form of the indictment itself may need to be drafted by counsel before the Crown Court trial commences.

5.3   Classification of Offences and Choice of Court

For procedural purposes, criminal offences are classified into three categories, namely those triable only summarily; those triable only on indictment; and those triable either way. Figure 5.1 on p. 80 gives examples of these.

5.3.1   PURELY SUMMARY OFFENCES

These offences are those that can only be tried by a magistrates' court. They include almost all motoring offences and the vast bulk of regulatory offences. Good examples are the offences of careless, and inconsiderate, driving under s. 3 of the Road Traffic Act 1988 and taking a conveyance under s. 12 of the Theft Act 1968. Although in principle these are triable only summarily, that is they can be dealt with only in the magistrates' court, they can be added as extra counts to an indictment where connected offences are being tried by the Crown Court (see **8.2.4.1**).

5.3.2   OFFENCES TRIABLE PURELY ON INDICTMENT

These are the more serious offences at the opposite end of the spectrum which can only be tried before a judge and jury in the Crown Court. They include murder, rape and robbery.

5.3.3   'EITHER WAY' OFFENCES

This group of offences consists of crimes which may be tried either in a magistrates' court or in the Crown Court. These are offences whose nature and seriousness is not necessarily indicated merely by the name of the offence. Thus, for example, 'theft' can cover a whole spectrum of behaviour from shoplifting a tin of peaches to stealing a Leonardo da Vinci.

Type of Offence	Triable only on Indictment	Triable Either Way	Triable only Summarily
1. Offences against the person	Murder Manslaughter Attempt to procure an abortion Causing grievous bodily harm with intent	Inflicting grievous bodily harm Unlawful wounding Assault occasioning actual bodily harm Assault with intent to resist arrest	Common assault Assault on a police constable in the execution of his duty
2. Sexual offences	Rape: Intercourse with a girl under 13 Buggery Incest	Unlawful sexual intercourse with a girl under 16 Indecent assault Living on the earnings of a prostitute	Soliciting
3. Theft Act offences	Robbery Aggravated burglary Blackmail Assault with intent to rob Burglary comprising commision of, or intention to commit, an offence only triable on indictment Burglary of a dwelling with threats to occupants	All Theft Act offences not being in the other two categories	Taking a motor vehicle without consent Taking a pedal cycle without consent
4. Criminal damage	Damage or arson with intent to endanger life	Damage where the value involved is over £5,000	Damage where the value involved is £5,000 or less
5. Road traffic	Causing death by dangerous driving	Dangerous driving	Most other traffic offences, e.g.: Speeding Failing to report an accident Driving while disqualified Driving without insurance Drunk in charge of a motor vehicle Failing to stop at a red traffic light
6. Miscellaneous	Perjury Attempt to pervert the course of justice Possessing a firearm with intent to endanger life Using a firearm to resist arrest Carrying a firearm to commit an indictable offence Collecting, communicating, etc. information intended to be useful to an enemy Riot	Making false statements on oath not being in judical proceedings Carrying a loaded firearm in a public place Shortening a shot gun Having an offensive weapon in a public place Using, communicating, etc. information entrusted in confidence to a person holding office under the Crown Violent disorder Affray Stirring up racial hatred All offences under the Forgery & Counterfeiting Act 1981 Offences under the Misuse of Drugs Act 1971	Interference with vehicles Being drunk and disorderly Obstructing police Using threatening words or behaviour Dropping litter Failure to pay TV licence All offences under the Factories Act 1961

Figure 5.1

If a defendant appears before a magistrates' court charged with an 'either way' offence, there will be a *mode of trial* hearing. The practice of the courts varies as to when this takes place. It may sometimes happen at the very first appearance of the accused before the court, but more commonly will happen at an adjourned hearing. Before the mode of trial hearing, the court should be satisfied that the defendant is aware of the requirement on the prosecution under the Magistrates' Courts (Advance Information) Rules 1985 to disclose certain advance information about the nature of the prosecution case. We shall return to this shortly.

5.4 Procedure at a Mode of Trial Hearing: ss. 18–21, Magistrates' Courts Act 1980

The mode of trial hearing is the hearing in the magistrates' court at which the decision will be made as to whether the case is to remain in the magistrates' court to be dealt with subsequently by summary trial, or whether the case should be sent to the Crown Court. Substantial criticisms of the previous procedure were made, to the effect that magistrates sent for trial at the Crown Court a large number of cases which they should in fact have tried themselves and that many defendants were opting for trial by jury, but then deciding to plead guilty in which case they could more cheaply and conveniently have been dealt with before the magistrates. The problem was caused because, until 1997, the accused was not invited to indicate his plea at the mode of trial hearing. These and other criticisms led to a substantial change in the previous procedures implemented by the Criminal Procedure and Investigations Act 1996 which inserts three new sections, ss. 17A, 17B and 17C into the Magistrates' Courts Act 1980. Section 17A deals with the mainstream case where the accused is present in court and ss. 17B and 17C cover cases where the accused is not present because of his disorderly conduct but is legally represented, and with the court's powers to adjourn or remand.

The charge is read to the accused who is then asked to indicate how he would answer the following hypothetical question:

Whether (if the offence were to proceed to trial) he would plead guilty or not guilty?

Before he is asked this question the court is required to explain to him in ordinary language that if he indicates that he will plead guilty, the magistrates' court will proceed to deal with sentencing him and will treat him as actually having pleaded guilty and there will therefore be no trial and no calling of evidence. If the magistrates' court then considers that its sentencing powers are inadequate to deal with the accused, they have the power of remanding him to the Crown Court for sentence.

In other words, where a person is charged with an offence triable either way, the accused is given the opportunity to plead guilty at the mode of trial hearing. The mode of trial hearing will therefore only need to proceed to determine the place of trial if the accused indicates that he will plead not guilty. It remains possible, of course, for an accused to plead not guilty at this stage to keep his option for the Crown Court open, but to plead guilty at some subsequent stage. It may be that the case is a very complex one on matters of law and it cannot be decided until thorough advice has been obtained, e.g., whether the accused's activities amounted to 'dishonesty' within the meaning of the Theft Act in which case a late change of plea is unlikely to be penalised in any way. There may also be other reasons, for example, the desirability of obtaining full disclosure of the prosecution evidence or the possibility of negotiating a reduction to a lesser charge.

If there is to be a plea of not guilty, then after the reading of the charge and the indication of plea the procedure is that the prosecution and the defence each has an opportunity to make representations as to mode of trial. If the prosecution is being carried on by the Attorney-General, Solicitor-General or Director of Public Prosecutions and he applies for trial on indictment, the magistrates must comply with his wishes. In other cases however it will usually be the case that the prosecution in a marginal matter will for considerations of cost and speed favour the magistrates' court. Their representations will often consist of no more than saying something along the lines of 'there seems nothing special about this case to warrant the time of the Crown Court and it would appear that the magistrates' sentencing powers are adequate'. The prosecution will take the opportunity to explain to the court the background features of the case where the charge itself does not make it apparent, e.g., where the charge does not describe the seriousness of the assault or the value of the goods.

The defence will have already decided which mode of trial they prefer and will now present their arguments. For example, if the prosecution are contending that there is something very serious about the matter so that it should be tried in the Crown Court, then the defence may need to meet this by suggesting to the magistrates that it is less serious than it may appear and that the magistrates' sentencing powers are adequate should they convict. If the defence have already decided to ask for trial at the Crown Court, they will then make their representations as to why this should be so. A number of factors which might make the Crown Court preferable are suggested below.

5.4.1 THE STATUTORY FACTORS

Thereafter, the magistrates consider the matter and, by s. 19 of the Magistrates' Courts Act 1980, they have to take into account the following:

(a) the nature of the case;

(b) whether the offence is of a serious character; and

(c) whether the punishment which a magistrates' court would have power to inflict for it would be adequate;

(d) any other circumstances which make the case more suitable for one method of trial rather than the other.

5.4.2 NATIONAL MODE OF TRIAL GUIDELINES

The court should also take into account the further considerations set out in *Practice Direction (Mode of Trial: Guidelines)* [1990] 1 WLR 1439 (often referred to as the 'National Mode of Trial Guidelines'). These were revised in 1995 and re-issued.

A number of named offences are described in the Mode of Trial Guidelines and relevant aggravating factors described in respect of each. The presence of such a factor might make them appropriate for committal to the Crown Court. So, for example, in the case of a charge of theft the fact that it was allegedly committed in breach of trust, i.e. by a person in authority, or has been committed or disguised in a sophisticated manner, or is committed by an organised gang, or the victim is particularly vulnerable, e.g., the elderly or infirm, or the property has not been recovered and is of high value may justify committal to the Crown Court. In the case of driving offences the fact that dangerous driving is alleged to have occurred and involved, for example, grossly excessive speeds or racing on a public road or that alcohol or drugs have contributed to it would be exacerbating features. In these kind of cases therefore magistrates should look closely at the possible eventual sentence as a factor in their decision about mode of trial. The Mode of Trial Guidelines are set out in full at the end of this chapter.

At this stage the court does not have the defendant's previous convictions before it and therefore it must act on the basis that it is dealing with a person who is of previous good character. The reason for this is that in principle the magistrates may proceed from the mode of trial hearing to the trial of the offence itself and they should not of course be aware of any criminal record of the accused. In fact, more commonly, there will be an adjournment whatever they decide, in one case for summary trial and in the other for committal proceedings. The reason for this need to adjourn is simply the saving of time and costs. The prosecution would be foolish to call their witnesses to court in the expectation of summary trial if it might in fact be the case that the accused will elect trial on indictment.

5.4.3 THE DECISION AND AFTER

The magistrates retire if necessary and return to announce their decision. If the magistrates consider that trial on indictment is more appropriate, the accused is then told of their decision and committal proceedings take place, either then or more probably at some later date. The accused has no choice in the matter. The question of bail may arise again at this stage if the accused has hitherto been refused bail or if some new matter has arisen which leads to the police now objecting to bail (e.g., it is suggested he has tried to intimidate a prosecution witness in the interim).

If the court decides that summary trial is more suitable, then there is an obligation on the clerk of the court to give the defendant certain information. The clerk must carefully explain to the defendant personally (even if he is legally represented) that he has a choice as to which court he may be tried in but that, if he does consent to summary trial, is found guilty by the magistrates and, then in the light of certain factors, the magistrates consider that greater punishment should be imposed than they have power to inflict, they may commit him to the Crown Court to be sentenced. In other words, the accused is being told that, if his only reason for preferring the magistrates' court is his knowledge that the maximum sentence that they can normally inflict is six months' imprisonment for any one offence, then he need not think that is conclusive. If he is convicted, the magistrates may still after further consideration commit him to the Crown Court for sentence and there he may receive the maximum which the Crown Court is empowered to impose. This is by virtue of s. 38, Magistrates' Courts Act 1980 as inserted by s. 25, Criminal Justice Act 1991. The procedure on committal for sentence after summary trial is described at 7.9.

Thereafter, the accused is asked where he wants to be tried and he has a final say. He may say that he prefers to be tried in the Crown Court or that he is content to accept magistrates' court trial.

5.4.4 WHY MAKE REPRESENTATIONS?

Why bother making representations to the magistrates if the accused has already made up his mind to 'overrule' the magistrates, no matter what, and opt for Crown Court trial? Frankly, many consider that there is little point in making detailed submissions in favour of Crown Court trial where the accused has already decided (on legal advice) to opt for Crown Court trial whatever the magistrates' preliminary decision is. However, there is one advantage in doing so. If the case does go to the Crown Court, let us say on a relatively trivial shoplifting charge, and one has successfully managed to persuade the magistrates themselves to choose that as the more appropriate forum (let us say because of some alleged difficulty in a matter of evidence which can be more satisfactorily dealt with before the higher court) then if the accused is convicted in the Crown Court, the record will reveal that it was the magistrates themselves who decided to send the case there. The accused will not then be subject to any criticism.

Suppose, however, that one had not tried, or, having tried, had failed to persuade the magistrates themselves to send the case to the Crown Court for trial and had in fact 'overruled' the magistrates' preliminary decision to try the case themselves. In those circumstances, the Crown Court judge may feel that it was wrong for the accused to overrule the magistrates' decision and involve the higher court's time in a trivial matter. Although it is certainly wrong in principle for him to impose a greater *sentence* to take into account his disapproval of this course of action, he is perfectly entitled to make the order which he imposes in respect of *costs* reflect his view of the waste of time of the higher court. He will therefore probably impose a higher costs order than he would otherwise have done.

5.4.5 CHANGE OF FORM OF PROCEEDINGS

Section 25 of the Magistrates' Courts Act 1980 (as amended by sch. 4, Criminal Justice and Public Order Act 1994) allows the court to change from summary trial to committal proceedings and vice versa. This may either be on its own motion or on the application of either party. What was a summary trial may become committal proceedings at any time before the close of the prosecution case. The most common example is likely to be, however, where the accused having previously consented to summary trial, perhaps on an occasion when he was unrepresented, now in the light of legal advice wishes to elect in favour of trial on indictment. In such a case the magistrates have a wide discretion as to whether or not to permit the change of election for trial. It will only very occasionally arise that after hearing prosecution evidence in a summary trial the nature of the offence seems to take on a greater seriousness than formerly, so as to merit the magistrates wishing of their own motion to send the case to the Crown Court. This should only happen rarely because of the opportunity which the prosecution had at the outset to stress factors which made the offence more suitable for trial on indictment.

An accused who has elected trial on indictment may also wish to change his election. The magistrates may permit this change, if proper. Again, it is more likely to occur before any kind of hearing has started. An example might be where an accused now wishes to change his plea to guilty and would naturally wish to stay in the magistrates' court with its lesser sentencing powers. It is important to remember that a mode of trial hearing will still be necessary in the case of an 'either way' offence even though the defendant intends from the outset to plead guilty.

5.4.6 MORE THAN ONE ACCUSED

If there is more than one accused, then the previous practice under which where any of them opted for trial in the Crown Court that election bound the rest is now not followed. In such a situation the magistrates are entitled to take into account the wishes of each co-accused. In *R* v *Brentwood Justices ex parte Nicholls* [1992] 1 AC 1 the House of Lords held that the court need not necessarily be influenced by the fact that one of the accused was electing Crown Court trial, and might still try summarily any accused who elected summary trial. The reason for this is that the proper interpretation of s. 20(3) of the 1980 Act gives the right of election to each accused individually.

5.5 Choice of Court

We have so far described the procedure by which the magistrates' court makes a preliminary decision as to which court will try the case. As we have seen, in cases of offences triable either way, the accused is always in a position to ensure that he has jury trial, either by persuading the magistrates to choose trial on indictment themselves or by overruling their preliminary decision against it. We will now consider the factors which his solicitor will take into account in advising an accused on choice of court.

5.5.1 FACTORS IN FAVOUR OF THE CROWN COURT

5.5.1.1 Acquittal rate

Despite somewhat inconclusive statistical evidence and local variations there is no doubt that many lawyers feel that in certain kinds of case the accused stands a much better chance of acquittal from a jury than in a magistrates' court. The magistrates are believed to become 'case hardened' in certain types of case. An example is shoplifting where the likely defence is that the accused forgot to pay or put the object into the wrong basket. Magistrates will have heard such defences on dozens of occasions and may generally be disinclined to believe them because the frequency with which they are advanced appears to make them improbable in any individual case. A jury is very likely to be hearing such a defence for the first time and to take the judge's direction on 'proof beyond reasonable doubt' more to heart when considering the case. Juries are thus more open minded (or perhaps more naive!) and, with this kind of offence anyway, the accused would generally seem to have a better chance before a jury.

It is also sometimes suggested that, particularly in some locations, magistrates have a belief in the invariable truthfulness of policemen which the ordinary layperson no longer has and therefore that on a jury of 12 people, there are likely to be a higher proportion of sceptics about police evidence.

Allied to these points there is also the undoubted factor that 'sympathy' verdicts are not impossible. This means a verdict based on the personalities involved, on the jury's regard for the personal circumstances of the accused, or on some other legally irrelevant matter. An example is generally thought to be the trial of the civil servant Clive Ponting on Official Secrets Act charges in 1986 where, in the face of a clear direction from the judge on the issues, the jury chose to acquit the accused. In such cases a feeling that the accused has been oppressively treated by the State, be it the police or even sometimes the harsh treatment an accused may have received when testifying from prosecuting counsel, may contribute to this possibility.

5.5.1.2   Matters of law or evidence

In a case which involves difficult legal points, many lawyers doubt whether magistrates, even with the expert assistance of a clerk, really do grasp the legal niceties involved. There are no such problems in the Crown Court where the judge will certainly be capable of grasping them. More important still is the question of evidence. As we shall discuss below at **14.1** the device of having a judge and jury with separate functions in relation to evidence proves to be a very happy one in the common law system. Thus, the fact that matters of admissibility are generally dealt with by the judge with the jury excluded from court means that the jury never hear evidence which is excluded.

In the magistrates' court, there is unfortunately no equivalent to this and one needs to make submissions about admissibility which inevitably involve discussing, describing or hearing the evidence in question in front of the very magistrates whose minds may well be affected by it even if they do rule in favour of exclusion.

There are other cases where in the magistrates' court matters of evidence have to be dealt with in what is, at best, a clumsy manner. Applications to cross-examine the accused on his criminal record under s. 1(f)(ii) of the Criminal Evidence Act 1898 (see **20.3.3.2**) are necessarily difficult. In the Crown Court, the judge might, having considered the application in the absence of the jury, refuse it, or perhaps limit cross-examination to certain parts of the accused's record. In the magistrates' court, merely to make the application for leave to cross-examine under s. 1(f)(ii) tells the magistrates that the accused does have a record. There can be no equivalent of letting the prosecution cross-examine on only part of the record, since the magistrates themselves will need to see the record to rule on any such application.

Likewise, the fact that directions about evidence are given to the jury in open court, e.g., on identification evidence, etc., must inevitably be more favourable to the accused than the somewhat bodged counterpart in the magistrates' court where the defence advocate in effect tells the magistrates what rules of evidence they ought to apply and how, and hopes that his submission is understood and remembered and perhaps repeated by the magistrates' clerk.

These procedural distinctions together constitute the most significant factors favouring Crown Court trial in any case where a matter of evidence arises.

5.5.1.3 Knowing the prosecution case in advance

Formerly, this was perhaps the greatest factor in favour of the Crown Court, namely that the prosecution had to disclose their evidence before trial. In the magistrates' court, it was sometimes possible if one had a reasonable relationship with the prosecuting solicitor to persuade him to let one look at the prosecution statements in advance, but this would inevitably be only shortly before the trial and the position was considered much less satisfactory.

Now, however, this has been resolved by the bringing into force of the Magistrates' Courts (Advance Information) Rules 1985. Before the court considers the mode of trial, the defendant or his representative may request that the prosecution furnishes him with advance information and on receipt of such request, the prosecution shall, as soon as practicable, furnish either:

(a) a copy of those parts of every written statement which contains information as to the facts and matters which the prosecution propose to adduce in evidence; or

(b) a summary of such facts and matters.

In fact, since it is obviously quicker and more convenient to send a simple photostat of the statements, this will often be what the prosecution do, rather than separately preparing a summary of the relevant matters. If only a summary is provided then it can later be a source of disputes, in that it would be open to the defendant to suggest that vital matters had been omitted from the summary. It seems, however, that, despite the extra work involved, in many areas of the country Crown prosecutors supply summaries, and brief ones at that, rather than copies of their witness statements. In any event, in every case of an offence triable either way, whether proceeding in a magistrates' court or the Crown Court, there will now be prior disclosure of the prosecution case.

5.5.1.4 Committal proceedings

Committal proceedings are a stage at which a magistrates' court may be called upon to scrutinise the prosecution evidence. Although the defence are neither allowed to insist on witnesses attending to give oral evidence, nor even allowed to submit any evidence of their own, however strong it may be, at least submissions may be made about the sufficiency of the evidence which the prosecution have put forward. There is therefore a chance of having the case thrown out during the committal proceedings. Alternatively, it may be possible to submit to the magistrates, even if they cannot be persuaded to dismiss the case at this early stage (and they will be understandably very reluctant to take this step), that the facts disclose only some lesser offence than that which the prosecution is presently charging (e.g., theft rather than burglary because it can be contended that the accused had permission to be in the premises). What is clear is that there may be some advantage to be derived from this procedural stage.

5.5.1.5 Marginal factors

The one certain feature about trial on indictment is that it will take a good deal longer to happen. Accordingly, in some cases there may be some use to which the delay can be put. The best example would be where some considerable time was necessary perhaps to trace witnesses or explore some difficult avenue of evidence. It may also be easier to obtain expert evidence if there is a lengthy delay, especially in the case of psychiatric evidence. A delay could also be useful with matters relevant to mitigation, although in that case one would be anticipating the conviction of the accused. For example, if the accused can put the delay to some use such as compensating the victim of the offence or in a way which changes the pattern of his life for the better, such as getting married, settling down, or acquiring a job after a lengthy period of unemployment, those things would be useful at the stage of mitigation.

5.5.2 FACTORS IN FAVOUR OF THE MAGISTRATES' COURT

5.5.2.1 Guilty plea

If the defendant firmly intends to plead guilty then unless he can use the delay inherent in Crown Court trial to provide mitigating factors for himself, the lesser sentencing powers of magistrates would normally be a conclusive factor in their favour.

5.5.2.2 Speed

A magistrates' court trial will come on significantly faster than a Crown Court trial. If the accused is nervous, or in custody, this may be a vital factor in favour of the former.

5.5.2.3 Defence statement

In the Crown Court there is a positive requirement on the accused to provide a 'defence statement' at an early stage and failure to do so may allow adverse comment by the prosecution or by the judge in directing the jury. In the magistrates' court giving a defence statement is a purely voluntary matter and failure to do so cannot lead to adverse comment. There is therefore still rather more of an opportunity for the defendant to 'ambush' the prosecution at trial with the exact nature of the defence. Whether this is actually of any advantage will depend upon the facts of every case.

5.5.2.4 Stress

There can be no doubt that the actual trial itself is a greater ordeal in the Crown Court. Not only is it likely that there will be many more people present in court, but the atmosphere, the greater deference accorded to the Crown Court judge, the wigs and gowns, and the feeling that the accused is being constantly scrutinised by the 12 jurors, the judge and the prosecuting counsel, will all put a greater stress on the accused. This is something that should not be dismissed lightly in the case of an accused who is in any way vulnerable.

5.5.2.5 Publicity

It is difficult to generalise about this. The press will have more representatives at a busy Crown Court centre but all of these may be in the same court where something particularly newsworthy is happening. Whether the press will be present in the smaller courts where individuals are being tried on, say, minor theft charges is doubtful. A local worthy, e.g., a local councillor or clergyman, is likely to be regarded as newsworthy and may be lucky to escape the attention of the press wherever he is tried.

It is fair to say that the press take less interest in magistrates' courts; however, much will depend on the locality. If it is a small country town with the magistrates' court only sitting two days a week, the press, if there is a local newspaper, will generally have a representative present throughout every case. It is not unusual, for example, to see in the local press headlines such as 'Barchester Man's Day of Shame' and on reading the report find that it concerns only a motoring offence. In a major conurbation, however, there may well be more chance of escaping any press report at all in the magistrates' court.

5.5.2.6 Sentence

Magistrates have limited sentencing powers. In principle, they can only sentence a person to a maximum of six months' imprisonment for one offence and a maximum of 12 months for any number of offences. Their powers to fine are also limited to £5,000 for each offence, except those for which there is some different statutory maximum. However, it must be noted that if, after trying an 'either way' offence summarily and convicting, they conclude that their sentencing powers are inadequate in view of what they have heard about other offences and the accused's criminal record, they do then have the power to commit the accused for sentence to the Crown Court, which may impose any sentence authorised by law for the offence. Therefore, sentence would only make a difference where the accused concluded that he might receive a sentence which would be longer than six months in prison, but not so much longer that the magistrates would be minded to commit him to the Crown Court. In other words, he is gambling on the magistrates not doing the latter.

It must be said that much will depend on one's knowledge of the bench of magistrates and local Crown Court judges. Certainly any advocate in the Crown Court can tell you of judges who are notoriously 'hard' or 'soft' but there is no controlling which judge will deal with which case and there must be many cases where it would be preferable to be dealt with by a 'soft' judge in the Crown Court, rather than a 'hard' local bench of magistrates. A Crown Court judge dealing with a relatively trivial offence may anyway prove more lenient than magistrates, if only because his usual daily diet involves considerably more serious crime.

5.5.2.7 Cost

Trial in the Crown Court will inevitably be more expensive, perhaps many times so, than summary trial. For a privately-paying client this may be a major factor. Even for a legally-aided client this is not a negligible matter, bearing in mind his contribution towards the costs of his case and a possible costs order in favour of the prosecution on conviction. Whilst such a costs order rarely amounts to the realistic costs of the prosecution it will naturally be larger in the Crown Court than in the magistrates' court.

5.6 Special Procedure in Criminal Damage Cases

There is a unique procedure in cases of alleged criminal damage. Somewhat anomalously, any charge of theft is triable either way and thus an accused may elect Crown Court trial notwithstanding that only a small amount is involved. The rationale of this is said to be that a charge of theft, carrying as it does an element of dishonesty, is of such crucial importance to a person's reputation that he is entitled to be dealt with by a jury of his peers. Criminal damage, notwithstanding that much larger amounts may be involved, and that the mental attitude of the offender may be no less blameworthy, is treated differently. The legislature apparently believes that wilful vandalism for its own sake of something worth £1,000 in some sense carries less of a stigma than shoplifting a tin of peaches. Accordingly, by s. 22, Magistrates' Courts Act 1980 (as amended by s. 46, Criminal Justice and Public Order Act 1994), there is a special provision which is as follows:

(a) Where an accused is charged with criminal damage contrary to s. 1(1), Criminal Damage Act 1971 or attempts to commit such offences, then unless the offence involves damage or attempted damage *by fire*, the magistrates must hear any representations made by the prosecution or the defence about the value of the goods involved in the offence. Documentary evidence, e.g., about repairs, may be produced.

(b) If the value involved is then considered to be £5,000 or less, the magistrates treat the case as if it were triable only summarily and the accused has no right to a trial on indictment.

(c) If the value involved is clearly over £5,000 the case is dealt with like any other 'either way' offence and there is a mode of trial hearing.

(d) If the case is dealt with as purely summary, then the maximum sentence available to the magistrates is three months' imprisonment or a £2,500 fine. The magistrates then have no power to commit for sentence to the Crown Court under s. 38 of the 1980 Act.

(e) If the case, notwithstanding being dealt with as an 'either way' offence, is tried summarily, the maximum sentence is six months' imprisonment and a £5,000 fine and the magistrates may, in those circumstances, commit for sentence under s. 38.

(f) If it is unclear whether the value of the goods involved is more or less than £5,000, the clerk of the court should ask the accused for his consent to summary trial. If he does consent to summary trial and is then convicted, the maximum penalty is £2,500 and three months' imprisonment and he cannot be committed for sentence under s. 38.

5.7 National Mode of Trial Guidelines

The purpose of these guidelines is to help magistrates decide whether or not to commit 'either way' offences for trial in the Crown Court. Their object is to provide guidance not direction. They are not intended to impinge upon a magistrate's duty to consider each case individually and on its own particular facts.

These guidelines apply to all defendants aged 18 and above.

General mode of trial considerations

Section 19 of the Magistrates' Courts Act 1980 requires magistrates to have regard to the following matters in deciding whether an offence is more suitable for summary trial or trial on indictment: (1) the nature of the case; (2) whether the circumstances make the offence one of a serious character; (3) whether the punishment which a magistrates' court would have power to inflict for it would be adequate; (4) any other circumstances which appear to the court to make it more suitable for the offence to be tried in one way rather than the other; (5) any representations made by the prosecution or the defence.

Certain general observations can be made: (a) the court should never make its decision on the grounds of convenience or expedition; (b) the court should assume for the purpose of deciding mode of trial that the prosecution version of the facts is correct; (c) the fact that the offences are alleged to be specimens is a relevant consideration; the fact that the defendant will be asking for other offences to be taken into consideration, if convicted, is not; (d) where cases involve complex questions of fact or difficult questions of law, the court should consider committal for trial; (e) where two or more defendants are jointly charged with an offence each has an individual right to elect his mode of trial; (f) in general, except where otherwise stated, 'either way' offences should be tried summarily unless the court considers that the particular case has one or more of the features set out in the following pages <u>and</u> that its sentencing powers are insufficient; (g) the court should also consider its powers to commit an offender for sentence, under section 38 of the Magistrates' Courts Act 1980, as amended by section 25 of the Criminal Justice Act 1991, if information emerges during the course of the hearing which leads them to conclude that the offence is so serious, or the offender such a risk to the public, that their powers to sentence him are inadequate. This amendment means that committal for sentence is no longer determined by reference to the character or antecedents of the defendant.

Features relevant to the individual offences

<u>Note:</u> *Where reference is made in these guidelines to property or damage of 'high value' it means a figure equal to at least twice the amount of the limit (currently £5,000) imposed by statute on a magistrates' court when making a compensation order.*

[Note: Each of the guidelines in respect of the individual offences set out below (except those relating to drugs offences) are prefaced by a reminder in the following terms 'Cases should be tried summarily unless the court considers that one or more of the following features is present in the case and that its sentencing powers are insufficient. Magistrates should take account of their powers under s. 25 of the Criminal Justice Act 1991 to commit for sentence'.]

Burglary

1. *Dwelling-house*

   (1) *Entry in the daytime when the occupier (or another) is present.*

   (2) *Entry at night of a house which is normally occupied, whether or not the occupier (or another) is present.*

   (3) *The offence is alleged to be one of a series of similar offences.*

   (4) *When soiling, ransacking, damage or vandalism occurs.*

   (5) *The offence has professional hallmarks.*

   (6) *The unrecovered property is of high value [see above for definition of 'high value'].*

Note: Attention is drawn to para. 28(c) of schedule 1 to the Magistrates' Courts Act 1980, by which offences of burglary in a dwelling cannot be tried summarily if any person in the dwelling was subjected to violence or the threat of violence.

2. *Non-dwellings*

   (1) *Entry of a pharmacy or doctor's surgery.*

   (2) *Fear is caused or violence is done to anyone lawfully on the premises (e.g., nighwatchman; security guard).*

   (3) *The offence has professional hallmarks.*

   (4) *Vandalism on a substantial scale.*

   (5) *The unrecovered property is of high value [see above for definition of 'high value'].*

Theft and fraud

   (1) *Breach of trust by a person in a position of substantial authority, or in whom a high degree of trust is placed.*

   (2) *Theft or fraud which has been committed or disguised in a sophisticated manner.*

   (3) *Theft or fraud committed by an organised gang.*

   (4) *The victim is particularly vulnerable to theft or fraud (e.g., the elderly or infirm).*

   (5) *The unrecovered property is of high value [see above for definition of 'high value'].*

Handling

   (1) *Dishonest handling of stolen property by a receiver who has commissioned the theft.*

(2) *The offence has professional hallmarks.*

(3) *The property is of high value [see above for definition of 'high value'].*

Social security frauds

(1) *Organised fraud on a large scale.*

(2) *The frauds are substantial and carried out over a long period of time.*

Violence (sections 20 and 47 of the Offences Against the Person Act 1861)

(1) *The use of a weapon of a kind likely to cause serious injury.*

(2) *A weapon is used and serious injury is caused.*

(3) *More than minor injury is caused by kicking, head-butting or similar forms of assault.*

(4) *Serious violence is caused to those whose work has to be done in contact with the public or who are likely to face violence in the course of their work.*

(5) *Violence to vulnerable people (e.g., the elderly and infirm).*

(6) *The offence has clear racial motivation.*

Note: The same considerations apply to cases of domestic violence.

Public Order Act offences

1. *Cases of violent disorder should generally be committed for trial.*

2. *Affray.*

(1) *Organised violence or use of weapons.*

(2) *Significant injury or substantial damage.*

(3) *The offence has clear racial motivation.*

(4) *An attack upon policemen, prison officers, ambulancemen, firemen and the like.*

Violence to and neglect of children

(1) *Substantial injury.*

(2) *Repeated violence or serious neglect, even if the physical harm is slight.*

(3) *Sadistic violence (e.g., deliberate burning or scalding).*

Indecent assault

(1) *Substantial disparity in age between victim and defendant, and the assault is more than trivial.*

(2) *Violence or threats of violence.*

(3) *Relationship of trust or responsibility between defendant and victim.*

(4) *Several similar offences, and the assaults are more than trivial.*

(5) *The victim is particularly vulnerable.*

(6) *Serious nature of the assault.*

Unlawful sexual intercourse

(1) *Wide disparity of age.*

(2) *Breach of position of trust.*

(3) *The victim is particularly vulnerable.*

<u>Note</u>: *Unlawful sexual intercourse with a girl under 13 is triable only on indictment.*

Drugs

1. <u>Class A</u>

(a) *Supply; possession with intent to supply: these cases should be committed for trial.*

(b) *Possession: should be committed for trial unless the amount is consistent only with personal use.*

2. <u>Class B</u>

(a) *Supply; possession with intent to supply: should be committed for trial unless there is only small scale supply for no payment.*

(b) *Possession: should be committed for trial when the quantity is substantial and not consistent only with personal use.*

Dangerous driving

(1) *Alcohol or drugs contributing to dangerousness.*

(2) *Grossly excessive speed.*

(3) *Racing.*

(4) *Prolonged course of dangerous driving.*

(5) *Degree of injury or damage sustained.*

(6) *Other related offences.*

Criminal damage

(1) *Deliberate fire-raising.*

(2) *Committed by a group.*

(3)   *Damage of a high value [see above for definition of 'high value'].*

(4)   *The offence has clear racial motivation.*

<u>Noe:</u> *Offences set out in schedule 2 to the Magistrates' Courts Act 1980 (which includes offences of criminal damage which do not amount to arson) <u>must</u> be tried summarily if the value of the property damaged or destroyed is £5,000 or less.*

SIX

BAIL

6.1   Introduction

Bail is the release of a person subject to a duty to surrender to custody in the future. We have already briefly considered the nature of 'police bail', that is when the police make the decision to release from custody either in the course of their enquiries with a duty to report back to the police station at some subsequent time or after charging (see **4.7**). When the question of bail arises in that context, the time for the suspect or accused to surrender to custody is fixed by the police either, in the former case, telling him when to return to the police station, or in the latter, specifying on the charge sheet the date on which the case will first come before the magistrates' court. The provisions of the Bail Act 1976 which we are about to consider in detail do not apply strictly in those situations, although the matters which the police will take into account when deciding whether to release a suspect who has been charged on bail, will largely correspond to the provisions of the 1976 Act.

On occasions when magistrates grant bail, they will specify the date of the next hearing, with the exception of the occasion when they commit an accused for trial in the Crown Court. The date of trial in the Crown Court is not fixed by the magistrates and thus bail is, so to speak, open-ended and the duty to surrender to custody comes about when the accused is notified of the date for the commencement of the Crown Court trial.

The question of bail therefore arises from time to time in the magistrates' court when they adjourn proceedings, either when the case is adjourned to be heard on some later date or when the case is part heard and is adjourned overnight or for a longer period, even, in principle, over the lunch adjournment.

Until the coming into force of the Bail Act 1976, it was common practice to grant an accused bail 'on his own recognisance'. This was a fixed sum of money which the accused did not have to provide at the time of granting bail but which, should he fail subsequently to surrender to custody would be forfeited. This practice has been abolished and in its place s. 6 of the Bail Act 1976 provides that 'a defendant who fails without reasonable cause to surrender to custody is guilty of the offence of absconding'. The burden of proving reasonable cause lies on the defendant. It is easy to imagine things which might give a defendant reasonable cause to fail to appear on the date to which he had been bailed, for instance, sudden serious illness or being involved in an accident on the way to court. Absconding is therefore now a separate offence which may lead to punishment quite separately from any imposed in respect of the charge on which the offender is due to stand trial.

The penalty on summary conviction is three months' imprisonment and/or a fine up to £2,000. In the Crown Court the offence is punishable as a criminal contempt with an unlimited fine and/or up to 12 months' imprisonment. If a defendant fails to surrender to bail the court may (and usually will) issue a warrant for his arrest.

6.2 The Right to Bail under s. 4, Bail Act 1976

Section 4 of the 1976 Act gives an accused person what might be described as a prima facie right to bail. However, it must be remembered that this section does not apply at every stage of the criminal process. It does not apply in particular where:

    (a)   the custody officer has to consider the question of granting a person bail at a police station after he has been charged; or

    (b)   the magistrates, having convicted a person, commit him to the Crown Court for sentence; or

    (c)   a person has been convicted by the magistrates and wishes to appeal to the Crown Court against either conviction or sentence; or

    (d)   by virtue of sch. 1, para. 2A, Bail Act 1976 (as inserted by s. 26, Criminal Justice and Public Order Act 1994),

        (i)   the offence is an indictable offence or an offence triable either way, and

        (ii)   it appears to the court that he was on bail in criminal proceedings on the date of the offence.

Similarly, sch. 1, para. 2A of the 1976 Act (as inserted) merely indicates that there is no *right* to bail. It does not necessarily indicate that in every case, notwithstanding that the present alleged offence was committed whilst on bail for other alleged offences, that the court would, automatically, on hearing all the circumstances, refuse bail.

Although s. 4 of the 1976 Act does not apply in any of these situations, the custody officer or court will consider the nature of the situation and whether on the broad common-sense criteria contained in the Act generally, it seems appropriate to grant bail. Thus, if there is in reality little risk of the defendant absconding, offending further, or interfering with the course of justice, and he has a fixed address, there may be little likelihood in any of those situations that the accused would actually be refused bail. The point is, however, that he is not granted the protection of s. 4 and has no prima facie *right* to bail.

In essence the court has the prima facie obligation to grant bail to all accused who do not fall within any of the three excluded categories above. In other words, the court has to consider the question of bail and the prima facie right to it:

    (a)   for all defendants at all stages of the criminal process up to conviction;

    (b)   even after conviction, where the court adjourns the case for reports or enquiries; or

    (c)   in sundry other circumstances, in particular where an accused is brought before a magistrates' court for breach of a probation or community service order.

6.2.1   EXCEPTIONS TO S. 4, BAIL ACT 1976

6.2.1.1   An offence punishable with imprisonment

To the prima facie right contained in s. 4 of the 1976 Act, there are naturally exceptions. The exceptions we shall consider are those contained in part I of sch. 1 to the 1976 Act. This provides that where an accused is charged with an offence which is punishable with imprisonment, he need not be granted bail if any of the following circumstances apply, namely:

(a) the court is satisfied that there are substantial grounds for believing that if released on bail he would:

    (i) fail to surrender to custody; or

    (ii) commit an offence while on bail; or

    (iii) interfere with witnesses or otherwise obstruct the course of justice, whether in relation to himself or some other person;

(b) the court is satisfied that he should be kept in custody for his own protection or, if he is a juvenile, for his own welfare;

(c) he is already serving a custodial sentence for some other reason;

(d) the court is satisfied that it has not been practicable to obtain sufficient information for the purpose of taking the decisions required by the 1976 Act for want of time since the commencement of proceedings against him;

(e) having been released on bail in connection with the proceedings for the same offence, he has been arrested for absconding;

(f) where the case has been adjourned for enquiries or a report, it appears to the court that it would be impracticable to complete the enquiries or make the report without keeping the defendant in custody.

In addition, by virtue of sch. 1, para. 2A, Bail Act 1976 (as inserted by s. 26, Criminal Justice and Public Order Act 1994) a defendant need not be granted bail if:

(a) the offence is an indictable offence or an offence triable either way; and

(b) it appears to the court that he was on bail in criminal proceedings on the date of the offence.

6.2.1.2 An offence not punishable with imprisonment

The above exceptions apply where an accused is charged with an offence *punishable with imprisonment*. Where the offence is one which is *not punishable with imprisonment* (e.g., careless driving) then different conditions apply and these are contained in part II of sch. 1 to the 1976 Act. These provide that a defendant need not be granted bail if:

(a) it appears to the court that having been previously granted bail in criminal proceedings, he has failed to surrender to custody in accordance with his obligations under the grant of bail and the court believes, in view of that failure, that the defendant if released on bail would fail to surrender to custody;

(b) the court is satisfied that he should be kept in custody for his own protection or, if he is a child or young person, for his own welfare;

(c) he is already in custody in pursuance of the sentence of any court;

(d) having been released on bail in connection with proceedings for the present offence, he has been arrested already for absconding.

To take first the latter cases of the refusal to grant bail in the case of a non-imprisonable offence. It is apparent that these are not of great practical importance. They would for example apply in the case of someone charged with careless driving who persistently failed to appear before the court. We shall now consider the matter of an application to the magistrates' court for bail in the case of someone charged with an imprisonable offence.

6.2.1.3 Application for bail in respect of an imprisonable offence

The basic requirement is self-explanatory. The phrase 'substantial grounds for believing that' implies that the court must satisfy itself to a reasonably high standard of proof. Referring back to the grounds listed in **6.2.1.1**:

(a) The three subdivisions of the first ground ((i), (ii) and (iii)) are self-explanatory. They are by far the most important in practice.

(b) The ground of 'custody for his own protection' might apply to the alleged perpetrator of some highly unpopular kind of offence, for example a sexual attack on a young child where the alleged offender would return to live in the same locality as the victim's parents or relatives.

(c) This a matter of common sense. If someone is already in custody in respect of some other offence when the fact of his alleged guilt of the present offence first comes to light so that he is actually charged while still in custody, it would obviously be ridiculous if the prima facie right to bail in the Bail Act 1976 could override the fact that he is already legitimately in custody.

(d) The ground that there has not yet been time to obtain the necessary information is one relied on very frequently by the police. It will be remembered that when the accused is produced before the court, he may well have been in police hands for only a matter of hours. The police will often contend in such circumstances that the kind of information necessary to enable the magistrates to reach an informed conclusion when considering the grant of bail is not as yet available until further enquiries are made.

(e) On ground (e) it is a matter of the defendant being rearrested after already having absconded in the present proceedings, in which case naturally there would be no further presumption of bail as such, though it is by no means impossible on some proper explanation being given for the failure to surrender to custody (e.g., sudden illness) for further bail to be granted.

(f) This ground concerns the case where proceedings have been adjourned for enquiries but it may be clear that it will be difficult to complete these enquiries because of the nature of the accused. For example, it might be suggested that one cannot complete a psychiatric report upon the accused because it is unlikely that he will voluntarily attend at a hospital to be psychiatrically examined. He may, therefore, be remanded in custody for the purpose of a medical report being prepared. Remands in custody for reports however, may not be for a period exceeding three weeks.

6.2.1.4 The factors to be considered

In considering whether or not the grounds for refusing bail apply, one must have regard to the following matters which are contained in para. 9 of part I of sch. 1 to the 1976 Act. This provides that in taking decisions (i.e. whether or not to grant bail) under sch. 1, paras 2 and

2A of the 1976 Act, the court shall have regard to such of the following considerations as appear relevant:

(a) the nature and seriousness of the offence and the probable method of dealing with the defendant for it;

(b) the character, antecedents, associations and community ties of the defendant;

(c) the defendant's record in respect of the fulfilment of his obligations under previous grants of bail (if any) in criminal proceedings;

(d) except in the case of a defendant whose case is adjourned for enquiries or a report, the strength of the evidence of his having committed the offence;

(e) any other matters which appear to be relevant.

6.2.1.5 Persons previously convicted of homicide or rape and charged with similar offences

By s. 25 of the Criminal Justice and Public Order Act 1994 it is expressly provided that where a person is charged with, or has already been convicted of and is awaiting sentence in connection with, one of certain offences and has previously been convicted of any such offence, then he shall not be granted bail. This section is therefore stronger than merely denying the presumption to the right of bail and positively states that a court may *not* grant bail whatever the surrounding circumstances. The relevant offences are:

(a) murder;

(b) attempted murder;

(c) manslaughter;

(d) rape;

(e) attempted rape.

In the very exceptional circumstances therefore where the person presently charged with one of these offences has already been convicted previously of such an offence, whatever sentence was imposed on the previous occasion and however distant in time from, or different in circumstances to, the present alleged offence, there will be no bail.

6.3 Procedure for a Bail Application

It is now appropriate to consider the procedure by which the bail application is made on the first or any subsequent appearance in the magistrates' court.

Generally, the accused will already be in custody, having been arrested, and will be produced from the police station. He is brought before the court and the court will first need to consider the future course of the proceedings. Local practice varies, but in some courts hardly anything other than the question of bail is dealt with on a first appearance. Sometimes, however, a defendant who is pleading guilty in a straightforward case may be dealt with on first appearance.

Let us assume, however, that the defendant is proposing to plead not guilty. The question of an adjournment inevitably arises since contested trials never proceed on first appearance, if only for the reason that the prosecution will not yet be prepared or have their witnesses available. Where the court adjourns a matter it will *remand* the defendant. 'Remand' merely means 'specify whether the accused is to be on bail or in custody at this stage'.

The question of bail must be considered, therefore, in the light of the 1976 Act. The court is granted an inquisitorial function by the Act so that it ought really to enquire as to whether bail is appropriate in every case. However, if the police themselves do not object to bail, it is highly unlikely that the magistrates will raise objections or require to hear any more about the matter. In that case, only a formal application for bail needs to be made. If there are objections to bail, however, the court will go on to consider them. The course of the proceedings will then be as follows:

(a) The prosecution will put forward their objections. Practice tends to vary from court to court and from case to case. Sometimes the Crown Prosecutor will put forward the nature of the objections to bail; sometimes the officer in charge of the case goes into the witness box and gives evidence concerning the question. The rules of evidence do not apply. Indeed, as the criteria to be considered when assessing the question of bail make clear, the accused's criminal record is highly relevant to the question of the grant of bail and therefore will become known to the magistrates at this stage. Quite apart from that, however, much of the policeman's evidence will amount to hearsay (e.g., 'I was told by the victim that ...'). Moreover, much of the officer's evidence may be merely speculative. A common objection to bail is that the police are investigating other matters in which they suspect the accused might be involved. Clearly, this is highly prejudicial to the accused's prospect of obtaining bail.

(b) Although the rules of evidence do not apply, some attempt may then be made to cross-examine the officer. It is, naturally, difficult to cross-examine effectively about matters to do with other enquiries because the officer may legitimately refuse to answer (for instance because it may alert the defendant and his associates to the course of those further enquiries).

(c) The accused's advocate then makes his application for bail. This ought to be in the form of a considered response to the precise objections put forward by the prosecution. There is prima facie no need to respond to potential grounds for objection which the prosecution have not relied upon, although it is often as well for the sake of clarity in the minds of the magistrates to just pass through other grounds for objection if only to dismiss them.

6.3.1 CONTENTS OF BAIL APPLICATION

The contents of the bail application will mainly consist of a discussion of the objections in the light of the considerations referred to in para. 9 of part I of sch. 1 to the 1976 Act. It is perhaps now as well to consider these points individually.

6.3.1.1 Nature and seriousness of the offence and the probable method of dealing with the defendant for it

In fact, there is no rule as such that a defendant charged with very serious offences cannot have bail. Bail on a murder charge is far from unknown. However, a new para. 9A was inserted into part I of sch. 1 to the 1976 Act by the Criminal Justice Act 1988; this requires a court granting bail to an accused charged inter alia with murder, manslaughter or rape, or attempts to commit those crimes, to give reasons for granting bail and cause those reasons to be entered into the record of court proceedings.

The criterion is simply one of common sense. If it is inevitable that the accused, if convicted, is going to receive a custodial sentence, perhaps a very lengthy one, then clearly, as a matter of human nature, the temptation to abscond, or perhaps to commit further crimes whilst at liberty with the object of providing for his dependants during the period of custody, will be stronger than in the case of someone charged with a relatively trivial crime.

The discussion of the probable method of dealing with the defendant may involve the defending advocate speculating (somewhat optimistically on occasion) that, despite an apparently serious criminal record, it is by no means sure that the defendant will receive a custodial sentence even if convicted because of mitigating factors to do with the offender's personal circumstances or the sentencing provisions of the Criminal Justice Act 1991 discussed below at **10.9**.

6.3.1.2 Character, antecedents, associations and community ties

(a) 'Character' means in this sense, criminal record. 'Antecedents' means the accused's history and background, e.g., upbringing, education, job record and so on.

(b) 'Associations' means the type of person with whom he mixes. It may well be contended by the prosecution, for example, that the accused is a member of a gang of professional criminals and habitually mixes with them. The accused's address may itself indicate this to magistrates with local knowledge in some cases. The method of meeting this particular objection, with others, will be referred to below.

(c) 'Community ties' means matters which tend to cement the accused to his present place in terms of family circumstances and location. It is self-evident that a family man with a mortgage and a regular job is considerably less likely to think it is worthwhile uprooting and going 'on the run' than a casual worker living in a bedsitter. Of course, even this is not conclusive and much will depend upon the intermixing of the various criteria. For example, it may be suspected that even a family man with a mortgage and job may well 'abscond' if the offence with which he is charged is serious enough.

6.3.1.3 The accused's record if previously granted bail

If the accused has not been charged with any offence before, this is something which will be to his credit under other criteria but is of no help on this one. If he has committed a number of previous criminal offences and always received bail and always turned up, this provides a reasonably powerful argument for bail. Again the intermix with other matters must be considered. If he has indeed had bail on previous occasions, then clearly he is likely to have a bad criminal record. This may, in its turn, make it more likely that he receives a substantial custodial sentence this time and thus will weaken his argument on the objection to do with the probable method of dealing with him for the offence.

6.3.1.4 The strength of the evidence

This is naturally extremely hard to assess at such an early stage in the proceedings. The prosecution themselves will say in general terms that they have substantial evidence, but will certainly not be called upon to name their witnesses or give the gist of what the witnesses will say. Any kind of forensic evidence will probably not be available at the stage of a first bail application, e.g., the results of fingerprinting or blood sample tests. All one can do is respond in general terms to whatever evidence is alleged to exist by the prosecution by saying, for example, that the admissibility of an alleged confession is strongly disputed, or that the case turns on weak identification evidence.

6.4 Conditions of Bail

Although a defendant prima facie has a right to bail, and to unconditional bail at that, the court may, where it considers it appropriate, impose conditions. These conditions are of three kinds, namely:

(a)   sureties;

(b)   security by the accused;

(c)   miscellaneous conditions.

By s. 3(6) of the 1976 Act a defendant may be required by a court to comply with such requirements as appear to the court to be necessary to secure that he:

(a)   surrenders to custody;

(b)   does not commit an offence while on bail;

(c)   does not interfere with witnesses or otherwise obstruct the course of justice;

(d)   makes himself available for the purpose of enabling enquiries or a report to be made to assist the court in dealing with him for the offence.

In other words, the court may not impose conditions merely because it has some general sense of unease about the grant of bail. It must only impose conditions specifically tailored to coping with the problems it foresees in the grant of what would otherwise be unconditional bail. We shall now consider the nature of conditions.

6.4.1   SURETIES

A surety is a person who enters into a recognisance to ensure that the accused appears at court. Accordingly, if the accused does fail to appear, the surety is liable to have his recognisance *estreated* (i.e. forfeited). In other words, a surety is someone who guarantees the accused's appearance in court in a specified sum of money (which does not have to be provided in advance). If the person does not surrender to custody, then prima facie the amount of money is forfeited to the court. The surety, therefore, has every interest in ensuring first that he does not undertake his duties lightly and secondly that he does what he can to ensure that the person does appear at court.

The court does have a discretion where the accused does not appear as to whether or not to order forfeiture of the sum. The court will generally require to be satisfied that the surety has exercised extreme diligence in the matter before refusing to order the sum to be forfeited; the surety might escape forfeiture by keeping a very close watch on the accused so as to assist the police by notifying them immediately should there be any hint of the accused absconding.

Strictly speaking a surety should only be asked for in order to meet the risk of absconding. It is improper for a surety to be asked for to ensure that further offences are not committed.

6.4.1.1   Suitability of a surety

In considering the suitability of a surety, the court must have regard to the matters contained in s. 8 of the 1976 Act, namely:

(a)   the surety's financial resources;

(b)   the character and previous convictions of the surety; and

(c)   the proximity (whether in point of kinship, place of residence or otherwise) to the person for whom he is surety.

Let us suppose, therefore, that one has a defendant whom one suspects may not be granted unconditional bail. A surety would seem to help the situation and one has come forward. The first thing the court will do is consider an appropriate amount and whether the proposed surety's resources are sufficient. In fact they will generally accept evidence from the surety that he has resources of that amount, whether in the form of savings or value of goods. If documentary evidence is available, then it is of course as well for the surety to bring it to court (e.g., building society accounts, bank statements).

The matter of suitability extends beyond resources, however, to the question of the surety's own standing. If he has a bad character or criminal record, then (while not necessarily absolutely fatal) it may make him less acceptable. Finally, there is the question of proximity between the surety and the accused. Basically the surety is 'keeping an eye' on the accused to ensure he fulfils his obligations. Obviously, therefore, a close relative or someone who lives very close by will be best for this purpose. However, a spouse is often considered not appropriate as a surety in some courts and, on the authority of a case which is more than a century old, it is also considered improper to accept the solicitor of an accused as surety.

It is not necessary for the surety to be present in court, although this is preferable. It is possible to obtain agreement from the magistrates to the grant of bail, subject to sureties, if the sureties come forward to a police station where their suitability can be investigated by the police; if the police are then satisfied the accused may be released from custody.

6.4.2 SECURITY

The giving of a *surety* does not imply payment of money in advance. However, under s. 3(5) of the 1976 Act, if 'it appears that the accused is unlikely to remain in Great Britain until the time appointed to him to surrender to custody he may be required before release on bail to give *security* for his surrender to custody ... the security may be given by him or on his behalf'. In this situation, therefore, money must be provided in advance, either by the accused personally or by someone else.

A common example is that of a wealthy foreign person accused of a substantial shoplifting offence (e.g., some very valuable item of clothing) from a West End store. It would not generally be appropriate to keep a first offender in custody but, equally, it is somewhat unlikely that he will wish to return to stand trial, especially if he lives thousands of miles away. In these circumstances, the informal practice is to set an amount of security which would roughly correspond to the potential fine and leave it at that. An alternative might be to require surrender of the defendant's passport but this may not be appropriate, e.g., the wealthy visitor may need to return home before the time fixed for the hearing, or may need to go to Paris to continue shoplifting.

6.4.3 MISCELLANEOUS CONDITIONS

The court may impose other conditions. Some of the most common are:

(a) surrender of passport;

(b) the observing of a curfew, that is being at home after a certain hour at night and until a certain hour in the morning;

(c) to reside at a particular place, or with a particular person;

(d) not to go to a particular place, or within a particular area (e.g., the area where the offence occurred). This condition is used very flexibly as a means of, for example, preventing an accused going to public houses or football matches;

(e) not to contact certain individuals.

6.5 Meeting Objections to Bail

It is now appropriate to consider how to meet objections to bail, assuming that these have been put forward by the officer in the case or the Crown Prosecutor. You must ensure that your argument, which should be soundly based on facts, deals with the specific objections. You must immediately assess the prospects of obtaining unconditional bail. Whilst no doubt it is in a sense a more clear cut 'victory' on the issue to obtain unconditional bail for a client, if there is any substantial risk of it being refused, then it is more prudent to examine what conditions might be offered to meet the objections raised.

For example, if the nature of the objection is that the accused, who is an habitual burglar, will continue to commit further burglary offences if allowed bail, there really is little point in offering that he will surrender his passport. In such a situation, the obvious suggestion is a curfew. If it is contended that he will abscond, the appropriate conditions will be that he should report to the police station daily and that he can provide adequate sureties. If the objection is that he will interfere with witnesses, then a condition that he will not go to certain places where those witnesses live or work, or will not contact them would be adequate to meet the suggested objection. The interplay between the various grounds set out for refusing bail and the criteria by which the existence of those grounds are to be judged is obviously capable of enormous variation in any given case.

It should be noted that the court may vary conditions imposed, on the application of either the prosecution or the defendant subsequent to the granting of bail, and that the police have power to arrest without warrant for breach of conditions under s. 7(3) of the 1976 Act.

When the prosecution and defence have put forward their arguments the magistrates will give their decision. If the accused is granted unconditional bail, he is merely notified of the date upon which he is required to surrender to custody. If he is refused bail, or given bail subject to conditions, then there must be a record made of the decision in the prescribed manner and a copy should be given to the defendant in the appropriate form.

6.6 Refusal of Bail

Where a bail application has been refused by the magistrates they will remand the defendant in custody. A court must give reasons for its decision and a note must be made of the reasons and a copy given to the defendant. Before conviction, or committal for trial, this first remand must be for a period which does not exceed eight clear days. In fact, the custom is usually to remand the defendant in custody for a slightly shorter period than this, often to the same weekday of the following week.

Whereas previously an accused was entitled to insist on appearing in court every eight days, that is no longer the position. An accused who is over 17 can be remanded in custody once a magistrates' court has set a date for the next stage of the proceedings, for a period of 28 clear days or to that date, whichever is the less. This may now be done even where the accused does not consent. This provision does not however apply on the occasion of a first remand in custody though it does apply subsequently. Thus the accused will have been able to make the two successive bail applications referred to below. This is by virtue of s. 128A of the Magistrates' Courts Act 1980 inserted by the Criminal Justice Act 1988. If they are however considering such an extended remand, the magistrates must have regard to the total period of time the accused would spend in custody if they were so to remand him. They will thus bear in mind, perhaps after a number of such extended remands where the prosecution are slow in preparing the papers for committal, that the remand in custody hitherto, e.g., for several months, may well come close to the likely eventual penalty for the offence should the accused be convicted. In such a case they may consider releasing him notwithstanding no change of circumstances, a possibility which may encourage the prosecution to greater haste in the preparation of the case for committal.

6.6.1 SUCCESSIVE APPLICATIONS FOR BAIL

We shall now consider what further applications for bail may be made where the initial one has been refused.

Until 1981, it was not uncommon for a full-length bail application to be made for a defendant on each successive appearance before the magistrates. It should not be supposed that on a defendant's second appearance he will be substantively dealt with either by summary trial or committal proceedings. There may be adjournments, sometimes many adjournments (especially a case of some substance), in order to enable the prosecution to collect evidence and prepare. The repetition of bail applications did have some point to it since the case might be heard each time before a new bench of magistrates, and arguments that did not impress the first bench might sometimes impress a more leniently-minded bench. However, there is now a restriction on the number of times that an application can be made, with the object of avoiding undue repetition and waste of court's time. By virtue of part IIA of the 1976 Act (inserted by the Criminal Justice Act 1988), if a court refuses bail it is under a duty at each subsequent hearing to consider bail providing that:

(a) the defendant is still in custody; and

(b) the right to bail under s. 4 of the 1976 Act still applies.

At the first hearing after that at which the court decided not to grant bail, the defence can put forward any argument (including those advanced previously) to support an application for bail. However, on each subsequent remand the court need not hear arguments as to fact or law which it has heard previously, although the duty to at least consider bail remains.

In essence therefore a defendant is allowed two 'full' oral applications for bail, that is one when he first appears in court and a second on his subsequent appearance after the defence solicitor has had longer to marshall his arguments, find sureties, discuss conditions with the defendant, investigate police objections to bail and so on.

At the end of committal proceedings, however often bail has been refused before, it is often possible to suggest new arguments in the light of the further evidence which will have been revealed by that stage. In particular the relevant criterion which requires consideration of 'the strength of the prosecution evidence' may well be viewed differently. Where an accused is committed in custody for trial at the Crown Court, then, notwithstanding that it may be some months before that trial takes place, the magistrates' jurisdiction ceases. Accordingly, if they commit him in custody he will not in principle be produced to any court before his Crown Court trial and further applications for bail, if any, must be made by him to the Crown Court.

6.7 Applications to Crown Court and High Court

If bail is refused by the magistrates after a full application, there are two separate methods for further applications. These are sometimes described as 'appeals' but they are not in truth appeals as such.

6.7.1 CROWN COURT

A defendant refused bail by the magistrates may apply to a Crown Court judge in chambers. Application is made on a prescribed form which is very straightforward to fill in. The person refused bail by the magistrates makes application on the written form and files with the application a so-called 'full argument certificate' from the magistrates' court, the purpose of which is to certify that the magistrates did hear full argument on the bail application. If legal aid has been granted it will cover one such application to a Crown Court judge.

The hearing takes place in chambers before a Crown Court judge and solicitors have right of audience. Usually the Crown Court will list the case for hearing before a judge in chambers before he starts the day's criminal work at 9.45 or 10 a.m. The Crown Court will usually give a hearing date as soon as the form is taken down to the court and notice of this must be served on the prosecution at least 24 hours before the application is made. In fact, it is not uncommon for a Crown Court to list such applications for the following day and for the prosecution to waive the strict requirement for a full clear day's notice.

The prosecution may either attend, indicate that they have no objection, or send in a written notice of objection. In most cases attendance is usual because the prosecution will naturally have many other cases in court that day and it is an easy matter for them to arrange representation by counsel instructed in some other matter. At the hearing, one may rehearse all the matters that were put before the magistrates, and indeed any new matters which have arisen or further arguments.

One may make this application to the Crown Court either immediately bail has been refused or at any stage up to committal for trial.

6.7.2 HIGH COURT

The second method of application is to apply to a judge of the High Court in chambers. This can either be straight after refusal by the magistrates (in which case no 'full argument certificate' is required) or after previous unsuccessful applications to a Crown Court judge. The application is considered to be within the civil jurisdiction of the High Court and is governed by RSC Ord. 79.

Application is made by way of a summons with an affidavit in support. The affidavit will be sworn by the defendant's solicitor and describe the background to the case and why it is suggested that the defendant ought to have bail. The summons will be issued at the nearest district registry and a hearing date will be obtained by agreement with the listing officer of the nearest High Court. Again, 24 hours' notice must be given to the prosecution, but again it is common practice for this to be waived. The hearing is in chambers and a solicitor will therefore have a right of audience

Legal aid issued for the criminal proceedings will not cover such an application, but a separate application may in principle be made for civil legal aid. The Legal Aid Board suggests that there is no firm policy of automatically refusing such applications, although the success rate of applications is not high. Bearing in mind, however, the criteria for the grant of legal aid in civil proceedings, very few such applications, bail having been refused by magistrates and perhaps by a Crown Court judge already, are likely to be considered meritorious. This application to a High Court judge in chambers is usually only made by privately-paying defendants. The costs however are not great, the work involved merely being the swearing of an affidavit and issuing of a summons and attending a relatively short appointment, usually with a fixed hearing time before the start of the day's court business. Thus the costs may not be prohibitive even to defendants of modest means.

6.8 Appeal by the Prosecution against Grant of Bail

Until 1993, where a magistrates' court granted bail the prosecution had no right of appeal against it. Sometimes the police would, quite simply, re-arrest the person outside court in connection with any other offences of which they suspected him, either genuinely, or as a pretext. This would be particularly so where they feared intimidation of witnesses or the destruction of evidence in connection with the first offence.

Now, however, by virtue of the Bail (Amendment) Act 1993 there is a power for the prosecution to appeal against the grant of bail by a magistrates' court.

This Act applies where a person has been charged with, or convicted of:

(a) an offence punishable by a term of imprisonment of five years or more; or

(b) an offence under s. 12 or s. 12A of the Theft Act 1968 (i.e., taking a conveyance without authority or aggravated vehicle-taking).

In such a situation the prosecution may appeal to a judge of the Crown Court against the grant of bail provided that:

(a) the prosecution made representation to the magistrates that bail should not be granted and

(b) the representations were made before it was granted.

Oral notice of appeal must be given to the magistrates' court at the conclusion of the proceedings in which bail was granted and before the person is released from custody. Thereafter written notice of appeal must be served on the magistrates' court and the defendant within two hours of the conclusion of those proceedings. On receipt of that notice of appeal the person will be remanded in custody until the appeal against grant of bail is disposed of. If by any chance the prosecution fail to lodge the written notice of appeal within two hours, then the appeal is deemed to have been disposed of and the accused must be released from custody.

Where the prosecution proceed by this method, the appeal to the Crown Court judge will normally be heard within two working days. If the judge decides to allow bail that decision is final. If the judge allows the appeal and revokes the preliminary grant of bail, then further applications for bail may be made to the Crown Court or to a High Court judge in chambers by the accused as previously described.

6.8.1 RECONSIDERATION OF DECISIONS TO GRANT BAIL

Section 5B of the Bail Act 1976 (as inserted by s. 30, Criminal Justice and Public Order Act 1994) allows for the possibility of a magistrates' court being asked by the prosecutor to reconsider a decision to grant bail for a non-summary offence, on the basis of fresh information which has come into the prosecutor's possession. The provisions of s. 5B permit the prosecution to request reconsideration of the decision to grant bail and ask the court either to withhold bail, vary the conditions of bail, or impose conditions where bail had previously been unconditional. The application may be made by the prosecution on appropriate notice to the person affected and to the court.

Thus, if conduct of the alleged offender comes to the notice of the prosecution, after bail has been granted, which might have caused the court to come to a different decision, but does not in itself permit the prosecution to rearrest for the conduct now complained of, application to the court may be made under this section. Obviously, if the hearing to which the accused was bailed was to be in the relatively near future anyway, the use of this section is superfluous; on the other hand, if bail has been extended for some period ahead and it comes to the prosecution's notice that the accused is already making preparations to abscond, or to interfere with witnesses, procedure under this section may be useful.

6.9   Powers of the Crown Court

We have already considered the Crown Court's powers in respect of applications after refusals by the magistrates. Once a case is committed to the Crown Court for trial (see **8.1**) the Crown Court obviously has other powers of its own. In particular it has jurisdiction to grant bail where:

(a)   a magistrates' court has committed an accused for trial or committed for sentence in custody;

(b)   an accused is appealing against conviction or sentence from the magistrates' court;

(c)   a person is appealing from the Crown Court to the Divisional Court or is seeking judicial review of its decision;

(d)   the Crown Court judge has certified that a case is fit for appeal to the Court of Appeal against conviction or sentence.

The powers to grant bail are contained in s. 81(1) of the Supreme Court Act 1981. In addition to those powers the Crown Court has inherent jurisdiction to deal with bail during the course of a trial before it. Thus, if an accused is on bail up to the time of his trial, it is normal practice to renew bail for overnight adjournments (and in principle during the lunch times though only rarely is this mentioned).

If circumstances change during the course of a case, bail may be withdrawn. Thus, for example, if the accused delays his trial by turning up too drunk to participate in it, or where the case is obviously going badly for the accused or additional aggravating factors have appeared, or there is some suggestion of interference with witnesses or jurors, bail may be withdrawn.

Where it is clear from the way in which a case is going that a custodial sentence is likely, bail may be withdrawn once the judge has commenced his summing up and therefore bail may be refused over any lunch adjournment, or even overnight if the summing up is a lengthy one or the jury are taking some time to consider. See in particular *Practice Direction (Crime: Bail During Trial)* [1974] 1 WLR 770.

SEVEN

SUMMARY TRIAL

7.1 Introduction

Where a defendant is charged with an offence which is triable purely summarily, or after a mode of trial hearing, has consented to summary trial of an 'either way' offence, then the trial will take place. As we have seen this is most unlikely to be at the first hearing. If the accused has been in custody, then the first hearing will be the day after he is charged; if he has not been in custody, it may be some time later, but even so the practice of most courts is to inform the defendant in advance that if he pleads not guilty the case will not proceed at the first hearing. Indeed, in the case of purely summary offences which have been commenced by the issue of a summons, i.e. so that no question of bail arises, the accused may be told that if he proposes to plead not guilty, he should notify the court in writing and then need not attend court on the first hearing because the prosecution will not have their witnesses present. Even after a mode of trial hearing there may well be other hearings before the actual trial takes place. This will particularly be the case over the summer months when police witnesses and others may be away on holiday, thus rendering a number of hearing dates ineffective. Eventually, however, the trial will take place on the date fixed for it and the accused will be expected to be there. Before we can discuss summary trial, it is important to consider a number of preliminary matters.

7.2 Joint Trials

Two or more accused may be charged in one information with having committed an offence jointly. Where this occurs then almost inevitably they will be tried together.

Where there are two or more informations against one accused, the magistrates may try the informations together if neither of the parties object. However, even if the defendant does object, the court still has power to try two or more informations together, if it is of the opinion that it is in the interests of justice to do so because they form part of a series of offences of a similar character.

The interests of justice include a consideration of the convenience of the prosecution, as well as the question of minimising any risk of injustice to the accused. This arises from the case of *Chief Constable of Norfolk* v *Clayton* [1983] 2 AC 473. This case overturned the former general rule that an accused had the right to object to being tried by the same court on different informations at the same time. In principle, under the old law, an accused was entitled to insist on separate trials for each of the informations no matter how many there might be. If the accused does successfully represent to the magistrates that a number of informations against him ought to be tried by different benches and the magistrates agree, those magistrates should not then proceed to try any of them because they will of course now know of the other alleged offences. See *R* v *Liverpool Justice ex parte Topping* [1983] 1 WLR 119. They would therefore adjourn the trials so that they could be heard successively by differently constituted benches.

7.3 Amendment of the Information

Section 123 of the Magistrates' Courts Act 1980 provides that a defendant cannot object to an information, summons or warrant on the ground of any defect in it in substance or form or because of any variance between it and the prosecution evidence. However, if the accused has been misled by a variance between the information and the prosecution evidence, he must be granted an adjournment if he requires one.

This section is worded in such a way that in principle it would seem to enable the court to continue with the trial, no matter how defective the information was. However, a restricted meaning has been given to the section by a number of cases. These establish that where the defect is trivial so that there can be no question of the accused being misled by it, the section applies, e.g., the misspelling of names, places or the giving of wrong dates due to typing errors. In such a case, there is probably no need for the court even to consider formally amending the information. If there is a more substantial variation, then the prosecution should apply for leave to amend. If the amendment has been such that the accused is prejudiced (e.g., if he had not collected and called his evidence to meet matters which are relevant to the amendment) he is entitled to an adjournment. An example is the leading case of *Wright* v *Nicholson* [1970] 1 WLR 142 where an information charged that an accused committed a certain offence on 17 August. The evidence of the alleged victim was vague as to when the incident happened and it could have been at any time in the month of August. W had called alibi evidence in respect of 17 August only but was convicted on the basis that he committed the offence some time in August. It was held on appeal that W had been misled and had been severely prejudiced since he had been unable to consider calling alibi evidence for other days in August.

Amendment of the information can remedy almost any defect if there is an adjournment granted to enable the accused to meet it. However, an information laid against completely the wrong person is so fundamental a defect that it cannot be cured by amendment. This is not to say however, that a mere misspelling in the defendant's name will bring the case within that category.

7.4 Absence of the Defendant

If the defendant is absent, then in cases begun by summons, he may be tried in his absence provided service of the summons has been proved to the satisfaction of the court. This is by virtue of s. 11 of the Magistrates' Courts Act 1980. A plea of not guilty will be entered and the prosecution will be required to prove their case strictly.

If the defendant is represented in court by counsel or a solicitor, he is normally deemed to be present unless he is on bail, in which case his personal attendance to surrender to custody is required. Thus, the accused must in principle be present at mode of trial proceedings and generally at committal proceedings. If he has been bailed to appear and does not do so, then the magistrates may issue a warrant for his arrest.

Where the trial proceeds in his absence and he is represented by counsel or solicitor, his representative may conduct the case on his behalf, cross-examine prosecution witnesses, call defence witnesses and make speeches, just as if the accused were present.

7.5 Plea of Guilty by Post

Under s. 12 of the Magistrates' Courts Act 1980 (as amended by sch. 5, Criminal Justice and Public Order Act 1994) the prosecution may give an accused of 16 or over the opportunity of pleading guilty by post where he is called to appear to answer an information alleging a summary offence for which the maximum penalty does not exceed three months' imprisonment.

In such a case, the prosecution serves on the accused, together with the summons, a notice explaining how he can plead guilty by post and what the course of events will be if he does so. In addition, the prosecution serve a brief statement of the facts as they allege them to be. The form sent to the defendant notifies him that, if he pleads guilty by post, he will only have evidence given against him to the extent of the reading out of the statement of facts in open court and no other evidence will be brought. The prosecution are usually quite happy to put the statement of facts in a fairly neutral form in the hope of persuading the accused to plead guilty and to save the court and the prosecution time.

The accused in such a situation should return the form to the court indicating that he proposes to plead guilty. There is space on the form for him to set out any mitigating circumstances and details of his means. He is informed, however, that he is not bound by his plea of guilty and may appear at court at any time up to the hearing of the summons and withdraw the plea of guilty and be tried on the basis of a not guilty plea. The procedure thereafter is as follows:

(a) The prosecution will read out the charge and the particulars of the offence as stated in the statement of facts, but may give no other information to the court about the crime.

(b) The defendant's form setting out his means and any mitigating circumstances is read out by the clerk of the court.

(c) The court will normally pass sentence straight away. If, however, it does propose to disqualify the offender from driving or imprison him, it must call him before the court and will adjourn the case for that purpose.

If there is something ambiguous in the plea of guilty by post, for example where the accused's statement of mitigating circumstances suggests facts which it seems would actually amount to a defence, rather than to mitigation, then the magistrates may refuse to accept the plea and may adjourn the case for a hearing.

If the prosecution do not offer the accused the opportunity to plead guilty by post, then there is nothing he can do to compel them to adopt this procedure. This is so even in the case of straightforward driving offences. The availability of fixed penalties for offences such as speeding has in some areas largely replaced pleas of guilty by post. The police however are still likely to lay an information rather than apply a fixed penalty in cases where they consider that a fixed penalty (currently £40, £30, or £20 depending on the offence) would be inadequate in the light of the road conditions, or the speed which the vehicle was doing. The prosecution, in the case of most driving offences, will usually opt to offer a plea of guilty by post unless it is obvious from the circumstances that the accused is likely to be disqualified.

Minor changes introduced by the Criminal Justice and Public Order Act 1994 permit the court to proceed where the defendant does not in fact write in to plead guilty but appears and informs the court of an intention to plead guilty. With his consent the court may then proceed to deal with the case as if such notification had been given and he were absent rather than formally calling him before the court. They may, however, give him the opportunity to make oral submissions in mitigation.

7.6   Disclosure

We have already referred to the requirement on the prosecution under the Magistrates' Courts (Advance Information) Rules 1985 to disclose advance information about the nature of the prosecution case. The provisions of the Criminal Procedure and Investigations Act 1996 ('the 1996 Act') with regard to disclosure are at their most important in the Crown Court and these are discussed at **9.6** below. Some elements of the disclosure provisions of the 1996 Act are also applicable in the magistrates' court. By virtue of s. 5 of the 1996 Act a prosecutor must undertake 'primary disclosure' that is to say that he must disclose to the accused any prosecution material which has not previously been disclosed to the accused, which in the prosecutor's opinion 'might undermine the case for the prosecution against the accused', or alternatively give to the accused a written statement that there is no such material.

In other words, the prosecution have a positive duty to assist the defence if there is such material in their possession. Such things might include, e.g., statements of witnesses whom the police have interviewed and who have given descriptions of the perpetrator which are significantly different from the appearance of the suspect; confessions to the offence by other persons which the police have chosen to disregard, perhaps because they disbelieved the person giving the alleged confession; the criminal records of any prosecution witnesses; and any other material which might indicate some doubt about the guilt of this suspect.

This material will of course be of most significance in the case of weightier crimes in the Crown Court, but given that many relatively serious crimes do remain for trial in the magistrates' court, if those crimes have given rise to lengthy investigations, this disclosure procedure may well be relevant.

Once the 'disclosure officer' who is a policeman in charge of this aspect of the investigation has given that disclosure, then by s. 6 of the 1996 Act the defendant has the opportunity (if he wishes) to undertake 'voluntary disclosure'. Where he does this he will supply a 'defence statement' which sets out in general terms the nature of the defence and indicates the matters on which the defendant takes issue with the prosecution and the reason why. In addition, a defence statement must disclose any alibi and particulars relevant to it, in particular which witnesses may be able to give evidence in support of the alibi, their names and addresses and any other information, e.g., which might assist in finding any such witnesses whose names and addresses are not known. Such further information may well be necessary where it is said, for example, that the accused spent the evening in a particular public house where there should have been many people who observed him, but whose names and addresses he does not know.

Whereas in a Crown Court case, if the accused fails to give a defence statement the jury may be invited to draw adverse inferences from his refusal to do so, there is no such provision in relation to voluntary statements in a summary trial. However, if the defendant has happened to give a voluntary statement, but at trial his defence is inconsistent with what is in that statement or he puts forward a defence which is different from a defence in that statement or he calls alibi evidence, but it was not disclosed in the statement, then the court may draw adverse inferences about those matters.

The second feature is that where a defendant does serve a defence statement there is an extra duty on the prosecutor to disclose to the accused any further prosecution material which might reasonably be expected to assist the accused's defence as disclosed by the defence statement.

It may therefore be that there is bona fide material the significance of which the disclosure officer did not appreciate because he was unaware of what the line of defence would be at the time when primary disclosure was undertaken. But in the light of the specific matters raised in the defence statement, he now sees the relevance of certain documents in his possession which he must now proceed to disclose. Therefore if one does not undertake service of a defence statement one will lose the advantage of the possibility of secondary disclosure.

For further detailed discussion see **9.6**.

7.7 Non-appearance of Prosecution

If the prosecution fails to appear at the time and place fixed for summary trial, the magistrates have discretion either to dismiss the information or adjourn. If the case has already begun and been adjourned as part heard, then the magistrates have the option to proceed in the absence of the prosecution, although this will only happen rarely.

7.8 Outline of Procedure

We shall now consider an outline of the procedure at summary trial of either a summary offence or an 'either way' offence on a not guilty plea.

(a) The charge will be read to the defendant and he will be asked whether he proposes to plead guilty or not guilty. In such a situation his plea must be unequivocal. The court has a discretion to allow a change of plea from guilty to not guilty at any time before sentence. Thus if, for example, as in the case of mistakenly pleading guilty by post, the accused pleads guilty, say, to a charge of theft but in stating his mitigation says something along the lines of 'I never knew I had it' or 'I thought it was mine at the time' the magistrates ought to allow him to withdraw his guilty plea, substitute a not guilty plea and either proceed with the hearing then and there, or, more probably, adjourn it so that he can receive legal advice and/or call evidence.

(b) The prosecution may make an opening speech stating the facts of the case and indicating which witnesses will be called to prove them. It is important to note that in the magistrates' court the prosecution do not in general have a closing speech and therefore this is the only chance the prosecution have to address the court. However, it must be remembered that magistrates are likely to be considerably more experienced than jurors and thus may need less in the way of introductory matter.

(c) The prosecution then call evidence which may consist of witnesses or written evidence tendered in the form of statements under s. 9, Criminal Justice Act 1967 (this topic will be dealt with in the section on hearsay evidence, see **16.10**). The witnesses will give evidence and are then subject to cross-examination and may be re-examined.

(d) At the end of the prosecution evidence, the defence may make a submission of no case to answer. This submission should be upheld if:

(i)   there is no evidence to prove an essential element of the offence charged; or

(ii) the prosecution evidence has been so discredited as a result of cross-examination or is so manifestly unreliable that no reasonable tribunal could safely convict upon it.

In other words, at this stage, the magistrates may simply decide whether on the basis of what they have heard so far, there is any possibility of them finding the case proved beyond reasonable doubt. The prosecution have a right of reply to this submission. If the submission is successful, the case is over. The magistrates discharge the accused and then go on to make any appropriate orders for costs or return of legal aid contribution. If the submission is not upheld the case continues and the defence may then present their case.

7.8.1 THE DEFENCE CASE

The procedure for the defence case is as follows:

(a) The defence may make an opening speech but in principle are limited to one address only and it is customary for the defence solicitor to make a closing speech rather than an opening one, for obvious reasons. Such a speech gives the advocate the opportunity to comment on all the evidence if made at the end, but if made at this time only gives a chance to comment on the prosecution evidence and to introduce the defence evidence.

(b) The defence witnesses are then called and the defendant testifies first.

(c) Exceptionally the court may grant the prosecution leave to call further evidence after the defence case for the purposes of rebutting defence evidence. Rebuttal evidence may only usually be called on a matter which could not reasonably have been foreseen and which arises suddenly. It will be recalled that the defence have no general obligation to give details of their case in advance of the trial. Accordingly, if, for example, a sudden allegation is made against a policeman and the prosecution are taken by surprise, they will now have the opportunity to call evidence to rebut it. A similar situation might arise in the case of an alibi. It will be recalled that in the magistrates' court there is no obligation to give advance notice of intention to call alibi evidence (whereas there is in the Crown Court as we have seen). Accordingly, the prosecution, if they have time to get the witnesses to court (and they may be allowed an adjournment for this purpose) may call rebutting evidence. If it is perfectly clear from the outset, however, that the trial is one in which evidence of a certain kind would inevitably be necessary, then the prosecution will not be permitted to call evidence in rebuttal. An example taken from a leading case is one which involved a charge of forgery where, at the close of the defence evidence after the defendant had denied the forgery, the prosecution applied for leave to call a handwriting expert to prove that the forged signature was written by the accused. It was held that it should have been obvious from the outset that in a case of alleged forgery handwriting evidence would be required and the prosecution were penalised for their lack of foresight by their application to call rebuttal evidence being refused. More recent cases seem to indicate a slightly more flexible approach, see 15.8.

(d) Finally, there is the defence closing speech, unless the defendant has already made an opening speech. The prosecution may only address the court after this with the leave of the court, but leave will always be granted where a point of law is raised on which the prosecution wish to reply. This is merely one aspect of the right either party has to raise a point of law and argue it at any stage during the proceedings. If exceptionally the prosecution were allowed to address the court on the facts or evidence, then the defence would always have the right to address the court last. The magistrates then reach their decision. They may retire for this purpose. Their verdict is by a majority. If there are only two magistrates and they disagree, they should adjourn the case for rehearing by a different bench. The magistrates may be advised by their clerk on matters of law or evidence, but not on issues of fact. Accordingly, if no matter of law arises in the course of the hearing, it is wrong for the clerk to retire with the magistrates.

If the defendant is acquitted, he will be discharged and may be able to make an application for costs (for the principles see 2.4.2). If he is convicted, the court will proceed to sentence after dealing with mitigation and other matters. These matters are dealt with at 10.1 onwards below.

If the accused has pleaded guilty at the outset, the prosecution will then read out a statement of how the offence occurred and the court will proceed to hear mitigation, consider the obtaining of reports, and sentence.

7.9 Committal for Sentence: s. 38, Magistrates' Courts Act 1980

The principles of sentencing generally are dealt with at **10.1**. It is important here, for the sake of continuity, to indicate the circumstances in which a magistrates' court, after having dealt summarily with an 'either way' offence where they have convicted an offender, have the power to commit him to the Crown Court for sentence because they feel that their own sentencing powers are inadequate. This may occur under s. 38 of the Magistrates' Courts Act 1980 in the case of an adult offender. There is a similar power under s. 37 in relation to persons aged between 15 and 17 when convicted in the youth court.

Section 38 of the Magistrates' Courts Act 1980 (as substituted by s. 25 of the Criminal Justice Act 1991) now provides:

> (1)   *This section applies where on the summary trial of an offence triable either way ... a person who is not less than 18 years old is convicted of the offence.*
>
> (2)   *If the court is of the opinion—*
>   (a)   *that the offence or the combination of the offence and one or more offences associated with it was so serious that greater punishment should be inflicted for the offence than the court has power to impose; or*
>   (b)   *in the case of a violent or sexual offence committed by a person who is not less than 21 years old, that a sentence of imprisonment for a term longer than the court has power to impose is necessary to protect the public from serious harm from him*
>   *the court may ... commit the offender in custody or on bail to the Crown Court for sentence*
>   *...*

The effect of these words is to focus upon the seriousness of the present offence and other offences associated with it rather than, as was previously the case, the offender's criminal record. The criteria reflect those in s. 2(2) of the Criminal Justice Act 1991 which is dealt with in more detail in **10.9**. As a result, committals to the Crown Court for sentence by way of s. 38 should be rare. The revelation of the accused's previous convictions ought not in principle to make a great deal of difference and thus committals are likely to be limited to cases where either the accused asks for further offences to be taken into consideration (which naturally may make the magistrates take a different view) or where facts about the offence charged come to light which were not drawn to the magistrates' attention at the time when they accepted jurisdiction. Thus if, for example, what they believed was a relatively trivial assault when accepting jurisdiction proves to have involved some serious or permanent injury to the victim, that might be a relevant factor. Such cases should also be rare since the prosecution, when urging the magistrates in matters of jurisdiction, have the duty to ensure that an outline of the full circumstances of the offence is made known to them.

EIGHT

COMMITTAL PROCEEDINGS

8.1 Introduction

As we have seen, criminal offences fall into three categories:

(a) Those triable only summarily in which case trial before the magistrates is inevitable and there is no option.

(b) Those triable only on indictment in which case trial is by the Crown Court before a judge and jury.

(c) Those triable either way, where there will be a mode of trial hearing to determine the manner in which the case is to continue.

With very few exceptions, not relevant to this text, all criminal proceedings commence in the magistrates' court. In the case of those triable only summarily or those triable either way where the magistrates opt for, and the accused is happy to accept, summary trial that is precisely what happens. In the case of those triable only on indictment and those triable either way where the magistrates themselves choose to send the case to the Crown Court or where the accused elects trial, there is still a preliminary hearing before the magistrates.

Crown Court trials are expensive and time-consuming. Moreover, there is always a considerable waiting list for trial on indictment which means that an accused remanded in custody may be detained for a substantial period before trial and even if released on bail will possibly be subject to stress and anxiety before the trial.

In order to filter out prosecutions with little prospect of success, almost all trials on indictment are preceded by a preliminary hearing before the magistrates which is known as committal proceedings. These proceedings are not a trial as such. They simply involve the prosecution demonstrating that it has a reasonable or prima facie case which it is proper to call upon the accused to answer before a judge and jury in the Crown Court. Magistrates conducting these preliminary hearings are referred to as *examining justices*, and contrary to the usual rule, one examining justice may sit alone for the purpose of committal proceedings.

The onus on the prosecution to show that it has a prima facie case is not a heavy one. The examining justices only have to be satisfied that there is sufficient evidence on which a reasonable jury *could* (not *would*) find the defendant guilty. In practice this means that most such hearings do result in a committal for trial.

Until 1997 the defendant had the choice of two different forms for committal proceedings. The first of these was under s. 6(1) of the Magistrates' Courts Act 1980 and involved a full hearing with prosecution witnesses giving evidence on oath and being subject to cross-examination. The defendant could also give evidence if he wished, and even call his witnesses if he thought his defence was so strong that it might assist in persuading the magistrates to throw the case out at that preliminary stage. Quite apart from hearing the evidence, the magistrates might be called upon to listen to lengthy submissions and argument including, e.g., arguments that the procedures used to obtain a confession were so flawed that the confession should be excluded, leaving the prosecution with insufficient evidence to take the case on to trial. In extreme cases such 'full' committals as they were known might last several days. Apparently about 8 per cent of all committals were in this format and amounted to around 8,000 such cases per year.

The alternative format, applied in the other 92 per cent of cases, was under s. 6(2) of the Magistrates' Courts Act 1980. This was an entirely formal procedure by which the prosecution produced their evidence in the form of written statements which were served upon the accused in advance of the committal hearing. If the accused accepted that on the face of those statements a prima facie case was disclosed then he could consent to a committal 'on the papers' and the hearing would only last a few minutes whilst ancillary administrative matters such as the issue of witness summonses, the decisions about the continuance of legal aid and bail and the like were made. The fact that an accused would accept committal in this 'short' form did not in fact necessarily imply that he accepted that there was evidence on which to commit him; it might well be a tactical acceptance which would allow him to reserve his evidence until trial at which time he could indeed 'ambush' the prosecution with a surprise line of defence.

The view of the government was that 'full' committals were unnecessarily time-consuming and expensive and that whilst they might assist in the disposal of some weak cases, the costs outweighed the advantages.

The Criminal Procedure and Investigations Act 1996 substantially amends s. 6(1) of the Magistrates Courts' Act 1980 and replaces 'full' committals with a very different and much shorter version; s. 6(2) remains basically unchanged and is still likely to be overwhelmingly the more common of the two. We now turn therefore to a consideration of the two kinds of committal.

8.2 Committals with Consideration of the Evidence

Where a committal in this form is chosen by either prosecution or defence (and the defence have the power to insist upon it if they wish), no witnesses are called to give oral evidence. Instead evidence in the form of written statements is tendered to the examining justices and must be tendered in the presence of the accused. The evidence must be in one of the following forms by virtue of s. 5A of the Magistrates' Courts Act 1980 (inserted by sch. 1, Criminal Procedure and Investigations Act 1996). The forms of statement are as follows:

(a) written statements signed by the person who made them and containing a declaration by that person to the effect that the statement is true to the best of that person's knowledge and belief, and that he made the statement knowing that if it were tendered in evidence he would be liable to prosecution if he wilfully stated anything which he knew to be false or did not believe to be true; or

(b) a *deposition*, that is a statement taken on oath before a magistrates' clerk in the case of a potential witness who would not voluntarily give a statement to the prosecution, but who has been summoned to do so under s. 97A of the Magistrates' Courts Act 1980; or

(c) statements which the prosecutor indicates would be admissible by virtue of s. 23 or s. 24 of the Criminal Justice Act 1988. The prosecutor must confirm that he has a reasonable belief that the statements might be admissible under those sections if the case came to trial on the information available to him at the time of the committal and that he has reasonable grounds for that belief and he gives the reasons for that belief; or

(d) any other document which by virtue of any other enactment is evidence in proceedings before a magistrates' court enquiring into an offence as examining justices.

All the prosecution evidence will therefore fall within one or other of those categories. In principle it should all be read out loud to the court unless the court otherwise directs. The following therefore is an outline of the procedure at such a hearing.

8.2.1 THE PROCEDURE

(1) The charge is read to the accused. He is not as such required to respond although it will be recalled that he was obliged to intimate his plea at the mode of trial hearing and unless a not guilty plea were intimated, the case would not go on in committal proceedings, but would be dealt with by the magistrates.

(2) The prosecution opens its case. The Crown Prosecutor may make a speech telling the examining magistrates what the case concerns, the charge or charges on which it is suggested the accused should be committed for trial and the nature of the evidence the Crown Prosecutor intends to tender. There is no requirement on the prosecution to tender all their evidence at this stage because all they need to do is provide sufficient evidence to establish a prima facie case. Thus if, e.g., there are several eye-witnesses to the same thing the prosecution may be content to tender the statements of only one or two of them at this stage.

(3) The prosecution evidence will then be tendered. Whether courts are likely to insist on it being read out remains to be seen because at the time of writing, this procedure has only just been instituted and applies only in respect of criminal investigations begun after April 1997. As cases which take this route will inevitably take several weeks from the commencement of the criminal investigation to reach committal proceedings, there is as yet no body of practice on which one can predict whether magistrates' courts are generally likely to see much benefit in having the statements read out rather than reading them themselves.

8.2.2 THE PROSECUTION MATERIAL

The statements must take one of the forms referred to above. Inevitably the majority of such statements will be those under s. 5B of the 1980 Act, that is witness statements containing a simple declaration as to their truth in the prescribed words.

In addition, documents that the prosecution will be seeking to put in evidence under s. 23 or s. 24 of the Criminal Justice Act 1998 (see **16.10.3**) will include such things as business accounts, other business documents, statements from absent witnesses and the like.

The other provision referred to above, permitting the use of sworn depositions before magistrates' clerks, would be very much an exceptional case where a witness has been summoned prior to the committal proceedings specifically for the purpose of giving the statement on oath. It would be very rare indeed that the prosecution would want to adopt this course because experience suggests that a witness who is unwilling to give a statement voluntarily will not prove to be very much use as a witness under compulsion. The possibility nonetheless remains.

Finally, there may be evidence under some other statute which permits documentary evidence in one or other form to be given. An example is the Bankers Books Evidence Act 1879 which permits banking records to be tendered in evidence in criminal proceedings in various circumstances and subject to certain procedural requirements. (See **16.10.2**.)

Thus a full committal now consists of the reading out or summarising, or reading by the magistrates, of the various witness statements and other items of documentary evidence. No witnesses will be present.

There is no provision for defence evidence to be called, whether from the defendant himself or from anyone else.

8.2.3 WHAT IS THE POINT OF A 'FULL' COMMITTAL?

The main advantage of a committal in this form, which will inevitably take longer than the more simple procedure under s. 6(2) of the Magistrates' Courts Act 1980 described at **8.3** below, will be where the case put forward by the prosecution seems so weak, even on the documents and bearing in mind the lack of any right now to challenge prosecution witnesses by cross-examination, that the defence think there is a realistic possibility of having the case dismissed by the magistrates. Probably there will be relatively few cases in this category. It will not be open, generally speaking, for the defence to contend that any part of the prosecution case will be inadmissible at trial and, providing that the evidence is put in the proper form, there cannot of course be any suggestion that the evidence would be inadmissible at the committal itself.

It may also be possible of course for submissions to be founded on matters of law, e.g., a submission that even if everything in the prosecution depositions is true, it does not for instance connote 'dishonesty' within its technical meaning, and therefore an important element of an offence is not made out. Likewise it may still be possible to submit that even on the prosecution's version the elements of some lesser offence only appear to be disclosed, e.g., theft rather than robbery because there is no apparent element of violence or threat of violence.

Committal proceedings in this form will therefore conclude with submissions about the sufficiency of the evidence and the magistrates will then make their decision about whether to commit.

What if the magistrates refuse to commit? If the magistrates decline to commit the accused is discharged. This does not however constitute an acquittal. The prosecution may, so to speak, make a further attempt to 'get their act together' and may re-charge the accused for the same offence or other offences and start the procedure again.

8.2.4 THE COMMITTING COURT'S CHOICE OF TRIAL VENUE AND CHARGES

If the magistrates decide to commit the accused to the Crown Court then they have to decide to which Crown Court they will commit him and on which charges. In relation to the first of these matters it is simply a matter of geographical convenience unless there is some special feature, such as that the incidents have provoked some local feelings which may make it better to have the accused tried out of the area.

As to the charges on which they commit the accused, these will usually be the charges which the prosecution brought against him at the outset. Sometimes however, the magistrates may decide that there is insufficient evidence of some aspect of those charges and commit him for some other offence disclosed by the evidence, as in the example given above of a charge of robbery being brought; if the magistrates are not satisfied that there was any evidence of force, they may commit only on a charge of theft.

8.2.4.1 Adding linked offences: ss. 40 and 41 Criminal Justice Act 1988

Quite apart from the above one should also have regard to the powers under ss. 40 and 41 of the Criminal Justice Act 1988. Under these sections an accused who is committed for trial at the Crown Court may also be dealt with in respect of 'linked' summary offences on the same occasion. The provisions are as follows:

(a) Section 40 of the 1988 Act provides that if the accused has been committed for trial in respect of an indictable offence, and the evidence that was before the committal court also discloses a summary offence, then the *prosecution* may include a count in the indictment for the summary offence. There are, however, two conditions that must be satisfied:

(i) the summary charge must either be founded on the same facts or evidence as the indictable charge or it must be for a series of offences of the same or a similar character; *and*

(ii) the summary charge must be one of those specified in the section or by subsequent statutory instrument: these at present include the charges of common assault; taking a motor vehicle without the owner's consent; driving while disqualified; and criminal damage.

It must be noted therefore that it is not a case of the *committing court* adding counts to the indictment. It is entirely up to the prosecution to do this at a later stage if the facts at committal disclosed the extra summary offence, and that offence is linked in one of the ways mentioned with the indictable offence for which committal has taken place. Once in the Crown Court the charges will be tried before the same jury. However, on conviction of the summary offence the Crown Court's power of sentence is limited to those which the magistrates would have had.

(b) Under s. 41 of the 1988 Act, magistrates who commit a defendant to the Crown Court for trial of an 'either way' offence, e.g., theft, may also commit for trial in respect of any summary offence which is:

(i) punishable with imprisonment or disqualification (such as careless driving or taking a conveyance); *and*

(ii) arises out of circumstances which are the same as or connected with the 'either way' offence.

This procedure is not strictly speaking 'committing for trial'. What happens in the Crown Court is that the defendant is tried on the indictable offence alone. At the end of that trial, if he is convicted, the summary offence is put to him, and if he pleads guilty to that then the Crown Court can sentence him for it, although its powers are again limited to the maximum sentencing powers of a magistrates' court. If however, the defendant pleads not guilty to the summary offence, the summary offence is remitted to the magistrates' court for trial.

This procedure then allows a linked offence of a certain degree of seriousness to be dealt with at the Crown Court but only where there has been a conviction for the 'either way' offence and a plea of guilty to that linked summary offence.

8.2.5 OTHER MATTERS

On the decision to commit for trial, then certain other matters require to be dealt with.

8.2.5.1 Publicity

The next matter to be dealt with is the question of publicity. Committal proceedings, even full committal proceedings, involve only the prosecution side of the case. If it were open to the press to report these proceedings then a one-sided view of the case might emerge and, moreover, matters highly prejudicial to an accused might come out. For this reason the press are prevented by s. 8 of the Magistrates' Courts Act 1980 from reporting anything more about committal proceedings than the names, addresses, ages and occupations of the parties and witnesses and the names of their legal representatives; the charges against the accused; and the outcome of applications for bail and legal aid. The reason for this restriction is that the persons in the area from whom the jurors will be chosen who eventually try the case in the Crown Court should not be prejudiced by reading a one-sided version of events (or preferably any version of events) in advance but should be open-minded when they judge the case on what they hear in the Crown Court at the appropriate time. Full reporting of what happens, that is of the allegations made and the evidence given, is allowed only if reporting restrictions are specifically lifted by the court. It ought to be said that s. 8 also applies to any previous hearings before the court, e.g., the mode of trial hearing or remands.

If the accused actually wants publicity however, for example so that a missing witness might come forward to give evidence on his behalf, then it is open to him to apply to the examining justices to lift reporting restrictions. If he does so they must comply, in which case the press (if it is sufficiently interested) may report more about the case. Where there is more than one accused and one wants reporting restrictions lifted and another or others do not then the magistrates should consider the interests of justice before deciding whether to grant the application. The burden is on the person who wishes the reporting restrictions to be lifted to show that his chance of a fair trial is prejudiced through lack of publicity.

8.2.5.2 Witnesses

Until April 1997 it was necessary at the end of a committal hearing to seek witness orders in respect of witnesses who would be required to attend the eventual trial. The 1996 Act repeals the power of magistrates' courts to make witness orders in respect of Crown Court proceedings and substitutes s. 2 of the Criminal Procedure (Attendance of Witnesses) Act 1965. There is now a simple administrative procedure to be undertaken by way of application to the Crown Court under Crown Court rules and application is made there after committal.

8.2.5.3 Bail

As we have seen, the mere decision to commit the defendant for trial will not in itself constitute a change of circumstances sufficient to ground the making of a third bail application if two full applications have already been made unsuccessfully. Despite the fact that the accused may after committal be in custody uninterruptedly for some weeks or months, that is not in itself a sufficient new feature. It may well be however, if the prosecution evidence has been thoroughly explored by cross-examination at the committal, that a submission can be made and that the court might take a different view of the strength of the prosecution evidence, which is of course one of the relevant considerations for deciding on a bail application. By virtue of s. 22 of the Prosecution of Offences Act 1985 there are regulations which lay down custody time limits between committal for trial and the start of the trial. The present time limit prescribed is a maximum of 112 days. Where that time limit expires then the accused in principle has an absolute right to bail and the exceptions to that right in the Bail Act 1976 do not apply. However, the prosecution have the power to apply for an extension of the time limit and this is commonly granted in difficult cases where the prosecution can justify the length of time which they are taking to prepare the case for trial.

8.2.5.4 Legal aid

Unless a 'through' order has been made for legal aid to cover the Crown Court trial, it is appropriate to apply to the magistrates for legal aid to be extended. In fact it is in principle a *new* legal aid order that is made but this is the terminology invariably used. If one forgets to do this at the committal proceedings one can in any event apply to the Crown Court directly by completing a straightforward application form. It is usual to tell the magistrates in committal proceedings that the accused's means have not changed since his earlier application for legal aid for the magistrates' court proceedings.

8.2.5.5 Prosecution costs

Under s. 17 of the Prosecution of Offences Act 1985, the Crown Prosecutor (who usually conducts the case before magistrates) need make no application for costs at the end of committal proceedings. There is no point in applying for costs from central funds, as was previously the practice, where the prosecution is anyway publicly funded. If there is a private prosecutor then it may be appropriate to make application for costs out of central funds. It would not of course be appropriate ever at this stage to claim costs from the defendant since his guilt has not been established.

8.2.5.6 Defence costs

If the defendant is discharged then defence costs may be claimed from central funds unless (by virtue of regulations made by the Lord Chancellor) the court concludes that the prosecution's unnecessary or improper conduct has put the defendant to expense, in which case the order may be made direct against the prosecution.

8.3 Committals without Consideration of the Evidence

These are provided for by s. 6(2) of the Magistrates' Courts Act 1980 as amended by sch. 1 to the Criminal Procedure and Investigations Act 1996. This section allows the accused to consent to being committed for trial and would be appropriate where although he intends to plead not guilty he accepts that on the prosecution evidence there is a prima facie case against him.

The section permits the accused to be committed without consideration of the evidence if:

(a) all the evidence to be tendered consists of written statements made in the proper form in compliance with s. 5A of the 1980 Act;

(b) and the accused (or where there is more than one, all the accused) is legally represented; and

(c) none of the accused wishes to make a submission of no case to answer.

In the case of a committal under s. 6(2) of the 1980 Act the accused will have been served (usually at his solicitor's office) with copies of the prosecution's statements in the appropriate form some time in advance of the hearing. Having received the statements with a view to committal under s. 6(2) it is always open to the defence solicitor to change his mind, in the light perhaps of how weak the prosecution evidence looks, and to insist on a full committal.

The defendant should attend, in principle, although (unless he is on bail) he need not do so provided that his solicitor is present. Thereafter the following is the order of events:

(a) The charge is read out though again no plea is taken.

(b) The clerk will ask the defence whether they wish for reporting restrictions to be lifted. The same considerations as before will apply although of course the press will not actually hear the substance of the prosecution evidence. It is open however, to the defence solicitor to mention any matter to the court on which press assistance might be required (e.g., the tracing of a missing witness).

(c) The clerk then asks the prosecution to confirm that all their evidence is in the appropriate form, that copies have been given to the defendant already and that the defendants are all legally represented. The clerk then asks the defence formally to confirm that they do not wish to submit that there is no case to answer.

(d) The prosecution statements are not read out to the court nor do the magistrates need to consider their contents. It is simply a matter of counting the number of statements presented. Thereafter, the magistrates announce the committal for trial to the Crown Court on the charges which the prosecution have brought. Since they do not examine the evidence at all they will naturally not need to consider whether all the elements are proved or whether some lesser charge might be appropriate. In fact, in some courts the magistrates' clerk deals with s. 6(2) committals under delegated powers.

(e) Thereafter, the procedure to be followed is the same as that in the case of a committal with consideration of the evidence (see **8.2** above).

8.4   Notice of Further Evidence

Finally, one further point should be noted. It has been stressed throughout that the prosecution are under no obligation to put in all their evidence at the committal hearing. All they need to tender is sufficient evidence to show a prima facie case. This does not however, mean that they are entitled to keep secret, and surprise the accused with, the evidence of other witnesses. After committal the prosecution are obliged to give the accused notice of the evidence of all the witnesses whom they propose to call at the trial. This is done by subsequently serving on the accused's solicitor copies of the statements comprising the additional evidence which is to be called at trial in the Crown Court.

8.5   Alternatives to Committal

There are two alternative procedures to committal though both are rarely used.

(a) *Voluntary bills of indictment*
Although this procedure is in principle available in any case, its use is limited by *Practice Direction (Crime: Voluntary Bills)* [1991] WLR 1633. The procedure should only be used where the interests of justice require it and where either committal proceedings have been held but have resulted in the discharge of the accused or the holding of committal proceedings would for some other reason be undesirable. Where the procedure applies, the prosecution apply direct to a High Court judge for a 'voluntary bill' and the case by-passes the committal stage. The application is usually made on written submissions.

(b) *Notice of transfer*
In the case of two exceptional kinds of crime, a 'notice of transfer' can be used to by-pass the committal stage and reduce delays. The two kinds of case are:

(i)   serious and complex fraud where the circumstances make it appropriate for the management of the case to be taken over by the Crown Court without delay (s. 4(1)(a), Criminal Justice Act 1987); and

(ii)   those involving child witnesses who are the victims of sexual offences or offences of cruelty or violence (s. 53, Criminal Justice Act 1991).

In both cases the notice of transfer may be lodged at any time between the accused being charged and the commencement of committal proceedings. It is given to the magistrates' court which would otherwise have conducted the committal. There is a procedure permitting the accused to challenge this notice by applying to the Crown Court to dismiss the transferred charges.

NINE

THE CROWN COURT: PREPARATION AND TRIAL

9.1 Introduction

The Crown Court is part of the Supreme Court. Its jurisdiction is to deal with:

(a) Trials on indictment.

(b) Offenders who have been committed for sentence by the magistrates' court under s. 37 or s. 38 of the Magistrates' Courts Act 1980.

(c) Appeals from magistrates' courts against conviction and/or sentence.

(d) Sundry miscellaneous civil matters (e.g., appeals on licensing matters).

9.1.1 THE JUDGES OF THE CROWN COURT

There are four categories of judge who sit in the Crown Court. These are:

(a) High Court judges, almost invariably from the Queen's Bench Division, who spend part of their time sitting in criminal cases.

(b) Circuit judges, who divide their time between criminal work in the Crown Court and acting as judge in the county court on civil or matrimonial matters.

(c) Recorders, who are part-time practitioners, usually barristers but also some solicitors, who sit for a fixed number of days each year as a judge of the Crown Court.

(d) Assistant recorders, who are in all ways equivalent to a circuit judge or a recorder and are likewise appointed from private practitioners at the Bar or solicitors to sit for a number of days per year.

9.1.2 MODES OF ADDRESS

High Court judges, all judges at the Central Criminal Court in London, and the judges who perform the honorary offices of Recorder of Liverpool or Manchester are addressed as 'My Lord' or 'My Lady'. All other judges in the Crown Court are addressed as 'Your Honour'.

9.1.3 DISTRIBUTION OF WORK

9.1.3.1 Geographically

The whole Crown Court in England and Wales is considered to be a single court sitting in different locations. The courts are grouped into six circuits each one with its own separately organised practising Bar. Cases may be transferred by the magistrates to any given location, which will not necessarily be the one nearest to the transferring court. Considerations will include the length of lists at individual Crown Courts and other special factors, e.g., the fact that a certain offence has aroused a lot of feeling locally may mean that it should be tried in some distant Crown Court, e.g., in London rather than in the Crown Court for the town where the transfer took place and the facts occurred.

Locations are classified as first, second or third tier. First-tier locations will always have a High Court judge available because they will also deal with a substantial amount of civil work. These include trial centres in the largest towns such as Manchester and Birmingham. Second-tier locations have no facilities for civil work but may draw on a High Court judge entirely for criminal work at times. Third-tier locations have neither High Court civil work nor High Court judges.

9.1.3.2 Classification by judge

Offences are classified into four classes by the *Practice Direction (Crown Court: Allocation of Business)* [1995] 1 WLR 1083.

(a) Class one is murder, treason and certain other offences, e.g., offences contrary to the Official Secrets Act.

(b) Class two are other very serious crimes including manslaughter, rape and intercourse with a girl under 13.

Those in class one and two must be tried by a High Court judge unless the presiding judge of the circuit releases a certain case for trial by a circuit judge.

(c) Class three offences consist of those triable only on indictment and not in any other class (there are very few of these), they may be tried by a High Court judge, a circuit judge or recorder in accordance with directions by the presiding judge of each circuit.

(d) Class four offences, which are the largest group by far, includes all offences triable either way plus robbery and wounding/causing grievous bodily harm. These will in general be handled by a circuit judge or recorder in accordance with directions given by the presiding judge.

9.2 Between Committal and Trial

After the committal one's client will have been remanded either on bail or in custody for trial at the Crown Court. Depending on local conditions and in particular the length of local lists, clients on bail may usually expect a wait of many months for their trial. Clients in custody will wait a somewhat shorter time, but in cases of any complexity or where a long trial is anticipated a wait of some months is also likely to be involved. It will be recalled that by virtue of s. 22 of the Prosecution of Offences Act 1985, as amended by s. 71 of the Criminal Procedure and Investigations Act 1996, in principle there should only be a maximum delay of 112 days between committal and commencement of trial where a defendant is in custody but the prosecution may apply for this period to be extended and extension is liberally granted.

There ought therefore, given adequate resources within the office, to be ample time to prepare thoroughly the defence case and moreover, given the delay between first obtaining instructions and the committal, one should be relatively well informed at this stage as to what the case is about and it may be that the final preparation for the trial only takes some fine tuning of information that is already to hand. We shall now consider some of the procedural and tactical features of the process between committal and trial.

9.3 The Indictment

The indictment is the formal document which contains a list of the charges against the accused to which he is invited to plead at the beginning of his trial. In principle a jury may only try one indictment at a time but the indictment may contain any number of counts. A form of sample indictment charging two counts appears below:

INDICTMENT   NO. 970115

THE CROWN COURT AT MIDDLEMARCH

The Queen v Stephen Woodward

STEPHEN WOODWARD is charged as follows

Count 1.   *Statement of Offence*

ATTEMPTED BURGLARY, contrary to s. 1(1) of the Criminal Attempts Act 1981

Particulars of Offence

Stephen Woodward on the 15th day of January 1997 attempted to enter as a trespasser a building known as 3 West Road Middlemarch with intent to steal therein.

Count 2.   *Statement of Offence*

HANDLING STOLEN GOODS, contrary to s. 22(1) of the Theft Act 1968.

Particulars of Offence

Stephen Woodward on a day unknown between the 3rd day of January 1997 and the 17th day of January 1997 dishonestly received certain stolen goods namely a Yakimura model 21 television belonging to Ian Grant knowing or believing the same to be stolen.

7 May 1997

M Jones
An Officer of the Crown Court

As will be observed, the heading is in a standard form describing the Crown Court and the parties and each count then contains a statement of the offence and the particulars of the offence. As will be observed the particulars are in an extremely brief format and give no details whatsoever of *modus operandi* or surrounding circumstances.

The indictment may charge two or more accused in a single count if the prosecution case is that they were acting together to commit the offence. If several persons were involved in some offences but not in all of them and the counts may properly be joined together (see below **9.3.2**), then it is still proper for them all to be charged within the same indictment.

129

Indictments are usually drafted by officers of the Crown Court and only in cases of considerable complexity are the papers sent to prosecuting counsel to draft the indictment. In fact, increasingly, a CPS lawyer after the committal will prepare a so-called 'schedule' which is in essence a draft of the potential indictment and is sent on to the Crown Court with the committal papers for the Crown Court officer formally to prepare the indictment.

It will be recalled that at the end of the committal the magistrates will have indicated the charges on which they are going to send the accused for trial (and this may involve them indicating that they are refusing to commit him on certain others for which the prosecution had argued). It may come as a surprise to find that the person drafting the indictment is not bound in any way by the magistrates' view as to the offences for which there was a case on which to commit. The Crown Court officer (or CPS lawyer) may include in the indictment counts for *any* indictable offence disclosed by the prosecution statements used at committal or which in his opinion is disclosed by the statements whether or not the magistrates committed on those charges (s. 2(2), Administration of Justice (Miscellaneous Provisions) Act 1933, as amended by sch. 1, para. 17, Criminal Procedure and Investigations Act 1996). Thus, for example, if the magistrates, in a case of handbag snatching, committed only on a charge of theft, but the CPS lawyer considers that there was a sufficient element of violence for the charge justifiably to be one of robbery, the indictment may include a count in the alternative for both theft and robbery. Even more commonly, alternative counts for theft and handling are inserted where stolen goods are recovered from an individual but it is unclear as to whether he was the thief or a handler. It makes no difference as indicated above even if the magistrates expressly refuse to commit on the more serious charge. It is suggested however, that the power to include a count for an offence which the examining justices have *expressly* refused to send for trial should be sparingly exercised (*R v Kempster* [1989] 1 WLR 1125).

9.3.1 DRAFTING THE INDICTMENT

Although the indictment is a fairly short document there are numerous pitfalls for the unwary. The drafting of indictments is governed by the Indictments Act 1915 and the Indictments Rules 1971. The essential rule is r. 6 which says that 'the particulars must disclose the essential elements of the offence but even failure to disclose an essential element may be disregarded if the accused is not thereby prejudiced or embarrassed in his defence' (r. 6(b) and (c)).

9.3.2 JOINDER OF COUNTS IN AN INDICTMENT

Several counts against an accused may be put in one indictment by virtue of the Indictment Rules, r. 9 which provides:

Charges for any offences may be joined in the same indictment if those charges are founded on the same fact or form or are part of a series of offences of the same or a similar character.

Thus in the well-known case of *R v Mansfield* [1977] 1 WLR 1102 where the accused started different fires in different hotels, in the course of one of which seven people died, the seven charges for murder were rightly put in the same indictment with the relevant charges of arson as they constituted a series of offences albeit that no personal injury was caused to anyone in the later fires.

Under this provision also, quite commonly gangs of professional bank robbers may be charged with a series of offences, even in some cases when committed over a period of some years. All participants may likewise be charged, including those who only drove the getaway car or handled the stolen money as well as the robbers themselves, even though not everyone is involved in each individual offence.

Despite this prima facie provision, the judge, if he is of the opinion that the accused may be 'prejudiced or embarrassed in his defence' through having all the counts against him tried in the same indictment, may make an order to 'sever the indictment' under s. 5(3) of the Indictments Act 1915. This applies where the joinder of counts is technically permitted by r. 9 but if a single jury dealt with the trial of all the counts there would be a risk of prejudice. The judge is under a duty to order separate trials where the evidence relevant to one count might become intermingled with that of other counts or where one or other of the counts is of such a scandalous or offensive nature that it would inevitably prejudice the jury against the accused in relation to the other matters even if proof was lacking on those other matters.

The principle is often applied to sever counts and order separate trials of different sexual offences involving different victims if there is insufficient probative value between them for the 'similar fact' principle to apply. Nonetheless the case of *R v Cannan* (1991) 92 Cr App R 16 (see also **20.2.2**) indicates that even in sexual cases where the 'similar fact' principle does not strictly apply a judge has a discretion whether to order severance or not and the Court of Appeal will not interfere with that discretion unless the judge has exercised it on improper principles.

9.3.3 JOINDER OF ACCUSED

All parties to any individual offence normally will be joined together in a single count. This applies, moreover, not only to the principal offenders but to everyone else involved including those who merely aid, abet, counsel or procure. The judge has a discretion to order separate trials of defendants who are accused of committing an offence jointly but this should be very rarely used. The Court of Appeal indicated in *R v Moghal* (1977) 65 Cr App R 56 that separate trials should only be ordered in very exceptional cases, the trial in that case having gone badly wrong because one of two accused had persuaded a judge at an early stage to let her be tried alone, had then alleged duress against the co-accused and been acquitted in circumstances where, had they both been tried together, that would have been an inconceivable outcome especially given that the allegation was of a particularly brutal murder. Had they both been tried together it seemed on the facts likely that she would have been convicted as the main perpetrator.

The judge will bear in mind the interests of justice, which include the costs involved in holding separate trials so that even in quite extreme cases, e.g., where one accused has made a full confession which would be inadmissible against the others but will inevitably be put before the jury in the course of the full trial, the prejudice of that alone may not be a reason for ordering separate trials (*R v Lake* (1976) 64 Cr App R 172).

9.3.4 SUMMARY

(a) An individual may be indicted on any offence disclosed by the evidence on committal to the Crown Court.

(b) An individual may be indicted on alternative counts where it is unclear from the facts whether the jury ought to convict of one offence or another, e.g., of theft or handling, so that it is proper to let the jury decide after hearing all the evidence.

(c) Two or more counts may be joined in any indictment if they form part of the same facts or a series of offences of the same or a similar character; the similarity need not be so close as to be within the similar fact rule.

(d) Two or more defendants may be charged in a single count with having committed a single offence, and two or more counts in an indictment may charge different individuals with separate offences even though there is no one count against them all collectively.

9.3.5 OVERLOADING THE INDICTMENT

A number of recent trials have demonstrated the problem of 'overloading the indictment'. Recognition of this is a matter of common sense and practice. In the well-known case of *R v Thorne* (1978) 66 Cr App R 6 there were 14 different defendants charged on numerous counts of robbery and related offences including conspiracy, handling and attempting to pervert the course of justice. The trial involved more than 20 barristers and ten firms of solicitors and lasted more than four months including a 12-day summing up. The Court of Appeal observed, whilst not allowing the appeal merely because the trial had been too long and complex, that the trial ought to have been split up into shorter trials.

9.3.6 APPLICATIONS IN RELATION TO THE INDICTMENT

The most important applications likely to be made are as follows.

9.3.6.1 An application by the defence to sever the indictment

Such an application is an attempt to persuade the trial judge to order that two or more counts in the indictment should be tried separately in respect of one accused, or that certain defendants should be tried separately from others and often in a particular order. This application is usually made at a plea and directions hearing or a preparatory hearing (see **9.5**).

9.3.6.2 Amendment of the indictment

It is likely to be the prosecution who apply to amend the indictment and this may be permitted even well into the trial, although an adjournment must then be allowed to the defence if the trial is put on a different footing. If the amendment is so vital that it substantially invalidates or makes useless some of the evidence given hitherto, that may be grounds for an appeal or for the jury to be discharged and a retrial ordered.

9.3.6.3 Appeals in relation to defective indictments

If there is an error in the indictment which is not corrected by an amendment during the trial there may be an appeal. Serious defects may lead to a successful appeal. Mistakes in the giving of names or dates are unlikely to be sufficiently material, the key test being whether the error prejudiced or embarrassed the accused. Probably the most likely basis for a successful appeal will be that the judge was wrong in refusing to sever and thus that prejudice has been caused to the accused, particularly in sexual cases.

9.4 Procedures before Trial

Until recently in the majority of cases there would be no court hearings between committal proceedings and the start of the trial. This could cause considerable inconvenience and expense since the Crown Court might not even know how the defendant proposed to plead and thus witnesses would be warned to be available and several days might be set aside for a case in which, in the event, the defendant would plead guilty, thus necessitating a hearing only a few minutes long. Accordingly many courts developed informally a form of 'pre-trial review' or 'plea and directions hearing' at which a defendant would be invited, through his advocate, to indicate how he proposed to plead. This system was formalised by virtue of a *Practice Direction* at [1995] 4 All ER 379 which sets out a series of rules establishing formal *plea and directions hearings* (PDHs) in the Crown Court. The system of PDHs was introduced gradually after piloting in a number of courts and eventually applied in all Crown Courts by 1997. It must be understood that the system of plea and directions hearings is a non-statutory one developed as a matter of practice. This non-statutory system will now exist alongside the formal requirements for disclosure, a defence statement, and the possibility of 'preparatory hearings' described below.

At the hearing the defendant will be asked for his plea and prosecution and defence will be expected to assist the judge in identifying key issues and providing additional information required for the proper listing of the case. It is expected that the counsel briefed in the case will appear in the PDH so that it may be as fruitful and thorough as possible. Usually 14 days' notice of the PDH will be given, and the PDH appointment will be taken early in the day's list, thus releasing counsel for availability for other cases elsewhere. In principle the PDH should be within six weeks of committal where the defendant is on bail, and within four weeks where the defendant is in custody. At the PDH hearing the defence must supply the court and the prosecution with a full list of the prosecution witnesses whom they require to attend the trial. The prosecution are expected generally to prepare case summaries for the judge to use in more serious cases. This case summary will indicate the nature of the case and the issues of fact and law likely to be involved together with an estimate of trial length. The PDH should be held in open court and the defendants should usually be present. There is a useful questionnaire to be answered which helps to identify the salient issues.

Despite the existence of plea and directions hearings, nothing can prevent a defendant who, whether to keep all his options open, or for some other reason, has intimated a not guilty plea from changing his mind at the start of the trial and pleading guilty. Thus a great deal of money may have been expended on the preparatory stages of the case by prosecution, and indeed defence, in the belief that it was to go ahead as contested possibly for a very lengthy hearing, only to find that all the work has been abortive. At present no sanction exists against a defendant who changes his mind in this way.

9.5   Preparatory Hearings

Sections 29–33 of the Criminal Procedure and Investigations Act 1996 set up a still more formal system of 'preparatory hearings' which a judge may order, if he considers that:

> the indictment reveals a case of such complexity, or a case whose trial is likely to be of such length, that substantial benefits are likely to accrue from a hearing for any of the following purposes:

(a) *identifying issues which are likely to be material to the verdict of the jury;*
(b) *assisting their comprehension of any such issues;*
(c) *expediting the proceedings before the jury;*
(d) *assisting the judge's management of the trial.*

At the hearing the judge may, in addition, make a ruling as to any question of admissibility of evidence or any question of law relating to the case. It follows therefore, that if preparatory hearings are undertaken on a wide scale, trials before the jury may be substantially shortened because important issues of contested evidence will have been ventilated well in advance. There are indeed provisions for an appeal to lie to the Court of Appeal from rulings of a judge at a preparatory hearing and for the trial before the jury to be delayed until after the Court of Appeal has ruled.

9.5.1   SUMMARY

The basic procedural background is therefore as described above. There will be a plea and directions hearing which will continue in the same way as before the 1996 Act came into force, albeit with slightly different issues to be considered, and there will also be the possibility of the judge taking the initiative, perhaps after a plea and directions hearing, to order a formal 'preparatory hearing'. This may be either because of the length of the case, its complexity, or perhaps because it is possible to identify individual difficult points of law or evidence which preliminary argument may assist to resolve with the object of shortening the trial. Against that background we must now consider the revolutionary provisions relating to disclosure between the parties, set up by the Criminal Procedure and Investigations Act 1996.

9.6 The Disclosure Procedure

Before the coming into force of the Criminal Procedure and Investigations Act 1996 ('the 1996 Act') there was no formal stage of discovery of documents in the criminal justice system and certainly nothing corresponding to pleadings. In the case of summary trials there is still no positive requirement for the defendant to indicate his case in advance. However, s. 1(1) of the 1996 Act taken together with s. 6 constitutes an attempt to apply the principles of the 1996 Act to summary trials, although disclosure is voluntary insofar as the defendant is concerned. It therefore remains to be seen to what extent defence disclosure in summary trials will be used. The rest of this section will deal with trials on indictment.

9.6.1 DISCLOSURE OF THE PROSECUTION EVIDENCE

It will be recalled that the prosecution will have tendered sufficient evidence to enable the magistrates' court to commit the accused for trial and thus much of their case may have already been disclosed. Indeed, in factually simple cases the whole of the prosecution evidence is likely to have been disclosed by the committal stage. Of course, it may well be that the prosecution will have obtained other statements or material which they did not think of any use to them and which they did not propose to use at trial. Such material is called 'unused prosecution material' and the principles formerly applicable at common law are described in the section on privilege at 21.3 below.

Under s. 3 of the 1996 Act, the prosecutor must disclose to the accused any prosecution material which has not previously been disclosed and which in the prosecutor's opinion 'might undermine the case for the prosecution', or give the accused a written statement that there is no such material. However, by virtue of s. 7(5), material must not be disclosed to the extent that the court, on an application by the prosecutor, concludes it is not in the public interest to disclose it and orders accordingly. It follows therefore that all the principles of public interest immunity, particularly in relation to evidence from police informers, evidence of police operational matters, and the like, apply as they did before.

The kind of material that will be disclosed and which might assist the defence will include such things as inconsistent statements, statements by witnesses who were thought to be of no use to the prosecution, but in whose evidence there might be something which will assist the defence, the criminal records of prosecution witnesses, and any other collateral material which might be used for attacking the credibility of prosecution witnesses.

9.6.2 THE DECISION AS TO WHAT TO DISCLOSE

It will be observed that the decision as to what to disclose is the prosecution's and it relates only to material which 'might undermine the case for the prosecution'. It does not of course follow that the prosecution are the best judge of this even when carrying out their duties scrupulously and honestly. Statements from witnesses which may appear to the prosecution to be virtually irrelevant to the case need not be disclosed, yet it may sometimes be that in such witness statements there are leads which if the defence were able to follow them up would provide very useful material. As has been noted earlier, the resources for investigation available to the prosecution far outweigh what can be called on by a defendant, or at least by a legally-aided defendant. Faced with the manpower, technical and forensic resources available to the police the defence may be very much at a disadvantage and very reliant on additional information from the police investigation. Unless, however, the person in charge of disclosure considers that the material 'undermines' the prosecution case, it appears it will not be disclosed.

9.6.3 THE CODE OF PRACTICE

There is a Code of Practice issued under s. 23 of the 1996 Act which imposes duties and requirements on the 'disclosure officer' who is the policeman in charge of the issues relating to disclosure. It will be noted that the Code gives responsibility to a policeman and not, as might possibly have been anticipated, to the Crown Prosecutor who may be left in ignorance of material held by the police which the disclosure officer has decided need not be disclosed on the basis that it does not undermine the prosecution case.

Once disclosure has been made, and that involves not merely the listing of the materials, but of course the opportunity to inspect the originals, or for the provision of copies of them in the form of, e.g., transcripts, tape recording or photocopies of documents, the procedure passes to the next stage.

9.6.4 COMPULSORY DISCLOSURE BY THE ACCUSED

By s. 5(5) of the 1996 Act once the accused has been served with the necessary documents and the prosecution have completed 'primary disclosure', the accused is required to give a 'defence statement' to the court and prosecutor. This statement must be in writing and must:

(a) set out in general terms the nature of the accused's defence;

(b) indicate the matters on which the accused takes issue with the prosecution case and the reasons why he does so; and

(c) give full particulars if the defence involves an alibi, namely the name and address, or other information, to assist the tracing of any witness who it is believed can give evidence in support of the alibi.

The defence of alibi presupposes that the accused was somewhere else when the offence happened. If he does not remember where he was, then he can give no particulars. If he was alone at the time, he must still give such particulars as he can of where he was and when.

9.6.5 TIME LIMITS

Curiously, there is at present no time limit for the defence to give disclosure. It is clear, however, that the later it is done the more likely it is that there will be adverse comment. Moreover, it is not until the defence case has been disclosed that a further burden is thrown on the prosecution to disclose additional documents (see below).

What if the defendant does not serve a defence statement?

There has of course been a gradual weakening of the so-called 'right to silence' in the recent past. Until 1995 the only defence that had to be disclosed in advance was that of alibi, and any defence which was dependent upon expert evidence, in which case the expert's report had to be disclosed. When the Criminal Justice and Public Order Act 1994 came into effect the court was for the first time permitted to draw such inferences as appeared proper from the failure of an accused to mention, in the course of police interview under caution when he was charged any fact later relied on in his defence; and likewise adverse inferences could be drawn from the fact that an accused did not testify.

Now in addition to these matters under s. 11 of the 1996 Act, adverse comment may be made and adverse inferences drawn in a variety of cases where the accused has not fully disclosed his defence.

The accused will be subject to inferences being drawn in a variety of circumstances, in particular:

(a) if he fails to provide a defence statement at all (s. 11(1)(a));

(b) if he gives a defence statement, but it is out of time as defined by s. 12 (which provides a mechanism for the Secretary of State to prescribe by regulations the time at which a defence statement is to be served). At present there is no such period, but it is expected that regulations will be forthcoming once there has been the opportunity to monitor the working of the Act and identify common problems;

(c) where the defence statement sets out inconsistent defences;

(d) where a defence is put forward at trial which is different from any defence disclosed in the defence statement;

(e) where there is an alibi defence at trial, but no particulars of it have been disclosed in the defence statement, and where an alibi witness is called without the necessary particulars of the witness having been supplied.

Where any of these matters apply, then by s. 11(3) the judge or any other party with the leave of the court may make such comment as appears appropriate and the jury may then draw such inferences as appear proper in deciding on guilt. However, s. 11(5) further provides that 'a person shall not be convicted of an offence solely on inference drawn under sub-section (3)'. It therefore follows in this case, as also with inferences to be drawn from silence during questioning or at trial, that failure to supply a defence statement, or supplying one involving inconsistent material cannot in itself discharge the prosecution's burden of proof.

It may be of course that the defendant has said nothing at any stage, in which case the judge will have to direct the jury on the weight of inferences to be drawn from failure to respond to police questioning, failure to supply a defence statement, and silence during the trial. More commonly, perhaps, difficult or cunning defendants will risk a direction inviting adverse inferences in relation to the silence during interview and the failure to supply a defence statement, but still decide to testify at trial, in which case there will indeed remain the possibility of an 'ambush' defence. Of course, insofar as matters take the prosecution completely by surprise, an adjournment may be allowed to enable the prosecution to call rebutting evidence under the court's general discretion (see 15.8).

9.6.6 **FOLLOWING THE DEFENCE STATEMENT — SECONDARY PROSECUTION DISCLOSURE**

Once the defence statement has been supplied, the prosecutor must make 'secondary disclosure' by virtue of s. 7 of the 1996 Act. It is important to note that whereas in relation to primary disclosure the subjective view of the prosecutor was all that was required as to what evidence might undermine the prosecution case, the test for secondary disclosure is an objective test because the prosecutor must disclose any material 'which might reasonably be expected to assist the accused's defence as disclosed in the defence statements' (s. 7(2)(a)). The duty remains on the 'disclosure officer', i.e., the policeman appointed for this purpose, rather than on the Crown Prosecutor. In principle the disclosure officer must look again at all retained material and then disclose anything that now appears relevant to the defence.

9.6.7 **APPLYING FOR DISCLOSURE**

Section 8 allows the defence to behave in a proactive way instead of merely waiting to see how thoroughly the prosecution carries out their duty of secondary disclosure. By s. 8(2):

If the accused has at any time reasonable cause to believe that—
    (a) there is prosecution material which might be reasonably expected to assist the accused's defence as disclosed by the defence statement given under section 5 or 6, and
    (b) the material has not been disclosed to the accused,
the accused may apply to the court for an order requiring the prosecutor to disclose such material to the accused.

Thus an application can be made to a judge who will have to determines in effect, the same kind of interlocutory issues common in civil proceedings where there are disputes about discovery and will have to consider issues such as privilege and, particularly, relevance.

9.6.8 SUMMARY

The above is a bare summary of difficult new legislation supplemented by a detailed Code of Practice under s. 23 of the 1996 Act, which will apply to the disclosure officer and prosecuting agencies. There are many difficulties still to be worked out including the interrelationship of these provisions, and the previous case law rules relating to voluntary disclosure by the prosecution, the extent to which in reality a disclosure officer given his workload can be expected to keep files under review where he hoped that long ago he had passed all responsibility for them to the Crown Prosecutor; the relationship between the disclosure officer, the investigating officers in the case, and the Crown Prosecutor; to what extent judges may regard applications for further disclosure as 'fishing expeditions' and the like.

The commencement day was 1 April 1997, but these procedures only apply to cases involving 'any alleged offence for which the investigation has not begun before 1 April 1997'. It will thus apply in effect only to crimes committed after 1 April 1997 or those rare cases where the prosecuting authorities were unaware that there was any crime to investigate until new facts came to light, e.g., discovery of the body of someone who had merely been treated as a missing person before 1 April 1997. That is a clear example, but there may be more difficult ones, e.g., systematic fraud on an employer over many years, perhaps by several individuals, where the employer had called in the police who had made a fruitless investigation, say two years ago, but now further evidence has come to light which makes it easier to establish a chain of criminal conduct. Is the investigation to be treated as having started at the earlier or the later time?

9.6.9 DEFENCE TACTICS

These provisions therefore require a detailed and formal, almost ritualistic, exchange of information between prosecutor and defence. Defence tactics will have to be varied from what has been commonplace hitherto to take a more proactive approach. An early view of the case must be formed. Of course, in thousands of mundane cases, involving for example minor assaults, driving offences, shoplifting etc., none of this will matter very much. In such cases the prosecution are likely to disclose all their evidence anyway. Nonetheless, one important way of looking at a case, common with American defence attorneys, is to form a 'theory of the case' which usually implies trying to work out the most plausible alternative hypothesis to the guilt of the client who is now charged. This may well involve a considerable effort in investigating the possible culpability of the next most likely perpetrator. It remains to be seen whether those who draft defence statements will commonly go further than indicating reasons why the accused is not the guilty person and present positive facts as to who else might have been the person involved.

A great deal of thought and skill will have to be used in drafting defence statements because it will be important not to jeopardise any aspect of the defence case at the eventual trial. However, the statement must be sufficiently detailed to prompt secondary disclosure or to justify applications to a judge for further disclosure. The greatest difficulty in some cases is the fact that if the police, acting honestly, have formed the view that they have the right man they will close their minds to every other avenue of investigation, screen out evidence which might tend to contradict their initial view, and in the process of questioning witnesses tend to lead witnesses towards the kind of answers they are hoping for. There may be exceptional occasions where this is done dishonestly, but there is evidence that policemen do this subconsciously where they are personally convinced of the guilt of their main suspect. Thus, e.g., witnesses who originally gave vague or uncertain answers about some aspects of their observations are led along to give very much more positive versions by the form in which police take their witness statements. It will become part of the skill of the defence lawyer to draft the statement in such a way as to maximise the opportunities for further disclosure.

9.7 The Arraignment

All trials on indictment begin with the 'arraignment' which consists of formally putting the counts in the indictment to the accused and inviting him to plead to each. The jury are not empanelled at this stage and in most courts the procedure is that matters are 'listed to plead' where nothing else is dealt with but the taking of the plea. This is an obvious effort to clarify matters, improve listing and avoid the situation where there is a late change of plea causing wasted time and inconvenience. Exceptionally, if solicitors write to the CPS and the court and indicate that there is categorically to be a not guilty plea, the matter may be listed for trial without this preliminary stage. Otherwise the accused is brought before the court with both counsel present and he is invited to plead to each of the counts in the indictment. If he pleads guilty to all the counts there is no need to involve a jury and the court will then proceed to sentence or adjourn for sentence in order that reports or enquiries can be made. If he pleads not guilty to all offences the matter will be adjourned for jury trial, often some months later, especially if the accused is not in custody. If the accused pleads guilty to some offences but not others, prosecuting counsel will consider whether the overall admissions of guilt are sufficient for the accused to be fairly dealt with in his view. If so, he may, in respect of the counts to which the accused pleads not guilty, invite the judge to 'leave them on the court file'. In such a case the counts remain open but may not be proceeded with without leave of the court or of the Court of Appeal and, although this does not amount to a formal acquittal, only very exceptionally would the court permit these charges to be reopened. If counsel is not satisfied that the accused could be satisfactorily dealt with overall, as for example where he has only pleaded guilty to one minor offence out of several, then the sentencing for that offence is likely to be postponed until the offences for which he has pleaded not guilty are dealt with.

If there are co-accused and one pleads guilty and the other not guilty, the usual but not inevitable practice is for the judge to adjourn the case of the one who has pleaded guilty so that he is sentenced at the end of the trial of the one pleading not guilty after all the facts have come out so that it can more clearly be seen, for example, who is the ringleader and who the mere follower or how responsibility should otherwise be apportioned. However, if the prosecution wished to call the accused who pleaded guilty as a prosecution witness it may be preferable to sentence the accomplice before he testifies so that he is aware that there is no purpose in him changing his evidence to receive a more favourable outcome. In trials of professional criminals however it may be better to leave the sentencing of all to the end, even where one is to testify for the prosecution, so that the judge can assess their relative culpability (see especially *R v Weekes* (1982) 74 Cr App R 161 and **15.2.3.1**).

9.8 Plea Bargaining

As indicated earlier, there is a certain amount of scope for negotiating techniques in the criminal process. It may be possible for example to persuade the CPS not to charge at all, to withdraw a charge once made, to charge a lesser offence, or to caution (see **4.8.3**). Once matters have reached the Crown Court however then any 'negotiations' are likely to involve counsel.

The term 'plea bargaining' is used in a number of different senses. It may involve:

(a) An agreement that if the accused pleads guilty to certain offences his sentence will not exceed some given maximum, or will take some particular form (typically that he will not receive a custodial sentence).

(b) It may involve an agreement by the prosecution that if the accused will plead guilty to certain offences they may refrain from putting other or more serious offences to him.

(c) It may involve the prosecution agreeing with the defence that they will accept a plea of guilty to a lesser offence than the one charged.

(d) It may refer to the prosecution undertaking not to proceed on certain counts in the indictment if the accused will plead guilty to the remainder.

The position in England and Wales in relation to plea bargaining is that:

(a) The first of these situations ((a) above) is governed by the case of *R v Turner* [1970] 2 QB 321 which clearly establishes that any improper pressure by or in the presence of the judge to plead guilty in the expectation of a certain sentence renders a guilty plea a nullity and thus the conviction is liable to be quashed on appeal.

(b) The second form of undertaking ((b) above) is improper though in reality it merges somewhat into the third form ((c) above) which *is* proper, as is the fourth ((d) above). Usually it involves a discussion between prosecuting and defence counsel, with or without the solicitors present. It is unclear in the case law whether the judge's approval is strictly required in law. According to *R v Coward* (1980) 70 Cr App R 70 the onus is on prosecuting counsel to decide what pleas to accept. In effect it is difficult for a judge to force the prosecution to proceed, but other cases have indicated that a judge may express his disapproval so strongly that prosecuting counsel is likely in effect to be forced to go on. Unlike in civil cases any arrangements must really be struck before the trial has commenced, because once it has commenced and the prosecution evidence has established a case to answer, discontinuance or the acceptance of lesser pleas do require the consent of the judge.

9.9 The Jury

The trial will commence with the jury being empanelled. Jurors may be challenged by the defence 'for cause' so if there is any reason to suspect impropriety or overt bias such challenges may still be made, but the defence now no longer has the power to make 'peremptory challenges' without reason. The prosecution may ask any juror to 'stand by' but in the light of guidelines issued by the Attorney-General, reported at (1989) 88 Cr App R 123, such challenges are rarely made. The judge has a power to remove a juror from the jury and might exercise it, e.g., where it is clear that a juror cannot read or write and much of the trial depends on documentary evidence. There is much case law as to the extent to which, if at all, a judge should seek to intervene to ensure racially or sexually balanced juries.

9.10 The Course of the Trial

The evidential rules relevant to the course of a trial are discussed in **Chapter 15**. Procedurally the following is the order of events:

(a) After the jury have been informed of the charges to which the accused has pleaded not guilty, prosecuting counsel will open the case. He will summarise the facts and the evidence he proposes to adduce and explain, in factual and reasonably simple language, the way in which he proposes to establish his case and how well his evidence pieces together. He will introduce the witnesses that he proposes to call and say what each is likely to say and will indicate in outline the relevant law and the elements of the offence which he must establish whilst always reminding them that it is the judge who will give them a final direction on matters of law.

In the opening speech counsel must *not* refer to any matters of evidence whose admissibility he knows will be challenged by the defence and he will have received intimation of this by exchange of letters from the solicitors or by discussion with defence counsel immediately before the start. There is provision in the Criminal Procedure and Investigation Act 1996 for preliminary matters of admissibility of evidence which are challenged by the defence to be dealt with by way of preliminary hearing before the judge who will eventually take the trial. For a fuller discussion see **9.5** above.

(b)   The prosecution will then call its witnesses one by one and each in turn is subject to examination-in-chief, to cross-examination by or on behalf of each of the defendants, and to re-examination where appropriate. Counsel will also put in evidence any formal admissions which have been agreed under s. 10, Criminal Justice Act 1967 and witness statements which are admissible under some principle of evidence, e.g., under s. 9, Criminal Justice Act 1967 or ss. 23 and 24, Criminal Justice Act 1988.

If at any stage the prosecution wishes to introduce evidence the admissibility of which is challenged by the defence there will be a *voir dire*, or trial within a trial, at which the prosecution will need to establish to the judge's satisfaction that the relevant exception to the hearsay rule is made out or that a confession is reliable and thus admissible under s. 76, Police and Criminal Evidence Act 1984; that notwithstanding s. 78 of the 1984 Act it does not make the trial unfair if a given item of evidence is introduced; that one of the reasons for unavailability of a witness under s. 24, Criminal Justice Act 1988 applies; or as the case may be. All these matters are more fully discussed in the chapters on evidence.

(c)   At the end of the prosecution case there may be a submission of no case to answer. The nature of this submission and the principles on which it should be allowed are described more fully at **14.3.1**.

(d)   If there is a case to answer, the defence present their case. It may be that the defence need adduce no evidence at all and that defence counsel wishes merely to make a closing speech. The defence may make an opening speech if they wish unless only the accused and character witnesses are to be called in which case defence counsel does not have an opening speech (s. 2, Criminal Evidence Act 1898).

The accused may testify but is not compelled to, but if he does he must testify before his witnesses unless the judge otherwise orders (s. 79, Police and Criminal Evidence Act 1984). The other witnesses of fact and/expert witnesses will be called and each in turn will be subject to examination-in-chief and cross-examination, not only from the prosecution but from the counsel for every other defendant who has not called the witness.

(e)   Counsel then have closing speeches. Prosecuting counsel sums up the case to the jury and at this stage, as throughout, he must act as a 'minister of justice' and must not strive at all costs for a conviction. He will remind the jury of the most cogent parts of the prosecution evidence and comment upon inconsistencies or contradictions in the defence evidence. He may now comment upon the failure of the accused to give evidence. The prosecution do not in fact invariably choose to make a closing speech.

The defence then have their closing speech and may comment in any way appropriate on the whole of the case that is justified by the evidence. It is not appropriate however for counsel to suggest fanciful explanations unsupported by any actual evidence.

(f) The judge then sums up. Explanations of various aspects of what should appear in a judicial summing up appear throughout the chapters on evidence. There should be clear explanations of the respective roles of judge and jury, of the law, of the burden and standard of proof, and of any other relevant point of evidence on which a specific form of direction is required, e.g., identification evidence, the need to consider the case against each of two or more accused quite separately, the use of their knowledge of the defendant's bad character if any, or the relevance of the defendant declining to testify. The judge may comment on the evidence but should not indicate so strongly what is credible and what is not that the jury are likely to adopt the judge's views. The judge may nonetheless comment on manifest implausibilities or contradictions.

Increasingly a judge may invite counsel to assist him on the law and form of a direction especially in matters where there are many technicalities. Defence counsel is under an obligation to assist at this stage rather than as was formerly the practice being entitled to sit tight in the hope of a successful appeal against a manifest misdirection. The point is however, not entirely clear and depends in part on the Bar's Code of Conduct. In *R v Edwards* (1983) 77 Cr App R 5 it was suggested that in principle defence counsel should not keep silent in those circumstances but should assist the judge to ensure that the present trial is a fair one by intervening if he notices a clear misdirection.

(g) The jury are then directed to retire and consider their verdict, which must be a unanimous one, and to appoint a foreman. If in the course of their retirement the jury wish to ask any question, both question and answer should be given publicly in open court and not, for example, by private note to the judge. It may be necessary for the judge to completely redirect the jury in the light of some question which may indicate that they have misunderstood some aspect of the case.

After a minimum of two hours and ten minutes (longer in complex cases) the judge may indicate to the jury that he will accept a *majority* verdict by no less than ten to two or if the jury is reduced below 12, a majority of ten to one, or nine to one. If the jury still prove unable to agree then, after what the judge considers to be an appropriate time, he may discharge them. He may not bring improper pressure to bear on them however to return with a verdict more quickly than they are able to. If the jury are discharged there may be a retrial, though the prosecution, depending on all the facts, may decide not to proceed, e.g., in view of the passage of time or the way certain evidence has come out.

If the jury return an unambiguous verdict it must be accepted by the judge. If the verdict on any count is ambiguous the judge should attempt to clarify it by questions (e.g., where the jury purport to find the accused guilty of both murder and manslaughter in respect of the same incident). The more confused that the jury's verdict is, the more likely it is that an appeal will be successful on the basis that they must have misunderstood their duty.

(h) At the conclusion of the trial, if the verdict on any charge is one of guilty, the judge will proceed to sentence and before doing so will deal with mitigation and other matters such as obtaining of pre-sentence reports (see **Chapter 10**). It may be necessary to remand the accused, on bail or in custody, until further information is available for sentencing. There may indeed be other trials involving the same accused which are being dealt with separately and later, and it may not be appropriate to sentence until the outcome of those trials.

(i)   In the event of a guilty verdict it will be necessary to consider the possibility of appeal (see **Chapter 12**).

If the verdict is not guilty the accused will be discharged and counsel for the accused will ask for any other appropriate orders, e.g., for costs from central funds, the remission of legal aid contributions, etc.

9.11   Preparation for Trial

We have thus far dealt with the procedure in getting to the outcome of a Crown Court trial. It is now appropriate to consider preparation for that trial.

Considerations relevant to managing a criminal practice have been discussed earlier in **Chapter 3**. The importance of keeping accurate records, proper file management, and the possibility of having to run substantial cases with teams of people have been dealt with there. Criminal practitioners whose main interest is advocacy may well not be involved any further in cases past the committal stage and, as suggested earlier, many of the most specialist criminal firms have quite separate sections dealing with cases between committal and trial.

The most important immediate procedural aspects include the following:

(a)   Undertaking the disclosure procedure discussed at **9.6**.

(b)   The possibility of agreeing the tape-recorded evidence under *Practice Direction (Crime: Tape Recording of Police Interviews)* [1989] 1 WLR 631. This will involve listening to the tape, and discussing it with the client, and possibly with counsel.

(c)   The indictment should be received in due course and should be checked for technical or procedural problems and if necessary counsel should be consulted.

(d)   Custody time limits should be borne in mind. If the client is in custody, no more than 112 days should elapse between committal and start of the trial. However, the prosecution may apply, in writing or if necessary orally, for that period to be extended and an extension will very commonly be needed in many Crown Courts in view of listing delays, even in quite routine cases.

9.11.1   FURTHER PREPARATION

9.11.1.1   Costs

If the case is going to the Crown Court clearly there will be substantial expense ahead. It is vital to ensure that an appropriate legal aid order has been obtained at the end of the committal stage or by a further application to the Crown Court. If the client has been paying privately hitherto it may be that an application to the Crown Court is now required in view of the substantial expense ahead and the depletion of the client's savings hitherto. One must bear in mind that applications for prior authorisation may be advisable in the case of substantial expenditure particularly on expert witnesses. Specific application will need to be made to use a Queen's Counsel at trial. It may be possible to arrange informal payments on account where cases are very substantial and a long delay is likely. It is necessary to write to the Chief Clerk at the taxing office at the Crown Court indicating what work has already been done, what work is involved ahead and what is an appropriate figure for costs and substantial disbursements.

9.11.1.2   The client

After committal it is appropriate, however familiar the client appears to be with the criminal process, to advise him further about the subsequent procedures up to the start of his trial. In the light of prosecution documents and perhaps the way in which an oral application to dismiss went, it may be necessary substantially to improve and update his own proof of evidence. This must be done not only in respect of matters of guilt or innocence but with a view to ultimate mitigation. It will be vital to deal with every single factual aspect of the prosecution statements insofar as the client is likely to know anything about them or can comment on them. Statements should be supplied to the client where necessary for him to consider thoroughly, although some discretion should be used in this. It is for example sometimes appropriate to delete witnesses' names and/or addresses from depositions and to delete details from statements in sexual cases which are supplied to a client in custody, where such papers may circulate and be misused.

9.11.1.3   Prosecution evidence

This will have been obtained in the form of statements. However, the prosecution have no obligation to disclose all their evidence at the committal stage or even to indicate who their witnesses are. They only need call sufficient evidence to show a prima facie case. That does not mean however that they are entitled to keep their evidence secret until trial in respect of any witness.

The prosecution will after committal need to serve a 'notice of additional evidence' in respect of any witnesses whom they did not use at the committal stage. This should be served on both the defence and the court and is usually served in a signed statement complying with s. 9 of the Criminal Justice Act 1967. One will need to consider carefully any new aspect of the case which this raises and whether the evidence is so uncontroversial that it can be agreed under s. 9 or whether new evidence needs to be found on the client's behalf to meet extra points made in this statement. It may be necessary to consult counsel as to his view of the evidential effect.

The implications of the disclosure procedure and the drafting of a defence statement have already been discussed at **9.6** above.

9.11.1.4   Additional evidence for the defence

It may be necessary to interview new witnesses or reinterview other witnesses in the light of what is learned by this stage and any additional evidence served by the prosecution.

9.11.1.5   Expert evidence

If the case is one where expert evidence seems likely to be required, an appropriate expert should be instructed as soon as possible to provide a report. Typical experts might be, for example, forensic document examiners, forensic scientists of other kinds, psychiatrists and the like. Expert evidence is the only example of evidence, apart from an alibi notice, of which an accused needs to give the prosecution warning before the Crown Court trial by virtue of the Crown Court (Advance Notice of Expert Evidence) Rules 1987. These apply to both defence and prosecution and require the prior disclosure of expert evidence in much the same way as is applicable in civil cases.

9.11.1.6   Plans

If the physical layout of the scene of the alleged crime is relevant (e.g., the interior of a public house) then it may be necessary to visit it, photograph it, or even prepare maps and plans.

Where these are done they should be served on the other parties with a statement under s. 9, Criminal Justice Act 1967 if necessary to indicate their authenticity.

9.11.1.7 Writing to the prosecution

It is worth writing to the prosecution, and this may well be done when sending the defence statement, about any outstanding matters. You should already have obtained your own client's criminal record and it will have been important to have gone through this with him at a far earlier stage to confirm that he accepts any recorded offences. It will be necessary to ask for the criminal record of any witnesses they propose to call; it may be necessary to correspond with them in an effort to have any particular statements which might otherwise be admissible edited. This also applies to the tape or the transcript of any tape which may be played in court so as, for example, to take out any references made in interview to a client's previous bad character.

9.11.1.8 Interviewing prosecution witnesses

Although it is perfectly proper to interview any witness it is often said, though on no particular authority, that it is unwise for a solicitor to interview prosecution witnesses without notifying the prosecution in advance. Some consider it best to have two persons present to provide a corroborated note of what is said to avoid any suggestion of attempting to influence a witness. It is the writer's view that this is somewhat over cautious and that no reputable solicitor would be likely to be accused of attempting to tamper with prosecution evidence merely by interviewing a witness.

9.11.1.9 Use of counsel

The purposes for which counsel may be used have been discussed earlier. Unless a solicitor has obtained the Higher Courts Advocacy Qualification only counsel may conduct a Crown Court jury trial and therefore an appropriate barrister will have been selected earlier. One will need to consider whether it is necessary to obtain advice on evidence or tactics; advice on plea; or perhaps to have a conference with the counsel of one's choice with or without the client present.

An appropriate brief should be prepared, as late in the day as possible to take account of any new developments, but not so late that counsel does not have time thoroughly to digest it.

9.11.1.10 Ensuring the attendance of witnesses

One must take all relevant steps to ensure the attendance of witnesses including the obtaining and service of necessary witness summonses. These are obtained from the Crown Court and conduct money ought in practice to be served although there is no strict requirement to do so. This should only amount to travelling expenses to court. The sum is reclaimed from the court with the witness expenses and therefore should be collected from the witness. If a witness on service of the summons seems extremely reluctant, even though he had given a proof of evidence before, one may need to reconsider the desirability of calling him. Relevant dates of, for example, holidays, hospital appointments and the like should be obtained. One should ask one's own witnesses at interview whether or not they have a criminal record and each witness statement should of course be signed in case of problems with the witness later whereupon it may become necessary to treat the witness as hostile. Witnesses should be told about the course that the evidence will take and the role of judge and prosecuting counsel, although this may happen outside court. Witnesses will need to be told that they may only be warned the night before of the date of the trial.

9.11.1.11 Date of trial

When the case comes into the warned list the client should be notified and if he is on bail he should be asked to keep in daily touch unless a fixed date is given. In the Crown Court a fixed date some weeks or months ahead may be given for very substantial trials or where there is a good deal of expert evidence.

9.11.1.12 Sentence and mitigation

It is usually appropriate to give some consideration to sentence and mitigation however good the defence case seems. It may be appropriate to obtain references from character witnesses, who can also be used on questions of guilt so long as the accused has no criminal record, and expert evidence from, for example, doctors may be necessary on matters of mitigation also. The client should be advised of the likely range of sentences and of the risk that conducting the case in certain ways may increase those sentences (e.g., by scandalous or improper imputations on prosecution witnesses) although one should not shrink from making any appropriate imputation which is essential for the defence.

9.12 At the Trial

It is important to attend by a responsible representative. The witnesses should be marshalled and any other assistance that counsel requires given. It is vital to take as full note of the evidence and other events as possible especially when counsel is conducting cross-examination and may not be able himself to make full notes, e.g., not merely of what the witnesses say but of the judge's comments or other interventions. One should be in such a position as to be able to take instructions from the client in the dock during the trial. It will be necessary to assist witnesses to claim on expenses forms from the appropriate office of the Crown Court.

If the trial lasts more than one day it is important to see that the client's bail is extended overnight and counsel should be reminded to make this application strongly, though it may be refused once the judge has commenced summing up.

After the trial the client should be advised fully as to what has occurred if he has been acquitted. It may be that in the light of what has happened he may wish to consider some form of civil action, although there is no action available as such for inconvenience or distress caused by a failed prosecution unless it can be brought within the heads of one of the normal torts, e.g., malicious prosecution. If the client has been convicted he should be advised about the effect of any sentence passed on him, e.g., time for payment of a fine, compensation order or other penalties. If the client is in custody he will need to be visited in the cells, usually with counsel, to receive advice about the precise terms of imprisonment which he has received and is likely to have to serve. Advice then and there will need to be given about appeal but it is usually better to say that this needs to be considered when the heat of the moment has passed and perhaps to arrange to see him on some subsequent occasion or to give him written advice (a legal aid order covers initial advice on appeal).

9.12.1 ACTION WITH OTHERS

Where a client has been sentenced to imprisonment it will be well known to the solicitor to which prison he will be taken immediately but after assessment he may quite shortly be transferred to some other prison. Enquiries may be made from the prison to which he has initially been taken or otherwise at the Home Office Prison Index, 11th Floor, Calthorpe House, Birmingham. It may be appropriate if the accused has a family or friends to inform them of the nature of the sentence, the client's whereabouts and the procedure for prison visits. Counsel may be asked to advise in writing on appeal and settle initial grounds (pending receipt of transcript).

9.12.2 COSTS

Once the case is concluded if it is a 'standard fee' case the application form should be completed and lodged by post at the Crown Court and payment should then take place very swiftly. If the case is not a case for standard fees then a proper bill must be prepared for determination by the Crown Court taxing officer and that should be lodged within three months. Full supplementary documentation may need to be supplied just as with a civil bill, e.g., attendance notes, disbursement vouchers and the like.

TEN

SENTENCING AND PROCEDURES AFTER CONVICTION

10.1 Introduction

In this chapter we shall be considering sentencing and procedures after conviction. We will consider what will happen initially after a guilty verdict is returned, or a plea of guilty entered. We shall then consider the range of sentences available to the courts in the usual case before turning to the regime imposed by the Criminal Justice Acts 1991 and 1993 which indicates the processes through which a court must go before selecting a certain type of sentence, and in deciding upon its length or severity. A discussion of the principles underlying the making of a plea in mitigation follows and the chapter concludes with a brief outline of the Crime (Sentences) Act 1997 which at the time of writing had not yet been brought into force.

A conviction may follow either a plea of guilty or a plea of not guilty. In neither case need the court proceed to sentence immediately. It may, and in some cases must, adjourn the proceedings and sentence at a future date for a number of reasons. Examples would be:

(a) Where a pre-sentence report (formerly called a social enquiry report) or a psychiatric or medical report needs to be prepared so that the court has more information available.

(b) Where there is insufficient information to enable the court to proceed immediately to sentence.

(c) In cases where the defendant has been convicted in his absence and the court has in mind either to disqualify him from driving or imprison him they must adjourn the case to enable the defendant to be brought before the court.

When the court does propose to adjourn proceedings for sentence for any reason the defendant will be remanded. In other words, the court will have to consider the question of bail or custody pending sentence. It must be remembered that the prima facie presumption in favour of bail contained in the Bail Act 1976 does *not* apply at this stage except where the court is adjourning to obtain reports on the offender. Even here the court may well now impose conditions even if bail has previously been unconditional. The initial procedures are likely to include one or all of the following matters:

(a) Outlining the facts of the case.

(b) The defendant's antecedents.

(c) Offences taken into consideration.

10.1.1 THE FACTS OF THE CASE

If the defendant has been convicted after a not guilty plea then the court will have been made aware of all the evidence in the case. In addition to deciding the issue of guilt or innocence they will know which version of the facts they are minded to believe. In other words they may have already heard matters relevant to sentencing. For example, suppose that the accused is charged with an assault arising out of a fight and his defence has been self-defence. It may well be that although the court convicts him, having found that his actions did not amount to self-defence, it will nonetheless be apparent that there was gross provocation and this may clearly be a matter relevant to the sentence which it will impose.

There is more difficulty where the defendant has pleaded guilty. In this case there will be no evidence on oath but the prosecution will summarise the facts of the case. In a straightforward case there is no problem, but what if the defendant, whilst admitting his guilt, wishes to give some entirely different version of how matters occurred? What if there is a substantial difference between how the prosecution says an incident occurred and what the defendant has to say?

At this stage it must be remembered that the prosecution is supposed to be acting as a 'minister of justice'. They should maintain a relatively neutral attitude about matters and in particular never press for any particular sentence nor explain the facts of the crime in an emotive or exaggerated way. If it appears that there is a genuine and material dispute about how an incident occurred, then the advocates for prosecution and defence should each make their submissions about the matter, but thereafter the sentencing court should either:

(a) accept the defence account, or

(b) allow prosecution and defence to call evidence about the matter. This is called a 'Newton' hearing from the leading case *R* v *Newton* (1982) 77 Cr App R 13.

In the Crown Court where this happens after a guilty plea there is no jury, the judge himself deciding which version of the facts he prefers to believe. The sentencing court will therefore now be aware so far as possible of the facts of the crime itself.

10.1.2 THE DEFENDANT'S ANTECEDENTS

These are usually presented to the court by the Crown Prosecutor or one of the policemen involved in the case. The 'antecedents' are details of the offender's age, upbringing, education, employment record and domestic circumstances. Also there is some account of his previous criminal record, although this is not in substitution for the actual printout of his criminal record which will also be supplied, but the antecedents officer will give more background information, for example, he will mention the actual date of release from each previous sentence and deal with whether or not the accused had bail and the like.

The rules of evidence do not apply at this stage but the antecedents officer may be cross-examined by the defendant's advocate in an effort to elicit more favourable details about the defendant's past, for example that he cooperated with the police from the outset, that he has now found a job or got married. It must be remembered that the Rehabilitation of Offenders Act 1974 does not apply in criminal proceedings, but pursuant to *Practice Direction (Crime: Spent Convictions)* [1975] 1 WLR 1065, details of 'spent' convictions should not be read out in court unless the court gives leave to do so.

Procedure varied greatly in respect of the presentation of antecedent evidence and eventually a *Practice Direction (Crime Antecedents)* [1993] 1 WLR 1459 was promulgated in order that matters could be standardised. It is particularly important to ensure that if an officer is called to give evidence relating to antecedents he does not make allegations of a generalised and prejudicial nature. For this purpose it is good practice to give the defence notice of the proposed evidence of the antecedents officer in those cases where a policeman is called rather than the information given directly by prosecuting counsel.

10.1.3   OFFENCES TAKEN INTO CONSIDERATION

In the course of being questioned about the present offence the offender may well have been questioned also about other offences. Where the offender proposes to plead guilty then he may well have admitted other past crimes. There is no need for the prosecution to charge him with each of the crimes which he has admitted. One option available to the prosecution is merely to charge him with a few selected crimes and allow him to have the others 'taken into consideration'. This is a somewhat informal procedure, although sanctioned by long usage, in which the prosecution have the advantage of clearing up unsolved crimes and the defendant has the advantage of having the slate wiped clean insofar as these other offences are concerned so that he could not be prosecuted for them after his trial for the present offences is concluded.

The offences to be taken into consideration should be prepared in a proper schedule with all relevant details by the police. They should be offences of a broadly similar nature or of a less serious nature than the present charge. The sentencing court cannot specifically impose a sentence in respect of offences which are to be taken into consideration (although it may order compensation to the victims of those offences) but such offences will be taken into account in a general way when deciding on sentence.

It may be helpful to give an example. A very common type of crime which is taken into consideration is house burglary. Suppose that the offender has made it his habitual practice to go out to one of the wealthier suburbs of the city in which he lives and break into houses at weekends. He may well have done this over a period of a year or more before he is caught. When he is caught he may admit the most recent crimes in the course of interrogation. As other incidents which have not been solved by the police are put to him he may well be prepared to admit those also.

It is very important to stress when acting for a defendant that the list of offences to be taken into consideration should be gone through very carefully with the defendant to ensure that he is right in admitting those other offences. For example, in the incidents just cited it is most unlikely, if regular weekend burglaries had been carried out over a year, that the defendant will any longer remember the precise locations or addresses of the houses which he has burgled or the exact goods which he took away from each. There may be a tendency on the part of the police to slip in anything conceivably likely, in order to improve their detection statistics. On the assumption however, that the defendant admits, let us say, 30 such burglaries, the probable practice of the prosecution would be to charge him only with a selected four or five and to have the others 'taken into consideration'. Whilst it may at first sight appear that to admit a course of conduct of regular burglary involving say 30 houses is a very significantly different scale of crime to admitting only the four or five with which one is actually charged, the sentencing practice of the court is such that very little in the way of an extra sentence will be imposed for the other offences. The maximum penalty for one burglary is 14 years and therefore in relation to the five offences to which the accused specifically pleads guilty the maximum is ample and would far exceed anything the court would realistically be minded to impose. The consideration of the other offences referred to in the example would probably make very little difference.

It ought to be mentioned that 'TICs', as they are called, may also be relevant for a defendant who has been convicted after pleading *not guilty*. In the nature of things however such cases will be rare and the usual case of offences taken into consideration occurs where the offender is prepared to admit the crimes with which he is presently charged in advance of trial and the prosecution will thus have ample opportunity to put the other matters to him.

We shall now go on to consider remaining matters in the following order:

(a) Reports (**10.2**).

(b) Types of sentence (**10.3**).

(c) Other orders including compensation and costs (**10.8**).

(d) The structured approach to sentencing under the Criminal Justice Acts 1991 and 1993 (**10.9**).

(e) The plea in mitigation (**10.11**).

10.2 Reports

There may be some situations where the court, even with the offender's criminal record and a detailed and helpful plea in mitigation made by the defence advocate, feels it is unlikely to have sufficient information about the convicted person to enable it to pass sentence. In such a situation it may obtain reports on the offender from a variety of sources and we shall now consider these.

10.2.1 PRE-SENTENCE REPORTS

Such reports are prepared, in the case of adults, by the probation service. They are not usually prepared in advance of trial unless the defendant has already indicated a guilty plea or is already on probation. The report is prepared after one or several interviews between a probation officer and the offender, sometimes in the offender's home environment. The offence will be discussed with the offender and the report will deal with his background, education, upbringing, circumstances, financial position and any particular personal, medical or social problems which he seems to have. Such a report is needed in almost every case before a custodial sentence or before the majority of forms of community sentence can be considered. Unlike the old 'social enquiry report' which often was obtained with an eye to the welfare of the convicted person, a pre-sentence report is expressly to assist the court in deciding on punishment. It will often conclude with a recommendation for a particular type of sentence and may especially deal with the offender's likely response to probation or community service.

If there is no report prepared before conviction then inevitably there will have to be an adjournment to enable one to be prepared and the usual term of such adjournment is three weeks. It is generally considered more satisfactory to have such a report prepared whilst the offender is at liberty, though it is not conclusively the case that when adjourning for a pre-sentence report the court should never remand in custody. Everything will depend upon the facts of the case, remembering that the prima facie right to bail in the Bail Act 1976 *does* apply at this stage.

When considering the regime imposed by the Criminal Justice Act 1991 we shall consider specifically the occasions when a pre-sentence report is required at **10.9.1.3**.

10.2.2 MEDICAL AND PSYCHIATRIC REPORTS

It may be that the court will consider that the occurrence of the offence is connected with some medical condition, in which case they may require the making of medical reports on the accused. A common example is where there is some suggestion of a drug habit or alcoholism which is relevant to why the offender committed the offence, e.g., to provide money to sustain the habit or whilst under the influence of alcohol or the drug. In such a situation the court has power to remand the offender (in custody or on bail) for the preparation of such reports, bearing in mind again that the prima facie right to bail does apply at this stage. Alternatively, the offender may be remanded to a hospital for a report to be prepared under s. 35 of the Mental Health Act 1983. The court is likely to do this either if the offender appears dangerous or if it seems he will not cooperate with the making of a report voluntarily.

Section 4(1) of the Criminal Justice Act 1991 requires a court sentencing an offender who 'is or appears to be mentally disordered' to obtain and consider a medical report before passing a custodial sentence in almost every case.

Both pre-sentence reports and medical reports are prepared in order to be presented to the court, but will be disclosed on a confidential basis in advance to the offender's legal representative.

10.2.3   REPORTS FOR THE DEFENCE

Although reports in both the instances so far considered are made by order of the court it should not be forgotten that it is always open to the legal representative of an offender himself to commission suitable reports. Such reports would be particularly appropriate where it is already apparent that the prosecution have medical evidence to the effect that the offender should be committed to a secure hospital. It may be that the offender is meanwhile receiving treatment from his own consultant who may be prepared to make a different recommendation, e.g., that the offender could safely be released into the community provided he voluntarily agrees to adopt a certain course of treatment. The possibility of the defence commissioning its own reports should not be overlooked.

One important thing to consider is the stage at which reports might be requested. Suppose that an offender has been convicted and there is no pre-sentence report available (as there will not normally be in the case of an offender pleading not guilty). One can make a lengthy plea in mitigation as part of which one might suggest that the court ought to obtain more information before finally sentencing the offender.

More usually an attempt will be made to save the court's time by asking the court to form a preliminary view as to whether it is likely to require a pre-sentence report. This may be done quite early on. The defendant's advocate may simply say that there appear to be matters to do with the offender's upbringing or home circumstances which have contributed to the problems which led to the offence and in view of the relative scarcity of information, and the likely range of sentences which the court will be minded to impose, that the court should obtain a pre-sentence report. One can then ask the court (whether magistrates or Crown Court judge) for a preliminary indication of whether it is in sympathy with that view. If it is not, then that is a clear indication that a custodial sentence, and most types of community sentence, are not in the court's mind and thus one can address the rest of the plea in mitigation to the other possible outcomes. If a pre-sentence report is then ordered the full plea in mitigation can be made when the report is to hand. It may be that otherwise there will be a great deal of repetition of material which is anyway contained in the eventual report.

10.3   Types of Sentence

We shall now consider the types of sentence which the court has the power to impose. It should not be forgotten that sentencing may have a number of purposes, some of which are mutually contradictory. They are generally considered to be:

(a) *Deterrence*

That by seeing that an accused is caught, convicted and punished in some disagreeable way for a crime, like-minded people may be deterred from committing such offences.

(b) *Retribution*

To express society's dislike for or outrage at the type of conduct for which the offender has been convicted.

(c) *Prevention*

Where the offender is a menace to society then by incarceration he is at least kept out of circulation for the period of that incarceration and society's welfare improved by his being prevented from committing further offences during that time.

(d) *Rehabilitation*

This aims at the reform of the offender, to help him to return to ordinary social living and to mend his ways and become a useful member of the community.

Until 1991, in pursuance of these diverse aims, sentences could be classified into two categories, namely *tariff* sentences, which represent so to speak the 'going rate' for the type of crime involved and which look to the punishment pure and simple of the offender, and *individualised* sentences which look in some way to treat the needs of the offender. The offender's needs will generally be treated by a rehabilitation-type sentence, e.g., community service or probation, although it should not be overlooked that rehabilitation may on occasion be prompted by something that also appears a deterrent to future misconduct. The aims of deterrence and rehabilitation are to some extent merged by the concepts in the Criminal Justice Act 1991 which treats most kinds of community sentences as 'punishment' as well as rehabilitation.

10.4 The Courts

We shall now consider the sentences available to the particular courts.

10.4.1 CROWN COURT

The Crown Court may impose any penalty up to the maximum prescribed by law for the offence. Thus in the case of a theft which is punishable under the Theft Act by a penalty of up to seven years' imprisonment the court may impose seven years or less and/or a fine of an unlimited amount or any other penalty prescribed by law which is applicable up to the maximum for that type of penalty, e.g., community service up to the maximum. Moreover, where the Crown Court tries more than one offence in relation to the same offender, it may in principle impose *consecutive* prison sentences each within the maximum prescribed by statute for the offence or it may make those sentences *concurrent* so that they run together.

Example An offender is charged with theft (maximum seven years) and burglary (maximum 14 years) and is convicted of both. The Crown Court (having a potential maximum of 21 years in total available) may decide to impose a sentence of two years in respect of the theft, and one year in respect of the burglary and make them *consecutive*. The total term to be served (subject to early release, see **10.5.1**) will be three years. If the court makes the terms *concurrent* the total term to be served will be two years.

10.4.2 MAGISTRATES' COURT

The magistrates' court has the power to impose a penalty of up to six months' imprisonment and/or a fine of £5,000 for any one offence unless the statutory maximum for the offence is less than that. An example is careless driving under s. 3 of the Road Traffic Act 1988 where the maximum punishment is a £1,000 fine and there is no power to imprison. Where magistrates try more than one offence against the same offender then their total powers are as follows:

(a) If all the offences are summary offences the aggregate total sentence imposed must not exceed six months.

(b) If however there are two or more offences both triable either way then the magistrates may impose up to a total aggregate sentence of 12 months.

(c) If the magistrates convict of one offence triable either way and one purely summary offence the maximum is six months.

10.4.3 WHICH COURT?

As we have seen, a magistrates' court may commit a person to the Crown Court for *trial* in the case of an 'either way' offence or an offence triable only on indictment. In addition, however, as we have seen a magistrates' court, after hearing a case triable either way and convicting the offender, may commit him to the Crown Court for sentence if the court is of the opinion that greater punishment should be inflicted than it has power to impose. Where this happens the Crown Court may deal with the defendant as if he had been convicted on indictment and thus impose a sentence on him up to the maximum provided by the statute concerned. By s. 38 of the Magistrates' Courts Act 1980 (inserted in redrafted form by s. 25, Criminal Justice Act 1991) a magistrates' court may now only commit for sentence if it is of the opinion:

(a) *that the offence or the combination of the offence and one or more offences associated with it was so serious that greater punishment should be inflicted for the offence than the court has power to impose; or*

(b) *in the case of a violent or sexual offence that a custodial sentence for a term longer than the court has power to impose is necessary to protect the public from serious harm from him.*

10.4.4 THE POWERS OF ONE COURT TO DEAL WITH SENTENCES IMPOSED BY OTHERS

10.4.4.1 Suspended sentences

It should be noted that the Crown Court may deal with a suspended sentence of imprisonment imposed either by that or any other Crown Court or by any magistrates' court. Thus any Crown Court may decide whether or not to activate a previously imposed suspended sentence on further conviction. A magistrates' court however can only deal with a suspended sentence imposed by itself or by some other magistrates' court.

10.4.4.2 Probation

The Crown Court can deal with an offender who has reoffended whilst on probation no matter which court imposed the probation order. However, if a probation order was made by a magistrates' court the Crown Court's sentencing powers in respect of the breach of probation and its powers of resentencing in respect of the original offence are limited to those of the magistrates. A magistrates' court can in general only deal with probation orders imposed either by itself or by some other magistrates' court, and in the case of other magistrates' courts the consent of the supervising court must be obtained. This is not generally a difficult matter and consents may be obtained by relatively informal means.

10.5 Sentencing Offenders Over 21 Years of Age

10.5.1 IMPRISONMENT

A person of 21 years or over may as we have seen be sentenced to imprisonment by the Crown Court up to the maximum length of the term fixed by the statute creating the offence in question, or by a magistrates' court within the limit of six months for any one offence or up to a maximum aggregate of 12 months when dealing with two or more offences triable either way. Time spent in custody before trial and during trial is treated as part of the term of imprisonment. The previous system of 'remission for good conduct' is replaced by a system of unconditional release, and release on licence, whereby prisoners of good behaviour may be released at certain stages during a sentence subject to recall in the case of further offending. In outline the system is:

(a) Offenders sentenced to 12 months or less are released after serving half of their sentence automatically and unconditionally if of good behaviour.

(b) Offenders sentenced to between 12 months and four years are released automatically on licence after having served half their sentence provided they are of good behaviour.

(c) Prisoners of good behaviour sentenced to more than four years are released automatically after serving two-thirds of their sentence but may be considered at the half-way point for release on licence by the Parole Board.

10.5.2 LEGAL AID AND CUSTODIAL SENTENCES

A person who has not previously received a custodial sentence and who is not legally represented at the time of sentence cannot be sent to prison unless he has had the opportunity to apply for legal aid and declines to do so or his application for legal aid has been refused only on the grounds of means (s. 2(1), Powers of Criminal Courts Act 1973).

Some general comment on what one should say in a plea of mitigation appears later. Obviously unless there is some very special consideration in the case (e.g., a foreigner who above all fears a deportation order from the court) an immediately effective term of imprisonment is the worst thing that may happen to an offender. The plea in mitigation will generally be aimed above all else at avoiding this.

10.5.3 SUSPENDED SENTENCES UNDER S. 22, POWERS OF CRIMINAL COURTS ACT 1973

A court which passes a sentence of imprisonment for a term of no more than two years may order that it be suspended for a period of between one and two years. This latter period is called 'the operational period' and if the offender does not commit an imprisonable offence during that time the suspended sentence lapses. If however he does commit an imprisonable offence during that period the sentence is brought into effect unless the sentencing court for the later offence decides that it would be unjust to do this.

This power is available to both magistrates' courts and the Crown Court although naturally in the magistrates' court the period of imprisonment imposed is subject to the maximum powers of the magistrates (see 10.4.2).

A suspended sentence is often seen by the layperson or by the popular press as a very easy option since it appears that the criminal has walked out of court a 'free' man whereas other, lesser offenders may have received substantial fines. A suspended sentence however should in principle only be imposed if the court *first* decides to imprison the offender and then carries on separately to consider whether that sentence can be suspended. Suspended sentences should not be used in order to intimidate petty offenders. The court's powers to suspend a sentence are now more restricted than previously because by virtue of s. 22(2)(b) of the Powers of Criminal Courts Act 1973 (as substituted by the Criminal Justice Act 1991) it is provided that a court shall *not* pass a suspended sentence unless it is of the opinion: 'That the exercise of that power can be justified by the *exceptional circumstances* of the case.' This makes it even clearer that the court will in effect have already chosen a sentence of imprisonment before passing on to consider special circumstances which make its suspension desirable.

10.5.3.1 Activation of a suspended sentence

In what circumstances should a suspended sentence be activated? Suppose that a person who is convicted of an offence of dishonesty and who has some previous convictions is sentenced to a term of imprisonment for six months suspended for one year. That sentence will be activated if during the year he reoffends unless the court considers it unjust to impose it. Circumstances which might make a court hesitate to activate the original six months' term even after a further offence would be where, for example, the subsequent offence is of a completely different type, say an assault arising out of football hooliganism whereas previous offences have been for dishonesty, or where the second offence happened very late indeed during the operative period, e.g., after 11 months of the year had elapsed. In principle, however, a suspended sentence represents something of a 'last chance' for an offender and thus ought generally to be activated, in addition of course to any further punishment imposed for the subsequent offence.

10.5.3.2 Suspended sentence supervision order

The Crown Court has a further power not open to the magistrates' court which is a useful addition to the sentencing options. It has the power to impose a suspended sentence supervision order under which the offender receives a suspended sentence but in addition there is a condition that he should be under the supervision of a probation officer. To all intents and purposes this may be seen as something like a period of probation allied to a suspended sentence. Until 1991 it was not possible to combine probation with a custodial penalty although this is now permitted under the Criminal Justice Act 1991 and therefore this combination is likely largely to replace suspended sentence supervision orders since it will have the same net effect and is available to magistrates' courts as well as the Crown Court.

It should be noted that this form of order can only be made when the circumstances justify a suspended sentence in the first place. It should certainly not be a routine order or treated as a 'probation order with teeth'.

10.5.3.3 The magistrates' powers to activate a suspended sentence

It ought finally to be noted that a magistrates' court does not have the power to activate a suspended sentence imposed by the Crown Court although it does have the power to activate a suspended sentence imposed by itself or by any other magistrates' court. Where an offender comes before the magistrates' court whilst still subject to the operational period of a Crown Court suspended sentence, the magistrates must either commit the offender in custody or on bail to the Crown Court in relation to that matter or notify the Crown Court in writing of the action they have taken. It is then up to the Crown Court to take action in relation to the offender, if the judge of the Crown Court so requires. The magistrates may go on to sentence for the new offence which has occurred within the operational period. By not committing the offender to the Crown Court the magistrates are impliedly indicating that they do not consider it appropriate to activate the sentence.

10.5.4 FINES

A magistrates' court may impose an overall maximum fine of £5,000 per offence unless the statute creating the offence prescribes a different figure as the maximum. If the offence is also punishable with imprisonment the statute will indicate whether the fine is an alternative to imprisonment or may be imposed with it.

The Crown Court may fine an offender any amount at all unless statute prescribes a maximum. Fines can be imposed as well as or instead of imprisonment and in combination with almost all other penalties.

Fines are obviously an appropriate method of dealing with trivial offences, especially motoring offences (in combination with other penalties). They may also be appropriate for offences of dishonesty or even violence where the offences are not serious and the offender has no substantial criminal record. They do however present obvious problems of fairness. For example, it may seem in principle wrong to fine an individual who is only in receipt of welfare benefits since by definition welfare benefits are generally taken to be at subsistence level and it would be wrong to depress a person below even this. Equally however it is wrong that wealthy persons should in effect be able to 'buy' their way out of a sentence of imprisonment because of their ability to pay a substantial fine.

In the Crown Court this problem has always been left to the judge to decide. In the magistrates' courts, however, s. 18 of the Criminal Justice Act 1991 attempted to impose a mathematical basis of fairness by providing so called 'unit fines' whereby a strictly mathematical formula was imposed depending upon the seriousness of the offence and the level of the offender's income. This system in its brief life gave rise to many allegedly ludicrous anomalies whereby, for example, relatively prosperous people were fined many hundreds of pounds for trivial driving offences, whereas impecunious persons were fined nominal amounts for quite serious offences, such as burglary.

The moral and computational difficulties caused by s. 18 of the 1991 Act have already been laid to rest because its provisions have been substituted by s. 65 of the Criminal Justice Act 1993 and the section now reads:

(1) Before fixing the amount of any fine, a court shall enquire into the financial circumstances of the offender.
(2) The amount of any fine fixed by a court shall be such as, in the opinion of the court, reflects the seriousness of the offence.
(3) In fixing the amount of any fine, a court shall take into account the circumstances of the case including, among other things, the financial circumstances of the offender so far as they are known, or appear, to the court.

This provision is supplemented by sch. 3 to the 1993 Act which enables the court to make a 'financial circumstances order' in respect of any offender whereby it will have the power to look carefully into his exact financial status in terms of income, outgoings and dependants. The new s. 18 therefore allows the magistrates' court to employ a wide and general discretion in making the level of fine fit the seriousness of the offence and the means of the offender without being hamstrung by the complexities of the unit fine system.

Payment of fines is usually permitted by instalments over a period of one year. A fine is enforced by the clerk to the magistrates' court (who now has extended powers for this purpose and who may make decisions independently of the magistrates) and a defendant may be arrested or summoned before the court and committed to prison for non-payment of fines.

10.5.5 COMMUNITY SENTENCES

A community sentence consists of one or more community orders (Criminal Justice Act 1991, s. 6). These community orders are as follows:

(a) probation order;

    (b)   community service order;

    (c)   combination order;

    (d)   curfew order;

    (e)   supervision order;

    (f)   attendance centre order.

Of these, the first four are available in respect of offenders aged 16 or over; a supervision order is available for an offender aged between 10 and 17; and an attendance sentence order is available for an offender aged between 10 and 20.

We shall now discuss in turn the orders which apply to offenders over the age of 21; those which apply only to persons under that age are dealt with at **10.6**.

10.5.5.1   Probation order

All the sentences so far discussed (with the possible exception of a suspended sentence supervision order in the Crown Court) are in the nature of tariff sentences. They look to punishment rather than reform. Probation however may be imposed by either magistrates or the Crown Court. Either court dealing with an offender who is 17 or over may, with his consent, place him on probation for a period of between six months and three years. The nature of probation is that a person must keep in touch with his probation officer and comply with the latter's directions and be of good behaviour. He must in principle visit the probation officer at times to be specified by the latter.

The court may additionally impose conditions in the probation order. Examples of additional conditions might be that the person resides at a fixed address, e.g., with his family or some other relative or at a probation hostel, or that he receives treatment for some medical condition or attends a day centre, i.e. premises where there are facilities and advice to assist in the rehabilitation of offenders. Also negative requirements may be imposed requiring the person on probation to refrain from certain activities during the term of the probation order.

The probation officer allocated to the person on probation will be one who is attached to the magistrates' court area in which the person on probation resides and this may be different from the area of the court imposing the sentence. The magistrates' court for that area then becomes known as the 'supervising court'.

Probation is a sentence in its own right and can now be combined with most other penalties, in particular a suspended sentence, a fine or a community service order. A probation order, like a suspended sentence, is not meant to be an easy option. It should only be imposed when someone seems to be the kind of person for whom probation would be useful in the sense of assisting his reform or rehabilitation. An offender must consent to a community order such as probation and the consent obtained from the offender must be genuine and must not be extracted, for example, by the judge indicating that the offender either consents or will as an alternative receive a custodial sentence. A probation order is only ever made after a pre-sentence report has recommended that probation would be helpful in the circumstances of an individual's case. It would be most obviously useful for someone who has some discernible social or family problem. It would not for example be imposed upon a mature person who is living in settled family circumstances without any apparent difficulty of adjustment to the community.

If there is a further offence committed during the period of the probation order or some other breach of its terms, then when the offender is brought back before the sentencing court or the supervising court, the individual may be sentenced for the original offence in addition to being sentenced for the new offence. The original probation order may be quashed and another sentence substituted for it, or the probation order may be left in force with a fine being imposed for the breach, or may be extended for a further term if the accused consents.

10.5.5.2 Community service order

Where the court is dealing with an offender aged 16 or over and the offence is an imprisonable one a community service order may be made. This is an order that the person perform without pay work which is deemed to be of value to the community. The order must fix the precise number of hours to be worked and there is a minimum of 40 and a maximum of 240 (120 if the offender is aged only 16). If the offender fails to comply with the order he may be fined up to £1,000 or the order may be revoked and the offender resentenced.

Before such a sentence can be imposed there must be a pre-sentence report from a probation officer indicating that the offender is suitable for the work and that he consents and that appropriate work is available in the locality. The type of work is usually gardening, improving public spaces, decorating old people's homes, etc. It must be performed under the supervision of a probation officer.

Whilst there is no prescribed maximum age, this sentence is often thought to be appropriate for young offenders. This is especially the case where the offender has been convicted of offences which are unpleasant but not necessarily extremely serious, e.g., vandalism of some kind. The work is meant to be both a temporary restriction on his liberty and to give him some sense of usefulness and social purpose.

A community service order may not be combined with most other penalties for the same offence although it may be combined with disqualification from driving, endorsement of driving licence and orders for compensation and costs. It may however, as in the case of probation, be combined with other penalties and imposed in conjunction with penalties for another offence where these have been tried together.

10.5.5.3 Combination order

A combination order is a mixture of a probation order and a community service order. It is particularly aimed at 'persistent property offenders', e.g., vandals and burglars. The probation element must be for a minimum of 12 months and the community service element between 40 and 100 hours. A pre-sentence report must be obtained which should specifically recommend this form of punishment.

10.5.5.4 Curfew order

The curfew order was introduced by s. 12 of the Criminal Justice Act 1991 (although at present its use is still confined to the courts of certain areas where the success of the order is being monitored before introduction nationally). It requires the offender to remain at a particular place (which is obviously likely to be at home) for between two and 12 hours on any days over a period which must not exceed six months from the date of sentence. It is specifically aimed, according to the White Paper which preceded the Criminal Justice Act 1991, at preventing some forms of theft of and from cars, pub brawls and other similar disorders. A curfew order may also be used to keep people away from particular places. The order must be preceded by a pre-sentence report which must consider the attitude of any person likely to be affected by the enforced presence of the accused! Electronic monitoring by tagging may be employed. The consent of the offender is required but refusal of consent may well involve an alternative custodial sentence.

10.5.6 **ABSOLUTE AND CONDITIONAL DISCHARGE UNDER S. 7, POWERS OF CRIMINAL COURTS ACT 1973**

The court may impose these penalties in relation to relatively trivial offences. A court dealing with an offender which does not wish to punish him at all, for example because his offence was merely technical, may give an absolute discharge. An example would be in the case of a driving offence of strict liablity where there is no real moral blame on the defendant. Take for example a defendant who has just had his vehicle serviced by a reputable garage when the brakes suddenly fail. He would be guilty of the offence of driving a car with defective brakes, for which no mens rea is required. However, in all the circumstances a court would not consider his offence sufficiently blameworthy to impose any punishment and an absolute discharge would suffice.

A conditional discharge is like a somewhat watered down version of a suspended sentence in that, if the offender does not offend during the period of the discharge, the conditional discharge lapses. Thus an individual who is conditionally discharged for a year and commits no further offence is then free of any punishment in respect of the original offence, but if he does reoffend then in principle he can be dealt with again for the first offence. Discharges are imposed where immediate punishment is deemed to be unnecessary and probation is not required by the circumstances. A conditional discharge may apply for a period of up to three years.

10.5.7 **BINDING OVER**

One final method of dealing with an offender should be mentioned. This is binding over to keep the peace. This ancient power was originally contained in the Justice of the Peace Act 1361 and is now in s. 115 of the Magistrates' Courts Act 1980. The way in which this power is used is subject to a great deal of local variation.

Its proper use is where a person before the court has by his behaviour led the court to believe that a breach of the peace might arise from his future behaviour. In such a case that person may be bound over to keep the peace and be of good behaviour in a given sum of money. If he fails to keep the peace within the period fixed by the court then the sum of money is forfeited. Refusal to enter into the recognisance may involve him being sent to prison for contempt of court. Some magistrates use this power, probably quite wrongly, in respect of almost any kind of offence including shoplifting, but its most appropriate use is in relatively petty disputes involving disturbances or minor violence, in particular quarrels between neighbours. Commonly in such cases the CPS decline to become involved, and the neighbours will issue private prosecutions against each other for minor assaults arising out of some fracas. When they come before the court, it is likely to bind both of them over to keep the peace. A bind over may be ordered in addition to any other penalty for an offence and indeed even where the person concerned has been acquitted. Anyone before the court may be subject to a bind over, even a witness, as is commonly the case in disturbances arising out of industrial disputes or disputes between hunt saboteurs and hunt followers.

10.6 Sentencing Offenders Between 17 and 20 Years of Age

10.6.1 **CUSTODIAL SENTENCES**

An offender within these age ranges is sentenced to detention in a young offender institution. Under s. 1A of the Criminal Justice Act 1982 a convicting court may impose such a sentence in respect of an imprisonable offence if it considers that the defendant qualifies. The maximum term is the maximum available to that court in respect of the offence in question, in other words a magistrates' court may impose detention for up to six months for each offence (up to the overall maximum of 12 months) unless the statute in question prescribes some other maximum, and the Crown Court may impose up to the maximum for the offence in question. The *minimum* term which the court may impose is, however, prescribed and is 21 days for an offender of 18 or more, and two months for a 17 year old.

These orders are broadly subject to the same provisions in respect of release on licence as sentences of imprisonment for persons of 21 or over in adult prisons. In addition it should be noted that the court which imposes a detention order must:

(a) give reasons why the defendant qualifies for an order; and

(b) explain to the defendant in ordinary language why it is imposing such a detention order.

It should also be noted that the courts have no power to *suspend* custodial sentences in respect of persons under 21. Accordingly when one is presenting a plea in mitigation for someone within this age group it is worth stressing in the plea in mitigation that if the offender were 21 or over the option of a suspended sentence would be available to the court and that therefore the court might consider that this offender merits a 'last chance' by virtue of some non-custodial sentence since the courts do not have the option of suspending the sentence which they might otherwise impose.

10.6.2 NON-CUSTODIAL PENALTIES

(a) Such offenders may be fined up to the same maximum as an adult (an attendance centre order may be imposed for non-payment of a fine in addition to any other powers).

(b) A community service order may be made in respect of an offender within this age group with his consent and subject to the same conditions as previously described.

(c) Probation may be imposed with the consent of a person in the 17 to 20 age group.

(d) A supervision order or attendance centre order may be made (see below).

(e) Absolute and conditional discharges may be imposed upon offenders within this age group, in the same circumstances and subject to the same criteria as in the case of offenders aged 21 or more.

10.6.2.1 Supervision order

These are available only in respect of offenders aged up to 17. The order may apply for up to three years and the supervisor is usually a social worker for the local authority in whose area the offender lives, although it may sometimes be a probation officer. It is the duty of the supervisor to 'advise, assist and befriend' the offender. In many ways it is similar to a probation order but the range of extra conditions is somewhat wider, for example the offender may be ordered to live away from home for up to 90 days at a time, e.g., on a useful course of training. It will be noted that there is an overlap between the age ranges so that an offender of 17 may be given either supervision or probation as the court sees fit in the light of any recommendations made.

10.6.2.2 Attendance centre order

The court dealing with an offender under the age of 21 for an imprisonable offence may make an attendance centre order if:

(a) the court has been notified that there is a suitable centre available; and

(b) the offender has not previously received a custodial sentence.

The number of hours attendance must be fixed by the court. It must be at least 12 and not more than 36.

Attendance centres are generally run by policemen in their leisure time. There is a certain amount of discipline and physical exercise and perhaps, depending on availability of staff, handicraft. The aim is partly to deprive the defender of leisure time but also to encourage more sensible use of leisure. Often such centres are held on Saturday afternoons. Although not primarily intended for football hooligans it has occurred to magistrates that by making attendance centre orders for one hour at a time over successive Saturdays they do have the power to prevent an offender attending football matches for virtually an entire season. More commonly, attendance centre orders in two-hour sessions are imposed. It should also be noted that an attendance centre order may be made for default in paying a fine or breach of a probation or supervision order.

10.7   Penalties in Road Traffic Cases

The Road Traffic Acts 1988 and 1991 and the Road Traffic Offenders Act 1988 provide a code for penalties in the case of criminal offences committed in connection with vehicles. In essence there are two types of offences, namely:

(a) Those punishable by disqualification which may be either mandatory or discretionary.

(b) Those where, in addition to some other penalty imposed (e.g., a fine), the offender's driving licence must be endorsed with a certain number of penalty points as prescribed in the Road Traffic Offenders Act 1988 and the Road Traffic Act 1991. In some cases the offence, however committed, is subject to a prescribed number of penalty points (e.g., using a motor vehicle with defective brakes — three points), in others there is a band of penalty points prescribed and the court may impose any number of points within that band depending on the gravity of the offence. Thus for careless driving, which may vary in circumstances from one isolated act of inattention to something only just short of dangerous driving, a band of between three and nine points is prescribed.

In principle when, within a period of three years the individual has had endorsed on his licence a total of 12 penalty points or more, he must be disqualified for at least six months unless there are certain circumstances which make the court think it appropriate not to disqualify him.

That is an outline of the code and we shall now consider the provisions in somewhat more detail.

10.7.1   DISQUALIFICATION

Certain offences carry mandatory disqualifications, e.g.:

(a) causing death by dangerous driving;

(b) dangerous driving;

(c) offences connected with driving with excessive alcohol in the blood or when unfit through drugs.

In general terms, where an offence carries obligatory endorsement, e.g., careless driving, there is a *discretion* in the court to disqualify the defendant for the offences alone. They would normally only do so if the facts of the offence were very gross indeed.

Quite separately from the above, an offender may be disqualified under the points system, still often called the 'totting up' system. Where an offender is convicted and a penalty is imposed which involves the number of points endorsed on the offender's licence within the preceding three years totalling 12 or more, the court must in principle disqualify him for at least six months unless it thinks it fit not to do so.

10.7.2 ENDORSEMENT OF DRIVING LICENCE

A driving licence must be endorsed with the appropriate number of penalty points within the limits set out in sch. 2 to the Road Trafffic Offenders Act 1988 unless there are circumstances permitting the court not to do so (to which we shall come in due course).

If the offender is disqualified for the offence itself (rather than under the 'totting up' provisions) then the licence is not endorsed with further penalty points although particulars of the offence for which the offender is disqualified are recorded on the licence. In other words, a person who is being disqualified for a specific offence does not receive any penalty points.

> **Example** An offender who has a clean licence is disqualified for a particularly gross case of speeding (say exceeding 100 mph on a motorway) for a period of six months. Speeding carries from 3 to 6 penalty points. However, in the present case these would not be endorsed on the offender's licence. Thus at the end of his period of disqualification, the offender still has no penalty points on his licence and so, if when he begins driving again he commits other offences for which the total penalty points are, say, 10 he will not be subject to disqualification for exceeding 12 penalty points as he would otherwise have been.

Some offences for which there are prima facie obligatory disqualification (such as dangerous driving) also carry an alternative number of penalty points (in the case of dangerous driving between 3 and 11 points). This is because if there happen to be special circumstances justifying not imposing the otherwise obligatory disqualification, the court then has open to it the power to impose a number of penalty points as an alternative.

It should be noted that where the defendant is convicted of two or more endorsable offences which arise out of offences committed on the same occasion, then only the highest number of penalty points will be endorsed and not the cumulative total, unless the court thinks fit to order otherwise in which case it must state its reasons in open court. Thus suppose an offender commits the offence of uninsured driving (6 to 8 points) and speeding (3 to 6 points) he only acquires 8 penalty points and not up to 14.

10.7.3 FOR WHAT PERIOD SHOULD THE OFFENDER BE DISQUALIFIED?

If the offence carries obligatory disqualification then generally this is for at least 12 months. Above that period then the court must weigh a number of important factors. It has been stressed in many cases that the court should be careful not to impose too long a disqualification from driving. In the case of young offenders, particularly those who are 'car mad', the effect of over-lengthy disqualification is to make them lose all hope of recovering their driving licence and to merely invite them to commit offences of driving whilst disqualified. This is not to say however that very lengthy disqualifications may not in some situations be appropriate. Indeed disqualification for life is possible and in some cases may be rightly applied.

It should also be noted that an offender who has been disqualified for a longer period than two years may apply to the court after two years or the halfway date of the period, whichever is the longer, for the disqualification to be lifted. The prosecution must naturally be informed of the application and there is a hearing in open court at which the prosecution will describe the circumstances of the original offence and may put forward their objections.

Under the 'totting up' system a disqualification is generally for at least six months. It may be for a longer period within the court's discretion. It should also be noted that periods of disqualification now always run concurrently and not consecutively. Therefore if an offender is convicted of a number of offences, whether or not committed on the same occasion, and is liable to disqualification either under the 'totting up' system and/or for the offences themselves, any disqualifications imposed must run concurrently. Of course the total length of the sentences imposed will affect the court's overall view of the gravity of the situation and thus whilst sentences of say 18 months' disqualification and six months' disqualification may be imposed for different offences it is the longer penalty which will reflect the court's overall view of what is appropriate for the whole 'disqualification package'.

Finally, it should be remarked that an offender cannot be disqualified unless he is given the opportunity to appear. Thus where an offender is invited to plead guilty by post, say to an offence of speeding, he will do so while sending his licence to the court as is required. If the points to be imposed for speeding take the points on his licence to a total of more than 12 then he is prima facie liable for disqualification. It does not inevitably mean that he will be disqualified because there may be circumstances in which the court will see fit not to impose that ultimate penalty, but certainly in such a case the matter will be adjourned to enable the defendant to attend court.

10.7.4 WHEN MAY DISQUALIFICATION OR ENDORSEMENT NOT BE IMPOSED?

Where disqualification for the offence itself (rather than under the penalty points system) is obligatory, or endorsement of penalty points is obligatory, they must on the face of it be imposed. However in either case if the defendant can show 'special reasons' for not disqualifying or for not imposing the endorsement at all, then the court may decline to do so. 'Special reasons' however in this context must relate to the circumstances of the offence itself *not* to the offender's personal circumstances and must not therefore be in the nature of mitigation generally. A good example of a reason which might justify non-disqualification is the case of a drink-driving offence where the offender's orange juice was 'laced' with vodka without his knowledge so that he was taken just over the legal limit (if of course he had any reason to suspect that he was drunk and that his drink had been laced, he could not argue this if he had then continued to drive). Another example might be on a charge of dangerous driving that the driver was taking someone to hospital in an emergency when the offence occurred. Likewise, in the case of a speeding offence where endorsement of penalty points is obligatory, if the offender admitted the offence but was able to show that he was driving a dangerously ill passenger to hospital at high speed, the magistrates, whilst finding guilt proved, might well impose only an absolute discharge and no endorsement.

It must be said that the courts have not been eager to find special reasons established. Evidence on oath must be given by the offender in each case and it is not sufficient for these matters to be advanced merely in a plea in mitigation. The offender may well be subject to searching cross-examination by the prosecution. Although the prosecution do not generally concern themselves at all with sentence, this is one occasion where they do have an overriding duty to see that justice is done and that any reasons put forward as justifying non-endorsement or non-disqualification are thoroughly examined.

In the case of *discretionary* disqualification (e.g., careless driving) then *general mitigation* can be advanced in relation to any proper matter, either the circumstances of the offence or the offender's personal circumstances, with a view to avoiding disqualification entirely or of obtaining a reduction in the period imposed.

10.7.5 DISQUALIFICATION UNDER THE PENALTY POINTS SYSTEM

If an offender is sentenced for an offence and penalty points are imposed which take his total to over 12 within the relevant period of three years he should in principle be disqualified for six months or longer. However, an offender need not be disqualified if there are 'grounds for mitigating the normal consequences of the conviction'. This is not the same as the case previously described where there are *special reasons* for not imposing penalty points or an endorsement. In the former case the matters must concern the circumstances of the *offence* itself. However, in connection with non-disqualification under the penalty points system the court may have regard to all the circumstances including the personal circumstances of the offender.

Part II of the Road Traffic Offenders Act 1988 however, provides that a court in deciding on this matter may only take into account hardship to the offender caused by loss of his licence where the hardship is 'exceptional'. Unfortunately there is no definition of 'exceptional hardship' and little guidance in case law. Circumstances which under previous law were considered appropriate for avoiding the consequences of disqualification often involved, for example: loss of a job because it depended on a driving licence, or where, because of the remoteness of the place of work, a car was necessary; the need to have a vehicle for important family reasons, e.g., transport of a disabled relative. Such things *might* still be sufficient. Hardship which is less than exceptional, e.g., for a private individual who does not need his motor vehicle for his job and who would be merely inconvenienced by having to use public transport, would not be an adequate reason for not imposing disqualification.

In addition the court may *not* take into account the triviality of the present offence. Thus the fact that the speeding offence concerned only involved exceeding the speed limit by, say, five mph would not in itself be a ground for mitigating the normal consequences. If three points imposed in this case takes the offender past a total of 12 then he ought still, in principle, to be disqualified.

It may well be that a person appears before the court and has penalty points imposed which takes his total over 12 but is able to persuade the magistrates that there is exceptional hardship and thus is not disqualified. What if a further offence is committed still within the period which would take his penalty points up by a further number? The 1988 Act provides that a person who has been excused disqualification because of mitigating circumstances on a previous occasion may not rely on any circumstances which the court took into account on that occasion. So, e.g., one cannot avoid disqualification on two consecutive hearings merely by arguing that loss of a licence will involve loss of a job. In such a situation, if that is the only mitigating circumstance, disqualification will be imposed on the second occasion.

Accordingly the court should carefully record the mitigating factors it found present when dealing with an offender so that these are available in any future case. All too often these mitigating factors are recorded in extremely short summary form and it may well therefore be the case that one can give a fuller version of the reasons on the second occasion. It also leads to the somewhat strange conclusion that if one has two separate excellent grounds for avoiding the normal consequences of the 'totting up' system it would usually only be wise to put one of them forward. Suppose for example that a person desperately needed his car because he lived in a remote place and needed to transport a disabled relative to and from hospital, and that he needed his driving licence for his job. If his penalty points were taken over 12 he would be well advised to put forward only one of these cogent reasons so that in the event of him offending on a further occasion he could then use the other.

It ought finally to be repeated that in driving offences, disqualification and endorsement may be combined with most other penalties. Very commonly they are combined with fines. It should not be overlooked however that driving penalties may be imposed in addition to custodial sentences, for example in the case of causing death by dangerous driving where both a lengthy disqualification and a custodial penalty would be usual.

Below is a list outlining some of the more common endorsable offences and the relevant available penalty points:

	Penalty points
Causing death by dangerous driving	3–11
Dangerous driving	3–11
Careless driving	3–9
Failing to stop after an accident	5–10
Speeding	3–6
Disobeying traffic lights	3
Using uninsured motor vehicle	6–8
Driving when unfit through drink or drugs;	
or with excess alcohol in blood	3–11

10.7.6 PROBATIONARY PERIOD FOR NEWLY QUALIFIED DRIVERS

The Road Traffic (New Drivers) Act 1995 introduces a probationary period of two years commencing from the day of qualification for newly qualified drivers. During that time a driver who acquires six or more penalty points will lose his licence and be required to present himself for re-testing before qualifying for a full driving licence. In fact the correct terminology is that his licence is 'revoked' rather than that he is 'disqualified' and the precise procedure for revoking the licence is different. There is no discretion involved as such, although it may be possible to urge 'special reasons' against endorsement, e.g., in circumstances where the driver admits driving at high speed when taking a dangerously ill person to hospital.

Although the Act received the Royal Assent in 1995 it did not come into force until June 1997.

10.7.7 DISQUALIFICATION FOR OFFENCES NOT INVOLVING DRIVING

Disqualification from driving cannot at present be imposed on offenders for crimes which do not involve the use of motor vehicles. More recently it has been seen that this might be a very effective general form of punishment and as and when the Crime (Sentences) Act 1997 is brought into force, there is the power under s. 39 of the Act to use disqualification from driving as a general punishment 'in addition to or instead of dealing with (an offender) in any other way...'. (See **10.12**.)

10.8 Other Orders

The court may also consider the following orders which may be imposed on an offender either additionally to or instead of other forms of punishment.

10.8.1 COMPENSATION ORDERS

Under s. 35 of the Powers of Criminal Courts Act 1973 (as amended by s. 104, Criminal Justice Act 1988), a court may order compensation for any personal injury, loss or damage (including payment for funeral expenses or bereavement) resulting from any offence (including any offences taken into consideration) when imposing any other penalty, or instead of imposing any other penalty on an offender. However a court cannot make any order in respect of injury, loss or damage arising out of the presence of a motor vehicle on a road unless:

(a) the offence concerned was one under the Theft Act 1968 and damage occurred to the property in question whilst it was out of the owner's possession (e.g., damage to a motor vehicle which was taken away for joy–riding); or

(b) the offender was uninsured at the time and compensation is not payable under the Motor Insurers' Bureau Schemes.

The court may make an order up to any amount in the Crown Court or a maximum of £5,000 in respect of any one offence in the magistrates' court but the court must have regard to the offender's means in the same way as they must have regard to those means in relation to imposing a fine. A compensation order may be made as an alternative to dealing with the offender in any other way and if the offender has not got sufficient income to pay both the fine and compensation the court ought to impose a compensation order to ensure that the victim is compensated. Compensation orders are enforced by the court in the same way as a fine with the ultimate penalty of imprisonment for non–payment.

The Magistrates' Association Sentencing Guidelines (April 1997) set out guidelines for awards for common types of minor injury, e.g., loss of tooth £1,000; sprain £100 to £1,000 depending on loss of mobility; bruise, depending on size, up to £75; black eye £100.

10.8.2   FORFEITURE ORDERS

Under s. 43 of the Powers of Criminal Courts Act 1973, where the court convicts an offender of an offence which is punishable on indictment with two years' imprisonment or more it may order forfeiture of any property which was in the offender's possession or control at the time of apprehension if the property was used for committing or facilitating any offence or was intended by the offender to be used for that purpose.

Thus for example the owner may be ordered to forfeit a car which has been used to transport stolen goods.

10.8.3   CONFISCATION ORDERS

Under s. 71 of the Criminal Justice Act 1988, as amended by the Criminal Justice Act 1993, a Crown Court may, in addition to dealing with a defendant in any other way, make a confiscation order in respect of the proceeds of the crime. The provisions initially were aimed only at the most serious kind of offenders so that a defendant must have benefited from the relevant offence in the sum of at least £10,000. That limitation has, however, now been removed by the Proceeds of Crime Act 1995. The amount that can be ordered is the benefit gained by the offender from the proceeds of crime. As well as more mundane offences there are express provisions applying this to offences involving breach of intellectual property rights. The provision does not however, apply to the proceeds of drug trafficking as to which there is a quite separate procedure laid out in the Drug Trafficking Offences Act 1994.

10.8.4   COSTS

A convicted offender may be ordered to pay costs to the prosecution as described earlier (see **2.4**).

10.9   The Structured Approach to Sentencing under the Criminal Justice Act 1991 (as Amended)

The Criminal Justice Act 1991 proposed a new structured approach to sentencing. As is well known, in its short life the Act gave rise to serious criticism and important reforms to it were introduced in the Criminal Justice Act 1993, and subsequently in the Criminal Justice and Public Order Act 1994.

Before the 1991 Act, there was wide-ranging consultation amongst practitioners, professionals, and other persons or bodies having an interest in the criminal justice process. The policies enshrined in the 1991 Act, particularly in regard to sentencing, were meant to carry out the policy formed in the light of that consultation process. Since that time there has been a Royal

Commission on Criminal Procedure and, most importantly, in the Criminal Justice Act 1993 a dramatic U-turn on major aspects of sentencing policy, also partly followed through in the Criminal Justice and Public Order Act 1994.

We shall now consider the present structured approach to sentencing, as varied by subsequent legislation. The 1991 Act commences with the most serious matters and we shall therefore follow that order.

10.9.1 CUSTODIAL SENTENCES

Section 1(2) of the 1991 Act, as substituted by s. 66, Criminal Justice Act 1993, provides that a court:

... shall not pass a custodial sentence on the offender unless it is of the opinion—

> (a) *that the offence, or the combination of the offence and one or more offences associated with it, was so serious that only such a sentence can be justified for the offence; or*
> (b) *where the offence is a violent or sexual offence, that only such a sentence would be adequate to protect the public from serious harm from him.*

In addition to this provision a custodial sentence may be passed if an offender refuses to consent to a community sentence proposed by the court of a kind which requires his consent.

The crucial change of emphasis here is away from consideration of the accused's previous criminal record and towards concentration entirely on the offence before the court and other offences associated with it.

10.9.1.1 The seriousness test

The court must have regard to the 'seriousness' of the offence and other associated offences at which it is looking. Thus notwithstanding that there are 10, or 50 offences dealt with at the same time, if they are all in themselves trivial, the court cannot conclude that the offender is simply such a pest that he ought to be given a custodial sentence. This requirement of 'seriousness' is said to provide a 'custody threshold requirement'.

10.9.1.2 Length of sentence

Section 2 of the 1991 Act deals with the length of custodial sentences and prescribes that the time imposed must be 'commensurate with the seriousness of the offence', or the combination of the offence and one or more *offences* associated with it; or in the case of violent or sexual offences for such longer term (not exceeding the maximum) as the court considers necessary to protect the public from serious harm.

10.9.1.3 Other important matters when imposing custody

(a) Any court passing a custodial sentence is obliged by s. 1(4) of the 1991 Act to explain in open court that either or both paragraphs of s. 1(2) apply to the case and to explain why it has formed that view. The explanation must be in ordinary language so that the offender understands why he is receiving a custodial sentence.

(b) *Pre–sentence reports.* Before giving the reason for selecting a custodial sentence, s. 3(1) of the 1991 Act requires that the court shall 'obtain and consider a pre-sentence report' in any case except where the offence is triable only on indictment. This latter provision avoids the court having always to have a pre-sentence report where the serious nature of the offence makes custody inevitable, though even in such a case the court has the option of obtaining a pre-sentence report.

The 1994 Act, sch. 9, para. 40 amends this rule as regards offenders aged 18 or over so that the court may dispense with the requirement to obtain a pre-sentence report before passing a custodial sentence if it is of the opinion that it is 'unnecessary'. For offenders aged under 18, the previous law remains, namely that a pre-sentence report is required except for offences triable only on indictment.

(c) Section 3(3)(a) of the 1991 Act provides that in addition to the pre-sentence report the court shall: 'take into account all such information about the circumstances of the offence (including any aggravating or mitigating factors) as is available to it'. This in turn imports consideration of ss. 28 and 29 of the 1991 Act which state: 'Nothing in [the relevant part of the Act] shall prevent a court from mitigating an offender's sentence by taking into account any such matters as, in the opinion of the court, are relevant in mitigation of sentence' (s. 28(1)). Section 29, as inserted by s. 66 of the Criminal Justice Act 1993, provides:

(1) In considering the seriousness of any offence, the court may take into account any previous convictions of the offender or any failure of his to respond to previous sentences.

(2) In considering the seriousness of any offence committed while the offender was on bail, the court shall treat the fact that it was committed in those circumstances as an aggravating factor.

In its short-lived first incarnation, the original s. 29 of the 1991 Act seriously constrained the right of the sentencing court to have regard to previous convictions. Indeed, it expressly said 'an offence shall not be regarded as more serious ... by reason of any previous convictions of the offender'. A number of well publicised cases in early 1993 concentrated on the supposed inability of judges to pass harsh sentences on frequent offenders because of this section and following other criticism by politicians and the higher judiciary this led to the amendment in the terms set out above. The effect is now to give the court a wide power to consider the whole of the past record of the offender when sentencing and, in particular, to take into account failure to respond to previous sentences (i.e. apparently lenient sentences such as probation), and the fact that the offence was committed on bail, if that is the case, is to be treated as an aggravating factor.

As indicated previously, however, one still only reaches a consideration of custodial sentences as a last resort and the basic framework of the 1991 Act is not affected. That Act requires the court previously to have considered 'community sentences'.

10.9.2 COMMUNITY SENTENCES

The policy under the Criminal Justice Act 1991 is that more offenders should be punished 'in the community' and thus the concept of community sentence has substantially developed by certain changes in status of probation, which previously did not count as a 'sentence' or 'punishment' at all, and by other developments, e.g., of the combination order and the curfew order. The principle of the legislation is that community sentences will be viewed as serious forms of punishment and not an easy option for sentencers nor an agreeable alternative to prison for offenders. Because of the supposed seriousness of these sentences, by s. 6 of the 1991 Act the court must not pass a community sentence unless:

(a) the offence (or the combination of the offence and one or more associated offences) is serious enough to warrant it; and

(b) the court has considered which order or orders are most suitable for the offender; and

(c) the restrictions on the offender's liberty imposed by the order or orders are commensurate with the seriousness of the offence or the combination of the offence and one or more offences associated with it.

In addition, the court must obtain a pre–sentence report, unless by virtue of sch. 9, para. 40 of the 1994 Act it concludes that, when it is dealing with an offender of 18 or over, the obtaining of such a report is unnecessary whenever it is considering:

(a)   a probation order which includes requirements additional to the standard conditions;

(b)   a community service order; or

(c)   a combination order.

A pre–sentence report is therefore *not* mandatory if the court is considering merely a probation order which does not include additional requirements, a curfew order or an attendance centre order, although in many cases it will be good practice for the court to obtain one.

The consent of the offender is required as we have seen in the case of probation orders, community service orders, combination orders and curfew orders.

10.9.3   DEVELOPMENTS BETWEEN THE 1991 ACT AND THE 1993 ACT

As mentioned above, the relevant sections of the 1991 Act and the sentencing policy they encapsulated came in for a great deal of criticism for improperly tying the hands of sentencers, especially by the statutory limitations in the former s. 29 of the 1991 Act on the extent to which previous criminal behaviour could be taken into account. The 1993 amendments restore a wide discretion to take past criminal behaviour into account when considering the seriousness of any offence. It still remains to be seen whether the courts will interpret this requirement strictly, so that the present offence is only rendered more serious by the fact that it clearly forms a continuing pattern of specific criminal behaviour (as in the case of a persistent burglar), or whether the courts will feel free to take into account the whole history of criminality, even for offences very different from the one presently under consideration.

Some useful decisions were given in guideline cases under the 1991 Act in the Court of Appeal on 27 November 1992 and these were aimed at establishing sentencing policy under that Act. They provide additional guidelines, some features of which will still be useful when considering sentencing under the 1993 amendments:

(a)   In *R* v *Cunningham* [1993] 2 All ER 15 the court observed that the purpose of the custodial sentence is primarily to punish and deter and therefore that the purpose of such a sentence must be commensurate with the punishment and deterrence required. The 'seriousness' of an offence means such things as the question of how many people it harms and to what extent. Thereafter, once a custodial penalty has been chosen, it would be a legitimate factor to take into account such matters as the prevalence of the type of offence.

(b)   In *R* v *Oliver* [1993] 2 All ER 9 the court considered to what extent regular dwelling–house burglary could be considered 'serious' and the relevance of the fact that some offences occurred in breach of a probation order.

(c)   In *R* v *Cox* [1993] 2 All ER 19 the court observed that for the purposes of s. 1(2)(a) of the 1991 Act an offence is 'so serious that only a custodial sentence can be justified' if it is such as to make all right–thinking members of the public, knowing all the facts, feel that justice would not be done by the passing of anything other than a custodial sentence. The prevalence of a particular class of offence and public concern are relevant to the seriousness of an offence (the offence was one of reckless driving (now dangerous driving) including going at 30 miles an hour along the pavement for some part of the time).

(d) In *R v Bexley and others* [1993] 2 All ER 23 the court explained the interrelationship of subss. (1) and (2) of s. 29 of the 1991 Act and the extent to which circumstances of other offences may be taken into account. The court observed that only those which disclosed some aggravating factor in the instant offence or its combination with another offence (e.g., deliberately targeting or selecting elderly victims; or persistently using stolen credit cards to acquire large amounts of luxury goods) would fall within the section.

(e) In *R v Baverstock* [1993] 2 All ER 33 the court indicated that a sentencing court must be given details of the 'circumstances' of previous convictions for offences committed by the defendant and that it is not for the prosecution to decide what circumstances of other offences may be relevant nor should there be argument between prosecution and defence about the relevance and admissibility of the material to be placed before the judge. The established procedure in relation to previous convictions from before the 1991 Act remains appropriate. The fact that an offence was committed whilst on bail is an aggravating feature of the present offence.

10.10 Guideline Cases

Quite apart from the cases which we have just considered on the interpretation of ss. 1, 2 and 29 of the Criminal Justice Act 1991, for some years the Court of Appeal has provided sentencing guidelines in respect of serious offences. The object of these is to lead to a greater consistency in sentencing in such cases. There is no space in this text to set out in detail the principles from each of these guideline cases though regard must be had to them where the offence with which one is concerned in practice is one for which guidelines have been given. The guideline cases include the offences of rape (*R v Billam* [1986] 1 WLR 349); offences involving breach of trust (*R v Barrick* (1985) 7 Cr App R (S) 142); drug importation and supply (*R v Aramah* (1982) 4 Cr App R (S) 407); armed robbery (*R v Turner* (1975) 61 Cr App R 61); and social security fraud (*R v Stewart* (1987) 9 Cr App R (S) 135).

By way of example, extracts indicating the nature of these guidelines are given from two such cases.

10.10.1 *R v BARRICK* (1985) 7 Cr App R (S) 142

This case deals with persons in a position of trust, e.g., accountants, bank employees and solicitors, who have used that trusted position to defraud partners, clients or employers of sizeable sums of money. Usually such people will have previous good character and it is virtually certain that they will never offend again as they will never again in their lives be able to secure similar employment. There is likely to be substantial disgrace and hardship for the offender and his family.

In such cases the guidelines indicate that the case will attract immediate custody unless the circumstances are exceptional or the amount is small. If the amount is less than £10,000 imprisonment for a short term up to 18 months is appropriate; between £10,000 and £50,000 the term should be about two to three years; for larger sums the term of three and a half to four years may be appropriate. In the event of a guilty plea a discount should be given.

In addition the court should take into account the period over which the thefts were committed; the use to which the money was put; the effect upon the victims; the impact upon the public and public confidence; the effect upon fellow employees or business partners; the effect on the offender; the offender's history; matters of mitigation special to himself; any help given by him to the police.

10.10.2   *R v BILLAM* [1986] 1 WLR 349

This case deals with the offence of rape. For rape committed by an adult with no special features a figure of five years is the starting point if there was a plea of not guilty. For a rape committed by two or more, or rape by a burglar, or by a person who is in a position of responsibility towards the victim, or by a person who kidnaps the victim, the starting point is eight years.

At the top of the scale is a defendant who has carried out a campaign of rape on different victims for whom 15 years or more is appropriate. In addition to this if the defendant's behaviour has been perverted or psychopathic such that he is clearly a danger for an indefinite time, a life sentence will be appropriate.

The following factors may also aggravate the crime: violence over and above the force necessary to commit the crime; use of a weapon to frighten or wound; repeated rape; a carefully planned rape; previous convictions for sexual offences; victim is subjected to indignities or perversion; victim very old or very young; physical or mental effect upon the victim. In all these cases the sentence should be substantially higher than the starting point.

A plea of guilty, since it will relieve the victim of embarrassment and distress, should result in some reduction from the appropriate sentence. The fact that the victim may have been foolish (e.g., by accepting a lift in a car from a stranger) is not a mitigating factor and her previous sexual experience is also irrelevant. If the victim has behaved in a manner which indicated to the defendant that she would consent to sexual intercourse that is of some mitigation. The offender's previous good character is of minor relevance.

10.11   The Plea in Mitigation

We have now considered the total package of orders which may be made against a convicted defendant. We have considered penalties on the defendant, the making of compensation orders, and the question of costs has previously been discussed in connection with the financing of criminal litigation (see **Chapter 2**).

It is now appropriate to consider the plea in mitigation which will be made in an attempt to persuade the court to impose some lesser sentence than the tariff for the offence might appear to warrant. The task of an advocate making a plea in mitigation is to persuade the court to view the offender or the offence in the most favourable light possible. The ultimate purpose is, so to speak, to get the offender as light a penalty as possible. From this point of view an immediate custodial sentence would generally be regarded as the most drastic penalty that could be imposed and it will often be the primary concern to avoid this. However, even if a custodial sentence is inevitable it is still important to make a full plea in mitigation so that the term imposed may be as short as possible.

10.11.1   THE 1991 ACT AND 'TRADITIONAL' MITIGATION

Before the 1991 Act came into force, mitigation would generally have been aimed at the features which we shall consider below. Thus one would have looked to the realistic penalty which a court would be minded to impose and then attempted to persuade the court to impose some lesser penalty, or if imprisonment was inevitable, to have made the period as short as possible. Now however, mitigation will take on a more technical aspect because one will first have to attempt to persuade the court to look carefully at the 1991 Act and to consider potential penalties in ascending order from fines and discharges through community senten- ces and up to custodial sentences. The technical requirements of the Act at each of these stages will have to be carefully considered and it may be that, whereas under the previous law a custodial sentence might have been feared as highly likely (e.g., a very persistent petty offender), under the new Act such a penalty would be unlawful and therefore one will have to consider what penalties short of imprisonment the court would be minded to impose.

Even if imprisonment is a possibility there are technical arguments which may be mounted under the 1991 Act, e.g., as to the true meaning of the word 'seriousness' or the proper way in which the court should approach 'aggravating factors' and the like, as discussed above. The plea in mitigation therefore will commence with this kind of technical discussion which formerly would have been unnecessary.

Having considered the matters in the 1991 Act with a view to likely sentence, one can then turn to 'traditional' mitigation, the need for which is expressly preserved by s. 28 of the 1991 Act, since s. 28(1) provides: 'Nothing ... shall prevent a court from mitigating an offender's sentence by taking into account any such matters as, in the opinion of the court, are relevant in mitigation'.

10.11.2   'KNOW THY JUDGE'

It is essential, when attempting to persuade a court towards a certain view of a penalty which it ought to impose, to make use of any knowledge of the personality or foibles of the sentencer. This is most easily done by counsel in the Crown Court where the same handful of circuit judges and recorders will appear in a given location time after time, and an experienced criminal barrister will be well aware that an argument which always appeals to judge A may be seen as positively aggravating by judge B. For solicitors the same may sometimes apply, bearing in mind that a solicitor has rights of audience on sentencing appeals from the magistrates' court to the Crown Court. However, in the context of the magistrates' court much will depend on local factors. In small rural courts it may indeed be that the same magistrates are seen time and time again. In larger urban courts the same stipendiary magistrate's predilections and preferences may become well known; in larger urban magistrates' courts however the rotating system by which lay magistrates sit in different combinations may make it unlikely that, save for those of the very strongest personality who live in the memory, the solicitor will be able to attribute known foibles to the faces before him. Where possible however it is vitally important to have regard to the personality of the sentencer. Thus, for example, to the writer's knowledge there are circuit judges who are sternly temperance minded and for whom any suggestion of drink being involved in the commission of an offence is not a mitigating factor showing impulsiveness, but an aggravating factor. Another circuit judge holds the apparently serious belief that the criminal classes should not be encouraged to procreate and thus the suggestion, which normally would be of some use in mitigation, that the offender's wife or girlfriend is pregnant will seriously irritate the judge (it goes without saying that a suggestion that both the offender's wife and his girlfriend are pregnant will be twice as bad). Similarly, different judges, or magistrates, take radically different views of the seriousness of offences involving cannabis. Some take the definite view that this is the first step on the rocky road to hard drugs; in another court, to the writer's knowledge, at least two of the magistrates, both of them practising doctors, take the view that cannabis is less harmful than tobacco and, both having strong personalities, impose their views on their colleagues so that in that court usually very lenient sentences indeed are passed for cannabis offences. Thus if one can obtain any knowledge of the sentencer it should be put to good use.

10.11.3   TRADITIONAL MITIGATION

Generally, it is best to divide a plea in mitigation into four sections and to treat these separately. This avoids putting forward a mishmash of unrelated matters which, albeit all favourable to a defendant, may give an unstructured impression. The four categories are:

(a)   the offence itself;

(b)   the offender;

(c) the offender's conduct in relation to the investigation of the crime and the proceedings; and

(d) the capacity to reform.

10.11.4 THE OFFENCE ITSELF

Here one should see what can be found in the immediate circumstances of the offence which makes it less serious than it might at first appear. A good example would be in the case of an assault where the offender had been subject to considerable provocation. One should not put forward one's mitigation so enthusiastically as to appear to indicate something which is in effect a defence, e.g., to suggest that it was self-defence rather than provocation. To do this is obviously to go behind either the plea of guilty and reopen the case or to impugn the jury's verdict. An example of something which might mitigate a dishonesty offence might be drink. This has to be advanced with some care. As mentioned above some sentencers have a view of drink which make them view it as an aggravating factor rather than as mitigation. It goes without saying of course that in any driving offence drink is unlikely to be a mitigating factor. It may well be, however, that on the facts of the case the element of drink can be presented in a favourable light, because as a general rule the court view it as some mitigation that an offence was committed on impulse rather than premeditatedly. Thus for example on a charge of say stealing £100, if the sum was left lying around and taken on a rash impulse, the offence would be regarded as rather less serious than for someone to procure the same amount by a cunning and premeditated plan. Since drink may well affect impulsiveness, to that extent it may be a mitigating factor.

10.11.4.1 Aggravation and mitigation

(a) An advocate must be alive to the fact that some features in an offence may be *aggravating*. These features are usefully dealt with in some of the 'guideline cases' in the Court of Appeal referred to above. In addition, the Magistrates' Association have issued a booklet of sentencing guidelines which features several 'seriousness indicators' which have an eye to the technical matters in the Criminal Justice Act 1991 but are also of general use. These 'seriousness indicators' deal with a number of matters which may aggravate an offence, e.g., breach of trust by person in authority; offence was cunning and premeditated; use of weapons; offence took place in a public place; the victim was particularly vulnerable; that it was an organised offence. Other common aggravating features are an element of professionalism in the crime; the use of excessive force; and gratuitous violence or destruction. By way of example, extracts from 4 pages of the Magistrates' Association Sentencing Guidelines (April 1997) are reproduced (see **10.12** and **10.13**) showing how magistrates should approach sentencing. The examples chosen are those of assault on a policeman and assault occasioning actual bodily harm; and burglary in a dwelling and non dwelling.

(b) Ordinary mitigating features are those which tend to demonstrate impulsiveness, e.g., acting on the spur of the moment; reduced mental capacity; good motive in what was done; genuine ignorance of the law; personal or social pressure akin to duress; that the offender played a minor role in the crime; and the like.

(c) In dealing with a crime one must therefore always have regard to aggravating features and attempt to deal with them rather than hoping that the court will not notice them. Thus for example if one is dealing with a senior employee who handles employer's money, such a person would be considered to have committed a much more serious offence if he stole that money than in the case of the same theft between strangers. Likewise if in the same instance the senior employee had involved another junior employee who was of previous good character in the crime this corruption would be

173

a further aggravating feature. One must take instructions from the client and address oneself frankly to this kind of problem.

10.11.5 THE OFFENDER HIMSELF

This is the point at which the advocate has the opportunity to discuss at length and in detail the personal circumstances of the offender. It will be remembered that if there is a risk of a custodial sentence, by this stage probably a pre-sentence report will have been obtained. This may in itself set out a number of matters relevant to the plea in mitigation. It may lengthily rehearse the offender's upbringing, education and background, and family circumstances and deal with personal problems. Bad advocates often merely parrot these, indeed sometimes actually reading them out despite the fact that the report is already before the magistrates. This is clearly boring and bad practice. One should seek to give the magistrates new information not already contained in the social enquiry report and if the social enquiry report is very full then one should refer the magistrates to it and stress or expand on the more favourable matters revealed. Matters which might be treated as being mitigation would be some of the following, if applicable.

10.11.5.1 Previous record

The best possible mitigation is no criminal record. It always gives a court pause for thought even in the case of a relatively serious crime that it is the offender's first offence. Thus, whilst previous criminal record may not inevitably be relevant in sentencing because of ss. 1 and 2 of the Criminal Justice Act 1991, absence of criminal record may still be particularly good mitigation. In addition to mere absence of criminal record however, positive features about the individual ought to be put forward such as any record of public service, service in the forces, good employment record, and settled family background. If the offence is one of dishonesty, reference to any positions of trust which the offender has had and faithfully carried out in the past, e.g., that he has handled a great deal of money for his employer for many years without shortages or discrepancies.

We have already considered the technical matters contained in the Criminal Justice Act 1991 and the way in which a previous record may be relevant to the present sentence. If an offender does have a criminal record then, bearing in mind the 1991 Act, it is important to deal with this so far as possible. For example, it may be possible to look back through the record and point to things which favour a particular course of action. Thus if, e.g., there are lengthy gaps in the record and these correspond to periods of employment and the offender is presently in employment this might be a feature worth putting forward. It might tend to show that his offences are born out of frustration and financial hardship when he is unemployed. Equally, if he has received some particular kind of penalty in the past and this seems to have worked for him, e.g., a period of probation where he kept out of trouble for some time, this should be stressed. Another point worth making is that if the bulk of his criminal record is for one particular type of offence and the present offence is of a completely different type, then under the 1991 Act one is entitled to suggest that the court ought to treat him as a first offender. Suppose, for example, that the offender has a bad criminal record for, say, offences of violence arising out of fights whilst under the influence of drink and the present offence is one of straightforward dishonesty. In such a case the court ought not to pay any attention to his record on the question of whether or not to choose a custodial sentence; and even if a custodial sentence is chosen there should be nothing in the previous conduct to aggravate it in terms of length.

10.11.5.2 Circumstances at the time of the crime

The offender's circumstances at the time of the crime should be described to the court if relevant. For example if the offence is one of dishonesty and occurred at a time of grave financial pressure on the defendant, especially if this was caused through circumstances beyond his own control, e.g., having been made redundant. Personal health problems or those of his loved ones may also be relevant, for example alcoholism or drug dependency, although the circumstances of this latter example must be treated with caution. Anything which in any way affected him at the time and made him more vulnerable or susceptible to pressures is worth stressing, such as bereavement or some personal tragedy. Perhaps connected to this is the next point.

10.11.5.3 The effect of his offence and punishment on others

The effect on others of his crime or potential punishment ought to be stressed. It is of course common place that if an offender goes to prison he will lose his job. Magistrates will hear this argument very often but it is still one worth putting forward. Another argument commonly advanced is that when considering the penalty to be imposed on the offender the court should have regard to its effect on society as a whole. Thus if he loses his job by being sent to prison it may be unlikely that he will easily obtain another one, so an additional point to make is that his family will be reduced to welfare benefits whilst he is there and indeed indefinitely afterwards. The cost to society of an individual being kept in prison has been variously estimated but the weekly cost of providing prison facilities alone is said to be over £400 depending on the type of institution in which he is detained. When one takes into account the additional cost to society of keeping his family. the cost is a very significant one. It has indeed been pointed out by one leading criminologist that it would in purely financial terms be considerably better for the state to pay persistent offenders to take extended holidays abroad rather than to imprison them in England. A sentencing court is unlikely to take any specific notice of the financial argument when presented in these terms, though it will of course always bear in mind the undesirability in every case of imprisoning an individual in terms of prison overcrowding and cost.

10.11.5.4 Other penalties suffered

Linked to this point of the effect on his family, one should stress other penalties which the offence has occasioned of a non-judicial nature, such as personal humiliation in the light of publicity, loss of job or status, perhaps the break-up of his family if his wife has left him because of the offence, loss of earnings in the future and possibly the effect of being totally unemployable in his chosen job, e.g., where he was employed as a cashier and dishonesty has led to his dismissal, the certainty that he will never again obtain a position of trust (but see *R v Barrick* at **10.10.1** above).

Until the 1991 Act it was sometimes possible to urge the effect on a family, e.g., through loss of job, as a particularly powerful reason for suspending any sentence of imprisonment. This argument ought to be less successful than previously because it will be recalled that, expressly by the terms of s. 2(2)(b) inserted in the Powers of Criminal Courts Act 1973 by the 1991 Act, the exercise of the power to suspend must be 'justified by the exceptional circumstances of the case'. Since most criminals have familes who will be affected by their imprisonment, any given case can hardly be called 'exceptional'.

10.11.5.5 Time in custody

Finally, one might stress, if one hopes to avoid a custodial sentence, any period in custody which the accused has already spent in consequence of the investigation of the crime or remands. For example if he has already spent some weeks in prison before conviction it might be suggested that this is in itself sufficient penalty and represents sufficient of a shock to him to amount to an effective deterrent.

10.11.6   CONDUCT IN RELATION TO THE INVESTIGATION OF THE CRIME AND CRIMINAL PROCEEDINGS

It is always a potent feature in favour of an offender if he has cooperated in the prompt and efficient disposal of his case. This may take two aspects, as follows.

10.11.6.1   Cooperation with the police

The earlier that this cooperation commences the better. The best case of all would obviously be relatively rare, that is a person who was not even a suspect but walked into a police station and made a full confession. Whilst this is unlikely, prompt cooperation with the police from the onset of questioning is almost as good, for example an offender who makes a full confession leading to the recovery of stolen property at an early stage. The fact that property is recovered for the victim of the crime is a potent consideration in favour of an offender. So is giving evidence against, or giving information leading to conviction of, his associates in crime, e.g., a thief who names the handler or vice versa. When advising a client one should leave this matter very much up to the client. Obviously giving information leading to the arrest and conviction of criminal associates may lead to a lesser penalty from the court, but it may have certain undesirable consequences of a personal nature in relation to the behaviour of those former accomplices towards one's client, as and when they are all at large again.

10.11.6.2   Proceedings in court

A guilty plea at the earliest opportunity is also a powerful mitigating factor. It saves a great deal of the court's time, costs to public funds, and may also save embarrassment to the victims of the offence especially in sexual cases. In an appropriate case, a guilty plea is said to lead to a reduction in custodial sentence on the apparent tariff figure of up to one-third, and a guilty plea together with giving useful information about co-offenders may, in the case of serious crime anyway, lead to a reduction in sentence of more than 50 per cent (see *R v Lowe* (1977) 66 Cr App R 122, 11½ years reduced to five years on appeal because of such mitigating factors).

This discount for a guilty plea has now been given statutory authority by s. 48 of the Criminal Justice and Public Order Act 1994 which is in the following terms:

(1)   *In determining what sentence to pass on an offender who has pleaded guilty to an offence ... a court shall take into account—*

(a)   *the stage in the proceedings of the offence at which the offender indicated his intention to plead guilty, and*

(b)   *the circumstances in which this indication was given.*

(2)   *If, as a result of taking into account any matter referred to in subsection (1) above, the court imposes a punishment on the offender which is less severe than the punishment it would otherwise have imposed, it shall state in open court that it has done so.*

The effect of this is to give a 'credit' not only for a guilty plea but in effect for an indication of a guilty plea at the earliest possible stage in the proceedings, presumably by early indication to the police that that is the defendant's intention thus saving police time in preparing a thorough prosecution file.

10.11.7   CAPACITY FOR REFORM

First it should be mentioned that the showing of contrition is an important factor. This can of course hardly be combined with conviction after a not guilty plea and must realistically only be urged in the case of a guilty plea. Factors which tend to show this might be that the offender has already made voluntary restitution to the victim in an appropriate case or has made a serious offer to do so by instalments and commenced paying them. Care should be taken to ensure that this is not seen as a sign of insincerity or an attempt to 'buy off' a sentence.

Other circumstances which show capacity to reform might be something in the offender's personal life which is about to change for the better to show that he is prepared to take on a more responsible role in society or in the family context. Factors which might be so regarded include finding a new job after a long period of unemployment; being about to get married; becoming pregnant in the case of a female offender; that a wife or cohabitee is pregnant in the case of a male offender.

The plea in mitigation should be structured and concise. It is better to avoid clichés, for example, the phrases 'victim of society' and 'he stands at the crossroads of his life' unless at least two of the magistrates have beards, wear sandals, or can otherwise be proved to be *Guardian* readers.

10.11.8   CHARACTER EVIDENCE

It is also open to the advocate to call character witnesses. The rules of evidence do not strictly apply at this stage and of course the accused's character is now known to the court. It is generally considered not of much use to call a close relative such as a mother or wife since she will inevitably say the same thing the sentencer has heard before, namely that the accused has always been a good, responsible and loving son/husband and deserves a last chance. There may be cases however where a suitably impassioned plea can have some effect and certainly does no harm. Much better is to call as a character witness someone such as an employer who is willing to hold the accused's job for him despite his knowledge of the conviction. The best of all of course and, perhaps surprisingly, by no means unknown, is to call as a character witness the employer against whom the theft was committed to say that notwithstanding this the employer will give the accused another chance. Where an employer is prepared to make this commitment it is a very powerful argument to put to the court that the court ought also to give the accused this further chance and not impose a custodial sentence.

Three final matters ought to be mentioned.

10.11.9   THE USE OF THE PRE-SENTENCE REPORT

As has been previously suggested, the pre-sentence report may often contain a great deal of useful background information. It is pointless to read this to the court and one should merely refer the court to the relevant passages. To an extent a report does a good deal of the mitigator's work for him. Commonly reports end with a recommendation for a particular type of sentence. There should be such a recommendation as to suitability for a community sentence where one is to be imposed. Where the probation officer who will have completed such a report does in fact make a recommendation for dealing with an offender by one or other particular type of sentence, and this is acceptable to the offender, then one may at the end of the plea in mitigation suggest that the court adopt the course recommended. Indeed the whole procedure of a plea in mitigation may in an appropriate case be short-circuited by an early enquiry of the court as to whether it would agree to adopt the recommendation of the probation officer. If it indicates that it will then no more need be said.

If the probation officer makes no particular recommendation for a type of sentence then in some courts this will be treated as equivalent to the probation officer saying that there appears to be no other method of dealing with the offender than custody. In such a case one needs to try even harder in a plea in mitigation to avoid the offender receiving a custodial sentence. It is fair to say that whilst most courts regard the contents of a pre-sentence enquiry report with great seriousness, it is a notorious fact that individual probation officers may on occasions recommend wholly unrealistic alternatives, e.g., in a very serious case may recommend probation where it is clearly inappropriate. If the advocate independently forms the view that the probation officer's recommendation is hopelessly optimistic, then it may well not be enough simply to ask the court to adopt that recommendation but a full plea in mitigation stressing all possible factors in the defendant's favour may need to be made. It is sometimes good tactics in such a case to be seen to side with the sentencer against the probation officer and to indicate that one views the recommendation as optimistic. A striking opening to such a plea in mitigation might, for example, say:

> Contrary to the probation officer's suggestion most people might see this as a nasty spiteful crime by a man who for 10 years has made little contribution to society and whom it might appear that you would be highly justified in sending to prison immediately. On the other hand, despite that preliminary view I would urge you to consider the following ...

10.11.10 SHOULD THE ADVOCATE RECOMMEND ANY PARTICULAR TYPE OF SENTENCE?

In cases where the probation officer in a report is not recommending any particular type of sentence there is nothing to stop the advocate from doing so, or indeed anyway from recommending one different to that recommended by the probation officer. Thus one may suggest to the court that a fine is an appropriate way of dealing with the offender and in that case details of the offender's means and outgoings should be given. Whilst one may recommend the type of sentence it is not generally considered appropriate to recommend a specific term or the amount of a fine. One would not for example suggest to a court that a case merited say nine months' imprisonment rather than some longer term or a fine of any particular amount. One merely recommends a type of sentence and asks the court to impose the minimum it sees fit. In this connection and in connection with mitigation generally it is appropriate to mention one further matter.

10.11.11 DEFERRED SENTENCE

Advocates who make pleas in mitigation often make some relatively optimistic claims on behalf of offenders concerning some change in lifestyle and capacity to reform. For example it may be suggested that a person will stay out of trouble if he is able to get a job and that he has an interview for a job in a few days' time. Likewise, claims may be made that an offender will pay compensation to the victim of the offence.

The court has the power under s. 1 of the Powers of Criminal Courts Act 1973 to defer passing any sentence for a period of up to six months. The main reason why a court might defer sentence is to enable it to take into account the offender's conduct after conviction and any change in circumstances that comes about.

When a court defers sentence the offender is released until the date when he is instructed to reappear, which should preferably be fixed by the court there and then. Moreover, in principle, the offender should return to be dealt with by the same judge or magistrates who have dealt with the case hitherto. When the offender does reappear before the court he or his advocate will be expected to explain what has occurred in the meantime, in particular with regard to any promises or undertakings given on the previous occasion. If the offender has carried out his promise, e.g., to obtain a job or pay compensation and has not in the meantime reoffended, he should be safe from a custodial sentence. However merely staying out of trouble on its own is not sufficient to ensure that an offender will not be sent to prison. It is also important to consider whether the offender has done the best he can to change his lifestyle in the way suggested on his behalf at the mitigation stage. If the sentencing court does impose an immediate custodial sentence it should state precisely in what respect it considers there has been a failure to comply with the undertakings previously given.

10.12   Crime (Sentences) Act 1997

What follows is a very brief account of some of the main provisions of the Act. The most important and controversial provisions are those which take away some of the general discretionary sentencing powers of the judiciary and indicate certain minimum custodial sentences. The hostility of the judges to these provisions, particularly when the Bill was debated in the House of Lords, received considerable comment in the legal and other press. However, the Act did not prove very controversial in party political terms. At the time of writing it has not been implemented. Some of the provisions are not particularly controversial and are of only administrative interest. There are, e.g., detailed provisions relating to transfers of prisoners to and from the Channel Islands.

The following are the most important mainstream provisions:

(1)   Mandatory minimum custodial sentences

(a)   *'Serious offences'*

By ss. 1 and 2 of the Crime (Sentences) Act 1997, where a person is convicted of a second 'serious offence', then the court 'shall' impose a life sentence unless the court is of the opinion that there are exceptional circumstances relating to either the past offence or the present offence or to the offender which justifies not doing so, in which case the court must give in open court a statement of what the exceptional circumstances are.

'Serious offences' are

(i)   attempts to murder, and conspiracies, incitements and soliciting murder;

(ii)   manslaughter;

(iii)   wounding or causing grievous bodily harm with intent contrary to s. 18 of the Offences Against the Person Act 1861;

(iv)   rape or attempted rape;

(v)   having sexual intercourse with a girl under 13;

(vi)   possession of a firearm with intent to injure or to resist arrest or carrying a firearm with criminal intent;

(vii)   robbery where the offender had in his possession a firearm or imitation firearm.

The object of this section therefore is to reduce substantially the court's discretion in relation to the sentences it may impose in respect of these offences, so that imposing anything other than a life sentence should only happen where there are 'exceptional circumstances'. It should not be assumed that a generous interpretation will be given to the words 'exceptional circumstances' because where the same words are used in the context of suspended sentences, case law demonstrates that there really has to be a very unusual feature present. An example might be where perhaps the previous offence was, say, 30 years ago since when the accused had led a relatively blameless life before the new offence and there are also mitigating features about one or both of the crimes concerned.

(b) *Drug trafficking*

Section 3 of the 1997 Act provides that there will be a minimum of seven years' imprisonment for a person convicted of a drug trafficking offence involving Class A drugs (e.g., heroin or cocaine) where the person convicted has been convicted twice previously on separate occasions of trafficking in Class A drugs. If the court is of the opinion that there are specific circumstances which relate to any of the offences or to the offender and which would make the prescribed custodial sentence unjust in all the circumstances, the court need not impose such a sentence, but must state what the specific circumstances are.

The section is aimed at habitual drug trafficking offenders and applies irrespective of the quantity of drugs involved. The application of s. 3 is arguably unnecessary where the offence concerns substantial quantities of drugs because the Court of Appeal guidelines on sentencing Class A drug traffickers (see **10.10**) would, in any case, inevitably lead to a sentence of more than seven years.

(c) *Domestic burglary*

Section 4 provides for a minimum sentence of three years' imprisonment where a person is convicted of a domestic burglary and has been convicted of two other previous domestic burglaries on separate occasions, both of them having been committed after the coming into force of the 1997 Act.

Again, the court need not impose the minimum term of three years where it is of the opinion that there are specific circumstances which relate to any of the offences or to the offender and would make the prescribed custodial sentence unjust in all the circumstances. Those circumstances are to be stated in open court.

(2) **Release of offenders**

The second part of the Crime (Sentences) Act 1997 also deals with the technically difficult issue of when offenders are actually released, in other words the relationship borne between the sentence as passed by the judge and the actual term served. Detailed consideration is unnecessary for this book, but the rules are re-stated in more specific terms as to the circumstances in which a prisoner may be released on compassionate grounds; that periods of remand in custody should be credited against custodial sentences; and that where a prisoner is serving a term of more than two months and less than three years he may be awarded 'early release days' for good behaviour. The net effect of these rules is to impose a much more restrictive regime and to reduce considerably previous periods of remission for good behaviour and the like.

Section 12 relates to prisoners who are serving a sentence of three years or more and provides that such prisoners may be released when they have served five-sixths of their sentence if the Parole Board recommends that course.

Section 17 of the Act provides a system of 'release supervision orders' so that certain offenders, on release, are subject to supervision for specified periods following their release from custody. This supervision will be by a probation officer and will require the offender to comply with such conditions as are specified, although certain conditions, e.g., that the offender lives in an approved probation hostel or is subject to a curfew order can only be made following recommendations of the Parole Board after an oral hearing. Breach of any 'release supervision order' is a specific offence.

(3) **Release on licence of persons sentenced to life imprisonment**

Chapter II (ss. 28–34 of the 1997 Act) sets up a new regime for the release of life prisoners following consideration of their cases by the Parole Board and deals with the duration and condition of the licences on which they may be released and the situations under which their licences may be revoked and they may be recalled to prison.

(4) **Miscellaneous provisions**

Part III of the 1997 Act contains a number of miscellaneous sections, in particular:

(i) Section 34 sets out a regime to be applied to fine defaulters who may be required to undergo a community service order up to certain prescribed maxima, depending upon the amount of the fines outstanding.

(ii) Section 37 prescribes a regime to be followed in relation to 'persistent petty offenders', that is those who have a number of convictions for minor offences for which they have received a fine and where the fine has not been paid. If any further fine would be beyond the offender's means, then the court may make a community service order or curfew order instead of imposing a fine if the provisions of the section are met.

(5) **Driving disqualifications**

In the past, driving disqualification as a punishment has always related to conduct involving a vehicle. To be deprived of one's driving licence, however, would be generally viewed as a considerable punishment and in order to add a further flexibility to the way in which offenders may be punished, s. 39 of the Act provides that a court may order disqualification for such periods as it thinks fit, in addition to or instead of dealing with an offender in any other way.

It remains to be seen to what extent the courts will consider it appropriate to impose this further level of punishment on someone convicted of offences relating to misconduct in unrelated criminal activity, e.g., offences of dishonesty, or violence, not involving motor vehicles.

10.13   The Magistrates' Association Sentencing Guidelines: Assault — Actual Bodily Harm; Assault on a Police Officer

Offences Against the Person Act 1861 s.47 Triable either way - see Mode of Trial Guidelines Penalty: Level 5 and/or 6 months	Assault — Actual Bodily Harm

CONSIDER THE SERIOUSNESS OF THE OFFENCE
(INCLUDING THE IMPACT ON THE VICTIM)

GUIDELINE: ➤

IS COMPENSATION, DISCHARGE OR FINE APPROPRIATE?

IS IT SERIOUS ENOUGH FOR A COMMUNITY PENALTY?

IS IT SO SERIOUS THAT ONLY CUSTODY IS APPROPRIATE?

ARE MAGISTRATES' COURTS' POWERS APPROPRIATE?

 ### CONSIDER AGGRAVATING AND MITIGATING FACTORS

for example

Racial motivation
Deliberate kicking or biting
Extensive injuries (may be psychiatric)
Group action
Offender in position of authority
Premeditated
Victim particularly vulnerable
Victim serving public
Weapon

Offence committed on bail
Previous convictions and failures to respond
to previous sentences, if relevant
This list is not exhaustive

for example

Impulsive
Minor injury
Provocation
Single blow
This list is not exhaustive

CONSIDER OFFENDER MITIGATION

for example

Age, health (physical or mental)
Co-operation with the police
Voluntary compensation
Remorse

CONSIDER YOUR SENTENCE

*Compare it with the suggested guideline level of sentence and reconsider
your reasons carefully if you have chosen a sentence at a different level.
Consider a discount for a timely guilty plea.*

DECIDE YOUR SENTENCE

NB. COMPENSATION - Give reasons if not awarding compensation

Remember: These are GUIDELINES not a tariff

Assault on a Police Officer

Police Act 1996 s.89
Triable only summarily
Penalty: Level 5 and/or 6 months

CONSIDER THE SERIOUSNESS OF THE OFFENCE
(INCLUDING THE IMPACT ON THE VICTIM)

IS COMPENSATION, DISCHARGE OR FINE APPROPRIATE?

IS IT SERIOUS ENOUGH FOR A COMMUNITY PENALTY?

GUIDELINE: ➤   *IS IT SO SERIOUS THAT ONLY CUSTODY IS APPROPRIATE?*

 ## CONSIDER AGGRAVATING AND MITIGATING FACTORS

for example
> Any injuries caused
> Gross disregard for police authority
> Group action
> Premeditated
>
> Offence committed on bail
> Previous convictions and failures to respond
> to previous sentences, if relevant
> *This list is not exhaustive*

for example
> Impulsive action
> Unaware that person was a Police Officer
> *This list is not exhaustive*

CONSIDER OFFENDER MITIGATION

for example
> Age, health (physical or mental)
> Co-operation with the police
> Voluntary compensation
> Remorse

CONSIDER YOUR SENTENCE

*Compare it with the suggested guideline level of sentence and reconsider
your reasons carefully if you have chosen a sentence at a different level.
Consider a discount for a timely guilty plea.*

DECIDE YOUR SENTENCE

NB. COMPENSATION - Give reasons if not awarding compensation

Remember: These are GUIDELINES not a tariff

10.14 The Magistrates' Association Sentencing Guidelines: Burglary — Dwelling; Burglary — Non Dwelling

Theft Act 1968 s.9 Triable either way - see Mode of Trial Guidelines Penalty: Level 5 and/or 6 months	Burglary (Dwelling)

CONSIDER THE SERIOUSNESS OF THE OFFENCE
(INCLUDING THE IMPACT ON THE VICTIM)

GUIDELINE: ➤

IS COMPENSATION, DISCHARGE OR FINE APPROPRIATE?

IS IT SERIOUS ENOUGH FOR A COMMUNITY PENALTY?

IS IT SO SERIOUS THAT ONLY CUSTODY IS APPROPRIATE?

ARE MAGISTRATES' COURTS' POWERS APPROPRIATE?

 ### CONSIDER AGGRAVATING AND MITIGATING FACTORS

for example
- Racial motivation
- Deliberately frightening occupants
- Group offence
- People in house
- Professional operation
- Forcible entry
- Soiling, ransacking, damage

Offence committed on bail
Previous convictions and failures to respond
to previous sentences, if relevant
This list is not exhaustive

for example
- Low value
- Nobody frightened
- No damage or disturbance
- No forcible entry
- Opportunist
- *This list is not exhaustive*

CONSIDER OFFENDER MITIGATION

for example
- Age, health (physical or mental)
- Co-operation with the police
- Voluntary compensation
- Remorse

CONSIDER YOUR SENTENCE

*Compare it with the suggested guideline level of sentence and reconsider
your reasons carefully if you have chosen a sentence at a different level.
Consider a discount for a timely guilty plea.*

DECIDE YOUR SENTENCE

NB. COMPENSATION - Give reasons if not awarding compensation

Remember: These are GUIDELINES not a tariff

Burglary (Non-dwelling)	Theft Act 1968 s.9 Triable either way - see Mode of Trial Guidelines Penalty: Level 5 and/or 6 months

CONSIDER THE SERIOUSNESS OF THE OFFENCE
(INCLUDING THE IMPACT ON THE VICTIM)

GUIDELINE: ➢

IS COMPENSATION, DISCHARGE OR FINE APPROPRIATE?

IS IT SERIOUS ENOUGH FOR A COMMUNITY PENALTY?

IS IT SO SERIOUS THAT ONLY CUSTODY IS APPROPRIATE?

ARE MAGISTRATES' COURTS' POWERS APPROPRIATE?

CONSIDER AGGRAVATING AND MITIGATING FACTORS

for example	for example
Racial motivation	Low value
Deliberately frightening occupants	Nobody frightened
Group offence	No damage or disturbance
Night time	No forcible entry
Professional operation	*This list is not exhaustive*
Forcible entry	
Soiling, ransacking, damage	
Serious harm to business	
Offence committed on bail	
Previous convictions and failures to respond	
to previous sentences, if relevant	
This list is not exhaustive	

CONSIDER OFFENDER MITIGATION

for example
- Age, health (physical or mental)
- Co-operation with the police
- Voluntary compensation
- Remorse

CONSIDER YOUR SENTENCE

*Compare it with the suggested guideline level of sentence and reconsider
your reasons carefully if you have chosen a sentence at a different level.
Consider a discount for a timely guilty plea.*

DECIDE YOUR SENTENCE

NB. COMPENSATION - Give reasons if not awarding compensation

Remember: These are GUIDELINES not a tariff

ELEVEN

JUVENILES IN THE CRIMINAL PROCESS: THE YOUTH COURT

11.1 Introduction

In all other parts of this text we have dealt with the problem of adult offenders. It is inevitable however in the conduct of a criminal litigation practice that one will come across younger offenders. In the main, adults are persons of 18 or over and all are dealt with the same procedurally, except that for those between the ages of 18 and 20 inclusive there are certain kinds of *sentence* which may be available to the courts which are not available for those over 21. In this chapter we are concerned with those of 17 or younger who are collectively called 'juveniles', a non-technical term which encompasses 'children', aged 13 or under, and 'young persons', aged up to 17 inclusive.

11.2 At the Police Station

When a juvenile is kept at a police station, the Codes of Practice require (Code C, para. 1.7; Code D, para. 1.6) that 'an appropriate adult' should be present. In the case of a juvenile this means:

(a) a parent or guardian or, if he is in care, a representative of the care authority or voluntary organisation; or

(b) a social worker; or

(c) failing either of the above, another responsible adult aged 18 or over who is not a policeman or employed by the police.

A solicitor himself however may not act as 'the appropriate adult'. The appropriate adult should also not be someone suspected of involvement in the offence. Similarly, if the parent or guardian has received admissions from the juvenile he should not be the appropriate adult. If the parent of a juvenile is estranged from him he should not be the appropriate adult if the juvenile does not want him. The police must use a good deal of initiative in this situation and the choice of the wrong 'appropriate adult' may invalidate any confessions subsequently made by the juvenile, e.g., as in *R* v *Blake* (1989) 89 Cr App R 179 where the accused did not want her father to be present but rather her social worker and the police proceeded nonetheless with the father; or *R* v *Morse* [1991] Crim LR 195 where the juvenile's father had an IQ of below 70 and was incapable of appreciating the situation, evidence of the confession was excluded because the father would have been of no use to his son.

A custody officer must, as soon as practicable after the detention of a juvenile, inform the appropriate adult of the grounds of detention and the juvenile's whereabouts and ask the appropriate adult to come to the police station. His function there is to ensure that there is an impartial adult to safeguard the rights of the juvenile. The appropriate adult may then exercise the juvenile's right to legal advice, but the juvenile may anyway consult a solicitor straight-away, and it is usually better to take instructions direct from the juvenile rather than the appropriate adult, although proper consultation is of course required. The juvenile has the final decision whatever his age. It is vital of course to ensure that the juvenile understands any allegations made and has given a full and coherent account. If the custody officer will not grant bail to the juvenile, the local authority should be contacted and the appropriate adult or parent/guardian informed.

Save in respect of the most serious offences, juveniles are not usually charged immediately but are bailed for a report to, and decision by, the Juvenile Bureau. It is vital to explain this procedure to the juvenile and discuss the possible outcomes, in particular the possibility of a caution. The importance of the juvenile admitting the crime, and only admitting it honestly, must be carefully explained.

11.3   Detention Pending First Appearance

By virtue of s. 38 of the Police and Criminal Evidence Act 1984 (as amended by s. 59, Criminal Justice Act 1991, and subsequently by ss. 20 and 21, Criminal Justice and Public Order Act 1994) a custody officer must now ensure that the juvenile is moved to local authority accommodation unless:

(a) it is impracticable for him to do so (in which case he must give reasons why this is so); or

(b) in the case of children or young persons aged 12–17 inclusive, no secure accommoda-tion is available and it appears that local authority accommodation would not be adequate to protect the public from serious harm from that child or young person.

It should be noted that this latter provision is not confined to offences of violence or serious offences and may be appropriate even in other cases since the phrase 'serious harm' is not defined and could extend to the risk of property damage alone.

It should also be noted that a further adjustment is made by s. 23 of the Criminal Justice and Public Order Act 1994 which provides that if a juvenile is remanded or committed to local authority accommodation, then conditions may be attached to the remand or committal, requiring the juvenile to comply with any conditions which might have been imposed on an adult under the Bail Act 1976.

11.4   Courtroom Procedure

A juvenile is likely to make his first court appearance before magistrates. This is likely to be in the youth court unless he is charged jointly with an adult in which case both will come before the adult magistrates' court initially. The decision on whether a juvenile is tried summarily or on indictment is taken by the magistrates and the juvenile does not have the right to elect trial on indictment.

Section 24(1) of the Magistrates' Courts Act 1980 provides that a juvenile must be tried in a youth court (or in an adult magistrates' court if tried jointly with an adult) unless either:

(a) He is charged with homicide.

(b) He is charged jointly with an adult who is going to be tried on indictment *and* the magistrates consider that it is in the interests of justice to commit them both for trial.

In deciding whether to hold committal proceedings in respect of both an adult and a juvenile so as to send the juvenile for trial with the adult, the magistrates must consider the whole interests of justice, including the undesirability of putting a juvenile through the ordeal of Crown Court trial. The younger the juvenile is and the less serious the offence, the more likely it is that the magistrates will decide to commit only the adult to the Crown Court and allow the juvenile to plead to the charge in the magistrates' court. If the juvenile pleads not guilty the adult court will then remit him to the youth court to be tried. If he pleads guilty the adult court will consider sentence but its powers in this respect are limited and it will again usually remit the case for sentencing to the youth court.

(c) He has attained the age of 14, is charged with a grave offence (principally offences punishable with 14 years' imprisonment or more), and the magistrates consider that he could probably be sentenced under s. 53(2) of the Children and Young Persons Act 1933 if he were convicted. This power is concerned with the most serious kinds of offence and governs the case where a Crown Court may sentence a juvenile to detention for a term not exceeding the maximum prison term available in the case of an adult. A sentence under s. 53(2) is only possible where there has been a conviction on indictment. Thus even if a youth court commits a juvenile to the Crown Court for sentence under s. 37 of the Magistrates' Courts Act 1980, the Crown Court cannot then pass a s. 53(2) sentence because there has been no trial on indictment. Thus the magistrates must consider the possibility of committal for trial if they think the allegation is one of sufficient seriousness to warrant a substantial sentence of detention.

11.4.1 TRIAL OF JUVENILES IN AN ADULT MAGISTRATES' COURT

A juvenile who is to be tried summarily is to be tried in a youth court unless:

(a) he is charged jointly with an adult; or

(b) he appears before the magistrates together with an adult and has been charged separately but the charges are that he aided and abetted the commission of the offence alleged against the adult or vice versa; or

(c) he appears before the magistrates together with an adult, and the charge against him arises out of circumstances the same as or connected with the circumstances giving rise to the charge against the adult; or

(d) the trial has started against him in the erroneous belief that he was an adult (it may then be continued).

11.4.2 TRIAL OF JUVENILES IN A YOUTH COURT

The youth court (formerly known as the juvenile court) consists of magistrates drawn from a special youth court panel.

The following differences in procedure apply:

(a) A youth court must sit in a room which has not been used as an adult court within the last hour so as to avoid the mixing of juveniles and adult offenders.

(b) The general public have no right of admission to youth courts (where proceedings against juveniles take place in the adult courts this is however usually in open court).

(c)   The bench of magistrates must include one of each sex.

(d)   There is a certain change in terminology so that witnesses in the case 'promise' rather than 'swear' to tell the truth and if the magistrates decide that the juvenile is guilty they do not 'convict' but 'record a finding of guilt against him'. Likewise the term used after the finding of guilt is not 'sentence' but 'the making of an order upon a finding of guilt' (s. 59, Children and Young Persons Act 1933).

(e)   The court may require the attendance before it of the parent or guardian of the child (s. 34, Children and Young Persons Act 1933).

(f)   The media may not report the name or any other identifying details of the juvenile unless it is necessary in order to avoid injustice.

(g)   There is no dock and the juvenile usually sits on a chair or bench facing the magistrates with his parents beside him. The magistrates are usually seated at the same level as the juvenile and will usually call him by his Christian name.

11.5   Sentencing of Juveniles

11.5.1   CROWN COURT

The Crown Court may pass any sentence appropriate in the case of a juvenile. Section 56 of the Children and Young Persons Act 1933 provides that, except in cases of homicide, the Crown Court must remit a juvenile convicted on indictment to the youth court to be sentenced, unless satisfied that it will be undesirable to do so. However, guidelines given in leading cases indicate that a Crown Court judge need not remit for sentence if inter alia remitting would cause delay, unnecessary duplication of proceedings, and unnecessary expense; the effect of this is that in most cases, since he will be familiar with the facts, the Crown Court judge is likely to sentence a juvenile himself rather than remit the case to the youth court.

Where a juvenile of 15, 16 or 17 years is guilty of an indictable offence and the court considers that he should be sentenced to more than the six months' detention, which is the maximum available to a youth court by virtue of s. 37 of the Magistrates' Courts Act 1980, it may commit him to the Crown Court to be sentenced. The Crown Court may then pass a sentence of up to 24 months for the offence or deal with the offender in any way in which the youth court could have dealt with him.

11.5.1.1   Secure training orders

Sections 1–4 of the Criminal Justice and Public Order Act 1994 create a completely new form of sentence available for those aged 12–14 at the date of the offence (*not* at the date of sentence).

The requirements are that the offender:

(a)   must have been convicted of an imprisonable offence (other than murder for which the penalty is fixed by law);

(b)   must have been convicted of three or more imprisonable offences;

(c)   must previously, or in relation to the present offence, have breached a supervision order or have committed an imprisonable offence while subject to such an order.

Section 1(6) of the 1994 Act provides that this sentence is a 'custodial sentence' for the purpose of the Criminal Justice Act 1991. Thus in deciding to impose it the sentencing court will be required to take into account all the relevant procedural provisions, including the 'custody threshold' rules, i.e. the decision to impose a secure training order must be based upon the 'seriousness of the offence or the combination of the offence and one or more associated offences'. Obviously the number and nature of previous convictions can assist with satisfying the 'seriousness' criterion.

The length of the sentence (minimum six months, maximum two years) must also be justified having regard to the seriousness of the offence and the other relevant criteria in s. 2(2) of the Criminal Justice Act 1991. The sentencing court must always have the benefit of a pre-sentence report.

11.5.1.2 The nature of the penalty

The secure training order comprises a period of detention followed by a period of supervision. The custodial part of the sentence and the supervision part of the sentence are meant to be equal in length. The supervision part will be served in the community under the supervision of a probation officer or social worker.

As yet these provisions are not in force because no secure training centres have been built.

11.5.2 ADULT MAGISTRATES' COURT

An adult magistrates' court's powers are limited in respect of juveniles. Apart from fines, and sentences of disqualification and endorsement, the adult court must remit a juvenile to the youth court to be sentenced by virtue of s. 7 of the Children and Young Persons Act 1969. The adult magistrates' court cannot commit a juvenile to the Crown Court under s. 37 of the Magistrates' Courts Act 1980 but must remit him to the youth court which then does have the power of considering that option.

11.5.3 YOUTH COURT

The youth court has the following powers:

(a) It may pass a sentence of detention in a young offender institution on those aged 15 and 16 for up to six months for any one offence; up to six months for any two or more offences which are purely summary; and up to 12 months for two or more 'either way' offences.

(b) It may make a secure training order subject to the magistrates' maximum powers to impose custodial sentences of six months for any one offence and up to 12 months for two or more 'either way' offences.

(c) It may fine up to £1,000 in the case of those aged 15, 16 or 17 and up to £250 in the case of an offender of 14 or younger. For obvious reasons it is highly unlikely that a fine will be appropriate for a juvenile in any event.

(d) It cannot pass a sentence of detention under s. 53 of the Children and Young Persons Act 1933. These sentences are appropriate only in the minority of serious cases and in such cases clearly the case will be sent to the Crown Court.

(e) By s. 34A of the Children and Young Persons Act 1933 (inserted by s. 56, Criminal Justice Act 1991) the parent or guardian of a juvenile is required to attend before a court when the juvenile appears. The parent or guardian may be required to enter into a recognisance to take proper care of him and exercise proper control over him and a sum of up to £1,000 may be ordered to be forfeited when that recognisance is breached. In addition, parents may be required to pay fines, costs or compensation orders imposed by the criminal courts on juveniles.

TWELVE

APPEALS IN CRIMINAL CASES

12.1 Appeals from the Magistrates' Court to the Crown Court against Conviction and/or Sentence: ss. 108–110, Magistrates' Courts Act 1980

It should first be noted that if there are adequate grounds shown by virtue of s. 142, Magistrates' Courts Act 1980 (inserted in amended form by s. 26, Criminal Appeal Act 1995) a person convicted by a magistrates' court may apply to the court that in the interests of justice the case should be heard again by different justices. If that application is made the court may make a direction for a retrial. This might occur, e.g., where, after conviction, a defence witness who had not appeared arrives at court late, or subsequently where new evidence is found. It is also an appropriate way of dealing with the situation where an accused has pleaded guilty by post in ignorance of some defence open to him.

If that is not appropriate then an appeal must be considered by one or other of the following methods.

A defendant who has been convicted in the magistrates' court following a plea of not guilty may appeal against either conviction or sentence or both to the Crown Court. This is done by giving notice of appeal in writing to the clerk to the magistrates' court concerned and to the prosecution within 21 days of sentence being passed. The notice of appeal need not go into any detail on the grounds and indeed it is usual to use a standard form of appeal which merely states that 'the defendant proposes to appeal on the grounds that the magistrates erred in fact and in law in convicting him', or 'the defendant appeals against sentence on the grounds that the sentence imposed was excessive in all the circumstances'.

There is no filtering mechanism, as with appeals to the Court of Appeal, so there is no discretion to refuse to accept the appeal nor is any application for leave to appeal necessary. If notice of appeal is not lodged within the prescribed time there is a discretion to extend the time for giving notice of appeal on application in writing to the Crown Court judge. Reasons for the lateness in appealing need to be supplied (r. 7(5), Crown Court Rules 1982).

12.1.1 BAIL PENDING APPEAL

It should be remembered that if an immediate custodial sentence has been passed on a convicted person a bail application pending appeal may be made to the magistrates' court although the presumption in favour of bail does not apply. Accordingly in those circumstances a verbal notice of appeal should be given immediately sentence is passed, but this must still be supplemented by a written notice within the prescribed period. In similar circumstances an application to suspend a disqualification from driving pending appeal may also be made.

12.1.2 THE HEARING

The appeal is heard by a circuit judge or recorder sitting with an even number of magistrates (usually two) but with no jury *(Practice Direction (Crown Court Business: Classification)* [1987] 1 WLR 1671 and s. 74, Supreme Court Act 1981). The form of the appeal is a complete rehearing. The parties may call the same evidence as in the court below in the hope that the higher court will take a different view of it or may call different evidence including not calling witnesses whom they did call in the court below. Matters of law may also be argued and new or different points of law may be raised.

12.1.3 APPEAL FOLLOWING PLEA OF GUILTY

A person who has pleaded guilty in the magistrates' court may appeal against sentence to the Crown Court following the same procedure as outlined above, but may not appeal generally against conviction. However it may be open to a person to argue that his plea of guilty was equivocal, that is to say that although he pleaded guilty, matters were put before the court then or subsequently, probably as mitigation, which actually undermined the plea. For example an accused who when charged with theft says 'guilty but I only took it because I thought it was mine'. In these circumstances the words which accompany the plea are such as to indicate a full defence and the plea should not have been accepted. In such a case an appeal against a conviction may be heard and the case will then be remitted by the Crown Court to the magistrates' court with the direction that the matter be treated as if a plea of not guilty had been entered. There will then be a retrial before the magistrates' court. It should be noted however that this jurisdiction only applies where there is something which occurs at the time which renders the plea clearly equivocal. If it later comes to light that the defendant had an arguable defence which was unknown to him at the time he is generally bound by his plea.

12.1.4 POWERS OF THE CROWN COURT

The powers of the Crown Court when hearing an appeal from a magistrates' court are contained in s. 48 of the Supreme Court Act 1981. The Crown Court may, having heard the appeal:

(a) confirm, reverse or vary the decision appealed against; or

(b) remit the matter with the court's opinion to the magistrates (for example where it found that the plea was equivocal); or

(c) make any such other order as the court considers just, and by such order exercise any power that the magistrates might have exercised (e.g., make appropriate orders for costs); or

(d) award any sentence whether lesser or greater than that which the magistrates actually awarded provided that the sentence is one which the magistrates' court had power to award. It should be noted therefore that there is a possibility of an *increase* in sentence which may act as some deterrent to frivolous appeals.

It is important not to confuse the procedure for appeals to a Crown Court with the powers of the Crown Court where magistrates commit an accused to the Crown Court for sentence under s. 38 of the Magistrates' Courts Act 1980 having tried the case summarily. Where this occurs the Crown Court has the power to impose any sentence up to the maximum sentence permitted by law for the offence in question.

Only the defence has a right of appeal from the magistrates' court to the Crown Court. If the prosecution thinks it has a basis for appeal on a point of law against an acquittal it must use the procedure next described.

12.2 Appeals from the Magistrates' Court to the Queen's Bench Division, Divisional Court

As we have previously seen, an appeal to the Crown Court may be on any matter of fact or law and may be brought by the defendant alone. There is an alternative avenue of procedure which is open to either side and this is by virtue of s. 111(1) of the Magistrates' Courts Act 1980 which provides that:

> *Any person who was a party to any proceedings before a magistrates' court or is aggrieved by the conviction, order, determination or other proceeding of the court may question the proceeding on the ground that it is wrong in law or in excess of jurisdiction.*

The appeal may therefore be made by either party, prosecution or defence, as long as it concerns a matter of law or an allegation of excess of jurisdiction. The procedure commences by requiring the magistrates to 'state a case' for the opinion of the High Court. The aggrieved party applies in writing to the magistrates within 21 days of the acquittal or conviction or sentence; the application may be by letter and should identify the question of law on which the High Court's opinion is sought. The application is sent to the magistrates' clerk. The kind of matters which may be raised by way of case stated are such things as whether the magistrates had power to try the case; whether they were right to find that there was a case to answer; whether inadmissible evidence was received or admissible evidence excluded, and the like.

A 'statement of case' is prepared by the court which will outline the facts called in question, state the facts which the magistrates found and then state the magistrates' finding on the points of law in question, listing any authority cited and finally posing the question for the High Court. The case is drafted by the magistrates' clerk in consultation with the magistrates. Drafts of the case are sent to the parties who may suggest amendments. The final form of 'case' is then sent to the appellant who must lodge it at the Crown Office of the Royal Courts of Justice in London. Notice must then be given to the respondent with a copy of the case.

The appeal is subsequently heard by the Divisional Court of the Queen's Bench Division in London in which at least two judges, but more usually three, sit. Evidence is not called and the appeal takes the form of legal argument for the appellant and respondent based solely upon the facts stated in the case. The Divisional Court may reverse, affirm or amend the magistrates' decision or may remit the matter back to the magistrates with its opinion, e.g., with a direction that they continue the hearing, convict, acquit, or the court may remit the case to a different bench of magistrates. Costs may be awarded to either party out of central funds.

It should finally be noted that, where an individual has been convicted in the magistrates' court and appeals to the Crown Court by the procedure previously described, there is a subsequent appeal on a matter of law only by way of case stated from the Crown Court to the Divisional Court. This should not be confused with an appeal from the Crown Court after trial on indictment (i.e., before a jury) (for which, see **12.4**).

12.3 Application for Judicial Review

Instead of either of the methods of appeal previously mentioned, it may be open to a person to apply for judicial review of the decision of the magistrates' court, with the object of seeking the quashing of the magistrates' court decision. On making a decision by the prerogative order, certiorari, to quash the magistrates' decision, the Divisional Court also has the power of remitting the case to the magistrates with a direction for them to proceed in an appropriate manner, in accordance with its own ruling. Alternatively the whole decision may be quashed so that and conviction and sentence are overturned.

Judicial review will generally lie where:

(a) the order made by the magistrates' court was made in excess of jurisdiction; or

(b) the magistrates' court acted in breach of the rules of natural justice. This is a vague and widening part of the principles of judicial review so that in recent cases examples of breach of the rules of natural justice have included the following: failure to give the accused reasonable time to prepare his defence (*R v Thames Magistrates' Court ex parte Polemis* [1974] 1 WLR 1371); refusing to issue witness summonses (*R v Bradford Justices ex parte Wilkinson* [1990] 1 WLR 692); or where the accused had pleaded guilty under a misapprehension as to the facts because blood samples given by them might have been contaminated by swabs containing alcohol used by police surgeons (*R v Bolton Justices ex parte Scally* [1991] 1 QB 537). In all these cases the convictions were quashed by certiorari;

(c) where there is an error of law on the face of the record. This is relatively rare however, because the error must be *on the face of* the record and magistrates do not, in the main, give reasons for their decision.

In all these cases, the decision may be quashed by certiorari. As an alternative to certiorari, the other prerogative orders are available. These are mandamus and prohibition, which as their names imply, are orders requiring the magistrates' court to act, or not to act, in a certain way.

12.3.1 PROCEDURE

The procedure to apply for judicial review is in s. 31 of the Supreme Court Act 1981 and RSC, ord. 53. It is a two-stage procedure whereby:

(a) The applicant must obtain leave to apply for review. This is obtained on affidavit with written grounds for review filed by the applicant and put before a single judge. It is possible for this to be supplemented by oral argument.

(b) If leave to apply is granted, the application is dealt with by the Divisional Court which will hear argument from the applicant and anyone else affected by the outcome. Where the application is in effect brought against the magistrates' court, although the magistrates' court may supply any affidavit as to its reasoning or some other aspects, it is usual for the other party to be the CPS or the Home Office depending on the nature of the alleged error.

At the end of the hearing the court makes its decisions granting or refusing the order sought by the applicant and either bringing the case to an end or remitting the matter to the lower court for reconsideration. The grant of remedies by judicial review is always discretionary.

12.4 Appeals from the Crown Court to the Court of Appeal (Criminal Division)

A person convicted of on offence on indictment may appeal to the Court of Appeal either with the leave of the Court of Appeal or if the judge of the court of trial grants a certificate that the case is fit for appeal.

The Court of Appeal:

(a) shall allow an appeal against conviction if it thinks that the conviction is unsafe; and

(b) shall dismiss such an appeal in any other case.

Introduced in 1996, this important amendment abolishes the more complicated form of wording contained in s. 2 of the Criminal Appeal Act 1968 and provides a test that, even if there has been some mistake or irregularity or even a wrong decision of law in the trial in the Crown Court, if the Court of Appeal thinks the conviction remains safe the appeal may be dismissed. In other words the Court of Appeal has to consider whether, if the trial had been free of any mistakes, the only reasonable and proper verdict would still have been one of guilty and, if it concludes that this is so, it will affirm the conviction.

In fact the leave of the trial judge is only rarely sought and most appeals to the Court of Appeal follow leave given by the Court of Appeal itself.

A convicted person who has legal aid for his trial is covered by legal aid for initial advice on appeal and the drafting of the grounds of appeal if his counsel recommends that an appeal be pursued. The procedure is as follows:

(a) Within 28 days of conviction or sentence the appellant must serve on the Registrar of Criminal Appeals a notice of application for leave to appeal accompanied by draft grounds of appeal.

(b) If the appeal is against conviction then there will probably need to be a transcript provided, either of the judge's summing up or perhaps of some part of the evidence at the trial. The court shorthand writer will then be asked by the Registrar of Criminal Appeals to transcribe the appropriate part of his notes, or a transcript will be made from the automatic recording equipment.

(c) The papers are then put before a single judge who may be either a Lord Justice of Appeal or a High Court judge sitting as a member of the Court of Appeal. The papers will include the grounds of appeal, transcript and any other relevant documents.

This is a filtering stage at which the single judge considers whether leave ought to be given. There is no hearing and the matter will be decided simply on the papers. If he does grant leave to appeal he will grant legal aid (if necessary) for the hearing itself and the case then proceeds to the full court. If the single judge refuses leave to appeal the appellant has 14 further days in which to serve notice upon the Registrar if he wishes to continue with the case, that is to renew the application before the full court. The papers are then put before the full court. Again an oral hearing is not normal, at least in legal aid cases, and the full court reaches its decision by reading the papers in the case. The single judge is meant to act as a filtering mechanism and if he refuses leave to appeal and the appellant persists before the full court, the full court is empowered to give a so-called 'direction concerning loss of time' under s. 29 of the Criminal Appeal Act 1968. By virtue of this section and *Practice Direction (Crime: Sentence: Loss of Time)* [1981] WLR 270 the full court may direct that time in prison served between the single judge refusing leave and the full court refusing leave may not count as part of any custodial sentence imposed. Such a direction is normal unless the appellant received a written opinion from counsel that there were grounds for appeal. If the full court grants leave to appeal they may also grant legal aid for the hearing of the appeal proper.

As an alternative to the above procedure, if the Registrar of Criminal Appeals, after preliminary consideration of the grounds of appeal, considers that the appeal has a prima facie chance of success he may by-pass the single judge procedure, grant legal aid himself and list the application for leave to appeal for hearing by the full court. He will notify the prosecution and invite them to be represented and the court will then, whilst considering the issue of leave to appeal, usually treat the application for leave as the hearing of the substantive appeal.

12.4.1 THE HEARING OF THE APPEAL

At the hearing of an appeal against conviction the Court of Appeal will listen to argument and may exceptionally hear fresh evidence under s. 23 of the Criminal Appeal Act 1968 if that evidence:

(a) appears likely to be credible; and

(b) would have been admissible at the trial on indictment; and

(c) it was not adduced at the trial on indictment but there is a reasonable explanation for failure to adduce it.

Thereafter, whether or not there is fresh evidence, the court will determine the appeal in accordance with s. 2 of the Criminal Appeal Act 1968, as amended by the Criminal Appeal Act 1995, which provides simply that:

(a) it may quash the conviction and, in effect, enter a verdict of acquittal;

(b) it may quash the conviction and order a retrial;

(c) it may dismiss the appeal.

Accordingly the test now is simply whether the conviction is unsafe. If, despite the fact that there is merit in some of the points raised on appeal, the Court of Appeal comes to the conclusion that it would have made no difference to the outcome in the hands of a properly directed jury, the conviction may be affirmed. If it concludes that the original trial was flawed in some way, whether by misdirection by the trial judge, wrong application of the law or as the case may be, or in cases where new evidence has been discovered which the court feels ought to be considered by a jury together with the original evidence, it may direct retrial. Although until recently it was only likely to direct retrial if very little time had passed so that the memories of the other witnesses would be relatively fresh, recent cases would seem to indicate that the court is now willing to direct retrial even when some years have gone by (as in the recent Sara Thornton case). Only therefore, if for some reason a retrial would be unfair or inappropriate is the court likely simply to quash the conviction.

12.4.2 APPEALS AGAINST SENTENCE

An appeal to the Court of Appeal is also possible against sentence and the leave of the court is always required. It will be necessary at the hearing of the appeal to indicate that the trial judge erred on a matter of principle; that the sentence is manifestly excessive; or that the sentence was wrong in law in some respect. Simply that the Court of Appeal might have imposed a different sentence within the appropriate range will not be sufficient for an appeal against sentence to succeed. The Court of Appeal does not have the power to *increase* the sentence imposed by the court below by virtue of s. 11(3) of the Criminal Appeal Act 1968. This should however be distinguished from the relatively rare cases where the Attorney-General considers that the offender was dealt with unduly leniently in which case he may refer the sentence to the Court of Appeal for review under s. 36 of the Criminal Justice Act 1988. In that specific case the Court of Appeal *does* have the power to increase the sentence.

12.5   Appeals to the House of Lords

Under s. 33 of the Criminal Appeal Act 1968, either prosecution or defence may appeal to the House of Lords from a decision of the Criminal Division of the Court of Appeal provided:

(a) the Court of Appeal certifies that the decision involves a point of law of general public importance; and

(b) either the Court of Appeal or the House of Lords gives leave to appeal. Such application for leave to appeal should be made immediately after the court's decision or at the latest within 14 days of the decision.

PART II
THE EUROPEAN CONVENTION ON
HUMAN RIGHTS

PART II
THE EUROPEAN CONVENTION ON HUMAN RIGHTS

THIRTEEN

THE EUROPEAN CONVENTION ON HUMAN RIGHTS

13.1   European Law

The importance of the European Union in a criminal law context ought to be understood by a competent criminal lawyer and the differing functions of the relevant institutions appreciated. Although the European Court of Justice has no real competence in criminal matters, its sphere of activity being confined largely to economic aspects, sometimes it may be possible to challenge criminal procedures or penalties because they might be held to be in some way inimical to the basic economic purposes of the European Union. Thus, to take a relatively mundane example, in Case C–193/95 *Criminal Proceedings against Skanavi and another* (1996) *The Times*, 8 March 1996 the European Court of Justice held that for Germany to impose a penalty of imprisonment on a driver who had failed, contrary to German law to exchange his home country's driving licence for a German driving licence within a year of taking up residence in Germany, was grossly disproportionate to the gravity of the offence and provided a significant fetter on the rights of free movement of labour.

Other cases which concern matters of criminal law have involved the courts considering the right to order deportation of community nationals from one State of the European Union to another (see, e.g., *R v Bouchereau* [1978] QB 732). In addition, in the case of *R v Kirk* [1985] 1 All ER 452, the Newcastle Upon Tyne Crown Court referred aspects of criminal proceedings to the European Court of Justice. That case decided that an attempt to punish a Danish national for conduct which was not, at the time when he committed it, criminal, under a statute with retrospective effect, was contrary to the basic principles of law acknowledged by the European Community, which expressly had regard to Article 7 of the European Convention on Human Rights (see **13.9.2**).

However, cases where the criminal process will give rise to any issue of community rights will be rare, and we turn now to the much more mainstream aspect of the uses of the European Convention on Human Rights and the organs of the Council of Europe in Strasbourg which have a direct impact upon criminal justice.

13.2   The Council of Europe and the Convention

The Council of Europe is an organisation of European states which is quite independent of the European Union and of any other political or economic body. At the time of writing, the membership is 39 strong and, in order to join, a State must demonstrate that it has a

201

commitment to parliamentary democracy. Applications for membership are outstanding from a number of States which were formerly within the Eastern bloc.

The Council has permanent premises at Strasbourg and is organised into a number of divisions including a Directorate of Legal Affairs much of whose work is involved in the harmonisation of European law in a number of areas. The work of the Council of Europe which has the highest profile, however, is that of the European Commission of Human Rights and the European Court of Human Rights. The purpose of these bodies is to implement the European Convention for the Protection of Human Rights and Fundmental Freedoms ('the Convention').

The Convention was signed by the countries who were then members of the Council of Europe in November 1950. It was intended to be a statement made by the signatory governments who were said to share the common philosophical and democratic traditions of Western Europe.

Article 25 of the Convention provides that:

> *The Commission may receive petitions ... from any person, non-governmental organisation or group of individuals claiming to be the victim of a violation by one of the High Contracting Parties of the rights set forth in this Convention provided that the High Contracting Party against which the complaint has been lodged has declared that it recognises the competence of the Commission to receive such petitions.*

The Convention thus was and remains unique in that, in cases where the contracting parties have accepted the *right of individual petition*, the European Commission and the European Court of Human Rights are given a competence to adjudicate on complaints made by individuals within the jurisdiction of the contracting States, whether those individuals are citizens or aliens, and irrespective of any other international agreement or treaty.

Of the member countries of the Council of Europe, at the time of writing, all but four have ratified the Convention and accepted the right of individual petition. The remaining four are widely expected to ratify in the immediate future. In considering present applications for membership from former Eastern bloc countries, the Council of Europe has made it clear that it will treat new States' willingness to ratify forthwith the European Convention and accept the right of individual petition as a crucial test of commitment to democracy, on which the success of an application for membership will depend.

The Council of Europe, has, for virtually the first time, encountered widespread public criticism throughout Europe in permitting Russia to join the Council at a time when it is, because of the conflicts in part of its territory, arguably unable to comply with the appropriate requirement to observe the human rights of people within its territory.

13.3 The Effect of the Convention

The Convention therefore provides an opportunity for any individual within a member State to challenge the legal or political actions or institutions of the State concerned where he alleges that his rights under the Convention are breached. Apart from this right of individual petition, there is a possibility for applications to be brought *between* States although this has only happened in 18 cases since 1950. The overwhelming majority of applications (more than 30,000 by 1996) are brought by individuals against member States.

The Commission and Court cannot of course strike down national laws as such, but rulings may be given which must inevitably lead to the amendment or repeal of national laws or a change in administrative practices which have been found to have been in conflict with the principles of the Convention. In addition to the change in a State's laws or practices, compensation may be obtained by the individual adversely affected by the original breach.

In principle, a State cannot defy a ruling of the Court and remain a member of the Council of Europe, and the political pressure to remain a member is very strong. Exceptionally, by virtue of Article 15:

> *In time of war or other public emergency threatening the life of the nation, any High Contracting Party may take measures derogating from its obligations under this Convention to the extent strictly required by the exigencies of the situation.*

The effect of this is that if there is a genuine state of emergency a State may obtain a temporary reprieve from implementing a decision of the Court. The United Kingdom for example has made such a derogation in respect of some aspects of police powers in Northern Ireland.

In many of the countries within the Council of Europe, the Convention has been incorporated into their domestic constitutions. The effect of this is that the Convention rights become directly enforceable in the domestic courts of the country in question so that the first port of call for an aggrieved individual is the courts of his own country. Only if no satisfactory redress is obtained there need he take his case to Strasbourg. As is well known this is not the case in the United Kingdom. The status of the Convention in the UK will be discussed below but first it is appropriate to mention the UK's record in proceedings before the Commission and Court.

13.4   The 'League Table'

As is well known, until 1992 the UK had been condemned by the Court for breaches of the Convention on more occasions than any other European State. In 1992 the UK was, however, overtaken by Italy as the worst offender.

The UK's position in the league table is nothing to be proud of but very few would consider that in reality this means that there are wholesale flagrant breaches of human rights occurring on a daily basis as a matter of governmental practice in the UK. Whilst the UK is in many respects arguably an undemocratic society and executive powers are often arbitrary, unaccountable, and exercised in secrecy, it is transparent nonsense to suggest that the human rights of individuals are worse protected in the UK than in, say, Turkey. The UK's unfortunate position in the league table reflects the fact that we have accepted the right of individual petition for several decades, whereas other member States of the Council of Europe have accepted the right of individual petition only relatively recently (e.g., as in the cases of Malta and Turkey).

Moreover, it is possible for States, when indicating that they will acknowledge the right of individual petition to incorporate into the declaration reservations under Article 64 of the Convention in respect of some aspect of their activities. Thus, for example, Turkey has made such a reservation in respect of matters to do with its armed forces. Whilst no doubt the conduct of the Turkish armed forces may be a byword for tolerant civility and good manners, it is self-evident that if a State puts a major area of its potentially contentious activities beyond the scope of applications under the Convention then its problems will be reduced.

In addition, if one prepares a different league table based on successful applications per capita of population then a very different position is shown. On this league table the UK does not come at the top, first place being contested by Austria, Switzerland and Belgium. Regard must also be had to the competence of national lawyers in their imaginative uses of the Convention. There is no doubt that there is presently a high level of awareness in the UK of the potential of using the Convention as a further avenue of appeal. Press reports indicate that disgruntled complainants about almost every aspect of English life, legal or administrative, claim to be 'taking their cases to the European Court' although the press reports, and indeed the disgruntled parties themselves, are usually unclear about whether they mean the European Court of Justice or the European Court of Human Rights. The fact, moreover, that the Convention is not directly applicable in the UK courts whereas it is in other countries means that disputes involving the rights guaranteed under the Convention inevitably take place on a European stage in UK cases, whereas they may well be litigated to a satisfactory conclusion in the domestic courts of those countries which have incorporated the Convention into their domestic law. (See also 13.12 below.)

13.5 The Status of the Convention

A much discussed current question is the extent to which the Convention affects English law directly. The use of the Convention as an aid to interpretation of English authorities or to resolve problems of conflicting authorities in the common law has been problematic. Thus in an early case, *Ostreicher* v *Secretary of State for the Environment* [1978] 1 All ER 591, the High Court said that one article of the Convention '... was of little assistance ... it is in vague terms'. The Convention was better received by Lord Denning in *R* v *Chief Immigration Officer Heathrow Airport ex parte Salamat Bibi* [1976] 3 All ER 843:

The position as I understand it is that if there is any ambiguity in our statutes or uncertainty in our law, then the courts can look to the Convention as an aid to clear up the ambiguity and uncertainty ... but I would dispute altogether that the Convention is part of our law.

Later, in *Ahmad* v *ILEA* [1978] QB 36 he said:

The Convention is not part of our English law but ... we will always have regard to it. We will do our best to see that our decisions are in conformity with it. But it is drawn in such vague terms that it can be used for all sorts of unreasonable claims and provoke all sorts of litigation. As so often happens with high sounding principles they may have to be brought down to earth. They have to be applied in a work-a-day world.

The status of the Convention has been partly resolved in the context of statutory interpretation by the House of Lords in *R* v *Secretary of State for the Home Office ex parte Brind* [1991] 1 AC 696. The House of Lords held that, although in general terms in construing domestic legislation which was ambiguous in that it was capable of a meaning which either conformed to or conflicted with the Convention the courts would presume that Parliament intended to legislate in conformity with the Convention, there was no corresponding presumption that, as a matter of domestic law, the courts would review the exercise of an administrative discretion on the basis that such discretion had to be exercised in conformity with the Convention. Accordingly, the Convention could not be a source of rights and obligations in English law and resort could not be had to it for the purpose of construction unless there was an obvious ambiguity in the relevant statute. In the Court of Appeal in that case the Convention received an even less warm reception, Lord Donaldson indicating that it was up to the government of the day whether or not to ensure that new statute law was consistent with the Convention and Ralph Gibson LJ indicating that a court should only apply the English rules of construction of statutes and that only if no ordinary rule of construction assisted could the Convention be used.

The Convention received a somewhat warmer reception in *Derbyshire County Council* v *Times Newspapers Ltd* [1993] AC 534, where the House of Lords referred to Article 10 of the Convention (which guarantees freedom of speech) but noted with satisfaction that the common law was consistent with the Convention in any event.

Despite these cases the Convention continues to be cited with enthusiasm by some judges as at least a highly persuasive authority. For example, the Court of Appeal in *Middlebrook*

Mushrooms Ltd v *Transport and General Workers Union* [1993] ICR 612 adverted favourably to Article 10 of the Convention in support of their judgment notwithstanding that that article had not been relied on by either party in the appeal.

More recently the House of Lords has acknowledged that in cases which depend to some extent on the consideration of 'human rights' as an element within the decision-making process some consideration of the status of the Convention may legitimately be undertaken. Thus, in *R* v *Secretary of State for the Home Department ex parte Launder* (1997) *The Times*, 26 May the House of Lords took account of the Convention whilst upholding a decision made by the Home Secretary that there would not be a breach of the Convention in permitting the government of Hong Kong to extradite a man for trial on corruption charges, it having been contended that the fact that he would stand his trial at a time when the People's Republic of China had taken over Hong Kong did not mean he could not be guaranteed a fair trial.

In 1996 the status of the Convention was subject to further considerable comment in the British press following the decision of the Court of Human Rights in the case of *Ernest Saunders* v *United Kingdom* (Case–43/1994/490/572). In this case the court held that statements obtained under compulsion by Inspectors of the Department of Trade and Industry investigating the notorious Guinness takeover were obtained in breach of the Convention in that the right not to incriminate oneself lies at the heart of a proper criminal procedure, and applies to all types of criminal proceedings. Consequently, when such statements were used at Ernest Saunders' subsequent criminal trial there was an infringement of his right not to incriminate himself.

It may be noted, however, that this decision was less far-reaching than had perhaps been hoped by the appellant. In particular, it certainly does not open any further way for an appeal to the Criminal Division of the Court of Appeal in respect of his conviction nor can it necessarily be argued by implication that the provisions in ss. 34–37 of the Criminal Justice and Public Order Act 1994 which could be said to compel, in effect, an accused to answer police questions at the risk of adverse inferences being drawn at trial, are necessarily in contravention of Article 6 of the Convention.

An earlier important case concerning a similar point was that of *John Murray* v *United Kingdom* ((Case–18731/91), January 1996) in which the applicant's complaint concerned provisions in the Criminal Evidence (Northern Ireland) Order 1988 which affect the right to silence. Perhaps, bearing in mind the similarity of these provisions to those in ss. 34–37 of the Criminal Justice and Public Order Act 1994, the UK government thought this case so important that it chose to be represented by the Attorney-General in person in the Strasbourg proceedings. In the event, the outcome of the case was somewhat fudged, the Euorpean Court of Human Rights deciding that Murray's rights had been breached in respect of his being refused legal advice when in custody, but that provisions permitting adverse inferences to be drawn from the defendant's silence do not inevitably involve a breach of the Convention (i.e., Article 6 of the Convention which provides for a presumption of innocence). The decision was somewhat suprising in view of clear precedent to the contrary in the earlier jurisprudence of the Court, but it was no doubt a welcome relief to the UK government which might anticipate some success in any case brought by applicants from the UK claiming that ss. 34–37 of the 1994 Act are in breach of the Convention.

13.6 The Style of the Convention

Although British lawyers played a prominent part in its drafting, the Convention is drafted in a somewhat 'European style' as Lord Denning's earlier criticism indicates. Thus, for example, Article 8 of the Convention prescribes:

> *(1) Everyone has the right to respect for his private and family life, his home and his correspondence.*

(2)   *There shall be no interference by a public authority with the exercise of this right except such as is in accordance with the law and is necessary in a democratic society in the interests of national security, public safety or the economic well being of the country, for the prevention of disorder or crime, for the protection of health or morals, or for the protection of the rights and freedoms of others.*

This comprehensive article, usually described as the 'right of privacy' article, has provoked a vast volume of applications to the European Commission of Human Rights in matters to do with, inter alia, telephone tapping; a claimed right to privacy; illegal search; abortion; the refusal of abortion; the right to a homosexual relationship; the right to refuse medical examination; the right to refuse blood testing; contraception; the refusal of contraception; divorce; custody; child care; immigration; deportation; and in a large number of cases to do with the rights of prisoners, including the right to refuse to wear prison clothing, to receive daily visits and to free correspondence. The article is so widely framed both in the statement of the right and in the acceptable derogation from it as to appear not much more than a pious exhortation. It is so wide that it is meaningless in the strict sense that no individual would know whether his own case was within or outside the protection conferred but for the very considerable jurisprudence which the Commission and Court have developed in applying the article.

In general, however, when construing Article 8 or any other article, it is fair to say that rights which are guaranteed in the Convention are to be construed in the broadest sense and any restrictions on those rights in the narrowest. Thus it is always for a State which maintains that a particular restriction is necessary under Article 8(2) (or any other article) to demonstrate why that is so and to show that the restriction on the right is proportional to the mischief envisaged. This is clearly likely to be a nice balance.

13.7   Procedure under the Convention

The most important kind of case brought under the Convention is an individual application against a member State. An application must be sent in writing and is usually initially by letter; thereafter an application form is sent to the applicant or his representative and the application is registered. A report is then prepared by the Secretariat of the Commission of Human Rights and presented by a member of the Commission (the rapporteur) to the Commission itself or sometimes to a committee of three members. There will then be an opportunity for the respondent government to provide written observations. The extent to which an individual rapporteur takes an active role or is content to leave matters to the Commission's full-time legal secretariat will vary. If the rapporteur considers that there appears to be some merit in the application, the secretariat prepare a summary of the facts including a section dealing with the 'relevant domestic law and practice' and possibly a set of questions that the rapporteur suggests be posed to the State in question.

The Commission, or a chamber of seven members, will often deal with a relatively large number of applications at a single sitting. When deciding whether an individual application is *admissible* the Chamber will consider four important aspects, namely:

(a)   An application must not be *incompatible* and thus only the rights guaranteed by the provisions of the Convention can be invoked. Thus in past case law it has been established that the Convention does not provide, e.g., a right to a university degree; a right to asylum; a right to start a business; a general right to free legal aid; a right to a passport; or the right to a promotion. Nonetheless one must also bear in mind that although no article protects any of the aforementioned rights, a right which is not set forth expressly in the Convention may still be protected indirectly via one of the provisions in it. Thus, for example, although the Convention does not recognise a right to a pension, violation of an existing right to a pension may be contrary to Article 1 of the First Protocol, in which the right to enjoyment of possessions is protected.

(b) An applicant must have sufficient locus standi, that is he must in some sense be a victim of the act complained of and not merely an officious bystander who would like administrative practices or legal rulings changed as a point of principle. The Commission has however given a generous construction to the concept of 'indirect' victim, e.g., the complaint of a mother about the treatment of her detained son (Y v Austria (Case–898/60)) and even someone who complained that a perfectly lawful act by a Convention country might expose him to a breach of the Convention outside Europe has been held to have locus standi (Kirkwood v United Kingdom (Case–10479/83), where the applicant was objecting to extradition to California where he would be likely to receive the death sentence). Although the Convention expressly permits the death penalty, Kirkwood successfully argued that the 'death row' phenomenon of excessive delay would constitute inhuman and degrading treatment contrary to Article 3.

(c) By virtue of Article 26: 'The Commission may only deal with the matter after all domestic remedies have been exhausted, ... and within a period of six months from the date on which the final decision was taken'. We shall now consider both elements of this principle:

   (i) 'Exhausting domestic remedies'. This rule in essence means that an applicant must have taken his case to the highest relevant tribunal or administrative authority in the country concerned before he may even commence proceedings in Strasbourg. Thus there may well have been a very considerable delay whilst a case is taken to the highest court of appeal. It is fair to say that respondent governments commonly and quite shamelessly take the preliminary point that the appellant has not exhausted every conceivable route of appeal and challenge through all the judicial and administrative processes available. In one case which the writer observed in Strasbourg, which had to do with the improper revocation of a planning permission thus depriving the owner of the land affected of a substantial sum of money, the respondent government complained before the Commission (and repeated its complaint before the Court) that the applicant had not exhausted domestic remedies because there were no less than eight alternative routes through the various judicial and administrative planning appeal processes in the country concerned, and the applicant had only exhausted five of them. (The Court considered this spurious.) It is fair to say that latterly the Commission and Court have taken a more relaxed view of this requirement and have said in particular in the case of Cardot v France (Case–24/1990/215/277) that this requirement must be applied with some degree of flexibility and without excessive formalism. Thus the unavailability of legal aid for an appeal or the existence of binding case law against an appellant from the highest court in the country (see also Boschet v Belgium (Case–10835/84)) have been held to be adequate reasons not to have attempted to take the case to the very highest tribunal.

   (ii) 'The application must have been submitted within a period of six months from the date on which the final national decision was taken.' This means the decision of the highest court or highest administrative body. Occasionally however there is no available administrative challenge. For example, in the case of Christians Against Racism and Fascism v United Kingdom (Case–8440/78) the applicants complained about a regulation prohibiting public processions during a certain period. The Commission decided that as there was no way of challenging that regulation before any court the relevant date was the date when the applicants were actually affected by the measure concerned.

(d) An application must not be 'manifestly ill-founded'. This ground of inadmissibility really indicates that the Commission is a filtering mechanism. The word 'manifestly' is clearly a nonsense because many of the cases which have been rejected as 'manifestly ill-founded' are very close to the borderline indeed and certainly could have gone either way. In many cases the Commission does not differentiate very sharply between the question of manifestly ill-founded and the question of incompatibility with the Convention and the case law is far from consistent.

13.7.1 THE PROCEDURE AFTER AN APPLICATION HAS BEEN DECLARED ADMISSIBLE

After the Commission has declared an application admissible, it subjects the complaint therein to an examination of the merits. The application is initially examined by a rapporteur and there will be an attempt to try to achieve a 'friendly settlement' which shows respect for human rights. Often this involves a monetary payment with or without an amendment to the domestic legal order. The parties are invited to make written observations and subsequently to submit oral arguments at one or several hearings. Usually these will be supplementary rather than essential because the fundamental arguments will have been put forward during the admissibility stage. At such a hearing any member of the Commission may, with the consent of the President, put questions to the parties.

Article 31 of the Convention provides:

If a solution is not reached, the Commission shall draw up a report on the facts and state its opinion as to whether the facts found disclose a breach by the State concerned of its obligations under the Convention.

Thus if a friendly settlement is not obtained the Commission will give its decision in an 'Article 31' report.

13.7.2 THE PERSONNEL OF THE COURT AND COMMISSION

The European Commission is comprised of a number of members, one from each of the Convention countries. They are in effect nominated by their member governments although there is a notional election by the 'Committee of Ministers' that is the foreign ministers of each of the member States or their deputies. The members of the Commission are elected for a period of six years but may be re-elected. The members are invariably lawyers and although each country nominates one, the members of the Commission are most certainly *not* there to put the case for their own country. Indeed, on appointment, members of the Commission must swear an oath that they: 'will exercise their powers and duties honourably, impartially and conscientiously'.

The members of the Court 'shall be of high moral character and must either possess the qualification required for appointment to High Judicial office or be jurisconsults of recognised competence'. Members of the Court are elected for a period of nine years but may be re-elected. Whereas the Commission works in Strasbourg full-time, members of the Court work only part-time, typically about ten days each month. There is no requirement for a member State to appoint its own nationals as its chosen judge and indeed Liechtenstein for some years has appointed a Canadian academic as its judge, the rest of Liechtenstein lawyers presumably being fully engaged in secreting the assets of sundry Third World despots.

All Article 31 reports are forwarded to the Committee of Ministers which is an organ of the Council of Europe which has certain functions under the Convention and is comprised of foreign ministers of the member States or their deputies. The case may within three months be sent to the Court by the Commission or by a government involved. If the case is not sent to the Court the Committee of Ministers will pass a resolution as to whether or not the Convention has been violated and compensation can be awarded at this stage. This procedure is however extremely rare, and what we shall consider is the procedure when the case comes to the Court.

Before the case goes before the Court there is often a further exchange of 'memorials' (i.e., written submissions) and there is then an oral hearing. The Court has a registrar who deals with preliminary procedural matters and convenes the hearing. The Rules of Procedure specify that there shall be nine judges chosen by lot, in addition to the President (who is currently from Norway), and the judge from the member State affected. In addition, the Rules require the selection of a further four judges who sit on the substitute's bench, receive the papers and are ready to step in if any of the principal judges cease to be available. They do not vote if they are not required as substitutes.

As indicated above, the judge from the State concerned is expected to exercise an impartial jurisdiction, and is most assuredly not there to look after the interests of his own country but to provide the other judges with any necessary expertise about his domestic legal system.

Exceptionally, if the case before the court raises one or more serious questions affecting the interpretation of the Convention, the chamber may relinquish jurisdiction in favour of the plenary court and indeed may even do so after proceedings have ceased.

The court sits in a semi-circular formation in the exciting new British designed 'Human Rights Building' which resembles a giant saucepan, with the President at the centre. The other judges sit in no particular order save that the German judge may well come down the evening before and put his towel over the chair of his choice.

13.7.3   PROCEDURE BEFORE THE COURT

The European Commission attends the hearings — indeed, strictly speaking, it is the Commission which is bringing the case to the Court — and acts as a sort of *amicus curiae*, introducing its own findings in the case and making observations upon them and upon any other matter arising. The respondent government is invariably represented by a very senior lawyer and the applicant by his own lawyer who may be either a practitioner, or sometimes an academic.

The proceedings are subject to simultaneous translation for the judge by the interpreters of the Court and headphones are also provided for those in the public gallery. The interpreters, whilst technically perfect, all appear to be on secondment from the planet Vulcan and most wear long hair to conceal their pointed ears. They chant their interpretations in a mesmeric robotic way, often in a slight assumed American accent. Even if one speaks French sufficiently to be able to follow the proceedings without interpretation, it remains the best free entertainment in Strasbourg to listen in on the headphones to the English version.

The Court will decide, after representations, on the order of speeches. Because lengthy written submissions are received in advance, speeches are expected to be very brief (typically under half an hour). Usually the proceedings are introduced by the European Commission whose representative will discuss its report; thereafter the applicant will speak and then the respondent government. After that the applicant will usually be given the brief right of reply. The proceedings are thus remarkably swift with very substantial cases being over in under a half day.

Considering that this, in a real sense, is the most important and effective court in the world, the quality of advocacy is extremely variable. Indeed, the writer was told by a member of the staff of the European Court that the reason why so many British cases reach the Court is that the Court likes to see British advocates because of their competence. (The advocates of Holland and Italy were singled out for particularly unfavourable mention.)

The proceedings are somewhat unstructured and the judges exercise little control over the advocates. Often even preliminary facts appear not to have been clearly established and the advocates sometimes lapse into giving evidence themselves. In one case involving Sweden, which the writer observed, the Swedish government's counsel began asserting that the applicant was wrong about some material matter in terms that 'I spoke to the Ombudsman about this only last week and he told me ...'. At a later stage the applicant's representative, an academic lawyer, sought to put in evidence his own Ph.D thesis to demonstrate the essentially fascist nature of the Swedish state.

In cases where compensation for the individual is sought, what happens may vary considerably from case to case. In some cases there appears to have been no pre-hearing discovery or production of documents and very little formal proof of amounts in question, the advocate often merely stating the sum which his client thinks would be fair recompense. Latterly, somewhat more formality has been brought into the proceedings with the advocates being expected to produce some justification for the sums claimed. Nonetheless, matters of quantum which in England might be expected to occupy a court for many hours are often dealt with very briefly, with the court allocating round sum figures for injury to feelings, periods of wrongful imprisonment and the like. Quite often the biggest element in a case, financially speaking, is the claim for costs. Even if legal aid has been granted by the Commission or Court for the proceedings in Strasbourg, legal aid is in fact little more than reimbursement for actual expenses incurred in conducting the proceedings in Strasbourg. There is usually then a supplementary claim for the full legal costs involved. There is no formal taxation process and again the court usually ends up giving round sum figures which are, in the main, far below the amounts claimed by the advocates.

As indicated above, the proceedings are remarkably fast, largely because of the written submissions which precede the hearing. Questions from the judges are rare. The Court invariably reserves its decision.

13.8   Articles of the Convention

The subject matter of the articles of the Convention of major importance are as follows:

(a) Article 2 The right to life.

(b) Article 3 The right not to be subject to torture or inhuman or degrading treatment or punishment.

(c) Article 4 The right not to be held in slavery or servitude or to be required to perform compulsory labour.

(d) Article 5 The right to liberty and security of the person.

(e) Article 6 The right to a fair trial.

(f) Article 7 The right not to be prosecuted retrospectively.

(g) Article 8 The right to respect for private and family life.

(h) Article 9 The right to freedom of thought, conscience and religion.

(i) Article 10 The right to freedom of expression.

(j) Article 11 The right to freedom of peaceful assembly and free association.

(k) Article 12 The right to marry and found a family.

(l) Article 13 The right to an effective remedy before a national authority.

(m) Article 14 The right to have one's other rights under the Convention secured without discrimination on the grounds of sex, race, language, religion, national origin, property or birth.

(n) Protocol 1 The right to peaceful enjoyment of possessions; the right to education; the right to free elections.

13.9 The Convention and Criminal Justice

There is no space in this book to consider the case law under all the articles of the Convention. For the criminal justice system the important articles are Article 13 and Articles 5, 6 and 7. The text of these articles appears below:

Article 5

1. Everyone has the right to liberty and security of person. No one shall be deprived of his liberty save in the following cases and in accordance with a procedure prescribed by law:

(a) the lawful detention of a person after conviction by a competent court;

(b) the lawful arrest or detention of a person for non-compliance with the lawful order of a court or in order to secure the fulfilment of any obligation prescribed by law;

(c) the lawful arrest or detention of a person effected for the purpose of bringing him before the competent legal authority on reasonable suspicion of having committed an offence or when it is reasonably considered necessary to prevent his committing an offence or fleeing after having done so;

(d) the detention of a minor by lawful order for the purpose of educational supervision or his lawful detention for the purpose of bringing him before the competent legal authority;

(e) the lawful detention of persons for the prevention of the spreading of infectious diseases, of persons of unsound mind, alcoholics or drug addicts or vagrants;

(f) the lawful arrest or detention of a person to prevent his effecting an unauthorised entry into the country or of a person against whom action is being taken with a view to deportation or extradition.

2. Everyone who is arrested shall be informed promptly, in a language which he understands, of the reasons for his arrest and of any charge against him.

3. Everyone arrested or detained in accordance with the provisions of paragraph 1(c) of this Article shall be brought promptly before a judge or other officer authorised by law to exercise judicial power and shall be entitled to trial within a reasonable time or to release pending trial. Release may be conditioned by guarantees to appear for trial.

4. Everyone who is deprived of his liberty by arrest or detention shall be entitled to take proceedings by which the lawfulness of his detention shall be decided speedily by a court and his release ordered if the detention is not lawful.

5. Everyone who has been the victim of arrest or detention in contravention of the provisions of this Article shall have an enforceable right to compensation.

Article 6

1. In the determination of his civil rights and obligations or of any criminal charge against him, everyone is entitled to a fair and public hearing within a reasonable time by an independent and impartial tribunal established by law. Judgment shall be pronounced publicly but the press and public may be excluded from all or part of the trial in the interest of morals, public order or national security in a democratic society, where the interests of juveniles or the protection of the private life of the parties so require, or to the extent strictly necessary in the opinion of the court in special circumstances where publicity would prejudice the interests of justice.

2. Everyone charged with a criminal offence shall be presumed innocent until proved guilty according to law.

3. Everyone charged with a criminal offence has the following minimum rights:

(a) to be informed promptly, in a language which he understands and in detail, of the nature and cause of the accusation against him;

(b) to have adequate time and facilities for the preparation of his defence;

(c) to defend himself in person or through legal assistance of his own choosing or, if he has not sufficient means to pay for legal assistance, to be given it free when the interests of justice so require;

(d) to examine or have examined witnesses against him and to obtain the attendance and examination of witnesses on his behalf under the same conditions as witnesses against him;

(e) to have the free assistance of an interpreter if he cannot understand or speak the language used in court.

Article 7

1. No one shall be held guilty of any criminal offence on account of any act or omission which did not constitute a criminal offence under national or international law at the time when it was committed. Nor shall a heavier penalty be imposed than the one that was applicable at the time the criminal offence was committed.

2. This Article shall not prejudice the trial and punishment of any person for any act or omission which, at the time when it was committed, was criminal according to the general principles of law recognised by civilised nations.

Article 13

Everyone whose rights and freedoms as set forth in this Convention are violated shall have an effective remedy before a national authority notwithstanding that the violation has been committed by persons acting in an official capacity.

13.9.1   ARTICLE 13

It is worth dealing first with Article 13 which *appears* to be of vital general importance.

It provides that there should be an effective remedy before a national authority even if the violation of the Convention has been committed by persons acting in an official capacity. In short this requires a national political system to have effective courts or other bodies capable of making decisions and providing remedies for violations. Article 13 is usually seen as ancillary to other violations of the Convention and very often in cases where breaches of Article 13 with some other article have been brought, if there is a finding of a violation of that other article, the court does not go on to consider Article 13. Thus, for example, in the case of *Malone* v *United Kingdom* (judgment 26 April 1984; A95) which had to do with unlawful telephone tapping and a violation of Article 8, the Court, having found that there was a violation of Article 8, did not go on to consider the violation of Article 13 alleged.

A further problem is the question of whether Article 13 guarantees a remedy which allows a contracting State's laws to be challenged before a national authority on the ground of being contrary to the Convention. The case of *Leander* v *Sweden* (judgment of 26 March 1986; A116) decided, in a very confusing judgment, that Article 13 does not guarantee any such remedy and therefore it is not incumbent upon member States to provide mechanisms for adjudication on Convention rights within their domestic legal systems. Article 13 viewed alone is therefore virtually without effect.

13.9.2   ARTICLE 7

We will now turn to the articles more directly relevant to criminal justice, taking first Article 7. This appears relatively uncontroversial and provides a prohibition on retrospective prosecution in respect of acts which were not criminal at the time that they were committed. A good example of the way in which the Court deals with such matters is the case of *R* v *R* [1992] 1 AC 599 under which the crime of marital rape was on one view 'created' after centuries during which it was not a crime. In that case the Law Lords held that the historic exemption which provided that a husband incurred no criminal liability for raping his wife should be conclusively removed (this case law development was in due course overtaken by the Criminal Justice and Public Order Act 1994 which redefined rape so as to remove the marital exemption). However, it was a cogent argument on behalf of the applicant that as marital rape was not a crime until he was convicted of it, and that was affirmed by the Law Lords, he was being punished retrospectively for conduct which was not criminal when he committed it. On the face of it his success in the European Court of Human Rights would have appeared assured under Article 7, but matters under the Convention are rarely so straight-forward. One possible hurdle for the applicant would have been Article 7(2) which provides that 'this Article shall not prejudice the trial and punishment of any person for any act or omission, which at the time when it was committed, was criminal according to the general principles of law recognised by civilised nations'. When the case was argued in the European Court of Human Rights on 20 June 1995, counsel for the UK government, perhaps curiously, chose not to attempt to rely on the saving provision in Article 7(2) which would have led to a debate as to what 'civilised nations', whoever they may be, thought to be the position about marital rape. Rather the UK government argued the case on the basis that the common law was constantly developing and that at the time of his action the husband involved could not possibly have believed that the circumstances of his forced intercourse with his wife were lawful. To the writer's surprise this argument was upheld by the judgment of the Court given in November 1995 which concluded that the common law must be allowed to develop and that the UK government's position on this was a proper one, namely that given the surrounding circumstances the applicant could not have believed in the lawfulness of what he was doing and was properly convicted and punished for it, notwithstanding the apparent centuries-old law which prevented husbands from being convicted for raping their wives (to which, as the UK government pointed out, a number of common law exceptions had developed in any event over the years).

The Court rejected the applicant's apparently powerful argument that he could not have predicted that his conduct was criminal given that, in reported cases even after the occasion on which he had raped his wife, High Court judges in the United Kingdom had continued to uphold the historic 'marital exemption'.

13.9.3   ARTICLE 5

Article 5 deals with the right to liberty and security for the person and allows six different situations where that right may be restricted. Not surprisingly, the right to restrict liberty after conviction and while on remand pending trial are the most important provisions. In relation to the latter there are limits on the power to remand in custody, which is permitted only 'when it is reasonably considered necessary to prevent his committing an offence or fleeing after having done so'. Thus in decided cases the Commission and Court frequently had to consider such matters as reasonableness of grounds for arrest; length of detention on remand; the imposition of restrictions or conditions on bail. The rights in the article are further enforced by Article 5(3) which guarantees a right to be brought before a judge for a trial within a reasonable time or to release pending trial. The case law shows that even in the case of detention for remarkably long periods, no breach of the Convention may exist. Some of these delays are quite extraordinary by English standards, remands in custody of up to four years having been found acceptable on various grounds including the complexity of the case and the difficulties of collecting evidence. The reasoning in these decisions, which naturally reflect the domestic legal experience of the relevant members of the Commission or Court, appear highly questionable given that Article 6 provides a presumption of innocence until conviction.

It must however be conceded that, in balancing the various factors and the interests of continuity in the criminal justice systems in its many different States, the Commission and Court have been faced with an extremely difficult task. As a balance of what is politically acceptable and what is achievable it does nonetheless sometimes seem that the Commission and Court have shrunk from a proper application of the Convention. If even within the much criticised British criminal justice system it is possible to have a section of a statute (s. 22, Prosecution of Offences Act 1985) which in principle guarantees a period of no longer than 182 days between first appearance in the magistrates' court and commencement of Crown

Court trial, then there is no reason why that as a norm should not be sought elsewhere. In the UK the prosecution do of course have the right to apply to extend these time limits, but at least there is then a judicial process for investigating the merits of delay.

This criticism of the case law under the Convention must however be subject to the consideration that the greatest single group of all applications to the European Commission are persons involved in the criminal justice process who often see such applications as a further route of appeal, or just an opportunity to embarrass the officers of the criminal justice system concerned. Many such applications are utterly frivolous but still require a good deal of work from the Commission at the preliminary stage.

The other relevant parts of Article 5 need no further discussion. The Commission and Court have been inclined to accept that 'the right to have the lawfulness of deprivation of liberty by arrest or detention decided speedily and by a court' is susceptible of a wide variety of interpretations throughout the member countries and there is certainly no requirement that an accused on remand need be produced at frequent intervals to a court for them to reconsider his position. Nothing in the English criminal justice system is likely to offend these provisions.

13.9.4   ARTICLE 6

It is Article 6 which contains the most important and wide-ranging provisions governing the criminal trial. This article is closely modelled on the Sixth Amendment to the Constitution of the United States of 1791 but is rather more extensive than that amendment. When framing this article in particular, the authors of the Convention obviously faced enormous practical and theoretical problems. The eventual text needed to be a minimum statement of the rights of persons in the criminal justice system having regard to the very different conditions prevailing in Europe in 1950. It also required the accommodation of the different legal traditions of all the original signatories to the Convention. The principle that the proper purpose of criminal justice is to apprehend, convict and punish criminals is not a controversial one. Nonetheless the differences in procedures and indeed substantive law throughout Europe in ensuring this reasonable objective are considerable. These differences were a very important constraint on the degree of precision with which the relevant articles of the Convention could be drafted and thus the Convention does not deal at all with a number of very central matters.

In particular there is no consideration of what 'crimes' are as such. The Court has always held it inappropriate for it to decide whether a certain activity should or should not be criminalised in an individual country provided that there is no attempt merely to sidestep the Convention (e.g., by reclassifying the matter concerned so as to give what is really being prosecuted as a crime, the appearance of a civil or administrative dispute, for example between an individual and a local authority by a change in nomenclature).

The regimes in particular in the case of 'victimless' crimes such as drugs, prostitution, pornography, gambling and insider trading vary tremendously throughout the member States with these activities attracting substantial penalties in some and not amounting to crimes at all in others.

13.9.4.1   Criminal procedure in Europe

As is well known, European criminal justice systems have at least one fundamental difference from the common law system.

This is the inquisitorial nature of part of the process; this usually (at least in serious crimes) involves the existence of an *'instruction'* stage during which a dossier on the crime is prepared by a judge, sometimes with his own independent police force under his control with whose assistance he embarks upon an independent investigation. There is little real similarity to the committal process in England. In particular the judge may embark on comprehensive interrogation of the suspect with no lawyer present and no right to silence; may arrange confrontations between the suspect and witnesses or the victim; and can even undertake detailed reconstructions of the crime at the scene, often with the press or even television cameras in attendance. At this stage the rights of the accused appear very different to those in the English process. The nature of remands and criteria for the grant of bail may likewise be dramatically different.

There are equally striking differences in courtroom procedures. The judge usually runs the case and conducts much of the examination of witnesses himself; also the deference traditionally shown by English barristers to judges is usually lacking and it is a considerable culture shock to witness the often open hostility or contempt between the advocates and the sometimes young and inexperienced members of the professional judiciary. The procedures in multi-defendant trials also often contrast dramatically with English trials which are usually split so as to ensure manageable proportions. It would be unthinkable in England, as occurred in Italy in the Red Brigade and Mafiosi trials, that up to 80 defendants would be cooped up in a giant cage at the back of the court, often engaged in what seemed to be some kind of party whilst the proceedings in front of them dragged on for years. Another important difference is the intervention of the so-called 'civil party' (i.e., the victim) who often has the right to be represented at certain stages of the criminal trial and to argue for compensation, or even for a specific penalty to be imposed on the accused.

Courtroom procedure may arguably be a question of style, though inevitably the trier of fact must be influenced by such things. Of greater importance are evidential or procedural rules which must directly bear on the outcome of the trial. Thus for example in many countries the accused's criminal record is brought out at the start of the proceedings and placed before the trier of fact. As will be discussed in **Chapter 20**, complex English rules in the main prevent this happening on the basis that the trier of fact would be so dramatically influenced by his knowledge of the accused's criminal record as to make the so-called 'forbidden connection' between criminal record and present guilt. Similarly the UK system goes to considerable trouble by a variety of procedural rules backed by the ultimate sanction of contempt of court to ensure a minimum of pre-trial publicity. Other jurisdictions (and even the other main common law jurisdiction, the USA) have no such rules and give no attention at all to the risk of eventual jurors being prejudiced, so that press speculation, and worse, about the identity of the malefactor is very common. So for example in a much publicised French case the 'Villemin Affair' to do with the murder of a young boy in France, the Goncourt-prize-winning novelist Marguerite Duras published a novel before the trial had started purporting to describe the crime and naming the murderer. Other extraordinary developments in that case include the fact that the young examining magistrate, whose inexperience was said to have contributed to some of the problems, resigned and wrote a sensational book concerning his view of the case and his admiration for one of the leading suspects in it.

There is a wealth of case law on the application of Article 6 of the Convention and aspects of individual State's criminal justice systems have been subjected to the most minute scrutiny. Although the existence of a proper appeal procedure does not in itself remedy undesirable institutional aspects of a State's legal system, the Court has usually tended to look at the net outcome of the case rather than merely examining the trial at first instance. In considering what is a 'fair trial' the Court applies a variety of concepts, some of which are relatively vague, such as *proportionality* (a balance between remedy and wrong addressed), *equality of arms* (the concept that both parties are entitled to equal rights and adequacy of representation — a matter which cannot be too closely adhered to in some contexts), and *'margin of appreciation'* which allows that member States must have discretions in certain areas, amongst them criminal procedure.

13.9.4.2 Article 6 and the law of evidence

It is clear that the Court will not impugn individual State laws of evidence where these laws have to do with competence of witnesses or the actual assessment of evidence, for example the absence of corroboration requirements. The only strict requirements of Article 6 are 'a fair and public hearing by an independent and impartial tribunal', 'a presumption of innocence', and provisions in Article 6(3) which have to do with proper time to prepare and proper means to conduct a defence.

There is a great deal of case law, some of it confusing and contradictory, about various aspects of the conduct of a trial. Much recent case law has been under Article 6(3)(d) and as to whether the requirement that a person should have the minimum right 'to examine or have examined witnesses against him ...' indicates that hearsay by the production of out-of-court witness statements is inevitably contrary to the Convention. Even the interpretation of this apparently straightforward phrase has given rise to grave difficulties. The court often retreats behind a general formula that 'the assessment of evidence is a matter for national courts' and has declined to rule that statements from absent witnesses are contrary to the Convention (see *Isgro* v *Italy* (Case–1/1990/192/252) and *Asch* v *Austria* (Case–30/1990/221/283)). In other cases on virtually indistinguishable facts the court has held that the introduction of hearsay evidence from out-of-court witnesses was in breach of the Convention (see *Kostovski* v *Netherlands* (Case–10/1988/154/208) and *Unterpertinger* v *Austria* (Case–1985/87/134)).

The difficulty in such cases could again be interpreted as indicating that the Court shrinks from the apparently straightforward application of the clear wording of the Convention, which does indeed seem to prohibit hearsay, in the light of the possible political consequences of interfering so drastically in the criminal justice systems of the many European countries which appear to permit hearsay in the criminal trial (as of course does the United Kingdom under the many exceptions to the hearsay rule, e.g., ss. 23 and 24, Criminal Justice Act 1988).

13.10   The Future of the Court and the Commission

The Council of Europe's institutions have been the victims of their own success to the extent that cases now commonly take more than four years to get to a hearing in the European Court of Human Rights. This is moreover, as will be recalled, after domestic remedies have been exhausted which has the effect of meaning that the Court is often ruling on matters of complaint which happened nearly a decade before. A more streamlined procedure has therefore been under consideration and the text of a working party on this is incorporated in what is now known as the *Vienna Declaration* of 1993. This proposed a merger of the Commission and Court in one full-time body. There is now an 11th Protocol to the Convention designed to bring this into effect within the near future. The precise mechanisms and procedures have not, at the time of writing, been settled and for the immediate future the interrelationship of the Commission and Court will remain as described above.

13.11   Practical Use of the Convention

Challenges to the outcome of English cases are likely to prove increasingly popular. Articles 5 and 6 are both sufficiently vague as to leave a good deal of scope for interpretation and notwithstanding a great deal of case law (though some of it is inaccessible) on criminal justice systems there are usually individual features which make cases distinguishable. At present, legal aid is unlikely to be granted from Strasbourg until a reasonable amount of work has been done on a case and it is apparently the view of the Legal Aid Board that the Green Form cannot be used for work on applications to Strasbourg since such applications are not 'a question of English law'. One is however more likely to receive realistic instructions to take a case to Strasbourg in cases involving public law rights, e.g., under the more general articles such as Articles 8 and 10 where the scope for interpretation is even greater than in the case of criminal justice. Thus, recent cases in Strasbourg have held that the power of English juries to award unlimited libel damages may be a serious infringement of the right of free speech in Article 10; and in *Goodwin* v *UK* (1996) *The Times*, 28 March 1996 (Case–16/1994/463/544) it was held that the conviction of the applicant, a journalist, under s. 10 of the Contempt of Court

Act 1981 for refusing to betray his sources, infringed Article 10 in that the requirement that he disclose his sources was not necessary in a democratic society.

Nonetheless, it may be an important last resort to take a client's case to Strasbourg. In the most high profile of cases this is likely to result, at best, only in a change to the domestic legal order and monetary compensation because the delay in taking cases to Strasbourg is extreme, a period between the wrong complained of and the decision of the Court of several years being the norm. Thus if your client is subject to a period of imprisonment he is most likely to have served his sentence before any ruling is obtained from Strasbourg. The Commission does in fact have the power under rr. 27 and 28 of the Rules of Procedure in urgent cases to give precedence to a particular complaint and under r. 36 to 'indicate to the parties any interim measure the adoption of which seems desirable in the interest of the parties or the proper conduct of the proceedings before it' but this kind of recommendation (which is anyway not legally binding on the contracting States) is most unlikely to be used so as to procure the release from custody of a person pending his application to the Commission and Court.

13.12 Incorporation of the Convention into UK Law

The government has announced its intention to incorporate the Convention into English law, an intention which has the support of a number of eminent judges. The government has indicated that it will do this in a gradual way and after appropriate consultation. It is therefore safe to assume that in the academic year 1997/98 the Convention will not be incorporated in any workable way.

Whilst incorporation of the Convention has a number of significant advantages, in particular that the number of cases going through to Strasbourg may be substantially diminished by the fact that applicants can have the Convention taken into account before the UK courts, it must be realised that ultimately one cannot stop people who have exhausted their domestic remedies before the UK courts (even when the Convention has been considered and applied in the courts' decisions) carrying on with their cases to Strasbourg. Thus there will inevitably be perceived to be a further stage of appeal, even beyond the House of Lords.

In the end therefore nothing could stop a determined litigant from continuing with his case if he wanted to contend that the UK courts have misapplied the provisions of the Convention or taken it into account in some inadequate way.

It is suggested that incorporation of the Convention may lead to a number of difficulties which may well have an impact on the decision-making of the ordinary courts. Reference has already been made to the extreme generality of the way in which the Convention is drafted and one can only guess as to how a district judge, recorder or circuit judge is going to react when invited to consider the effect of individual articles of the Convention. Quite apart from those articles which are very wide-ranging and general, such as Article 8, it cannot be long before judges in the criminal courts are urged to take account of Article 6(3)(d) and exclude all hearsay evidence tendered by the prosecution on the basis of the clear wording of that article and the authority of cases like *Kostovski* and *Unterpertinger* (see **13.9.4.2**). What the reaction of such judges will be when invited to consider a plethora of Strasbourg case law remains to be seen. No doubt some of these issues will be addressed during the consultation period leading up to the gradual incorporation of the Convention.

PART III
CRIMINAL EVIDENCE

FOURTEEN

THE LAW OF EVIDENCE (1)

14.1   Introduction

The law of evidence as we know it today has come from a body of rules formulated by the common law judges of the 18th and 19th centuries, followed by a number of radical but piecemeal statutory reforms, in particular: the Criminal Evidence Act 1898; the Police and Criminal Evidence Act 1984; the Criminal Justice Act 1988 and the Criminal Justice and Public Order Act 1994.

The law of evidence has many aspects which today appear inconsistent or even bizarre and which originally came about for two reasons. The first of these was that, unbelievable though it now seems, the accused himself was not usually allowed to give evidence at his own trial until 1898. He would thus be faced with accusations which, in the draconian criminal climate of the 18th and 19th centuries, might lead to the death penalty for relatively minor offences, but he would not be allowed to testify against his accusers. A number of procedural and evidential rules were therefore adopted to protect the accused in that situation.

The second reason for some of the stranger rules is that a criminal trial takes place, as it has for centuries, before a jury of laymen who are the ultimate tribunal of fact. Because of the supposed inability of an inexperienced jury to evaluate certain kinds of evidence, complex rules were adopted which prevented certain kinds of evidence being put before a jury because the superficial attractiveness of such kinds of evidence would be too unreliable or prejudicial to the accused.

The result of this is that even today certain kinds of evidence are excluded although a layman would consider them highly relevant, or even virtually conclusive to showing guilt or innocence. Thus, complex rules generally prevent the prosecution bringing in evidence of an accused's previous record even where the criminal record is for offences which are similar to the present crime. Likewise, hearsay evidence is usually excluded even if it is of a relatively compelling kind, unless some specific exception to the hearsay rule permits it. This latter rule may in fact prejudice an accused rather than help him because in principle the rules of evidence are the same for the accused as they are for the prosecution; thus in general an accused is no more entitled to introduce evidence of hearsay than is the prosecution.

In this chapter we shall be considering the rules of criminal evidence mainly as they relate to a Crown Court trial. The rules in relation to magistrates' courts trial are almost the same, with minor exceptions which will be indicated where they arise.

The law of evidence is at its most vital where the person or body deciding on the *facts* is different to the one ruling on the *law*. It is therefore best seen in the context of a criminal trial in the Crown Court where the judge rules on the law, including the admissibility of evidence, and the jury decide what they make of the evidence which is presented to them, i.e. whom they believe. Consequently almost all modern case law of importance is from the Criminal Division of the Court of Appeal, hearing appeals from the Crown Court against alleged errors in rulings by the trial judge.

14.1.1   JUDICIAL CONTROL OF THE EVIDENCE

The judicial control of the evidence to be presented to the jury can be seen at the following stages.

(a)   The judge must apply rules concerning *which* witnesses may testify. Thus there are, e.g., special rules regulating whether children may give evidence, whether the prosecution may insist on the accused's spouse testifying, and so on.

(b)   There are rules concerning *how* witnesses must testify, e.g., about taking oaths and affirmations and about what questions may or may not be asked of the witness. The judge's control of a criminal trial at this stage includes not just the application of rules of law but also of discretionary rules and rules of practice which are very hard to formulate precisely. For instance the judge will permit counsel to cross-examine the opposing party's witnesses, often at great length and very fiercely, but the judge must see when aggressive questioning oversteps the permitted limits and becomes abusive or bullying and intervene to put a stop to it.

(c)   There are rules preventing certain types of evidence altogether, e.g., the well-known rule against hearsay evidence which has the effect that one witness may not testify to the court in terms such as 'X told me he saw the defendant stab the victim'. In some countries this evidence is permitted but the jury are then warned that hearsay may be unreliable, however in the United Kingdom such evidence simply cannot be given at all. Likewise, interesting and apparently relevant though the jury might well find it, no evidence can normally be given of the accused's criminal record, even if it is for similar offences. Because of the law's wariness of untrained jurors' drawing hasty conclusions (e.g., 'he's committed 20 previous burglaries so he's probably done this one') the law simply forbids such evidence.

(d)   If documents are to be used in a case then there are rules about whether and how they may be proved. Documents which are just statements, i.e. a written statement by a witness, usually cannot be used at all — the witness must be brought to court to testify in person. Other documents may be used, e.g., a will, business records or public documents, subject to certain procedures which the judge must rule upon.

(e)   Finally, and perhaps most importantly, the judge's control of the jury is shown when he sums up at the end of the case. Here he must give them firm rulings on points of law, but must tell them that they are the sole judges of matters of fact. He then reminds them (often at very great length) of salient points in all the evidence that they have heard, and as he goes through each witness's testimony he may, within limits, comment on factors which may make that witness more or less credible (e.g., he may point out that the witness had a motive to lie, or was trapped into inconsistencies in cross-examination, or even that he looked shifty and evasive while testifying). The judge must not go too far here and pre-empt the jury's decision, but judges often do contrive, by tones of voice and facial expressions (i.e. things which do not appear on the shorthand writer's official transcript of the summing up) to convey a definite view that a given witness is lying.

As the judicial summing up has evolved, various practices have now become settled rules of law so that a serious error in summing up will inevitably lead to a conviction being quashed on appeal. Judges must in some cases direct juries, often in very technical terms, about certain aspects of the rules of evidence. Thus there must be a clear direction on who has the burden of proof and to what standard; where certain things may have happened during the trial, for example it has become apparent that the accused has lied about an alibi, the judge must carefully warn the jury in certain terms, for example to the effect that innocent people do also invent alibis out of panic and that it does not indicate necessarily that the accused is guilty; if identification evidence by witnesses has been produced, the judge must warn the jury in the clearest terms about the risks of acting on eye-witness evidence of identification in such circumstances; and many other matters must also be specifically dealt with in the summing up.

Where there is a significant error in the judge's control of the evidence, whether on rulings of admissibility or in the course of his summing up, a resulting conviction will be quashed unless the Court of Appeal conclude that the conviction is still safe, i.e. it concludes that despite the error the accused would have been convicted anyway so that no miscarriage of justice has occurred.

14.2 Purpose of the Law of Evidence

The law of evidence has three purposes:

(a) it lays down rules as to what is admissible matter for the purposes of establishing facts in dispute;

(b) it regulates the ways in which such matters can be put before the court;

(c) it lays down rules as to how a judge may, or must, comment on the evidence.

For example, to establish the *actus reus* of a murder by stabbing:

(a) Direct eye-witness evidence is admissible matter; and

(b) It must (usually) be given to the court on oath by the eye-witness himself.

(c) The judge must in summing up remind the jury of what the eye-witness said and may comment on his evidence.

14.3 Burden of Proof and Standard of Proof: Introduction

'Burden of proof' has two main meanings:

(a) It is the duty of the prosecution or plaintiff to persuade the court (*by which is meant the person or persons who tries or try the facts*) by the end of the case of the truth of certain propositions. In this sense, therefore, the burden of proof falls on the party who will lose if at the end of the case the trier of fact is evenly balanced between belief and disbelief. This burden is known as the 'legal burden' or the 'persuasive burden'. The obligation to discharge this burden is expressed in the maxim 'he who asserts must prove'.

(b) Burden can also mean 'the evidential burden'. The evidential burden is also sometimes called 'the burden of passing the judge' and that phrase gives a good description of it. The evidential burden means the burden of satisfying the judge that there is sufficient evidence of a certain matter in order for him to direct the jury about it and treat it as a 'live' issue in the case. It is as well to consider separately how the evidential burden may arise for both prosecution and defence.

14.3.1   THE PROSECUTION'S EVIDENTIAL BURDEN

The prosecution have to prove *actus reus* and *mens rea*. They have to satisfy the jury of both to the usual criminal standard of proof. However matters may never get as far as the jury. The prosecution commences by calling its evidence and if by the end of all its own evidence it has failed to prove the crime sufficiently there will usually be a submission by the defence of 'no case to answer'. At that stage the judge sends the jury out of court and listens to the submission by the defence and the response to it by the prosecution. If he agrees that there is 'no case to answer' he will withdraw the case from the jury and direct an acquittal. The principles for consideration of a submission of 'no case to answer' are contained in *Practice Direction (Submission of No Case)* [1962] 1 WLR 227 as modified by *R v Galbraith* [1981] 1 WLR 1039. Such a submission should be upheld by the judge where:

(a)   there has been no evidence to prove an essential element in the alleged offence, or

(b)   where the judge comes to the conclusion that the prosecution evidence, taken at its highest, is such that a jury properly directed could not properly convict upon it.

In these circumstances it is the judge's duty to stop the case and discharge the defendant. In other cases, however, where the reliability of witnesses has merely been severely shaken it would now seem appropriate, following *Galbraith*, to leave the issue to the jury.

Where such a submission is successful the jury have never had the opportunity to hear the accused's evidence or that of its witnesses, nor has the accused had to make the often difficult decision about whether to testify at all. In other words the prosecution must rely entirely on the evidence which they themselves intend to bring to get past the middle stage of the case and cannot rely on any anticipated assistance they might get from cross-examining the accused if he should decide to testify.

If the prosecution do get past this stage in the case, then they have discharged their evidential burden. The jury are called back into court and the case goes on. The jury are not of course told why they were sent out of the court and the jury do not concern themselves at all with the question of evidential burden which in no way pre-empts or anticipates the eventual verdict of the jury after they have heard all the evidence including any that the defence choose to call.

14.3.2   THE DEFENCE'S EVIDENTIAL BURDEN

In contrast to the evidential burden borne by the prosecution, the defence's evidential burden arises somewhat differently. They do not have to *satisfy* the judge of anything as such. All that the defence have to do is to ensure that there is enough evidence about any defence that is to be raised to enable the judge to direct the jury upon the defence as a live issue. In other words the defence cannot invite the jury merely to speculate that there might have been, for example, provocation, self-defence or accident. There has to be some firm evidence about a defence before the judge will direct the jury in relation to it. This does not in any sense mean that the judge has to *believe* the evidence. There does not need to be very much evidence in support of a defence for a judge to be required to direct the jury on it; if a judge does wrongly withdraw a defence from the jury any resulting conviction is likely to be quashed. All that the judge has to find is that there has been *some* evidence, however flimsy, of a given defence so that he can direct the jury about it. The need to discharge this 'evidential burden' in relation to defence matters does not even mean that the accused must give evidence or call witnesses. Sometimes it is possible to obtain sufficient evidence from cross-examination of prosecution witnesses, e.g., as to the existence of provocation in murder. As we shall subsequently see a defendant must cross-examine prosecution witnesses on any matter in respect of which he disagrees with them and thus he must foreshadow any defence that he is to raise in due course by confronting prosecution witnesses with his version in cross-examination.

Again the jury do not concern themselves with questions of the evidential burden on the defence. Once a judge directs the jury about a defence then it falls within their province and if they find that there is a reasonable doubt as to whether or not the defence is true they should acquit.

14.4 Burden of Proof

The general principle is that the legal burden of proving facts lies on the person who asserts them. This protects the individual accused against the State. He need only answer a charge or claim when a reasonable case has been made out. The general rule therefore is that the prosecution or plaintiff bears the burden since each loses if the trier of fact is evenly balanced at the end of the case.

The leading criminal case is *Woolmington* v *DPP* [1935] AC 462 in which W shot his wife and his defence was accident. The trial judge directed the jury that once they were satisfied that W had pulled the trigger it was for *him* to prove his defence of accident. The Criminal Court of Appeal affirmed the conviction on the basis of this direction. In the House of Lords the conviction was quashed. It was for the prosecution to prove beyond a reasonable doubt both *actus reus* and *mens rea*. The jury did not need to be *satisfied* with the accused's explanation, it was sufficient if they were left in a reasonable doubt as to whether his explanation was true. The accused was entitled to be acquitted if they had such a doubt.

14.4.1 EXCEPTIONS TO THE GENERAL RULE IN CRIMINAL CASES

Normally, as we have seen, the prosecution must adduce sufficient evidence of the accused's guilt by the end of their case; otherwise there will be a submission of 'no case to answer' and the judge will direct an acquittal. The prosecution has to adduce sufficient evidence of actus reus and mens rea as prescribed by the substantive law, but does not have to negative every conceivable defence in advance nor deal with pure speculation.

There are four cases where an accused bears the *legal* burden of satisfying the jury of the *truth* of his defence (on the *civil* standard of proof — see later). The situations are as follows and are all to do with the mental state of the accused, and in practice relevant only on serious charges:

(a) Insanity.

(b) Unfitness to plead.

(c) Insane automatism.

(d) Diminished responsibility under s. 2(2), Homicide Act 1957.

The above exceptional cases are those where the *full legal burden* is borne by the accused. On all other normal defences an accused has only an evidential burden, that is, all he needs to do is raise sufficient evidence to make it appropriate for the judge to direct the jury that there is a live issue about the defence. This applies in cases, for example, of duress, accident, self-defence, provocation, alibi, mistaken identity and the like.

14.4.2   STATUTES AFFECTING THE BURDEN OF PROOF

It is not uncommon for criminal statutes to say that certain facts may be deemed to exist until the contrary is proved. There are many such statutes and the following are examples.

14.4.2.1   Prevention of Corruption Act 1916, s. 2

This provides that if on a charge under the Prevention of Corruption Act 1906, or the Public Bodies Corrupt Practices Act 1889, it is proved that a gift is given or money paid by a person holding or seeking a contract from a government department or public body to an employee of the department or body, the consideration is deemed to be given corruptly unless the contrary is proved. This is therefore an extreme measure because it requires the accused to prove innocent purpose in giving a gift once the fundamental facts, e.g., that the donor holds or seeks a contract from a government department or public body, have been established by the prosecution.

14.4.2.2   Magistrates' Courts Act 1980, s. 101

This provision (the section of the Magistrates' Courts Act 1952 which s. 101 replaced) applied only to magistrates' court cases until it was held in *R* v *Edwards* [1975] QB 27 that it was declaratory of the common law and therefore applied in the Crown Court as well.

Section 101 states:

> *Where the defendant to an information or complaint relies for his defence on any exception, exemption, proviso, excuse or qualification, whether or not it accompanies the description of the offence or matter of complaint in the enactment creating the offence or on which the complaint is founded, the burden of proving the exception, exemption, proviso, excuse or qualification shall be on him; and this notwithstanding that the information or complaint contains an allegation negativing the exception, exemption, proviso, excuse or qualification.*

The effect of this is that where the defendant claims to have a particular licence, permission or qualification to do something which would otherwise be criminal, it is for him to prove it, that is, he bears the *legal burden* not just the evidential burden.

See, for example, *R* v *Edwards*, where the accused was charged with selling intoxicating liquor without a licence. He did not give evidence at the trial but made an unsworn statement denying that he was the occupier of the premises concerned. He was convicted and appealed on the grounds that the prosecution should have proved *positively* that he had no licence whereas no evidence had been called about the matter. It was held on appeal that there was an exception to the fundamental rule of criminal law that the prosecution had to prove every element of an offence; the exception was limited to offences arising under enactments which prohibited the doing of an act subject to provisos or exemptions. In such a situation it was for the accused to prove that he was entitled to do the otherwise prohibited act and therefore it was for him to prove that he *did* have a licence not for the prosecution to prove positively that he did not.

14.4.2.3   The case of *R* v *Hunt*

The House of Lords considered in 1987 the whole question of burden of proof in a criminal trial under the rule in *Woolmington* v *DPP* [1935] AC 462 and the exceptions to it following *R* v *Edwards* [1975] QB 27.

In *R* v *Hunt* [1987] AC 352 the accused was charged with possession of a certain controlled drug. Regulations made under the Misuse of Drugs Act 1971 provided that no offence was committed if the proportion of the drug in any solution was not more than 0.2 per cent. The issue that arose was whether it was for the accused to prove that the strength of the drug in the solution was not more than that figure or whether it was for the prosecution to prove that it was higher. The House of Lords, whilst considering *R v Edwards* was a correct statement of law, held that as under the statute and regulations it was a criminal offence to have the drug in one form but not an offence to have it in another form, the strength was an element of the offence, which the prosecution had to prove, and the circumstances were not within *R v Edwards*. The House of Lords considered in particular that the fact that this was a very serious offence, unlike the purely regulatory offences mainly dealt with under the rule in *R v Edwards*, meant that the prosecution should retain the full burden.

It should be remembered that s. 101 of the Magistrates' Court Act 1980 and the corresponding principle in the Crown Court, expressed in *R v Edwards* are, in essence, rules of statutory interpretation. They provide a principle for examining the terms of other statutes to see whether key words in sections creating criminal offences either *define the offence* (in which case the burden of proving every element remains on the prosecution) or implicitly *provide an excuse or defence*, in which case one has to look carefully to see whether the effect is to switch the burden to the defence. There are many such statutes in the purely regulatory sphere concerned with matters such as food and drugs, health and safety and the like. Thus it will always be necessary to examine phrases in sections which create an offence such as 'without reasonable excuse', 'without lawful authority' and the like to see whether the legal burden of proving the defence is in fact switched to the defence.

14.5 Standard of Proof

One party has to prove the truth of the fact in issue. If he fails to do so he will fail overall; therefore he has to adduce more persuasive evidence than his opponent does. If he only adduces an equivalent amount of evidence to his opponent so that the judge of fact is left undecided, then the party who has the legal burden has not discharged it and will fail. Therefore the standard of proof concerns how much more (or better quality) evidence has to be adduced by one party than his opponent in order to be successful.

Cases from the second half of the 19th century show two standards of proof recognised by law:

(a) Proof on a preponderance of probabilities — the civil standard.

(b) Proof beyond reasonable doubt — the criminal standard.

So the standard of proof required of the prosecution is higher than that of a civil plaintiff and it is vital for the judge to direct the jury fully on the standard.

14.5.1 THE CRIMINAL STANDARD

The words 'beyond reasonable doubt' were at one time only one of a number of ways of explaining the criminal standard of proof to a jury. There are alternative versions which are acceptable, in particular, 'so that you are really sure', and the composite definition 'satisfied beyond doubt so that you feel sure of the defendant's guilt' has also been approved.

14.5.2 WHEN THE BURDEN IS ON THE ACCUSED

When the *legal burden is on the accused* in a criminal case, whether by common law rule or statute (e.g., insanity or diminished responsibility), the burden is not so heavy as that borne by the Crown on the general issue, i.e. it is on the civil standard. The accused must prove matters to the extent of persuading the jury that they are *more likely than not* true.

For example, see *R* v *Carr-Briant* [1943] KB 607. The accused was charged with corruption under the Prevention of Corruption Act 1906. It was proved that he had made a gift to a government employee. The trial judge, however, directed the jury that the onus of proving his innocence lay on the appellant beyond reasonable doubt. It was held, quashing the conviction, that although the appellant did have the burden of proof it was only to satisfy the jury of his defence upon the civil standard of balance of probabilities and not beyond reasonable doubt.

Moreover, standard of proof must be carefully explained. See *R* v *Swaysland* (1987) *The Times*, 15 April 1987 where the burden of proof was on the defendant it was not enough to tell the jury that he had to prove it on 'the balance of probabilities' for this might confuse them into thinking that it was, say, 75 per cent probable. The phrase 'more likely than not' was preferable.

14.6   The Importance of a Correct Direction

It is vital that the judge correctly directs the jury on the burden and standard of proof. In many cases where the point under appeal was the failure to give a proper direction on these vital matters. The cases establish that one must look at the direction as a whole. The unfortunate fact is that many judges give highly repetitive directions in which they repeat the point in several different ways and often at several different times throughout the direction. In principle a direction on matters of evidence should commence with dealing with burden and standard of proof but many judges deal with it briefly there, and then return to it at the end. It follows that there may be inconsistent things said in the course of a lengthy direction and the case law establishes that only rarely will the fact that one phrase, or short passage, misstates the burden or standard of proof matter provided that there is a correct explanation elsewhere in the direction.

There have been numerous recent cases in which misstatements by a trial judge of the principles of burden or standard of proof have led to convictions being quashed. Sometimes an otherwise impeccable direction is spoilt by one or two sloppy phrases. For example, in *R* v *Anderson* [1991] Crim LR 361 the judge unfortunately used the phrase: 'if you think the defendant's evidence and that of his witnesses is true or may be true, then ... acquit'. This clearly indicated that the jury should only acquit if they are satisfied with the truth of the defence. Likewise in *R* v *Bowditch* [1991] Crim LR 831 the judge included a number of unfortunate phrases, in particular 'if you accept the defence as a true explanation' which might also have led the jury to conclude that the burden was on the defendant. In *R* v *McDonald* (1987) *The Times*, 27 March 1987, the judge used the phrase 'the defence, if it is established' which also led to the conviction being quashed on appeal.

14.6.1   CAN A JUDGE DIRECT THE JURY TO CONVICT?

An interesting question is whether the judge is ever entitled to direct a *conviction*. He can of course direct an *acquittal* in a suitable case. An example is *R* v *Gent* (1989) 89 Cr App R 247 where the accused was charged with conspiracy to obtain drugs. His defence was that whilst he admitted all participation in the operation he had done so as a police informant on the instructions of a policeman who had now retired and was unfit to attend the trial. The judge directed the jury to convict because of the admissions made by G in the course of giving his evidence. On appeal the conviction was quashed. The appellant's evidence in the witness box was very strong evidence of guilt but he was entitled to the verdict of the jury not the judge.

14.6.2   JOINT ENTERPRISE AND BURDEN OF PROOF

One point which has arisen a number of times in reported cases and which provides an interesting conundrum is where there are two defendants (or more) and the facts are such that one or other of them, or possibly both together, must have committed the crime. The judge must first look to see whether there is any evidence of a joint enterprise. If there is then he can safely direct the jury that they have to be satisfied beyond reasonable doubt that one or other or both together did the crime.

The problem arises however where there is no evidence of joint enterprise and the crime was therefore committed either by A or B but there is little evidence pointing to which. The judge must of course sum up separately in relation to each defendant so he must tell the jury that they must be satisfied beyond reasonable doubt that A did it; he must then give the same direction in relation to B. Accordingly if the prosecution has been unable to show which of the two did it, even though one must have, the jury are perfectly right in acquitting both, considering each separately.

An interesting factual example is *R v Hyde, Sussex and Collins* (1991) 92 Cr App R 131. In this case three men combined to beat up another but one of the men went too far and gave him a fatal kick in the head. The defence submitted that the jury could not be sure whose act caused the death of the victim and thus none of them should be convicted as the killer, and convictions in respect of assault only should be brought in. The court held that there was sufficient evidence of joint enterprise to make them all guilty of murder.

A different result occurred in *R v Aston and Mason* [1991] Crim LR 701. In this case the victim was M's 16-month-old daughter. She was admitted to hospital showing a number of injuries consistent with having been beaten. A was not the child's father but had treated her as his own. Each testified that the child had been alone with the other for important parts of the day in question. The trial judge rejected the appellants' submission of no case to answer on a count alleging murder. They were eventually convicted of cruelty to a child under the Children and Young Persons Act 1933 and manslaughter. On appeal the convictions for manslaughter were quashed against each of them since there was no evidence at the close of the prosecution case which indicated which one of the appellants was responsible for the fatal injuries and each of them had had the opportunity. Neither was there any evidence that they had acted in concert.

14.6.3 WHAT IF THE TRIER OF FACT CANNOT DECIDE?

Where a jury cannot agree on an accused's guilt either unanimously or to the required majority, the judge will discharge the jury and normally order a retrial. Sometimes the prosecution choose not to proceed with a retrial particularly if there has been a long delay since the offence itself and the trial has been a long one.

If in the magistrates' court a case is being tried before only two magistrates and they disagree, the case should be remitted to a new bench for a fresh hearing: see *R v Redbridge Justices ex parte Ram* [1992] QB 384. Where however a bench of three magistrates are simply unable to make up their minds, this means that the prosecution have failed to discharge their burden and the result should be an acquittal. See, for example, *R v Bromley Justices ex parte Haymill (Contractors) Ltd* [1984] Crim LR 235. The accused firm were charged with using a vehicle with deficient steering. There was conflicting evidence about the steering. At the end of the case the justices refused to make a decision and decided to send the case for a rehearing by another bench. It was held that the three magistrates were required to proceed to a decision. If they were unhappy about convicting the accused then they should acquit.

14.7 Proof without Evidence

The general rule is that all facts in issue in a case, and all facts relevant to the issue, have to be proved by evidence brought at the right time. There are however three basic exceptions to this principle. These are:

(a)   Facts of which *judicial notice* is taken.

(b)   Facts which are the subject of some *presumption* so that they are taken as established unless some party proves to the contrary.

(c)   Facts which are *admitted* between the parties.

We shall now consider each of these briefly in turn.

14.7.1   JUDICIAL NOTICE

When a court takes judicial notice of a fact it declares that it will find that it exists even though no evidence has been called to establish it, e.g., that Christmas Day falls on 25 December. To be a proper fact for judicial notice to be taken, the fact must be so well established as not to be the subject of dispute amongst reasonable men. Facts may be judicially noticed either without enquiry or after reference to sources to which a judge may properly refer. Simple examples are:

(a)   14 days is too short a period for human gestation: *R* v *Luffe* (1807) 8 East 193.

(b)   In *R* v *Simpson* [1983] 1 WLR 1494 the accused was charged with having an offensive weapon outside the home. The relevant law is that certain kinds of articles will always be considered offensive weapons, but that whether others (e.g., a chisel) are offensive weapons must be left to the jury to decide after hearing evidence as to whether in the circumstances the item was an offensive weapon or held for some legitimate purpose (e.g., in the case of a chisel by a working carpenter on his way home). In this case the court took *judicial notice* (that is the judge decided as a matter of fact) that a flick-knife is always an offensive weapon.

Finally, it should be noted that in many cases the judge will take tacit judicial notice of many matters of worldly experience without the matter ever being referred to in the judgments, or evidence being called concerning it, e.g., that there are very few lawful uses for masks and jemmies, where these are found in the possession of an accused, or, as in *R* v *Thompson* [1918] AC 221, that a person who has powder puffs and indecent photographs of young boys in his possession is likely to be a homosexual.

14.7.2   PRESUMPTIONS

Presumptions are chiefly relevant in civil rather than criminal evidence. A presumption is 'a conclusion which may or must be drawn until the contrary is proved, once certain primary facts are established'. There were usually said to be three main categories of presumption, namely, presumptions of fact, irrebuttable presumptions of law, and rebuttable presumptions of law.

14.7.2.1   Presumptions of fact

This phrase is really an expression of the usual processes of reasoning and 'is, in reality no more than a slightly grandiose term for the ordinary processes of judicial reasoning about facts'. It describes the process whereby if stolen goods are found in the home of the accused the factual inference may be drawn (or presumption made) that he stole them. This 'presumption' is of course easily rebutted by other factual evidence (e.g., that they were stored there by someone else without his knowledge) but if no such evidence is given the jury *may* (not *must*) draw the inference and presume the theft.

To use the word 'presumption' to describe this kind of common-sense connection between primary facts (the goods being there) and he being the one who stole them is probably confusing since it is in effect a simple matter of common-sense connection.

14.7.2.2 Irrebuttable presumptions of law

These occur where conclusive inferences must be drawn from a given premise and no evidence in rebuttal is allowed. This is in truth substantive law: the 'presumption' simply defines the rights of the parties. An example is the presumption that a child aged under ten cannot be guilty of crime. Such irrebuttable presumptions may of course be varied by statute. Thus the former irrebuttable presumption that a boy under the age of 14 was incapable of sexual intercourse and thus could not be guilty of rape was reversed by s. 1 of the Sexual Offences Act 1993.

14.7.2.3 Rebuttable presumptions of law

The rebuttable presumptions of law such as presumption of legitimacy, presumption of death after seven years' absence and presumptions of marriage are of minimal importance in criminal litigation and for that reason will not be described further here. One such 'rebuttable' presumption is the well-known presumption of innocence in a criminal trial. This is in truth simply a way of indicating where the burden of proof lies rather than a true presumption as such.

14.7.3 MATTER WHICH IS ADMITTED

In a criminal trial, just as in a civil one, by virtue of s. 10 of the Criminal Justice Act 1967 matter may be formally admitted. This is often arranged between the parties to cut down the scope of a criminal trial to the true events in issue. Admissions must be made in writing unless made orally before the court itself and must be made by counsel or solicitor for the accused; admissions made under s. 10 may, with the leave of the court, be withdrawn.

The effect of s. 10 is that purely formal matters, such as the execution of documents, may be admitted between the parties at or before the trial. Alternatively, quite substantial admissions may be made which have the effect of limiting the scope of either the prosecution's case or of what the defence is seeking to contend. A defence lawyer will always need carefully to consider whether something is properly admitted where the proving of it might put the prosecution in such difficulties, albeit of a technical nature, that their case would be seriously in jeopardy. It is a recognised tactic in cases of considerable complexity (such as commercial fraud cases) to admit little or nothing so that the issues in front of the jury may be sufficiently voluminous to ensure the maximum of confusion. Sometimes however it may be to the advantage of an accused's defence that he should admit a substantial part of the facts. So, for example, where a householder is burgled and it is the essence of the accused's case that he was not the one responsible, he would gain little in the jury's eyes by failing to admit the formal facts that a burglary occurred. Similarly, on a rape charge, if the substantive defence is mistaken identity, it probably does the accused little good to make the complainant formally prove the fact of intercourse and absence of consent.

FIFTEEN

THE LAW OF EVIDENCE (2): COMPETENCE AND COMPELLABILITY: TESTIMONY

15.1 Introduction

A witness is *competent* if he can lawfully be called to give evidence, and *compellable* if he can be made to testify even if he is unwilling to do so.

The general rule, subject to the exceptions discussed below, is that all persons are competent to give evidence, and all competent persons are compellable.

One can compel a witness to attend court by a witness summons or witness order in criminal proceedings. Failure to attend court will result in arrest and/or proceedings for contempt being brought against the witness. If, having come to court, the witness refuses to answer questions, this will again be contempt of court leading to imprisonment either under the general law of contempt or under a specific statute (e.g., s. 97, Magistrates' Courts Act 1980, which permits the magistrates to imprison an uncooperative witness for up to seven days). A witness may claim *privilege* not to answer certain questions in certain situations which will be further discussed in **Chapter 21**. Subject to that, however, a witness, once called, must cooperate fully in the proceedings.

15.2 Exceptions to the General Rule

15.2.1 THOSE OF DEFECTIVE INTELLECT

(a) No witness is competent if prevented by 'lunacy', drunkenness, etc., from giving rational testimony. But the witness is only incompetent so long as the defect lasts, and if it is only temporary the trial may be adjourned provided application is made before the jury are sworn.

(b) In any given case it is for the judge to decide whether a person whose capacity is challenged can understand the nature of the oath. If the judge decides he does then it is for the jury to decide what degree of credit should be given to any such evidence. If the capacity of a witness is challenged, the judge should hear any relevant evidence about it in the presence of the jury so that they have the necessary information to assist them to decide how much credit to give to the witness. Note that for persons of low intelligence the same rules apply as used to apply before 1992 in the case of children (see **15.2.2**). In *R v Bellamy* (1985) 82 Cr App R 223 the accused was a man of low mental ability convicted of rape of a woman of similar capacity. When the victim gave evidence the trial judge investigated her competence, hearing evidence from her and a social worker. After questioning her as to her belief in and knowledge of God and the understanding of the importance of telling the truth he decided that she should affirm. It was held on appeal that the judge was clearly right to investigate her competence but having concluded that she was competent and did not object to being sworn she should have been sworn.

15.2.2 CHILDREN

In *criminal cases* until 1992 the provision as to the evidence of children was s. 38 of the Children and Young Persons Act 1933. This permitted a child to give unsworn evidence provided the child was possessed of sufficient intelligence and understood the duty of speaking the truth. It used to be for the judge to examine the child and decide whether or not the child had sufficient understanding. That exercise occurred in the presence of the jury so that they could see for themselves how intelligent the child was. Now, however, s. 52 of the Criminal Justice Act 1991 simply provides that all *children* (that is up to the age of 13 inclusive) shall give *unsworn* evidence in criminal proceedings; and persons above that age shall give *sworn* evidence. It was initially unclear whether there should nonetheless be an enquiry by the judge as to whether it was appropriate to take evidence in any form from any particular child in view of the child's apparent intelligence and state of understanding.

Section 33A(2A) of the Criminal Justice Act 1988, as inserted by sch. 9, para. 33, Criminal Justice and Public Order Act 1994, now provides:

> A child's evidence shall be received unless it appears to the court that the child is incapable of giving intelligible testimony.

In other words, there should now be no preliminary investigation or questioning of a child in advance to determine whether it is capable of giving intelligible evidence. It should be permitted to commence giving evidence and only if some matter arises that demonstrates that the child is incapable of giving intelligible evidence should the court consider, perhaps by questioning the child more widely about its state of understanding, whether the child should be prevented from continuing.

The competency of child witnesses was usefully reviewed in the case of *R v D and others* (1995) *The Times*, 15 November 1995 (albeit that this case was decided before s. 33A(2A) of the 1988 Act came into force). The court concluded that in deciding the competency of a child witness, the court should ask the child if he or she could understand questions and respond coherently and intelligibly, although it remained relevant also to enquire as to his or her ability to distinguish between truth and fiction and between fact and fantasy as part of that test. It is suggested that those matters might still be relevant, even though no specific test of 'ability to tell the truth' is mentioned in the new provisions. Once the court has decided that a child could give a comprehensible account, then whether the child is or is not telling the truth remains a matter for the jury.

15.2.2.1 Is there a minimum age?

In *R v Wallwork* (1958) 42 Cr App R 153 it appears that a five-year-old child was a witness and there is no particular age which has been held to be too young. The propriety of calling a five-year-old child was doubted in that case by the Court of Appeal especially as, in the event, the child proved too terrified to testify at all when in the witness box. It is not possible however to say with certainty what is the minimum age.

The competence of children has been further discussed in other more recent cases in one of which (*R v Z* [1990] 2 QB 355) a question arose as to whether a six-year-old child was too young to testify. The court observed that the policy of the legislature represented by the repeal of the requirement of corroboration in children's evidence (see **19.1.1**) showed that the public in general found the evidence of young children acceptable. It would be wrong to vet the discretion of the trial judge in such cases.

15.2.3 THE ACCUSED

Bizarre though it now seems, until the last century there were rules designed to stop the accused from giving evidence at all. The rationale was the risk of perjury and the fact that the obvious self-interest of the accused made his evidence specially untrustworthy. It has of course been obvious, at least since 1898, when the accused was first generally allowed to testify, that the fact-finding process represented by a criminal trial is substantially hampered, to the prejudice of the accused, by such a rule. Nonetheless there are still some restrictions on the accused's competence and these are described below.

15.2.3.1 As a witness for the Crown

In general, an accused is not a competent witness for the Crown. He cannot therefore be compelled to testify at his own trial. The rule is however much more important where there are several co-accused because the rule prevents the Crown calling any of several co-accused to testify against another. There are, however, several ways in which one of two or more co-accused may cease to be a co-accused and thus may become competent for the Crown:

(a) The Attorney-General may file a *nolle prosequi*.

(b) An order may be made for separate trials, but note that in such a case a co-accused from the first trial may be called at the second but not vice versa.

(c) The accused may be formally acquitted, e.g., if the prosecution offers no evidence.

(d) The accused may plead guilty and may then give evidence for the Crown against a former co-accused. It is usually considered desirable in such a case that the person should be sentenced before giving evidence thus demonstrating that he has nothing further to gain from lying to incriminate an innocent person. This is not of course in truth entirely logical because the fact that he is about to testify for the Crown will already have been mentioned in the plea in mitigation to the judge who sentences him and thus he is likely already to have been given full credit for his contribution and co-operation with the authorities. For this reason the court does have a discretion to postpone sentence on a person who is to testify for the prosecution and may well do so in cases of gang crimes where the precise degree of involvement of each of the participants may not be known until the end of the main trial.

15.2.3.2 For a co-accused

It will be rare for one co-accused to want to give evidence *for* another co-accused but not for himself, since he will thereby open himself to cross-examination which presumably is what he wanted to avoid by not testifying, although there could be such cases (e.g., on a *voir dire* as to admissibility of a co-accused's confession). A co-accused is *competent* but *not compellable*.

15.2.4 THE SPOUSE OF THE ACCUSED

The general rule until the coming into force of the Police and Criminal Evidence Act 1984 was that a spouse was not competent for the prosecution at the trial of the other spouse.

The law on competence of spouses is now contained in s. 80 of the Police and Criminal Evidence Act 1984 which provides:

(1)   In any proceedings the wife or husband of the accused shall be competent to give evidence—

    (a)   subject to subsection (4) below, for the prosecution; and

    (b)   on behalf of the accused or any person jointly charged with the accused.

(2)   In any proceedings the wife or husband of the accused shall, subject to subsection (4) below, be compellable to give evidence on behalf of the accused.

(3)   In any proceedings the wife or husband of the accused shall, subject to subsection (4) below, be compellable to give evidence for the prosecution or on behalf of any person jointly charged with the accused if and only if—

    (a)   the offence charged involves an assault on, or injury or a threat of injury to, the wife or husband of the accused or a person who was at the material time under the age of sixteen; or

    (b)   the offence charged is a sexual offence alleged to have been committed in respect of a person who was at the material time under that age; or

    (c)   the offence charged consists of attempting or conspiring to commit, or of aiding, abetting, counselling, procuring or inciting the commission of, an offence falling within paragraph (a) or (b) above.

(4)   Where a husband and wife are jointly charged with an offence neither spouse shall at the trial be competent or compellable by virtue of subsection (1)(a), (2) or (3) above to give evidence in respect of that offence unless the spouse is not, or is no longer, liable to be convicted of that offence at the trial as a result of pleading guilty or for any other reason.

(5)   In any proceedings a person who has been but is no longer married to the accused shall be competent and compellable to give evidence as if that person and the accused had never been married.

(6)   Where in any proceedings the age of any person at any time is material for the purposes of subsection (3) above, his age at the material time shall for the purposes of that provision be deemed to be or to have been that which appears to the court to be or to have been his age at that time.

(7)   In subsection (3)(b) above 'sexual offence' means an offence under the Sexual Offences Act 1956, the Indecency with Children Act 1960, the Sexual Offences Act 1967, section 54 of the Criminal Law Act 1977 or the Protection of Children Act 1975.

(8)   The failure of the wife or husband of the accused to give evidence shall not be made the subject of any comment by the prosecution.

(9)   Section 1(d) of the Criminal Evidence Act 1898 (communications between husband and wife) and section 43(1) of the Matrimonial Causes Act 1965 (evidence as to marital intercourse) shall cease to have effect.

15.2.4.1   Summary

(a)   *For the Crown*

Unless he/she is also a co-accused the spouse of an accused is always competent for the Crown and is also compellable for the Crown in the limited class of cases referred to in s. 80(3), namely where the offence charged involves an assault on or injury or threat of injury to the spouse or a person who was under 16, or the charge is a sexual offence involving a person under 16, or attempts to commit or aiding and abetting etc. these classes of offence, though *not* compellable in cases apart from those.

(b)   *For the accused*

Unless he/she is also a co-accused a spouse is always competent and compellable *for* his/her spouse.

(c) *For a co-accused*

Unless he/she is also a co-accused the spouse of one of two or more co-accused is always competent for a co-accused and is compellable in the limited class of cases in s. 80(3). Where spouses are co-accused one is never compellable for the other.

Note also:

(a) Section 80(5) provides that if spouses are no longer married at trial it is as if they were never married for the purpose of establishing competence and compellability.

(b) When a spouse is competent but not compellable, regard should be had to the case of *R v Pitt* [1982] QB 25. It held that it is desirable for a judge in such a case to explain to a spouse before she took the oath that she was not obliged to testify but that once she did commence to testify she could not pick and choose which questions to answer but was in the position of any other witness and to refuse to answer a proper question would be contempt. This should be explained to her in the absence of the jury.

(c) A 'spouse' to a polygamous marriage is to be treated as if not married to the accused and is thus competent and compellable in every case: *R v Khan* (1987) 84 Cr App R 44.

15.3 Testimony

15.3.1 OATHS

The general rule is that all evidence must be given on oath. The Oaths Act 1838 permits an oath to be administered in such a form and with such ceremonies as the person taking it may declare to be binding on him. A solemn affirmation may be administered instead if the witness is not a believer or taking an oath is contrary to his religion; also if it is impracticable to administer the oath in a manner appropriate to the witness's religion. So in *R v Kemble* [1990] 1 WLR 1111 a Muslim took the oath using the New Testament. K was convicted and appealed on the basis of material irregularity. At the appeal evidence was given by an expert in the Muslim faith. The appeal was dismissed. In the case of a person who is neither Christian nor Jew the oath may be administered in any lawful manner and in the present case the Muslim witness had given evidence that he considered the oath binding on him notwithstanding that it was sworn on the wrong book.

15.3.2 UNSWORN EVIDENCE

Unsworn evidence is only admitted in principle in the following situations:

(a) The unsworn evidence of a child under the age of 14 whose intelligence is sufficient to justify the reception of its evidence.

(b) Where the written statements of persons who are not present before the court are admitted under one of the exceptions to the hearsay rule (e.g., s. 23, Criminal Justice Act 1988) that statement is not on oath but it is nonetheless acceptable as testimony. (See **16.10.3**.)

15.3.3 EVIDENCE THROUGH TELEVISION LINK AND VIDEO

It is inherent in the usual rules of evidence that the witness giving evidence must be present in court. There are however, two exceptional situations provided for in recent statutes.

By s. 32 of the Criminal Justice Act 1988, evidence by live television link at a trial on indictment (and on appeal) may be given where either:

(a) the witness is outside the United Kingdom, or

(b) the witness is under 14 and the offence charged is one to which s. 32(2) applies — in general, these sections have to do with sexual offences and in any event the leave of the court is required.

The use of s. 32 is highly exceptional. Section 32 reads:

(1) A person other than the accused may give evidence through a live television link on a trial on indictment or an appeal to the criminal division of the Court of Appeal or the hearing of a reference under section 17 of the Criminal Appeal Act 1968 if—
  (a) the witness is outside the United Kingdom; or
  (b) the witness is under the age of 14 and the offence charged is one to which subsection (2) below applies,
but evidence may not be so given without the leave of the court.

(2) This subsection applies—
  (a) to an offence which involves an assault on, or injury or a threat of injury to, a person;
  (b) to an offence under section 1 of the Children and Young Persons Act 1933 (cruelty to persons under 16);
  (c) to an offence under the Sexual Offences Act 1956, the Indecency with Children Act 1960, the Sexual Offences Act 1967, section 54 of the Criminal Law Act 1977 or the Protection of Children Act 1978; and
  (d) to an offence which consists of attempting or conspiring to commit, or of aiding, abetting, counselling, procuring or inciting the commission of, an offence failing within paragraph (a), (b) or (c) above.

(3) A statement made on oath by a witness outside the United Kingdom and given in evidence through a link by virtue of this section shall be treated for the purposes of section 1 of the Perjury Act 1911 as having been made in the proceedings in which it is given in evidence.

(4) Without prejudice to the generality of any enactment conferring power to make rules to which this subsection applies, such rules may make such provision as appears to the authority making them to be necessary or expedient for the purposes of this section.

(5) The rules to which subsection (4) above applies are—
  (a) Crown Court Rules; and
  (b) Criminal Appeal Rules.

The second statutory exception to the requirement that the witness must be present in court is s. 54 of the Criminal Justice Act 1991, which inserts a new s. 32A in the Criminal Justice Act 1988. This provides for a video tape of an interview with a child witness by 'any adult' to be put in evidence and to constitute the examination-in-chief of the child. It is suggested that often this video tape will be very damning to the accused. Leave to put it in evidence is required and the leave will not be given if the child is not made available for cross-examination. There are substantial problems with the provision as yet unexplored in case law, in particular the likelihood that, in the course of the video-taped interview with the sympathetic adult, inadmissible material, e.g., hearsay, will be included which it will then be up to the defendant to insist should be edited under the authority of s. 32A(3). The section is concerned with interviews with a child witness, probably, but not necessarily, the victim, in relation to sexual offences of the kind referred to in s. 32 of the 1988 Act.

15.4   The Stages of Testimony

A witness is subject to three sets of questions: examination-in-chief (**15.5**), cross-examination (**15.6**) and re-examination (**15.7**). Each of these will be considered in turn.

15.5   Examination-in-Chief

The purpose of this is to obtain evidence to support the case of the person who calls the witness. The general rule is that *leading questions* cannot be asked. A leading question is one which:

(a)   assumes the existence of disputed facts as to which the witness is to testify, or

(b)   suggests the required answer.

The reasons why leading questions are prohibited are that a question in form (a) is improper because constant reiteration of facts which are in dispute may influence the jury to regard them as established, and a question in form (b) is improper because it 'coaches' the witness. Leading questions may be permitted for purely formal or introductory matter or where there is no dispute.

Three separate topics need to be considered in the context of evidence-in-chief (i.e. what evidence a party may obtain from his own witness). These topics are: refreshing the memory; previous consistent statements by the witness; and unfavourable and hostile witnesses.

15.5.1   REFRESHING THE MEMORY

15.5.1.1   Out of court

A witness may refresh his memory of the matters in issue by referring *out of court* (usually just before going into court) to any statement he has previously made, e.g., to the police. It is perfectly proper for the police to give a witness his statement to read through before the case, although it is desirable to inform the defence where this has been done: see *Worley v Bentley* [1976] 2 All ER 449.

It is said that, if this were not possible, testifying would become 'more a matter of memory than of truthfulness'. Any relevant statement may be used for this purpose, whenever written by the witness. An advocate has the right to call for and cross-examine on notes or statements used to refresh memory out of court even though they are not brought into court. See *Owen v Edwards* (1983) 77 Cr App R 191.

15.5.1.2   In court

A witness may 'refresh his memory' by referring to documentary records of the facts in issue but before he can do this four conditions must be satisfied:

(a)   *The document must have been made at substantially the same time as the occurrence of the events about which the witness is testifying*

This is a question of fact in each case. Certainly notes made within a few hours of an incident are likely to satisfy the condition. In cases of longer gaps it will be necessary for the witness to satisfy the judge that the events were still fresh in his or her mind when the record was written.

For the very common practice of policemen writing up their notes together see *R* v *Bass* [1953] 1 All ER 1064. In that case policemen giving evidence were allowed to refresh their memories from their notebooks. When the notebooks were examined it was observed that the notes were almost identical. The officers contended that they were not made up at the same time, and that one officer made his notes after the appellant had been charged and the other an hour or so later. The officers denied collaborating in preparation of the notes. The court observed that policemen nearly always deny collaboration in the making of notes and that there was no need for them to do so. Nothing could be more natural or proper where two persons had been present at an interview than that they should afterwards make sure that they had a correct version of what was said. Collaboration is a better explanation of almost identical notes than possession of a super-human memory.

(b) *The document was either supervised by, or read over to, the witness at the time*

It is not essential that the witness made it himself. See *Burrough* v *Martin* (1809) 2 Camp 112 where a captain who had inspected a ship's log throughout the voyage was allowed to refresh his memory from it although the entries had been made by the mate.

(c) *The document must be handed to the opposing advocate so that he may inspect it and cross-examine on it*

The jury may also see it. Note however that the document is not *in itself* evidence unless there is an allegation that it has been fabricated (see below as to 'recent fabrication'), or the advocate cross-examines on those parts of the document not used to refresh the memory.

(d) *The document should be the original*

With the decline of the 'best evidence' rule this may be less important but there seem to be no modern cases on the point.

The whole question of 'refreshing the memory' has been usefully reconsidered and principles reiterated in *R* v *Sekhon* (1986) 85 Cr App R 19. The accused was charged with drug offences. Observations had been kept by a team of officers who had kept a log. When the officers gave evidence they refreshed their memories from the log and were cross-examined as to the contents of the log. The jury asked to see the log and it was then made an exhibit and the jury retired with it. There was an appeal on the basis that this was improper. It was held that there was no difference between the log and notes used to refresh memory. The following points were established:

(a) The document could be referred to to refresh the witnesses' memory without necessarily being put before the jury.

(b) Such documents must be available for inspection by other parties who can cross-examine. Cross-examination will not make the record evidence and it will not be necessary for a jury to inspect it nor will it be appropriate for it to become an exhibit.

(c) Where the nature of the cross-examination involves a suggestion of fabrication the record may be admissible to rebut this suggestion, and if the nature of the record assists in showing whether or not it is genuine from its appearance.

(d) If the record is inconsistent with the witness's evidence it can be admitted as evidence of inconsistency.

(e) If it is difficult for the jury to follow the cross-examination of a witness who has refreshed his memory it may be appropriate for the record to be put before the jury.

(f) If the record goes before the jury it is not evidence as to the truth of the contents of the record and will not amount to corroboration. Its limited purpose is that of being a tool to assist in the evaluation of the truth of the witness's evidence.

(g) It would be wrong to conduct the case in such a way as to leave the jury to conclude that the document is evidence in itself.

(h) The document may become evidence of the truth of its contents in cases where it provides, because of its nature, material by which its authenticity can be judged in respect of that material and only for the purpose of assessing its authenticity. In that limited context it amounts to evidence in the case.

It seems apparent from recent cases that the formerly very strict rules about refreshing the memory are becoming progressively less important. This was so in *R v Sutton* [1991] Crim LR 836 where a prosecution witness was asked in evidence-in-chief about certain matters but the prosecuting counsel forgot to put a number of other matters to him during re-examination. Prosecuting counsel applied for leave for the witness to refresh his memory from a record of an interview with a policeman. On appeal it was argued that this should not be permitted since the witness's memory seemed to be adequate about most matters. The appeal was dismissed. The Court of Appeal held that the essential point was that the court should not deprive itself of the best chance of hearing the truth and provided the proper basis was laid a witness could be asked to refresh his memory either in evidence-in-chief or re-examination.

15.5.2 PREVIOUS CONSISTENT STATEMENTS

The general rule is that a witness cannot be asked in evidence-in-chief whether he made a prior statement, oral or written, consistent with his present testimony — nor can another witness be called to prove such prior consistent statement.

In *R v Roberts* [1942] 1 All ER 187 the accused shot his girlfriend in the course of an argument. His defence was that the gun went off accidentally. He wished to call evidence that, a few hours after being taken into custody, he had been visited in the cell by his father and that he had told his father that it was an accident. The trial judge refused to allow this evidence on the basis that it was of no probative value being merely a prior consistent statement. On appeal it was held that this ruling was correct.

The reason for the rule is that such a statement is self-serving and therefore valueless because so easily manufactured. There are, however, a number of important exceptions in criminal cases where a prior consistent statement is admissible because it has some special value in the circumstances.

15.5.2.1 The exceptions

(a) *Complaints in sexual cases*

Where absence of consent is among the facts in issue (e.g., rape) it was considered relevant to consider whether a complaint was made by the victim to raise a 'hue and cry' thus showing lack of consent. In more modern times the practice arose of limiting evidence of such complaint to *the fact* that it was made and not the words actually used.

Now, if two conditions are satisfied, evidence of the actual terms of complaint may be admitted; and this rule now applies even in sexual cases where the question of consent is not relevant, e.g., indecent assault on a (willing) child. This is established in *R v*

Osborne [1905] 1 KB 551. The accused was charged with indecent assault on a young girl. Two girls were in his shop and he sent one on an errand for him and assaulted the other. The victim then ran away and met the other girl in the street. The other girl asked the victim why she hadn't waited in the shop. The victim then made a complaint that the accused had sexually assaulted her. It was held that evidence of the complaint was admissible provided it was made at the first reasonable opportunity after the offence and that it was not elicited by questions of a leading and inducing or intimidating nature.

The conditions of admissibility of the terms of a sexual complaint are therefore:

(i)   that it should not be elicited by questions of a 'leading and inducing and intimidating character' and

(ii)   that it should have been made 'at the first opportunity that reasonably offers itself'.

So questions such as 'Why are you crying' would be in order but 'Did X assault you?' would not be.

One must take all the relationships and surrounding circumstances into account in applying these conditions. A delay of one week in complaining was not fatal on the facts of *R* v *Hedges* (1909) 3 Cr App R 262. The accused raped his own daughter, aged 15. At the time her mother was away from home. The girl did not complain until some eight days later when the mother returned. It was held that in all the circumstances evidence of the complaint was admissible.

Evidence of recent complaint is admissible only in sexual cases and may not be used in respect of other cases even where there is some analogy, e.g., in robbery (see *R* v *Jarvis & Jarvis* [1991] Crim LR 374).

(b)   *Previous consistent statement admitted to rebut an allegation of recent fabrication by the witness*

If it is alleged by the cross-examiner that the accused's story has been recently concocted, a previous statement concerning the nature of his defence becomes admissible. So too if it is suggested that a witness of the accused has made the story up after collaboration with the accused. To bring in this rule it is not enough merely to attack the whole of the witness's evidence — there must be a question in the nature of 'when did you invent this'.

See, for example, *R* v *Oyesiku* (1971) 56 Cr App R 240 in which the accused was charged with assault on a policeman. After the accused had been arrested and before she had been allowed to speak to him in custody, his wife went to see the family solicitor and made a statement about what had occurred which was to the effect that it was the police who had assaulted the accused. At the trial the wife was cross-examined to the effect that she had collaborated with her husband to make up her version. The judge refused to allow the defence solicitor to give evidence that the wife had been to see him and told him a version entirely consistent with what she had said in the witness box before she had had the opportunity of speaking to her husband about the case whilst he was still in custody. On appeal the conviction was quashed. It was held that this was an excellent example of a case where the prior statement should have been admitted to rebut the allegation of fabrication.

242

This rule does not however permit every defendant who is cross-examined as to the falsity of his version to produce his proof of evidence — *the time when he first made his statement* is what is material: *R v Okai* [1987] Crim LR 259.

Where a previous statement is admitted to rebut allegations of recent fabrication the status of the statement is the same as that in the case of evidence of complaint in sexual cases. In other words it is evidence only of the consistency of the witness and not of the facts. It is a distinction which will be lost on most juries.

(c) *Statements by accused when taxed with incriminating facts*

We are not here concerned with admissions of facts relevant to guilt to which the special rules relating to confessions apply. We are now considering things that the accused says on being taxed with incriminating facts where what he says is consistent with what he later says, denying guilt. These statements are not *evidence of the facts stated* but they are *evidence of reaction* and, if the accused later gives or calls evidence to the same effect, they can be relied on by him as *showing consistency* (i.e. it would then be proper for the defence counsel or judge to comment favourably on this aspect).

The leading case is *R v Storey* (1968) 52 Cr App R 249. The police broke into the accused's flat and found a large quantity of a controlled drug. In a statement then made to them she explained that the drug belonged to a man who had just brought it into her flat against her will. Her explanation was that the man had telephoned to ask if she wished to 'do business'. She was a prostitute and agreed. When he arrived, however, he tipped out a considerable quantity of the drug on the bed and it appeared that he had other 'business' on his mind. Just then the police burst in. A question that arose was the evidential value of the accused's statement to the police at the very time when they broke into the flat and accused her of the drug offence. It was held that her statement to the police was not evidence of the truth of the facts in it but only of her reaction — consequently, when she did not testify at her trial, it was wrong to attach any weight to the statement whose only use would have been to prove consistency.

The rule therefore is, where the accused does not testify, that, as the only use of the statement is to show consistency, there is no testimony for it to be consistent with, and therefore it is of no evidential value.

(d) *Statements forming part of the identification of the accused*

If a person is asked in court to identify a person he believes committed the offence, he will usually be asked if he has identified the person on some previous occasion. If he says 'yes' this is proof of a prior consistent statement. This may occasionally be part of the circumstances of the crime but usually is long after the crime, e.g., at an identification parade.

For example, see *R v Christie* [1914] AC 545. The accused was charged with indecent assault upon a little boy. At the trial, evidence was given that shortly after the offence the child and his mother and a policeman went up to the accused and the little boy said 'that is the man'. The accused replied 'I am innocent'. It was held that these words were all admissible as forming part of the identification.

The above exceptions have been grouped for convenience under the general heading of *consistent statements in evidence-in-chief* although sometimes the prior consistent statement will need to be proved at some different time, e.g., when rebutting an allegation of recent fabrications the prior statement will usually be adduced in re-examination after the cross-examiner has made the allegation.

15.5.3 UNFAVOURABLE AND HOSTILE WITNESSES

Parties prepare their cases by having their solicitors take a statement from each witness. This is written down and (if the solicitor is prudent) signed by the witness. This statement is called a 'proof of evidence'. A witness whose evidence in court is on the general lines of his statement is said to be 'coming up to proof'. The following sections deal with the situation where the witness fails to do so.

The rule at common law was that a *party may not impeach his own witness*, i.e. he cannot call evidence from another source to show that his own witness is mistaken, forgetful, or lying, although he can continue calling other (hopefully more favourable) witnesses to the same facts whose evidence may be better. Nor can one cross-examine one's own witness or attack one's own witness's character. The rules are now contained in the Criminal Procedure Act 1865, s. 3 which is declaratory of the common law and now governs the position.

There are two kinds of witness:

(a) An *unfavourable* witness is one who is not 'coming up to proof' and fails to prove some fact in issue or proves an opposite fact. Unfavourable witnesses cannot be attacked as to credit or have their previous inconsistent written statements put to them to show their lack of credibility. Unfavourable witnesses may be so because they are forgetful, mistaken or foolish.

(b) *A hostile witness* is one 'not desirous of telling the truth at the instance of the party calling him'. Where an advocate is examining in chief one of his own witnesses who appears hostile he should first ask the judge to rule that he may treat the witness as hostile. This application should be made in the absence of the jury. Whether or not the witness is hostile may be detected by the judge from his demeanour although his previous written statement is also shown to the judge so that he may see the extent of the inconsistency. If the judge allows the witness to be treated as hostile he may permit cross-examination of a party's own witness, e.g., by leading questions to test his memory and perception and by putting his previous inconsistent statements to him.

In *R v Fraser and Warren* (1956) 40 Cr App R 160 the accused were charged with a serious wounding on C. The victim had given a comprehensive statement in which he named both accused who were known to him and correctly described the weapons which they had. At the trial C gave evidence that he was now unable to identify his attackers and indeed that he was certain that the accused were not the men concerned. Prosecution counsel did nothing about this but the trial judge who knew that C had made a previous statement called for the statement and cross-examined C upon it. It was held that in such a case that it is the duty of counsel for the prosecution to show such a statement to the judge and ask the judge's leave to cross-examine the witness as hostile.

The position therefore is that:

(a) an *unfavourable* witness can be contradicted by other witnesses — otherwise the order of calling them would be all that matters! — but *cannot be cross-examined* or have previous statements put to him or have his character impeached;

(b) in the *case of hostile witnesses*, the judge has a discretion to allow them to be cross-examined and have previous inconsistent statements put to them. However, one still cannot attack one's own witness's character by putting in his previous criminal record, and thus such a witness is not entirely in the same position as an opposition witness to whom such matters may always be put.

15.5.3.1 What is the effect of the inconsistent statement?

The case of *R v White* (1924) 17 Cr App R 60 provides an example of the effect of a previous inconsistent statement. The accused was charged with riot. A witness G who had previously given sworn and unsworn statements to the effect that W was involved, testified at the trial that W was not involved. The Crown alleged that the witness had been terrorised and was allowed to treat G as a hostile witness. The judge appeared to direct the jury that thereafter they could choose between which of the witness's two versions they preferred to believe. It was held that it was one thing to say that in view of an earlier statement to the contrary a witness is not to be trusted but it is another thing to say that a witness's present testimony may be disbelieved and his earlier statement which he now repudiates be substituted for it. In the circumstances the correct direction was that the witness's evidence could be cancelled out to the extent of the inconsistency and the jury should not have been invited to choose between them.

So the net effect is that in a criminal case the judge must not leave it to the jury to say which of the witness's two versions they prefer — he must direct them that *the whole* of the witness's evidence on the inconsistent matter may be *totally disregarded*.

Despite this clear rule there have been more recent cases, albeit on unusual facts, which appear to have slightly modified the principle. So, for example, *R v Pestano* [1981] Crim LR 397 involved a witness where the inconsistent part of his testimony was clearly separable from the rest. The witness incriminated two of four defendants but resiled from his deposition in relation to two others. It appears that the prosecution were thereafter allowed to rely on the hostile witness's evidence insofar as it advanced their case in relation to the first two witnesses. On appeal it was held that there was no inflexible rule that a jury should be directed that all evidence contained in statements which were contradicted by previous statements should be regarded as unreliable. That principle was approved in the more recent case of *R v Nelson* [1992] Crim LR 653.

15.5.3.2 Hostile witnesses and s. 23, Criminal Justice Act 1988

One interesting problem in the case of hostile witnesses which will be commented on more fully in the section on criminal hearsay is the question of the status of previous statements given to the prosecution. As indicated above, in general the previous statement made by a witness who eventually proves hostile in criminal proceedings can only be used to discredit the witness and is not in itself evidence of the facts stated. Section 23 of the Criminal Justice Act 1988 makes certain kinds of statement admissible in cases where *inter alia* a witness does not give evidence 'through fear'. If therefore the reason for a witness becoming hostile is fear of the consequences of testifying, it may be possible not only to put in his previous statement under the procedures described here but that the status of that statement might be different from the status of statements admitted under s. 3 of the Criminal Procedure Act 1865. Such statements under the 1988 Act might actually be *evidence of the facts* stated in them.

15.6 Cross-examination

Almost all witnesses are liable to be cross-examined. All parties have a right to cross-examine any witness not called by them. Therefore one accused's witness can be cross-examined by the prosecution and by counsel for any co-accused. There are two objectives in such cross-examination:

(a) To elicit information about the facts in issue favourable to the party cross-examining.

(b) To test the truthfulness of, and where necessary cast doubt upon, the evidence given in evidence-in-chief by the witness.

When conducting cross-examination it is an advocate's duty to:

(a) Challenge every part of a witness's evidence which is in conflict with his own case.

(b) Put his own case to the witness insofar as the witness is able to say anything relevant about it.

(c) Put to a witness any allegation against the witness which it is proper to put.

15.6.1   IMPORTANT PRINCIPLES

(a) If one fails to challenge the evidence-in-chief on any point one *may* be held to have accepted it and not later be able to call witnesses to contradict it or to comment upon it in closing.

(b) Cross-examination is that part of the advocate's craft which tends most to impress the layman and mystify the novice advocate. It should be clearly remembered that every question must be asked with the specific intention of advancing one or other of the objectives mentioned above. Thorough preparation of cross-examination is absolutely vital to ensure a logical and constructive sequence of questioning and to avoid speculative rambling which takes the case no further.

(c) A defence advocate usually has the advantage of previous disclosure of prosecution evidence and therefore a structured and well planned cross-examination is possible, subject to unforeseen matters arising. In the early days of advocacy when all advocates fear 'drying up', a list of potential questions, in an appropriate order, may form a useful long-stop, though the use of such lists in the heat of the moment can sometimes create difficulties. One must develop the self-confidence to know when a question is not worth asking and it is even more important to be able to identify those questions which genuinely take your client's interests further, whether by being relevant to the very issues in the case or by undermining the credibility of the opposing witness. It is thus vital in the course of preparation to be thoroughly on top of all relevant facts and in addition to have a thorough grasp of the rules of evidence. Few things are more deflating than to be told by the clerk to the magistrates that your question is improper in some respect. In particular the usual exclusionary rules of evidence apply to evidence sought to be obtained by cross-examination as much as to evidence-in-chief. So, for example, the rule against hearsay applies and a question to a witness, the answer to which would inevitably be hearsay, would be disallowed: see *R v Thomson* [1912] 3 KB 19.

(d) You must also bear in mind at all times the risk of 'losing the shield' of a client who has a criminal record by inadvertent attacks on the integrity of prosecution witnesses. For a fuller discussion of this see 20.3.

(e) In cross-examination, leading questions may be asked, indeed they are often essential, much of the cross-examiner's time being taken up with attempting to establish the version of facts which he contends is true. The judge or clerk will control cross-examination and disallow questions he considers improper, abusive, vexatious or oppressive. Having said that, in cases where the liberty of the subject may depend upon the outcome, a good deal of latitude is usually allowed to the defence advocate even if the matter to be put to prosecution witnesses is highly offensive to them.

The two most important topics within the law relating to cross-examination concern previous inconsistent statements and cross-examination on collateral issues.

15.6.2   PREVIOUS INCONSISTENT STATEMENTS

We have considered prior inconsistent statements by one's own witness, and the effect of s. 3 of the Criminal Procedure Act 1865. We will now consider the situation where one knows that one's opponent's witness has made a previous statement inconsistent with his evidence-in-chief. Can one adduce evidence of his former statement?

The relevant sections are ss. 4 and 5 of the 1865 Act:

4.   *If a witness, upon cross-examination as to a former statement made by him relative to the subject matter of the indictment or proceeding, and inconsistent with his present testimony, does not distinctly admit that he has made such statement, proof may be given that he did in fact make it; but before such proof can be given the circumstances of the supposed statement, sufficient to designate the particular occasion, must be mentioned to the witness, and he must be asked whether or not he has made such statement.*

5.   *A witness may be cross-examined as to previous statements made by him in writing, or reduce into writing, relative to the subject matter of the indictment or proceeding, without such writing being shown to him; but if it is intended to contradict such witness by the writing, his attention must, before such contradictory proof can be given, be called to those parts of the writing which are to be used for the purpose of so contradicting him: Provided always, that it shall be competent for the judge, at any time during the trial, to require the production of the writing for his inspection, and he may thereupon make such use of it for the purposes of the trial as he may think fit.*

15.6.2.1   Section 4

Section 4 applies to *oral statements*. If a witness is asked during cross-examination about a former statement made by him which is inconsistent with his present testimony, then if he does not admit that he made such a statement proof may be given that he did in fact make it. However, two things must be done before such proof can be given:

(a)   the circumstances in which the alleged statement were made must be put to the witness, and

(b)   he must then be asked whether he made such a statement.

If he then admits the statement or it is proved under the section, the effect is precisely the same as in the case of a hostile witness's previous statement, i.e. *they cancel each other out* — the former statement is not itself evidence of the facts stated (see *R v White* above). (N.B. If the witness is the accused there are special rules as to the effect of a previous admission which is now denied — see below on confessions.)

15.6.2.2   Section 5

Section 5 applies where the previous statement is in writing. A witness can be cross-examined about such a statement without the statement actually being shown to the witness. However, if the cross-examiner actually intends to contradict the witness by using the written statement he must draw the witness's attention to those parts he intends to so use.

A cross-examiner *is not obliged* to put the statement in evidence (remember that to do so makes the *whole* statement available to the jury and there may be matter in it that the cross-examiner would prefer them not to see), and this is so even if he shows it to the witness — this is not 'putting it in evidence'. However, the cross-examiner must do so if he wishes to use the document as a contradictory statement made by the witness, and the witness must of course be given a chance to explain the contradiction.

In such a case, the usual procedure is that counsel asks the witness to read the statement to himself and asks him if he wishes to adhere to what he said in chief. If the witness says 'no', counsel has achieved his object — he has shown the jury that the witness is unreliable. If he says 'yes', then it is necessary for counsel to decide whether or not to use the statement to contradict the witness, and if he does so the whole statement becomes evidence in the case. It is only a witness's *own statement* which should be handed to him — this rule cannot be used as a way of making a witness look at other people's statements and comment on inconsistencies so that those other statements become evidence in the case. See *R v Gillespie and Simpson* (1967) 51 Cr App R 172.

15.6.3 CROSS-EXAMINATION ON COLLATERAL ISSUES

Cross-examination is directed either to the *issues in the case* or *collateral issues*. When it is directed to the issues in the case, what is asked is up to counsel (subject to the judges' control of improper questions), and there is an opportunity for counsel to call evidence in contradiction or rebuttal of what a witness says.

However, there are special rules relating to cross-examination on collateral issues, which are designed to stop a multiplicity of side-tracks being pursued in the interests of saving time.

15.6.3.1 Cross-examination as to credit

The chief collateral issue is credit of the witness, i.e. the extent to which his evidence is trustworthy. The general rule is that a witness's answers in relation to the *issues* in the case can be contradicted by further evidence but that answers relevant only to *credit* are final.

The test is sometimes difficult to apply and it is not always easy to see where the issues in the case end and credit begins.

An excellent general example is the old case of *R v Burke* (1858) 8 Cox CC 44. The accused was charged with rape. A witness was called on behalf of the accused and when being sworn the witness who was Irish professed that he could not speak English. Accordingly he was sworn in Irish and gave his evidence in that language through an interpreter. Later it came to the prosecuting counsel's notice that there were two other witnesses who knew the present witness; they told prosecuting counsel that the witness could speak English perfectly well, had often spoken to them in English, and had even sung a song to them in English. The witness was cross-examined on this matter and he denied again that he could speak English or ever had done so. The prosecution applied to call the two girls to contradict his evidence and thus to prove that he was an untruthful person. The judge refused leave to call the two witnesses. It was held that whether or not this witness could or could not speak English was an entirely collateral matter and nothing to do with guilt or innocence of the prisoner. Although this would have tended to totally discredit the witness it was not allowed; however, if the very issue in the case had been his knowledge of English, e.g., his authorship of some relevant document, it would have been permitted.

There are several exceptions to the general rule that answers as to credit are final; in the following cases evidence in rebuttal is allowed:

(a) *Evidence of general reputation as a liar*

At common law after a witness has given evidence the other side can call evidence to swear that the first witness has a general reputation as a liar and that his evidence should not be believed: see *R v Richardson and Longman* (1969) 52 Cr App R 317. This is a very old exception rarely used today. Indeed in the case of *Richardson and Longman* the judge indicated that he had never heard of the rule before authority was produced to him. Evidence as to the reputation for untruthfulness of a complainant in a sexual case was admitted under this principle in *R v Bogie* [1992] Crim LR 301.

(b) Physical or mental condition

Evidence of the physical or mental condition of a witness such as to show he is unreliable may be admitted. In *Toohey v Metropolitan Police Commissioner* [1965] AC 595 the House of Lords held that it was proper to call a medical witness to give evidence that the alleged victim of a crime had a hysterical personality, and when under the influence of alcohol (as was the case on the facts) might well misunderstand situations (e.g., as on the facts where he had accused two men who were helping him up from where he had fallen with attempting to rob him). The primary importance of *Toohey* is that it sanctions the calling of an expert witness to impugn the reliability of an opponents' witness on medical grounds. The point was made that, where appropriate, a medical witness might be called to swear to the fact that a previous witness had, for example, impaired vision or hearing and the situation in *Toohey* was said to be analogous.

(c) Previous convictions

By s. 6 of the Criminal Procedure Act 1865 (applicable to civil proceedings as well) a witness 'may be asked whether he has been convicted of any ... [crime], and if he denies it the cross-examiner may prove it'. This is so *however little relevant* it is to the issue of the witness's credibility, e.g., whether the conviction was for careless driving or perjury. This does not, of course, apply to the accused who usually cannot be asked this kind of question (see below on the character of accused).

(d) Bias

Bias generally means taking bribes from a party or having very close relations with one party. It can however also mean the opposite, that is bias *against* a party, e.g., because of a grudge. If such an allegation is put in cross-examination and denied, evidence in rebuttal may be called. For example, in *R v Shaw* (1888) 16 Cox CC 503 the accused was charged with forgery. The main witness against him was one P who stated that he had laid in wait and seen the accused forging the documents in question. He was asked, in cross-examination, whether he did not have an ancient grudge against the accused arising out of an incident some two years before. He denied this. The defence were then allowed to call a witness to whom P had sworn to get even with the accused because of the grudge.

(e) Previous inconsistent statements

The whole question of previous inconsistent statements could be seen as an exemption to the rule on finality of answers on collateral issues. The proof of the making of the inconsistent statement in a criminal trial goes of course to credit — a collateral issue.

(f) Victims of rape offences

As indicated above, questions to the complainant as to whether she had previously had consensual intercourse with the accused are relevant to the issue of consent and therefore evidence may be called by *the accused* to rebut a denial. Questions about sexual experience with *other men* were formerly treated as relevant to credit only and the answers were therefore final. If the allegation went beyond mere intercourse with other men and suggested that the alleged victim was actually a prostitute, evidence of her behaviour with other men might be admitted because the victim's profession as a prostitute was central to the issue of consent. See *R v Bashir and Mansur* [1969] 3 All ER 692; and *R v Krausz* (1973) 57 Cr App R 466. Now, however, s. 2(1) of the Sexual Offences (Amendment) Act 1976 provides that at a trial for a 'rape offence' (as defined) the complainant may only be *cross-examined* about her experience with men other than the accused with leave of the judge, such leave only to be given where the judge is satisfied it would be unfair to the accused to refuse it. The same applies where the accused wishes to *call evidence* of the complainant's sexual experience with other men. The leave of the judge will be required on the same basis. An alleged victim of rape may however be cross-examined freely about her sexual relations with the accused himself.

For an early application of the basic rule see *R* v *Mills* (1978) 68 Cr App R 327. The accused was charged with rape and he wished to call evidence of the victim's sexual experience with other men. The judge formed the view that this was nothing to do with the issue in the case and was entirely designed to blacken the character of the complainant. It was held that in all circumstances it was perfectly proper to disallow the cross-examination.

An interesting case showing a good example of when a court thought leave to call such evidence would have been appropriate is *R* v *Viola* [1982] 3 All ER 73. The accused was charged with rape. He knew the complainant slightly and whilst in her flat on another matter had intercourse with her. She alleged that the intercourse occurred only after a violent assault. There were a number of suspicious features in the case, *inter alia*, that the complainant did not report the rape for some three days. The accused wished to cross-examine the alleged victim on three separate matters, namely:

(i)   An allegation that very shortly before the rape occurred the victim had made sexual advances to two men who came to her flat.

(ii) Shortly after the rape the complainant had sexual intercourse with her boyfriend without mentioning the rape to him.

(iii) On the day following the rape a neighbour saw a man in the complainant's flat lying on the sofa wearing nothing except a pair of slippers. The trial judge refused to permit cross-examination on these matters.

It was held on appeal that, although these matters were very much ones of fact and degree, in all the circumstances and taken with the other suspicious elements it would have been proper to allow cross-examination of the complainant on these matters, and in the circumstances the conviction was quashed.

This concludes the section on collateral issues. It should finally be noted that where it is the *accused* who is being cross-examined, there may be other specific principles to be considered where his credit is being impugned in certain ways, e.g., by adducing evidence of previous convictions in those cases where this is permitted. (See below on the character of the accused.)

15.7   Re-examination

In re-examination of one's own witnesses leading questions may not be asked. Questions must be confined to matters which arise out of cross-examination. A new matter may only be introduced with the leave of the judge and leave will not easily be given.

Re-examination is usually an attempt to salvage evidence which has been shaken in cross-examination. It involves counsel asking his witness, obviously in a more sympathetic manner than that shown by the cross-examiner, to explain any ambiguities or confusion in his evidence. It is an attempt to allow the witness to clarify matters and to re-establish his credit generally. Because re-examination is within the discretion of the judge there is very little case law on it.

15.8   Evidence in Rebuttal

All the evidence which the plaintiff or prosecutor intends to call should be before the court before the end of his case. New evidence can only be called after the defence case with leave of the judge and he will only give leave if the evidence relates to a matter which could not reasonably have been foreseen.

A good example is the old case of *R v Day* [1940] 1 All ER 402. The accused was charged with forging a cheque. The prosecution called evidence and then the defence gave evidence denying the forgery. Thereafter counsel for the prosecution applied for leave to call the evidence of a handwriting expert. The judge permitted this. On appeal the conviction was quashed. It was held that the evidence was wrongly admitted as it was not evidence arising on a matter which arose *ex improviso* nor evidence the necessity for which no human ingenuity could have foreseen. It should have been obvious to the prosecution that they would need a handwriting expert from the outset. There had accordingly been a material irregularity.

The judgment is not really as harsh as it may appear. There is some possibility that the accused in such cases might be prejudiced if he did not then have a chance of finding and bringing to court an expert witness of his own to rebut the prosecution's expert witness; there would thus be delay, adjournments and inconvenience.

This rule has been applied with some firmness until relatively recently. However, there are now signs that the court is relaxing it. So in *R v Francis* [1990] 1 WLR 1264 prosecuting counsel in error failed to call a police inspector to prove the circumstances of an identification parade. Later the prosecution were allowed to call the police inspector to rectify his omission. The Court of Appeal agreed that there was 'a further flexible discretion to admit evidence in proper circumstances'.

The increasing willingness of the court to be flexible is also shown in also *R v Patel* [1992] Crim LR 739 wherein new evidence was admitted even after counsel's closing speeches. The court actually said that it was probably not helpful to use the *ex improviso* test in such cases. It was always a matter for the judge's discretion and, although the later in the trial an application was made to call such evidence the less likely it would be for a judge to agree, in the present case there was no injustice, especially as the judge had given counsel every opportunity to seek an adjournment or take further instructions or even to apply for the discharge of the jury.

A very unusual recent example occurred in the case of *R v O'Hadhmaill* [1996] Crim LR 509 where the appellant was charged with playing a controlling role in a planned IRA bombing campaign. Although there had been no cross-examination of prosecution witnesses about the matter, defence counsel in his closing speech based a submission on the fact that there was at the time an IRA cease-fire and thus the accused's purpose in keeping the explosives was not necessarily to use them for bomb-making. Thereupon the judge allowed the prosecution to recall certain witnesses for further examination and cross-examination and supplementary speeches. On appeal it was argued that the judge was wrong to allow the evidence in rebuttal because the prosecution should have anticipated the defence argument. The Court of Appeal dismissed the appeal holding that as no questions had been asked of prosecution witnesses about the matter, it was a total surprise when defence counsel's closing argument contained evidential implications to the effect that there had been no bomb activity in England during the relevant period. The court held that the interests of justice required the judge to permit the prosecution to rebut that evidence.

This concludes the notes on testimony, but it is appropriate to consider one further matter before leaving the subject.

15.9   The Judge's Right to Call Witnesses

It is an essential part of the adversarial process that the parties themselves decide which witnesses they wish to call and what questions to ask. In a criminal trial, the competitive nature of the adversarial process has some refinements to mitigate it. First, the prosecution do not have a duty to press ruthlessly for a conviction at any price, they should present evidence aimed at securing conviction but must also, e.g., tell the accused of matters helpful to him (e.g., if an identification witness has given a description of the suspect that does not fit the accused). The prosecutor ought to act as a 'minister of justice'.

Likewise in a criminal trial the judge has an overriding duty to see that justice is done and has the power to call a witness whom neither side has called (provided he is competent and compellable of course). This should happen very rarely: see *R v Harris* [1927] 2 KB 587, where several accused were charged with dishonesty. A number of the accused pleaded guilty at the outset and thereafter remained in the dock during the trial of the others. At the conclusion of the prosecution and defence cases the judge asked one of the accused who had previously pleaded guilty whether he was prepared to give evidence. The man said that he was, and the judge then called him to give evidence and his evidence strengthened the case against H. The resulting conviction was quashed on appeal. It was held that in order that injustice must not be done to an accused the judge should not call a witness in a criminal trial after the case for the defence is closed except in a case where the matter arises in such a way that no human ingenuity could foresee it. See also *R v Cleghorn* [1967] 2 QB 584.

The Court of Appeal has several times recently reaffirmed that a judge's right to call a witness should only be exercised very sparingly. It should only be exercised where the judge concludes that a certain witness should testify in the interests of justice and both parties are declining to call him. This may often occur where the defence would like the witness to be called for the purpose of cross-examination but, if the defence call the witness, they would be unable to cross-examine him since he is their own witness. In such a case the judge should consider an application to call the witness if he thinks the evidence will assist. A judge must be cautious however where neither party wishes to call a witness. So, for example, in *R v McDowell* [1984] Crim LR 486 a judge called a witness whom neither side wished to call in order to satisfy a query by a jury member after the jury had retired. The court held that as it was unable to assess the effect of this material irregularity the conviction had to be quashed.

In the rare case where the judge does call a witness he can be cross-examined by both sides but only with the leave of the trial judge. Leave will be given if the evidence is adverse to either party, and thus unless the witness in effect says nothing relevant to the case, leave will usually be given. Cross-examination may be restricted to the areas about which he has testified: see *Coulson v Disborough* [1894] 2 QB 316.

SIXTEEN

THE LAW OF EVIDENCE (3): THE RULE AGAINST HEARSAY

16.1   Introduction

The rule against hearsay used to be described as the great rule underlying the whole of the law of evidence. It is still of considerable importance but there are now very numerous exceptions to the basic rule forbidding hearsay which are applicable in criminal cases. *Cross on Evidence* gives a definition of the rule as 'A statement other than one made by a person while giving oral evidence in the proceedings is inadmissible as evidence of any fact stated.'

This rule applies to both oral and written statements and it applies even to what the person now giving evidence said out of court. When the rule applies to prevent a witness saying in court what *he himself* said on some other occasion it is usually called 'the rule against narrative' or 'the rule against self-corroboration'. It is important to remember that those occasions discussed in the earlier section on testimony, where a witness *may* repeat what he said on some previous occasion, e.g., sexual complaints, previous consistent statements used to rebut an allegation of recent fabrication, etc., do *not* infringe the hearsay rule because the previous statement is *not evidence of the facts stated* but of the maker's consistency.

There are many justifications of the rule against hearsay. As hearsay statements emanate from a person who is not under oath and is not before the court, that person's lack of truthfulness, defective memory or poor powers of observation cannot be called into question by cross-examination. In addition there is a danger of inaccuracy through repetition, especially of oral statements, and the problem that juries may attach too much weight to hearsay without realising its weaknesses.

There is no doubt that the strict application of the rule in criminal cases may lead to injustice. It means that a case will be decided without hearing all the available evidence, imperfect though some of it may be. It should also not be forgotten that the operation of the rule is not always for the protection of the accused — it may in fact prejudice him — see the facts of *Sparks* v R below.

16.1.1   ILLUSTRATIONS OF THE RULE

16.1.1.1   *R* v *Gibson* (1887) 18 QBD 537

A man was struck by a heavy stone and testified that, immediately after, a woman who could not be identified and who was not called at the trial had said, pointing to Gibson's house, 'the person who threw the stone went in there'. It was held that the conviction of Gibson would be quashed on the grounds that this hearsay evidence should not have been admitted.

16.1.1.2 *Sparks v R* [1964] AC 964

The accused, a white man, was charged with indecent assault on a four-year-old child. He wished to bring evidence that the child had said to her mother after the assault that 'It was a coloured boy who did it.' It was held that there is no rule that permits hearsay evidence merely because it relates to identity or because it favours the accused.

16.1.1.3 *Patel v Controller of Customs* [1966] AC 356

It was held that the words 'produce of Morocco' stamped upon bags of coriander were inadmissible to prove the country of origin of the coriander. The words were stamped on the bag with the express intention of asserting a fact and were thus hearsay.

16.1.1.4 *R v Muir* (1983) 79 Cr App R 153

The accused was charged with theft of a hired video. He contended that two unknown men whom he had assumed to be from the hire company had collected it from his house. The district manager of the company said that repossession of the equipment could be carried out by the local showroom or by the head office only. He said it had not been repossessed by the local office and that he had contacted head office and been told that no one from there had called on the appellant. It was held on appeal that the question was whether, as a matter of fact the video had been repossessed. As the district manager was the best person to give evidence of this his evidence was reliable. The court appears to have ducked the hearsay problem.

It is suggested with all due deference to the apparent common sense of the outcome that the evidence in question *was* hearsay. There are clearly very great difficulties about proving this kind of negative.

16.1.1.5 *Myers v DPP* [1965] AC 1001

The accused were charged with frauds involving dealing in stolen cars with false documents which actually related to scrapped vehicles. It was vital for the prosecution case to identify the actual cars involved which it was possible to do by reference to the number cast into the cylinder block. It was accordingly essential to prove the motor manufacturers' records to show the numbers which corresponded to the stolen cars. These records were microfilmed copies of record cards which had passed along the production line with the vehicle and on to which relevant numbers were enterd by workmen. It was held that these records amounted to hearsay and came within no recognised exception to the rule. The creation of new hearsay exceptions was for the legislature and accordingly the evidence was not admissible. In the circumstances, however, the proviso was applied and the convictions affirmed.

The actual effect of this final recognition of the truth that business records were all hearsay, and therefore inadmissible, was reversed by the almost immediate passing of the Criminal Evidence Act 1965.

16.2 Unnoticed Hearsay

It is apparent when reading reports of decided cases that courts do not always appreciate the existence of a hearsay problem. As Cross says this may sometimes be because the court regarded the applicability of some exception as too obvious to mention but there are also instances of the very existence of any problem at all being overlooked.

A clear case of this is *R v Cooper* [1969] 1 QB 267 where it is apparent that a considerable volume of hearsay which was not within any of the exceptions to the exclusionary rule, and therefore quite inadmissible, was allowed. Moreover, neither at first instance nor on appeal is there even any reference to the problem existing — the case as reported turning on quite a different point. The accused was charged with assault and whilst on remand in custody he was visited by two friends D and B. D gave evidence that one day whilst walking away from the prison B had confessed to him that he, B, and not Cooper had committed the assault. The trial court seems not to have appreciated that there was any hearsay problem with this evidence. Indeed the trial court subsequently permitted a photograph of B to be produced to prove the close similarity between the defendant and B.

16.3 Is It Hearsay At All?

When one is confronted by a statement made by someone out of court, whether oral or in writing, naturally one needs to consider the possibility that it is hearsay. It is by no means always the case that words said outside court and repeated in it will amount to hearsay. What matters is whether the statement from the speaker outside court is *tendered to prove the truth of its contents*.

The leading case clearly demonstrating this is *Subramaniam v Public Prosecutor for Malaya* [1956] 1 WLR 965. The accused was found in possession of ammunition contrary to an emergency regulation. He put forward the defence that he had been captured by terrorists and that at all material times he was acting under duress. He wished to give evidence of the threats made to him by the terrorists but the trial judge ruled that evidence of the conversation with the terrorists was inadmissible hearsay. The accused was convicted and on appeal the Privy Council held that evidence of words spoken is not hearsay and is admissible where it is proposed to establish by the evidence not the *truth* of the statement but the *fact that it was made* as being relevant to an event in issue namely the state of mind of the accused. The conviction was quashed.

16.4 Nature of Hearsay

It is suggested by Cross that you must ask two questions to find out if something is hearsay:

(a)   For what purpose is the statement put in evidence?

(b)   What fact is the statement tendered to prove?

If the statement expressly or impliedly *asserts a fact* the hearsay rule applies, and the *statement must be excluded as inadmissible* unless it comes within one of the exceptions.

16.4.1   EXPRESS ASSERTIONS

Express assertions occur where the witness who is not before the court has stated that a certain state of affairs is the case, e.g., as in the cases of *Gibson* and *Sparks* shown above. With express assertions there must be an intention to communicate, thus non-verbal behaviour such as nods, gestures, pointing or signs may well amount to an express assertion when what the person making the sign did is recounted to the court by another witness. As there must however, be some intention to communicate nobody has ever suggested that, say, a footprint, or yawning is subject to the hearsay rule.

16.4.2   IMPLIED ASSERTIONS

The reason why express assertions are excluded by the hearsay rule is obvious. They suffer from all the potential defects referred to above. The position may however be different with *implied* assertions. This is where the maker of the statement did not intend to assert any particular fact. An example is if the prosecution need to establish that X was present at a given place and time but no eye-witness has been found who can positively say he was there. However one person who was there heard someone shout out 'Hallo X'. Since shouting 'Hallo' is not an assertion of anything, would this fall foul of the hearsay rule?

The reason why it has often been suggested that these kind of statements ought to be admissible as exceptions to the hearsay rule is that there is a smaller risk of untruthfulness with implied assertions. It has been suggested for example that if in *R v Gibson* (1887) 18 QBD 537 the woman bystander had been heard to shout 'Hallo Mr Gibson where are you going?' This would have been admissible because the woman was not intending to assert anything to a third party. The authorities in England are not entirely conclusive. Consider the following cases.

16.4.2.1 *Teper v R* [1952] AC 480

The accused was charged with arson of his own shop in order to obtain insurance. Evidence was given by a policeman that some 26 minutes after the fire started and over 200 yards away from the fire he heard a woman's voice shouting 'your place burning and you going away from the fire' and thereupon a black car containing a man who resembled the accused went past. The woman could not be traced at the time of the trial. It was held that the words spoken by the woman were inadmissible hearsay. They asserted a fact, namely the presence of the accused at the time of the crime. The conviction was quashed.

16.4.2.2 *R v Lydon* (1986) 85 Cr App R 221

The case of *Patel v Controller of Customs* [1966] AC 356 has been referred to in **16.1.1.3**. A case often contrasted with that is *R v Lydon* (1986) 85 Cr App R 221 where the accused, Sean Lydon, was charged with a robbery at a post office in Oxfordshire. He lived in Neasden, North London. There was identification evidence from a taxi driver who identified him as a man he had taken on a journey from Oxfordshire to Neasden on the day in question. The car used in the robbery was abandoned near where the taxi driver had picked Lydon up and that car had been stolen from the Neasden area. A mile from the post office on the road between it and the place where the car was found abandoned, a gun was found on the grass verge similar to the gun used in the robbery. Near the gun were two pieces of rolled paper on which was written the name 'Sean'. Ink of similar appearance to that ink was found on the gun barrel. It was argued that allowing the pieces of paper to go forward was to permit hearsay evidence. The Court of Appeal held that it was not hearsay evidence but simply a piece of circumstantial evidence refuting the defendant's claimed alibi.

With all respect it seems that this case is dubious authority. Clearly the name written on the pieces of paper does not assert anything very much. But what surely matters is what the *prosecution* intend to assert by the use of the paper. Clearly they wish to 'assert' that Sean was the owner of the gun and was present at the time. Thus the evidence was tendered with a view to inviting the jury to draw conclusions which are of a hearsay nature.

16.4.2.3 *R v Korniak* (1983) 76 Cr App R 145

This is another difficult case. The accused was seen carrying a bag by policemen. It was found to contain valuable jewellery. At first the accused denied the bag was his and told lies but eventually admitted that he had bought the bag from a man who had at first asked £2,000 for it but eventually sold it for only £100. The accused then told the police they would have to 'do' him for receiving stolen property. He was charged with handling. He did not give evidence and at the time of trial there was no evidence to prove that the jewellery was stolen. The direction by the judge was that the jury could infer from the evidence that the jewellery was stolen. On appeal the grounds were that there was no evidence from which the jury could safely infer that the goods were stolen. It was held, rejecting the appeal, that there was ample evidence. Although the accused's own *belief* that it was stolen was relevant only to mens rea and not the fact there was sufficient circumstantial evidence of the fact of theft.

This case can be compared with *R v Marshall* [1977] Crim LR 106 where Marshall was charged with handling stolen goods and the only proof that they were stolen was that Marshall admitted that he had bought the goods from a man who had told him they were stolen. It was argued for the accused that such an admission was no more than hearsay and thus the status of the goods as stolen could not be proved. That submission was upheld. This case was not however cited in *Korniak*.

16.4.2.4 *R v Kearley* [1992] 2 AC 228

All these cases must be read in the light of this new leading case. It follows on from and in part resolves difficulties caused in two conflicting earlier authorities. The first of these is *Woodhouse v Hall* (1980) 72 Cr App R 316. In this case the Divisional Court held that evidence of conversation between policemen and women working in a massage parlour in which details of availability and cost of sexual services were discussed was admissible as non-hearsay and circumstantial evidence that the premises were operated as a brothel.

Subsequently, however, in *R v Harry* (1986) 86 Cr App R 105 the question was the admissibility of evidence of telephone calls made to certain premises by a person who apparently wished to buy drugs from those premises. In the case of *Harry* one of two co-defendants wished to adduce evidence that the callers had always asked for his co-defendant P in order to suggest that P and not Harry was the dealer. The Court of Appeal held that the proposed evidence was hearsay because it was being offered to prove the truth of facts asserted by the callers.

In *Kearley's* case the Court of Appeal followed *Woodhouse v Hall* rather than *Harry* and held that evidence of the contents of telephone calls received at premises to the effect that the persons calling it expected to be able to buy drugs from the premises was admissible and was not hearsay. In the House of Lords however by a majority of three to two the House held that the evidence of the caller's words were either *irrelevant* to prove that K was supplying drugs because it merely tended to show that the callers believed that he was supplying drugs; or in the alternative that evidence of the calls *was* hearsay because the usefulness of the evidence depended on the trier of fact believing in the implied truth of matters asserted in the calls, namely that the persons telephoning expected to be able to buy drugs from the person at the other end of the telephone. Many find that the reasoning of the House of Lords is less than convincing and the point is clearly nicely balanced since the Court of Appeal reached a different conclusion and the House of Lords only reached its conclusion by a majority of three to two.

We have so far considered the problem of ascertaining whether a given statement made out of court is, or is not, hearsay at all. If it is not hearsay then it is admissible unless it offends some other separate exclusionary rule. If it is hearsay then in principle it is excluded unless it fits one or other of the numerous following exceptions.

16.5 Exceptions to the Rule in Criminal Cases

A number of exceptions have grown up, under common law or statute, some of them dating back centuries. They are:

(a) Admissions and confessions (16.6 and 17.1).

(b) Statements made by deceased persons (16.7).

(c) Statements in former proceedings (**16.8**).

(d) Statutory exceptions (**16.9**).

(e) Statements admitted as part of the *res gestae* (**16.12**).

We shall now consider these exceptions in turn.

16.6 Admissions and Confessions

This topic is one of the most vital in practice. Because it is so important and lengthy it will be dealt with separately in **Chapter 17** together with the linked topics of questioning of suspects, the right to silence, and the Codes of Practice issued under the Police and Criminal Evidence Act 1984.

16.7 Statements made by Deceased Persons

Odd though it seems, the fact that the maker of an out-of-court statement has since died is not in itself a ground for the statement to be admitted in evidence. Thus it may well be, e.g., that the evidence of the only truly independent eye-witness of a crime is lost because of the rule against hearsay. A number of common law exceptions exist which do permit the evidence of persons who have died before the trial to be put in at the trial. These were developed by the common law judges and there is a different rationale applicable to each of the several exceptions. It must be borne in mind that under ss. 23 and 24 of the Criminal Justice Act 1988, see **16.10.3**, statements *in writing* by deceased persons are now generally admissible. The exceptions which we are about to consider therefore will be chiefly relevant in the case of *oral* statements made by persons who have died before the trial.

16.7.1 DECLARATIONS AGAINST INTEREST

In criminal cases, the oral or written statement by a person since deceased of a fact which, at the time of making it, the deceased knew to be against his or her financial or proprietary interest is admissible as evidence of the facts mentioned in it, provided the person now deceased had personal knowledge of such facts. The basis of the rule is the presumed likelihood of any such statement being true since people do not commonly make assertions contrary to their own interests unless they are true.

16.7.2 DECLARATIONS MADE IN THE COURSE OF DUTY

The oral or written statement of a person who has died since making the statement but which was made in pursuance of a duty to record or report his or her acts is admissible as evidence of the truth of the contents of the statement so long as the record or report was made roughly contemporaneously with the doing of the act and there was no motive to misrepresent the facts. Thus, for example, such things as plans drawn by surveyors, even from many years before, are likely to be admissible under this principle.

This old exception to the hearsay rule is still of use in modern times. For an interesting example see *R* v *McGuire* (1985) 81 Cr App R 323. The accused was convicted of arson by setting fire to his own hotel to obtain insurance monies. Evidence was provided by a Home Office scientific officer who had inspected the hotel soon after the fire. He had recorded certain facts and also given his opinion that the fire was likely to have started in a certain room. This was helpful to the accused's own explanation and at the trial he sought to admit the report both as to the facts and as to the opinion, the scientific officer having died since making this statement. It was held that the report would be admitted as to the *facts* only but not as to the opinion part which was excluded (now the whole of the evidence would be admissible under ss. 24 and 30 of the Criminal Justice Act 1988 — see **21.2.6**).

16.7.3   DYING DECLARATIONS

Oral or written statements of a deceased person are admissible evidence of the cause of his death at a trial for his murder or manslaughter *provided* he was under a settled, hopeless expectation of death when the statement was made *and provided* he would have been a competent witness if called to give evidence at that time.

So long as the expectation of death is firm it does not matter if the deceased takes some time to die, see *R* v *Bernadotti* (1869) 11 Cox CC 316 in which the victim made a dying declaration believing that he was about to die. He did not in fact die for nearly three weeks. It was held that there was no objection to the admission of the dying declaration. If a man believes himself dying it is equal to the solemnity of taking an oath.

But the expectations of death must be 'settled', see *R* v *Jenkins* (1869) LR 1 CCR 187 in which the victim's statement was taken down by a magistrates' clerk who added at the end the words 'made with no hope of my recovery'. The victim altered the words to read 'made with no *present* hope of my recovery' and it was held that the change of wording showed that the victim did entertain a faint hope and therefore the declaration was excluded.

There is no requirement that a jury should be warned that a dying declaration should be corroborated even if it is the only evidence against the accused. The words of the declaration must, however, be clear and unambiguous and the statement must have been completed before the person died. See *Nembhard* v *R* [1981] 1 WLR 1515.

16.8   Statements in Former Proceedings

A number of statutes provide for the reception of evidence of what was said in depositions and testimony at subsequent stages of criminal proceedings. There are also statutes which provide that subject to certain procedural safeguards, certain kinds of witnesses may have their statement taken on oath by a magistrate out of court and that such a statement may be used at a subsequent trial on indictment. The variety of common law and statutory rules relating to this have been largely superseded by s. 24 of the Criminal Justice Act 1988 which covers statements put in evidence in former proceedings which are contained in a record (i.e. the transcript of that evidence). It is worth noting a couple of examples, however, because the courts have developed a discretion to exclude such evidence, even though it may fulfil the strict criteria for admissibility and the exercise of that discretion is a good illustration of the way in which the court's other discretions under the Criminal Justice Act 1988 may well be used (see **16.10.8**).

In *R* v *Hall* [1973] QB 496, X gave evidence for the prosecution at the trial of the accused and the jury disagreed. Before the retrial X died. At the trial the defence wished to put in evidence the transcript of X's evidence at the first trial because X had shown himself to be a shifty and cantankerous witness and the prosecution case in part depended on X's evidence. The judge refused to permit this, holding that the evidence was inadmissible under the hearsay rule. It was held on appeal that the conviction would be quashed in that the deposition of the witness who had died before trial was admissible in evidence subject to the judge's discretion and the judge had wrongly exercised his discretion in the present case.

16.9   Statutory Exceptions

There are numerous statutes which provide exceptions to the hearsay rule.

16.10   Major Statutory Exceptions to the Hearsay Rule

16.10.1   CRIMINAL JUSTICE ACT 1967, s. 9

This is the most important section in practice. It is in daily use in thousands of criminal cases throughout the country. The section provides that statements in writing are admissible in criminal proceedings at trial provided the statements are signed and contain a declaration in specified words by the maker that they are true and that the maker knows he is liable to prosecution if he states anything untruthfully.

Before such a statement is admissible in evidence it must be served on the opposing party. That party (whether prosecution or defence) may then object to the statement and if he does object the statement is inadmissible. The objection may be made on any ground at all, or indeed without giving any ground. If a party objects to his opponent using the statement the court has no power to overrule the objection and to allow the statement to be put in. Accordingly the section is only used for uncontroversial statements.

A case which took prosecutors by surprise and showed that s. 9 should not be used for proving important matters is *Lister* v *Quaife* [1983] 1 WLR 48. In this case the accused was stopped leaving a branch of a chain store carrying a dress bearing a sale sticker. She could not prove that she had bought it but on being charged made a statement saying she had bought it at another branch of the chain store and had brought it back to change it. Before her trial the prosecution notified her that they would be tendering under s. 9 of the 1967 Act two written statements to the effect that no such dress would have been on sale at any of the store's branches at the sale price for three weeks after the date on which she claimed to have originally bought the dress and moreover that the branch at which she claimed to have bought it had no stocks of that particular dress. No objection to the s. 9 notice was served requiring the makers to attend. At trial their statements were read out. The defendant however persisted with her version that the officials of the chain store must be mistaken. The prosecution submitted that once statements were not objected to under s. 9 the defendant could not give evidence contradicting them. The defendant however was acquitted. On appeal by the prosecutor it was held that the statement under s. 9 was not deemed to be conclusive evidence of the matter stated in it but was treated in the same way as any other evidence. It would be better in a case where the evidence in question was crucial to the issue for s. 9 not to be used but the witness to be called in person.

The procedural requirements of s. 9 must be strictly complied with. Thus in *Paterson* v *DPP* [1990] RTR 329 the accused was convicted of driving with excess alcohol and as part of the case against him a seven-page statement by a policeman was tendered under s. 9 of the 1967 Act. The statutory declaration required by the Act was at page 7 and referred to '6 pages signed' by the officer. Also, the officer had not signed one of the pages. The prosecution argued that these errors were immaterial, but the court excluded the evidence, holding that the 1967 Act must be strictly complied with.

16.10.2   BANKER'S BOOKS EVIDENCE ACT 1879, ss. 3 AND 4

Section 3 provides that:

> ... *a copy of any entry in a banker's book shall in all legal proceedings be received as prima facie evidence of such entry, and of the matters, transactions and accounts therein recorded.*

Section 4 adds the qualification that the book in question must have been one of the ordinary books in the bank and the entries must have been made in the ordinary course of business. Most of the case law has involved definition of what is a 'bank' and what is meant by a 'banker's book'. This is a useful provision which may, in any case, be superseded where there is difficulty in the technicalities by evidence which would be admissible under s. 24 of the Criminal Justice Act 1988 which applies widely to any kind of business record (see **16.10.3.2**).

16.10.3 DOCUMENTARY EVIDENCE UNDER ss. 23–28, CRIMINAL JUSTICE ACT 1988; s. 69, POLICE AND CRIMINAL EVIDENCE ACT 1984

The facts of *Myers* v *DPP* [1965] AC 1001 are set out at **16.1.1.5**. The case was immediately followed by the passing of the Criminal Evidence Act 1965. This was a one-section Act which had the effect of creating a new exception to the hearsay rule whereby, in short, the records of a trade or business were admissible in evidence if the person supplying the information in the record was unavailable to testify for one of certain specified reasons, namely death, absence abroad, illness, he could not be traced or identified or even if found would have no recollection of the matters contained in the records. These last two reasons were the most important in practice and covered the common situation (as in *Myers* v *DPP* itself) where an employee made some kind of record at work and the record became relevant to a criminal trial, often some considerable time after its compilation. The employee (who may, as in *Myers* v *DPP*, be one of many engaged in the activity concerned) cannot then be identified, or if he can be identified would not be able to say that he had any genuine recollection of the circumstances of what he recorded, e.g., because he has made many such written records every day over a long period and has no reason to remember the one with which the criminal trial is concerned.

The 1965 Act worked reasonably well although the restriction of its scope to 'trade or business records' proved inconvenient. In a number of cases this prevented the records of certain bodies being used in evidence because they were not 'trades or businesses'. Thus the records of an NHS hospital, and even the Home Office, were excluded in decided cases even though their records would obviously be just as accurate as, say, the ledger accounts of a corner shop whose records would in fact have been admissible under the 1965 Act.

The 1965 Act was eventually replaced by s. 68 of the Police and Criminal Evidence Act 1984. Section 68 was a lengthy section which itself was supplemented by a lengthy Schedule and which extended the possibility of admitting documentary hearsay evidence to any situation where there was a documentary record compiled by a person acting in some kind of official or employment duty. Section 68 was, however, badly drafted in some respects. It gave rise to a number of difficult cases particularly in the context of evidence contained in police records.

Section 68 was repealed and replaced by the Criminal Justice Act 1988 which now contains the law on documentary evidence. There are two sections which deal with evidence in documents. Section 23 has to do with *first-hand hearsay* contained in such a document and that document may be of almost any kind. Section 24 has to do with *second-hand hearsay* made in a document in some kind of business or official context. When deciding upon what additional conditions would need to be satisfied before second-hand hearsay should be admitted, the legislature decided on a test fairly similar to that contained in s. 4 of the Civil Evidence Act 1968, that is to say that evidence provided in a business context is likely to be inherently more reliable than documentary evidence which comes about more casually. In the following parts of this text we shall consider three different aspects of ss. 23 and 24 where there are crucially different provisions which apply, namely:

(a) First-hand documentary evidence under s. 23.

(b) Second-hand documentary evidence under s. 24 in an ordinary business context.

(c) Second-hand documentary evidence under s. 24 which has been prepared expressly for the purpose of a criminal trial or investigation.

These provisions deal with evidence contained in a document. 'Document' is comprehensively defined to include maps, photographs, discs, tapes, videos and films as well as writing on paper. The sections read:

23. First-hand hearsay

(1)   Subject—

   (a)   to subsection (4) below;

   (b)   to paragraph 1A of Schedule 2 to the Criminal Appeal Act 1968 (evidence given orally at original trial to be given orally at retrial); and

   (c)   to section 69 of the Police and Criminal Evidence Act 1984 (evidence from computer records),

a statement made by a person in a document shall be admissible in criminal proceedings as evidence of any fact of which direct oral evidence by him would be admissible if—

   (i)   the requirements of one of the paragraphs of subsection (2) below are satisfied; or

   (ii)   the requirements of subsection (3) below are satisfied.

(2)   The requirements mentioned in subsection (1)(i) above are—

   (a)   that the person who made the statement is dead or by reason of his bodily or mental condition unfit to attend as a witness;

   (b)   that—

   (i)   the person who made the statement is outside the United Kingdom; and

   (ii)   it is not reasonably practicable to secure his attendance; or

   (c)   that all reasonable steps have been taken to find the person who made the statement, but that he cannot be found.

(3)   The requirements mentioned in subsection (1)(ii) above are—

   (a)   that the statement was made to a policeman or some other person charged with the duty of investigating offences or charging offenders; and

   (b)   that the person who made it does not give oral evidence through fear or because he is kept out of the way.

(4)   Subsection (1) above does not render admissible a confession made by an accused person that would not be admissible under section 76 of the Police and Criminal Evidence Act 1984.

24. Business etc., documents

(1)   Subject—

   (a)   to subsections (3) and (4) below;

   (b)   to paragraph 1A of Schedule 2 to the Criminal Appeal Act 1968; and

   (c)   to section 69 of the Police and Criminal Evidence Act 1984,

a statement in a document shall be admissible in criminal proceedings as evidence of any fact of which direct oral evidence would be admissible, if the following conditions are satisfied—

   (i)   the document was created or received by a person in the course of a trade, business, profession or other occupation, or as the holder of a paid or unpaid office; and

   (ii)   the information contained in the document was supplied by a person (whether or not the maker of the statement) who had, or may reasonably be supposed to have had, personal knowledge of the matters dealt with.

(2)   Subsection (1) above applies whether the information contained in the document was supplied directly or indirectly but if it was supplied indirectly, only if each person through whom it was supplied received it—

   (a)   in the course of a trade, business, profession or other occupation; or

   (b)   as the holder of a paid or unpaid office.

(3)   Subsection (1) above does not render admissible a confession made by an accused person that would not be admissible under section 76 of the Police and Criminal Evidence Act 1984.

(4)   A statement prepared otherwise than in accordance with section 29 below or an order under paragraph 6 of Schedule 13 to this Act or under section 30 or 31 below for the purposes—

> (a) of pending or contemplated criminal proceedings; or
>
> (b) of a criminal investigation,
>
> shall not be admissible by virtue of subsection (1) above unless—
>
> (i) the requirements of one of the paragraphs of subsection (2) of section 23 above are satisfied; or
>
> (ii) the requirements of subsection (3) of that section are satisfied; or
>
> (iii) the person who made the statement cannot reasonably be expected (having regard to the time which has elapsed since he made the statement and to all the circumstances) to have any recollection of the matters dealt with in the statement.

16.10.4 FIRST-HAND DOCUMENTARY EVIDENCE UNDER s. 23

Section 23 permits a statement made by a person in a document to be admissible as evidence of any fact of which direct oral evidence by him would have been admissible if one of the following reasons is proved:

(a) The person who made the statement is dead or by reason of bodily or mental condition is unfit to attend as a witness.

(b) The person who made the statement is outside the United Kingdom and it is not reasonably practicable to secure his attendance.

(c) All reasonable steps have been taken to find the person who made the statement but he cannot be found.

These reasons therefore would allow the putting in evidence of a witness statement of any kind made by a person.

Example W is on the way to the airport on holiday when he sees a robbery. He has no time to stop and carries on to the airport but whilst on holiday writes a letter to his mother describing the incident he saw. He comes back from his holiday but later dies in an accident. The prosecution appeal for witnesses to the robbery and his mother provides a copy of the letter he wrote to her describing the incident. This would be prima facie admissible.

(d) There is in addition a further provision, s. 23(3), for allowing the putting in evidence of a statement made to a policeman or some other person charged with the duty of investigating offences or charging offenders (such as a store detective or a Customs and Excise officer). In the case of such statements the additional ground is that the statement will be admissible if the person who made it does not give oral evidence through fear or because he is kept out of the way.

This provision allows the putting in evidence of first-hand hearsay in written form. However, its scope is severely limited by the application of two later sections, ss. 25 and 26 which we shall consider in due course. Before we do so it is now appropriate to consider s. 24.

16.10.5 SECOND-HAND HEARSAY CONTAINED IN A DOCUMENT, s. 24

A statement in a document may be admissible by s. 24 as evidence of any fact of which direct oral evidence would be admissible, even though it is second-hand hearsay, provided that the following conditions are satisfied:

(a) the document must have been created or received by a person in the course of a trade or business profession or other occupation or as the holder of a paid or unpaid office; and

(b) the information contained in the document must have been supplied by a person (whether or not the maker of the statement) who had or may reasonably be supposed to have had personal knowledge of the matters dealt with.

This provision therefore supposes that there will be either one or two people involved in the 'document-creating process'. If there is any other person or persons so that there is a chain of information ending up with the document, then there is further provision that each intermediary between the person who supplies the information and the person who compiles it in a document must have received it either in the course of a trade, business, profession or other occupation or as the holder of a paid or unpaid office.

We shall first deal with documents which arise in an ordinary business context as indicated above.

16.10.6 BUSINESS DOCUMENTS

Example 1 A, a delivery driver for a computer firm, delivers 20 computers to the premises of a retail company X Ltd. On his return to his own firm he tells his delivery manager Z that he completed the delivery and the delivery manager makes a note of this in his records. Sometime later, at the premises of the retail company two computers are believed to be missing from stock and an employee is charged with their theft. In order to prove the number of computers that were in fact delivered on this occasion the deliveries record of the computer manufacturers would prima facie be admissible under this provision.

Example 2 S is the unpaid social secretary of a rugby club. Part of his duties include the management and supervision of the bar of the club and the keeping of the accounts for it. The bar is managed by a part-time paid barman. S's job includes receiving deliveries and checking stock. It is suspected that the barman is pilfering from stock and he is eventually charged with theft of some spirits found in his car. At his trial the records of deliveries and accounts kept by S would prima facie be admissible under this provision to establish the pilfering.

Where a document is compiled in what might be described as the course of everyday life, without any regard being had at the time of its making to its usefulness in criminal proceedings, then there is no necessary requirement that the person who made the document or gained the information should be unavailable for any particular reason. A court would thus be able to admit in evidence any such document even though apparently the people involved in its creation were available to testify. However there is a general discretion under s. 25 of the 1988 Act to which we shall come shortly to disallow the giving in evidence of such documents on various criteria which we shall consider.

16.10.7 CRIMINAL INVESTIGATION DOCUMENTS

In addition to this, where the document was prepared for the purposes of pending or contemplated *criminal proceedings or a criminal investigation*, there is an express provision that the document shall *not* be admissible in criminal proceedings unless either the witness is unavailable for one of the reasons given above in the context of s. 23 for the absence of the original maker of the statement, or an additional reason provided by s. 24(4), namely that 'the person who made the statement cannot reasonably be expected (having regard to the time which has elapsed since he made the statement and to all the circumstances) to have any recollection of the matters dealt with in the statement'. In other words there is a presumption against admissibility of documents which amount to second-hand hearsay and which are prepared expressly for the purpose of criminal proceedings unless one of these particular reasons is shown for not calling as a witness the person who is the possessor of the original information which should be communicated to the court. This applies to both prosecution and defence, although of course in practice the section is much more likely to be relied upon by the prosecution. Quite apart from the need to demonstrate one of these reasons for unavailability the application to put in the evidence is still subject to the court's discretion (see below).

16.10.8   THE COURT'S DISCRETION TO EXCLUDE ADMISSIBLE EVIDENCE, ss. 25 AND 26

A person who wishes to put in documentary evidence under ss. 23 and 24 has first to jump the hurdle of strict admissibility based on the matters already discussed. Even where that hurdle is cleared, however, that does not mean that the evidence will be admissible. There is a further independent provision which needs to be considered. This is that the court has a set of discretions, contained in ss. 25 and 26 of the 1988 Act, which may lead it to exclude evidence which would be strictly admissible, in the interests of giving the accused a fair trial. The discretions in s. 25 of the Act govern ordinary statements admitted under s. 23 and business documents admitted under s. 24. The discretions in s. 26 govern documents prepared for a criminal investigation or trial.

16.10.9   THE DISCRETIONS IN s. 25

By s. 25 of the 1988 Act, it is provided that where the court is of the opinion that in the interests of justice a statement which is admissible by virtue of s. 23 or s. 24 nevertheless ought not to be admitted, the court may direct that the statement shall not be admitted.

The section goes on to provide that without prejudice to the generality of that, the court has the duty to have regard to the following matters:

(a)   to the nature and source of the document containing the statement and to whether or not having regard to its nature and source and not any other circumstances that appear to the court to be relevant it is likely that the document is authentic;

(b)   to the extent to which the statement appears to supply evidence which would otherwise not be readily available;

(c)   to the relevance of the evidence that it appears to supply to any issue which is likely to have to be determined in the proceedings;

(d)   to any risk, having regard in particular to whether it is likely to be possible to controvert the statement if the person making it does not attend to give oral evidence in the proceedings, that its admission or exclusion will result in unfairness to the accused or, if there is more than one accused, to any of them.

The court then has a broad discretion to exclude evidence which would otherwise be admissible in the interests of justice. This discretion no doubt will most commonly be exercised in the interests of the accused by means of excluding prosecution evidence.

16.10.10   THE DISCRETION IN RELATION TO CRIMINAL INVESTIGATION DOCUMENTS, s. 26

Section 26 of the 1988 Act goes on to provide that where a statement which is prima facie admissible under s. 23 or s. 24 appears to the court to have been prepared for the purposes of pending or contemplated criminal proceedings or of a criminal investigation then the statement shall *not* be given in evidence without the leave of the court and there is a *presumption against* admissibility unless the court is of the opinion that the statement should be admitted in the interests of justice. In considering 'the interests of justice' the court has the duty to have regard to the following matters:

(a)   to the contents of the statement;

(b) to any risk, having regard in particular to whether it is likely to be possible to controvert the statement if the person making it does not attend to give oral evidence in the proceedings, that its admission or exclusion will result in unfairness to the accused or, if there is more than one accused, to any of them; and

(c) to any other circumstances that appear to the court to be relevant.

This provides therefore a series of further tests. The drafting of the statute is somewhat odd in that parts of the discretion under s. 26 appear to repeat the discretions under s. 25, although without specific reference to other matters which might have been thought relevant, such as the criterion under s. 25 that the court should have regard to 'to the extent to which the statement appears to supply evidence which would otherwise not be readily available'.

16.10.11 MISCELLANEOUS MATTERS

(a) *Proof of the reason for absence*

It is for the party who wishes to put in some document under s. 23 or s. 24 to show by satisfactory evidence that one of the reasons is made out. Thus, for example, if it is suggested that the statement should be admissible because the witness is absent through fear, then by virtue of a case such as *R v O'Loughlin and McLaughlin* [1988] 3 All ER 431 the fact that the witness is afraid must be proved by admissible evidence and not by further hearsay. Similarly, as in *R v Bray* (1988) 88 Cr App R 354, the practicability of securing the attendance of a witness outside the United Kingdom will have to be proved by reasonable evidence (e.g., by evidence of attempts to trace and persuade the witness to return). A further example is *R v Case* [1991] Crim LR 192. This demonstrates that the court will give scrupulous attention to the preliminary proof of the acceptable reason for not calling a witness before allowing the statement. In this case there was a theft from Portuguese tourists and the Crown's case was based on the evidence of the arresting officers who sought leave to admit the tourists' statements under s. 23 of the Criminal Justice Act 1988. The accused's appeal was allowed on the basis that the judge's decision to admit the statements was materially irregular. There was no evidence in proper form as to when the tourists would have returned to Portugal or how long they might be in England, save for comments within the text of the statements themselves giving the tourists' address as that of a London hotel, but indicating that their stay was temporary. The court held that it was not proper to look at the statements themselves to see whether any reasons were supplied. The court went on to say that the word 'reasonably practicable' in the subsection implied that financial implications might be considered but there had been no proper prosecution evidence as to practicability. If the matter had been approached properly there might possibly have been such evidence but looking at the overall picture there was a material irregularity.

Where, however, it is the defence who seek to adduce the statement from the absent witness, then by virtue of *R v Mattey* [1995] 2 Cr App R 409 it is only necessary to establish the reason for absence on a balance of probabilities. In any event there is no bar on using the statement of one witness which is itself admissible under s. 23 to prove the inability of another witness to attend the trial (see *R v Castillo* (1995) *The Times*, 2 October 1995.)

(b) *Production of the document*

If a statement in a document is admissible under these provisions it may be proved either by production of the original document or by production of a copy authenticated in such matter as the court may approve. This marks a further weakening of the so-called 'best evidence' rule so that if it is for any reason inconvenient to produce the true document at court (e.g., a business ledger in daily use) a photocopy will be acceptable. 'Document' includes films, tapes and videos.

(c) Confessions

The 1988 Act cannot be used as a way of getting round the much stricter rules with regard to the admissibility of confessions. There are specific provisions excluding the application of these sections to confessions which would otherwise have been inadmissible under s. 76 of the Police and Criminal Evidence Act 1984.

(d) Using documents to discredit witnesses

By sch. 2 to the 1988 Act there is a specific provision that documents may be used not merely as to the issues in the case but to discredit witnesses who are not before the court. If, for example, the prosecution succeed in putting in evidence a document under s. 23 of the 1988 Act and the defendant has other evidence which would have discredited the absent witness, whether by proving a prior inconsistent statement or otherwise, he may use that evidence.

(e) The weight to be attached to documentary statements

By sch. 2, para. 3 of the 1988 Act 'in estimating the weight, if any, to be attached to such statement regard shall be had to all the circumstances from which any inference can reasonably be drawn as to its accuracy or otherwise'.

(f) Rules of court

There is a specific provision that rules of court may be made for the purposes of the 1988 Act. Thus rules may well be brought into force prescribing precisely how certain matters are to be proved. The coming into force of the Act however is not dependent on such rules being made and until any such specific rules are made the court will be able to admit documentary evidence under its usual procedures.

(g) Other discretions

Quite apart from the discretions to exclude evidence provided by the 1988 Act there is a specific provision in s. 28 that any other discretions which a court might have to exclude evidence are preserved. Thus discretions under s. 78 or s. 82(3) of the Police and Criminal Evidence Act 1984 will still apply. Of course all these discretions are likely to overlap in any event; so that since a court has a more or less unfettered discretion to exclude statements which would prima facie be admissible under s. 23 or s. 24 under the provisions of s. 25 or s. 26 of the 1988 Act that power would suffice anyway.

(h) Expert evidence

There is a further provision under s. 30 of the 1988 Act whereby expert reports may be admitted in criminal cases whether or not the author attends to give oral evidence. If the expert does not attend, leave of the court is required to admit the report. Section 30(3) gives various factors which would be taken into account when deciding whether to give leave to admit the report without calling the expert. This will be considered further in the context of opinion evidence at 21.2.6.

16.10.12   RECENT DEVELOPMENTS

A number of cases on documentary evidence came through the courts in 1990 and thereafter. These had to do with documentary evidence admitted under a variety of provisions, either in the last days of s. 68 of the Police and Criminal Evidence Act 1984, s. 13(3) of the Criminal Justice Act 1925 or others. All these cases stress that, as a vital preliminary stage in considering whether evidence which is strictly speaking admissible ought to be allowed to be given at trial, the court must examine the *quality* of the evidence. So in *R v Neshet* [1990] Crim LR 578 the evidence in written form from two very elderly ladies who were too frail to come to court was excluded because the very age and physical condition of the witnesses would show their unreliability. A similar result occurred in *Scott v R* [1989] AC 1242 when the Privy Council had to consider identification evidence in relation to a Jamaican statute. These cases will certainly be relevant as demonstrating that the court will always want to consider the quality of evidence sought to be admitted under ss. 23 and 24.

16.10.13   CASES ON CRIMINAL JUSTICE ACT 1988, ss. 23 AND 24

An early case was *R v Cole* [1992] All ER 109. The facts of that case could hardly have been more straightforward. It involved an assault witnessed by a number of people. One prosecution witness died before trial and the prosecution wished to put in his evidence under s. 24. The decision is extremely verbose and ultimately concluded that it was in order for the statement to be put in because the defence had witnesses who were going to controvert the dead witness's statement so there was no improper pressure placed on the defendant by allowing it in.

There have been two interesting cases on the tests to be applied where it is alleged that the witness does not give evidence 'through fear or because he is being kept out of the way' in s. 23(3)(b). In the most striking case, *R v Acton Justices ex parte McMullen* (1990) 92 Cr App R 98, the key witness, a boy of 16, was brought to court by the police but refused to enter court or give evidence because he was terrified of being identified by the accused. The Divisional Court held that the requirements of s. 23(3)(b) were fulfilled. In the case of committal proceedings the discretions in s. 26 of the 1988 Act have to be applied as to whether the statement should be admitted. Although in the instant case the magistrate had not fully appreciated the nature of his discretion, he had supplied an affidavit to say that the outcome would have been no different had he applied the proper discretions under the Act, and the court refused to quash the decision to admit the statements in the committal proceedings. Watkins LJ ruled that the matters of 'fear' and 'being kept out of the way' are disjunctive. He indicated that the test which a court should employ in determining whether there was fear sufficient to fall within the terms of s. 23 was that such fear would be found if on the evidence the court was 'sure that the witness was in fear as a consequence of the commission of the material offence or of something said or done subsequently in relation to that offence and the possibility of the witness testifying as to it'. In deciding whether this was made out the court would apply the criminal standard of proof. Watkins LJ went on to say:

> Whatever else may be seen to present difficulties for the court in these provisions, there is no doubt in my mind that the dual tests — admissibility and whether to admit — which have to be applied before a statement is admitted and read to the court will in many circumstances call for the most careful and scrupulous exercise of judgment and discretion.

See also *R v Ashford Magistrates' Court ex parte Hilden* [1993] QB 555 where the witness who was the victim of an alleged assault took the oath and gave evidence saying that she had no comment upon the alleged injuries. The accused's grandmother was in court and was said to have accompanied the victim to court. The prosecutor thereupon asked for leave to put in her written statement under s. 23(3)(b). The court found that the witness was in fear and admitted the statement. On application for judicial review it was held that for the subsection to apply it was not necessary for a witness to have failed to testify at all; and that it was open to the court to be satisfied that she was in fear by observing her demeanour.

16.10.14   COMPUTER RECORDS

Section 69 of the Police and Criminal Evidence Act 1984 provided for the admissibility in evidence of computer records. Now, since s. 68 of the 1984 Act is repealed, such computer records will have to fall within s. 23 or s. 24 of the 1988 Act to be admissible. A brief discussion of evidence by computer records is therefore appropriate.

Section 69 of the 1984 Act provided for computer records to be admissible in criminal cases. The word computer is not defined in the 1984 Act. In the 1968 Act the word 'computer' is defined and this definition is incorporated into the 1988 Act expressly by sch. 2, para. 5. The word computer means 'any device for processing or storing information'. As has been pointed out this somewhat woolly phrase could include a filing cabinet, a typewriter or even a cardboard file. Clearly it includes word processors, calculators, adding machines, etc., as well as computers.

The requirements of s. 69 are negative in form so that the person wishing to put in evidence a computer record must show absence of irregularity in the use of the computer, that is that there are no reasonable grounds for believing the computer records to be inaccurate because of improper use and that the computer was operating properly. Proof of this is to be subject to rules of court and may be given by a certificate purporting to be signed by a 'person occupying a responsible position in relation to the operation of the computer'. In addition the court may require oral evidence about the working of the computer to be given.

This is likely to be a growth area for case law and therefore it may help to summarise the position. Some of the difficulties are faced in the case of *R v Minors* [1989] 1 WLR 441. The facts of this case are not material and indeed it turns on s. 68 of the 1984 Act, which has now been repealed. Section 69, however, as we have seen, survives. It is not a self-contained code of admissibility because it lays down additional requirements for the admissibility of a computer record which has already passed the hurdle of what is now in s. 24 of the 1988 Act. The foundation requirements of s. 24 must be proved by oral evidence, in the absence of formal agreement between the parties. If there is a disputed issue as to the admissibility of the computer evidence, the issue should be decided on a trial within a trial at which the judge's function will be to decide whether the prosecution (or more rarely the defence) has established the foundation requirements of s. 24 and then of s. 616. It will be appropriate for the judge to give the jury a specific direction that the weight to be attached to documentary evidence produced by computer is entirely a matter for them to assess.

There are the following alternatives with regard to evidence produced by a computer printout:

(a) If the printout is tendered as evidence of any facts stated by any person, both s. 23 or s. 24 of the Criminal Justice Act 1988 and then s. 69 of the 1984 Act must be satisfied.

(b) If the printout is *the very fact* which is to be proved and the computer or machine has not 'added to its own knowledge' (such as a radar meter printout or an intoximeter printout) then the printout is *real evidence* and not hearsay and neither s. 69 nor any other section needs to be satisfied.

(c) If the printout is tendered as evidence of any fact actually observed by the computer itself or by a machine with which it is linked then everything will depend upon the nature of the additional information. For example, if the computer performs complicated calculations which depend on hearsay statements put into it and the computer then draws conclusions, the court will have to examine the nature of the information eventually supplied by the computer.

It is important to consider the case of *R v Spiby* (1990) 91 Cr App R 186. Here a computer installed in a hotel recorded, by mechanical means and without the intervention of human mind, information about telephone calls made by hotel guests. The case concerned conspiracy to import drugs and in the course of it the prosecution proved a number of telephone calls made by one of the accused from the hotel. It was proved that calls were made to others of the accused by production of a record showing printout sheets from a computer which metered guests' telephone calls, recorded them and worked out the charges. The manager of the hotel gave evidence that he was familiar with the function of the machine and that though he was not a computer engineer the machine had been working satisfactorily and no one in the relevant period had complained about the resulting bills. It was submitted that the evidence was subject to s. 69 of the 1984 Act and that the manager could not discharge the burden under s. 69 of showing that the computer was working properly. The trial judge held that the documents were real evidence and not hearsay. It was held on appeal that where information is recorded by mechanical means without the intervention of a human mind the record made by the machine is admissible in evidence provided it is accepted that the machine is reliable.

A computer differs from a thermometer or a camera only in that it can perform a variety of functions instead of only one. The records did not depend for their content on anything that had passed through a human mind. The record was entirely mechanical and fell within the class of real evidence. It would have been quite different if a telephone operator in the hotel had gathered the information and typed it into a computer bank and the printout was from that computer. In that case the sections would have applied. The court considered that it was entitled to apply the proposition from *Cross on Evidence* that, if the instruments were of a kind as to which it was common knowledge that they were more often than not in working order, then, in the absence of evidence to the contrary, the court would presume that they were in working order at the appropriate time.

There is an excellent commentary on the case at [1990] Crim LR 199. As Professor Smith points out, the court on the face of it is completely wrong in proceeding from the, no doubt correct, decision that the computer printout in *Spiby* was real evidence (if that phrase has any meaning) to the view that s. 69 has no application. Section 69 provides: 'In any proceedings a statement contained in a document produced by a computer shall not be admissible as evidence of any facts stated therein unless it is shown ...'. Clearly, whether you call it real evidence or not, the printout from this computer was tendered to prove some facts stated on it, namely the origin and destination of the telephone calls and the printout stated those facts. That does not mean that the printout is necessarily hearsay, but s. 69 clearly applies nonetheless and the court ought to have been satisfied by admissible evidence as to the proper working of the computer before the evidence could be put in. The point is further underlined by para. 12 of sch. 3 to the Police and Criminal Evidence Act 1984 which provides: 'For the purposes of paragraph 11 above, information shall be taken to be supplied to a computer whether it is supplied directly or *with or without human intervention* by means of any appropriate equipment' (emphasis added). The point of s. 69 is to provide for the court to be satisfied by admissible evidence about proper operation of the computer and whether the evidence is hearsay or not is irrelevant.

16.10.14.1 Proving the operation of the computer

It had been widely considered that there would be strict requirements for proof of the proper operation of the computer at the relevant time pursuant to s. 69(1). The requirement seems to have been weakened by the House of Lords in *R v Shephard* [1993] AC 380 where it was ruled that those certification provisions 'could be satisfied by the oral evidence of a person familiar with the operation of the computer who could give evidence of its reliability and such a person need not be a computer expert'.

Whilst the computer operation in that case was extremely simple (the court had allowed a store detective who had conducted an examination of till rolls to certify that the computer-linked tills were working properly on the day in question), many commentators have doubted whether the House of Lords was right to believe that a non-expert such as a store detective could properly certify the reliability of such equipment.

The Court of Appeal in *R* v *Cochrane* [1993] Crim LR 49, a case decided before the judgments in *Shephard* were known, ruled that the Crown needed to produce expert evidence as to each stage of the mode of operation of the computers involved in linked transactions in a case having to do with withdrawals from computer-linked 'hole in the wall' building society cash points. The cash point machines were linked to a branch computer which had back-up facilities in memory form before the information was transmitted to a central mainframe computer. None of the witnesses called for the Crown to testify about the operation could in fact say in which town the mainframe computer was located and the Court of Appeal quashed the conviction. None of the witnesses had testified adequately about the operation of the relevant machines.

16.10.15 WRITTEN STATEMENTS AND DEPOSITIONS FROM COMMITTAL PROCEEDINGS: CRIMINAL PROCEDURE AND INVESTIGATIONS ACT 1996, s. 68 AND sch. 2

As we saw earlier, written statements may be put in evidence at committal proceedings under s. 5B of the Magistrates' Courts Act 1980 together with depositions put in under s. 97A of 1980 Act. Section 68 of the Criminal Procedure and Investigations Act 1996 provides that those statements may be admissible at trial in accordance with sch. 2 to the Act. Paragraph 1(2) of sch. 2 to the 1996 Act provides that 'the statement may without further proof be read as evidence on the trial of the accused, whether for the offence for which he was committed for trial or for any other offence arising out of the same transaction or set of circumstances'.

The court of trial has a general discretion to order that the statement shall not be read and must listen to any objections to the giving in evidence of the statement, but may override those objections 'if the court considers it to be in the interests of justice so to order' (sch. 2, para. 1(4)).

This therefore raises the possibility of the court hearing written evidence in statement form from witnesses who are not called to the trial for cross-examination. It is a very surprising provision indeed because there is no requirement built into it that the witness concerned should be unavailable for any reason, nor are any of the specific discretions or limitations contained in ss. 23–26 of the Criminal Justice Act 1988 applicable. This very controversial provision was inserted into sch. 2 at a late stage with very little time for effective parliamentary scrutiny, although in a parliamentary answer the Minister concerned did say that 'it is anticipated that the courts will as now turn for guidance to section 26 of the 1988 Criminal Justice Act for assistance in applying the provisions of the new Schedule in the Bill'.

The possibility therefore arises of the prosecution (and of course it will only be prosecution evidence that is presented in this form because no defence evidence is tendered at a committal) applying at trial to put in evidence statements without being required to demonstrate the unavailability of the witness concerned or to satisfy any of the other criteria which would apply to statements under the 1988 Act. It is to be hoped, and perhaps anticipated, that the courts will, as the Minister's parliamentary answer indicates, have regard to the use of the discretions within the 1988 Act and the case law under them to determine whether or not such applications by the prosecution should succeed. It is therefore very important to notify the prosecution immediately upon receiving their committal statements that they are required to call the witnesses at trial. If you do not do this you may be held to have waived any objection.

16.11 Minor Statutory Exceptions

We have now considered the most important statutory exceptions to the hearsay rule. Apart from these there are numerous sections in a variety of statutes which make individual provisions for the reception of hearsay evidence in specific cases. These are of only minor importance.

Many of the statutory exceptions concern minor regulatory offences which provide for the proof of certain formal matters by the production of declarations, statements or certificates.

16.12 Statements Admitted as Part of the *Res Gestae*

The final group of exceptions falls within the so-called doctrine of *res gestae*. *Res gestae* means 'happening', 'series of events', or 'transaction'. Under this doctrine any statement relevant to an incident (usually the commission of a crime itself) may be admissible as an exception to the hearsay rule provided that the evidence arose spontaneously and contemporaneously with the incident.

The leading case was *Ratten v R* [1972] AC 378. The accused was charged with murder by shooting his wife. His defence was that the gun had gone off accidentally whilst he was cleaning it. The facts were that at about 1.15 p.m. a call was made from the accused's house to the local telephone exchange by a female speaking in a hysterical voice who sobbed and said 'Get me the police please'. The caller gave her address but then rang off. The police were thereupon informed of this by the telephone operator who telephoned the house and spoke to the accused who then asked them to come. The accused objected that the telephone operator's evidence was hearsay. On appeal, eventually to the Privy Council, it was held:

(a) That the jury properly directed might find that the telephone call was made by the deceased woman.

(b) That the evidence of the telephone operator was not hearsay and was admissible as evidence of fact relevant to an issue, i.e. that a call had been made by a woman in a hysterical state thus rebutting the suggestion of accident.

(c) That even if there was an element of hearsay the words were safely admitted under the *res gestae* principle being words spoken spontaneously under the overwhelming pressure of a contemporaneous event.

With all respect to their Lordships, it seems difficult to agree that there is no hearsay element in the words sought to be admitted. Their Lordships impliedly concede their doubts by going on to give a separate ground of admissibility — and this is the modern rule for admissibility. It is submitted that Mrs Ratten did assert a fact by implication in asking for the police, and certainly that the prosecution's wish in tendering the evidence was to assert that fact, i.e., her belief that police assistance was required in view obviously of some act or threat made by her husband. This consideration of the problems of implied assertion foreshadows the decision in *R v Kearley* referred to above.

The modern English authority is the case of *R v Andrews* [1987] AC 281, in which the House of Lords held that hearsay evidence of a statement made by a fatally stabbed man soon after he was attacked and naming his two attackers was properly admitted as evidence of the truth of the facts he had asserted under the *res gestae* principle. *Ratten v R* and *R v Turnbull* were expressly approved. The position was as follows:

(a) The primary question which the judge had to ask himself in such a case was: can the possibility of concoction or distortion be disregarded?

(b) To answer that question the judge first had to consider the circumstances in which the particular statement was made in order to satisfy himself that the event was so unusual or dramatic as to dominate the thoughts of the victim so that his utterance was an instinctive reaction to that event thus giving no real opportunity for reasoned reflection.

(c) In order for the statement to be sufficiently spontaneous it had to be so closely associated with the event which had excited the statement that it could fairly be said that the mind of the declarant was still in control of the event.

(d) Quite apart from the time factor there might be special features in a case which related to the possibility of distortion.

(e) As to the possibility of error in the facts narrated in such a statement: if only the ordinary fallibility of human recollection was relied upon that went to the weight to be attached and not to the admissibility of the statement and was therefore a matter for the jury.

There are relatively few modern cases on *res gestae* and most of them are in the context of very serious crime, e.g., murder. The courts always seem surprised when a point of *res gestae* comes up and often revert to analysing the position from first principles.

Res gestae has aptly been described as 'a lot of rag-tag-and-bobtail material', 'the dustbin of the law of evidence', 'an empty phrase encouraging looseness of thinking and uncertainty of decision'. It has often been, cynically but understandably, urged on young advocates that if they cannot justify to the court why a given piece of evidence, which is clearly hearsay is admissible 'say it is part of the *res gestae*'.

SEVENTEEN

THE LAW OF EVIDENCE (4): CONFESSIONS, EVIDENCE OF REACTION, AND THE RIGHT TO SILENCE

17.1 Confessions

The law on confessions is now contained in ss. 76 and 77 of the Police and Criminal Evidence Act 1984. These are to be read with the definition of 'confession' in s. 82 and reference must also be made to the Codes of Practice on the Detention, Treatment and Questioning of Persons and the Code of Practice on Tape Recording of Police Interviews issued under ss. 60 and 66 of the 1984 Act.

Before considering the statutory provisions and the case law under them we shall consider four preliminary matters, namely:

(a)   The procedure by which admissibility of a confession is determined.

(b)   Editing of confessions.

(c)   Confessions implicating others.

(d)   Confessions which also contain self-serving material.

17.1.1   THE PROCEDURE TO DETERMINE ADMISSIBILITY

17.1.1.1   The Crown Court

In opening its case to the jury the prosecution must refrain from referring to any item of evidence the admissibility of which will be challenged by the defence. The defence are of course aware of the nature of the prosecution's case because of the committal proceedings, at which stage the prosecution must reveal their evidence. If the opening speech is unintelligible without reference to the confession (i.e. if it is the only real evidence in the case) the admissibility issue may be taken as a preliminary matter before the opening speech. Otherwise after the opening speech the case proceeds with witnesses being called, examined and cross-examined until the item of disputed evidence is reached. In the case of a confession this will probably be quite early, the investigating officer usually being the second prosecution witness after the victim, although there is no real rule as to this. As soon as the question of the disputed confession is reached, the defence formally object and the jury are sent out of court (without of course knowing why) whilst the issue of admissibility is tried by the judge alone. This hearing is known as the *voir dire* or 'trial within a trial'.

Witnesses may be called and are cross-examined in the usual way, legal argument is presented by both sides, and the judge then decides on the admissibility of the confession. This will usually involve him deciding a dispute of fact (e.g., whose version as to what happened at the police station to believe) and then deciding admissibility as a question of law dependent on the facts as found.

If the judge rules that the confession is inadmissible under the above principles, either as being unreliable or under his discretion to exclude it as unfair to the accused, the jury when recalled to the court are never told of the existence of the 'confession' and the trial proceeds. If the confession is ruled *admissible* then the confession is put before the jury. It is still open to the defence to challenge it in any way, e.g., by trying to show the jury that it is untrue or unreliable because of the circumstances in which it was obtained. This may often involve them challenging the police evidence (e.g., as to intimidation of the accused at the police station) in exactly the same terms in which they have just challenged it before the judge on the *voir dire*. Indeed, often hours of cross-examination are repeated virtually word for word as the defence seek to show the jury that the confession is of no weight, the weight to be attached to it being, of course, entirely a question of fact for them.

The use of evidence given at the voir dire
The judge's function at the *voir dire* is to decide admissibility of the confession. If the judge excludes the confession then in principle the jury may not be told about anything that happened during the *voir dire*. Thus, if the accused has testified during the *voir dire* but declines to testify before the jury the prosecution are not allowed to tell the jury anything that the accused said during the *voir dire*. If on the other hand the judge rules the confession *admissible*, then if, e.g., the accused testifies and gives evidence which is inconsistent with what he or she said during the *voir dire*, the jury may be referred to the previous inconsistent statement.

17.1.1.2 The magistrates' court

In magistrates' courts before the 1984 Act came into force, it used to be considered pointless to hold a formal *voir dire* since the same magistrates decide admissibility as decide on the facts. Such a *voir dire* was held to be inappropriate following the case of *F v Chief Constable of Kent* [1982] Crim LR 682.

The terms of s. 76 of the 1984 Act however appear to require that a *voir dire* must always be held to determine admissibility:

(a) where the defence 'represents' that the confession is inadmissible (s. 76(2)), or

(b) where the court of its own motion requires proof of admissibility (s. 76(3)).

Following a certain amount of uncertainty it was held in *R v Liverpool Juvenile Court ex parte R* (1987) 86 Cr App R 1 that this literal construction should be adopted and therefore that in procedure by summary trial before magistrates the same thing should happen as in trial by jury, namely that there should be a separate and preliminary investigation into the admissibility of a confession. The difference however is that since the same magistrates will be present in court throughout there is no need to repeat the evidence after that stage if they rule the confession admissible.

17.1.1.3 What if the accused denies he confessed at all?

It should be noted that there only needs to be a *voir dire* if it is represented that the confession was obtained by oppression or is unreliable. If the accused denies that he ever made a confession, e.g., he says that the police forged his signature on a statement they themselves wrote or that he did not say any of the words attributed to him, this is a straightforward factual matter for the jury and there should not be a *voir dire*. See, e.g., *R v Flemming* (1988) 86 Cr App R 32.

There was an argument in *Flemming* as to whether the accused's signature was forged on certain notes of interviews with the police. The Court of Appeal confirmed that where it was alleged that signatures and initials were forged and there was expert handwriting evidence on that issue that it was simple matter of fact for the jury and there need not be a *voir dire*. The trial in this case happened at a time when the Police and Criminal Evidence Act 1984 was not in force but the same would apply under the Act.

17.1.2 EDITING OF CONFESSIONS

Suppose that the words of a confession refer to a previous offence or some other inadmissible matter? The rule is that where a confession is to be placed before the jury and it contains inadmissible matter (quite independently of any question of reliability) the confession may be 'edited' to omit the offending part.

In *R v Knight and Thompson* (1946) 31 Cr App R 52 the accused were charged with various offences and in the course of their confessions referred to other offences they had committed. The judge ruled that the confessions should be put in toto before the jury. It was held that this was wrong and the confessions should have been edited to exclude the references to other offences. Accordingly the defendants' convictions would be quashed.

If the editing is so substantial that the confession is unintelligible after it, the whole may need to be excluded. If the actual document is to be shown to the jury, it should be retyped without blanks or erasures which might lead the jury to speculate on the reasons for them. *Practice Direction (Crime: Evidence by Written Statements)* [1986] 1 WLR 805 explains the technical procedures to be followed.

17.1.3 CONFESSIONS IMPLICATING OTHERS

It should not be forgotten that a confession is an exception to the hearsay rule and is therefore evidence against *the maker* only. This leads to considerable practical difficulties in the case of trial of more than one accused. If A and B were charged with the same offence and A alone had made a confession that he and B carried out the crime, then if they are tried separately there will be no problem. The confession would be quite inadmissible at B's trial as hearsay, and of course at A's trial it would be evidence against A in the usual way. But the more normal procedure with co-accused is to try them together. What about A's confession which is clearly inadmissible as against B? The prejudicial effect as against B will *not* normally be a ground for ordering separate trials, see *R v Lake* (1976) 64 Cr App R 172 where the accused and two other men were charged with conspiracy to burgle. The accused applied for a separate trial on the grounds that confessions had been made by the other two accused which implicated him and that these would be inadmissible as against him. It was held that, although the confessions were inadmissible as against him and a strong warning from the trial judge would be necessary, the question of severance was primarily for the trial judge and there was no general rule that in such a case separate trials should be ordered.

It may be that reference to B can be edited out of A's confession without making it unintelligible and if so this should be done. If the reference to B is so prejudicial that it would affect B's chance of a fair trial, then the judge may exclude the whole confession (to A's advantage also).

If the judge rules that the confession can go before the jury he must give a strong direction to them to treat the confession as evidence only against A and not B. They are often assisted in this exercise in mental gymnastics by the judge explaining that it is clearly unfair to hold a statement made by A in B's absence against B who had no chance to reply, when A may have his own reasons for implicating B. Failure to give this direction is fatal to B's conviction.

It must be remembered that this is a rule relating to A implicating B *in his confession*. If A *goes into the witness box* and *gives evidence* implicating B then this is admissible evidence in the normal way.

17.1.4   CONFESSIONS WHICH ALSO CONTAIN SELF-SERVING MATERIAL

The difficulty here is that there is a general rule that where a statement is tendered to the jury, the whole statement must be tendered. There may thus be self-serving passages within confessions, especially if these are the record of interrogations rather than the accused's own written statement. The problem consists in the fact that the *confession part is evidence* against the maker, whereas the *self-serving parts are not evidence* of the facts which they state.

By s. 82 of the 1984 Act: '*Confession includes any statement wholly or partly adverse to the person who made it ... and whether made in words or otherwise.*' It must therefore be remembered that the term 'confession' covers things said by a suspect which are far weaker than an outright admission of involvement in the crime. It will encompass anything said by an accused which in any way assists the prosecution to establish their case, and thus quite minor partial admissions count in law as a 'confession' and thus require the prosecution to prove them strictly under s. 76 of the 1984 Act. For example, if, on being questioned about a murder, a suspect, whilst maintaining a complete denial, nonetheless conceded that he hated the victim, even that minor admission would need to be proved by the prosecution strictly under s. 76 if the circumstances in which it was obtained were called into question, because the suspect has admitted something (i.e. motive) which assists the prosecution to demonstrate his guilt. It often happens therefore that the court has to consider 'mixed' statements.

The jury must be told to consider the *whole* statement once the judge has decided that it could in law constitute a confession and is admissible, and to decide as a matter of fact whether they think it is a confession, i.e. whether the self-serving parts nullify any 'confessing' parts.

The correct direction to the jury in such a case seems to be as follows:

(a)   The whole statement must be considered in assessing whether it is a confession.

(b)   If so, adverse parts are evidence against the accused of facts stated in them.

(c)   Favourable parts are not evidence of facts stated in them but may be part of 'the general picture'.

A somewhat briefer and simpler direction, although one that arguably 'fudges' the real difficulty, was suggested more recently in *R v Duncan* (1981) 73 Cr App R 359 and this has been approved by the House of Lords in *R v Sharp* [1988] 1 WLR 7. In *R v Duncan* Lord Lane CJ said:

> where a mixed statement is under consideration ... the simplest ... method ... is for the jury to be told that the whole statement, both the incriminating parts and the excuses or explanations, must be considered by them in deciding where the truth lies. ... Equally, where appropriate, the judge may and should point out that the incriminating parts are likely to be true (otherwise why say them?), whereas the excuses do not have the same weight.

17.1.5   POLICE AND CRIMINAL EVIDENCE ACT 1984

It is important to consider the full text of ss. 76, 77, 78 and 82 of the Police and Criminal Evidence Act 1984. We have already considered s. 82; s. 78 will be dealt with in due course. It is important to consider the precise wording of ss. 76 and 77:

76. Confessions

(1)   In any proceedings a confession made by an accused person may be given in evidence against him in so far as it is relevant to any matter in issue in the proceedings and is not excluded by the court in pursuance of this section.

(2)   If, in any proceedings where the prosecution proposes to give in evidence a confession made by an accused person, it is represented to the court that the confession was or may have been obtained—

(a)   by oppression of the person who made it; or

(b)   in consequence of anything said or done which was likely, in the circumstances existing at the time, to render unreliable any confession which might be made by him in consequence thereof,

the court shall not allow the confession to be given in evidence against him except in so far as the prosecution proves to the court beyond reasonable doubt that the confession (notwithstanding that it may be true) was not obtained as aforesaid.

(3)   In any proceedings where the prosecution proposes to give in evidence a confession made by an accused person, the court may of its own motion require the prosecution, as a condition of allowing it to do so, to prove that the confession was not obtained as mentioned in subsection (2) above.

(4)   The fact that a confession is wholly or partly excluded in pursuance of this section shall not affect the admissibility in evidence—

(a)   of any facts discovered as a result of the confession; or

(b)   where the confession is relevant as showing that the accused speaks, writes or expresses himself in a particular way, of so much of the confession as is necessary to show that he does so.

(5)   Evidence that a fact to which this subsection applies was discovered as a result of a statement made by an accused person shall not be admissible unless evidence of how it was discovered is given by him or on his behalf.

(6)   Subsection (5) above applies—

(a)   to any fact discovered as a result of a confession which is wholly excluded in pursuance of this section; and

(b)   to any fact discovered as a result of a confession which is partly so excluded, if the fact is discovered as a result of the excluded part of the confession.

(7)   Nothing in Part VII of this Act shall prejudice the admissibility of a confession made by an accused person.

(8)   In this section 'oppression' includes torture, inhuman or degrading treatment, and the use or threat of violence (whether or not amounting to torture).

77. Confessions by mentally handicapped persons

(1)   Without prejudice to the general duty of the court at a trial on indictment to direct the jury on any matter on which it appears to the court appropriate to do so, where at such a trial—

(a)   the case against the accused depends wholly or substantially on a confession by him; and

(b)   the court is satisfied—

(i)   that he is mentally handicapped; and

(ii)   that the confession was not made in the presence of an independent person,

the court shall warn the jury that there is special need for caution before convicting the accused in reliance on the confession, and shall explain that the need arises because of the circumstances mentioned in paragraphs (a) and (b) above.

> (2)   *In any case where at the summary trial of a person for an offence it appears to the court that a warning under subsection (1) above would be required if the trial were on indictment, the court shall treat the case as one in which there is a special need for caution before convicting the accused on his confession.*
>
> (3)   *In this section—*
> *'independent person' does not include a policeman or a person employed for, or engaged on, police purposes;*
> *'mentally handicapped', in relation to a person, means that he is in a state of arrested or incomplete development of mind which includes significant impairment of intelligence and social   functioning; and*
> *'police purposes' has the meaning assigned to it by section 64 of the Police Act 1964.*

The prosecution must thus prove beyond reasonable doubt that a confession which is either impugned by the accused or where the court itself raises the issue was not obtained:

(a)   by *oppression* of the person who made it; or

(b)   in consequence of anything said or done which was likely, in the circumstances existing at the time, to render *unreliable* any confession which might be made by him in consequence thereof.

17.1.5.1   Oppression

This is defined by s. 76(8). It 'includes torture, inhuman or degrading treatment, and the use or threat of violence (whether or not amounting to torture)'.

The use of the word 'includes' causes difficulty. It presumably means that the matters referred to are not exhaustive as definitions of oppression, and that lesser conduct may qualify. The obvious problem is that whilst 'oppression' in previous case law usually meant relatively mild conduct which saps the free will (e.g., lengthy questioning etc.) the term now seems essentially to mean the most serious forms of conduct. The reference to 'torture and inhuman or degrading treatment' is borrowed from Article 3 of the European Convention on Human Rights and Fundamental Freedoms and a great deal of case law under that Convention has demonstrated that quite a high level of maltreatment is required to amount to torture etc. Indeed the United Kingdom has itself been found to have breached the Convention in its treatment of terrorist suspects in Northern Ireland.

A quite remarkable early case, which manages to discuss 'oppression' without once referring to the statutory definition, is *R v Fulling* [1987] QB 426. The accused was in custody and being interviewed concerning suspected dishonesty in a false insurance claim. After questioning had been unsuccessful a policeman told her that the man with whom she had been living, and with whom she was infatuated, had been having an affair for some years with a woman called Christine who was also in custody in connection with other matters and was in the adjoining cell to the defendant. Thereupon the defendant became very emotional and confessed because, to give her own explanation, she felt she wanted to say anything to get out of the police station. At her trial she applied for the confession to be excluded as having been obtained by oppression. The judge ruled the evidence admissible. Even accepting the accused's version of the interview with the police and the remark about her lover's unfaithfulness he held that this did not amount to oppression. On appeal the Court of Appeal discussed the meaning of the word oppression.

Most remarkably they made no reference at all to the definition of the term contained in the 1984 Act but instead referred to the dictionary definition of oppression which is 'the exercise of authority or power in a burdensome, harsh or wrongful manner; unjust or cruel treatment of subjects, inferiors etc., the imposition of unreasonable or unjust burdens'. The court also embarked on a discussion of the meaning of the term 'oppression' under the old law, though holding that the term under the 1984 Act did not necessarily mean the same thing. The court also observed that whilst a confession could be rendered *unreliable* without there necessarily being any impropriety on the part of the interrogator, it would be hard to imagine a case of oppression without some impropriety.

Assuming therefore that conduct by the person to whom the confession is given is not so extreme as to amount to 'oppression' we turn to the second test.

17.1.5.2   Unreliability

The use of the words 'circumstances', 'reliable', and 'anything said or done' appear to give the court a broad mandate to enquire thoroughly into the circumstances in which the confession was made. There is no requirement that anyone should have behaved *improperly* in any way for a confession to be held unreliable. The words in the section clearly imply a subjective test, i.e. in all the circumstances was anything said or done which was likely to render *this* confession by *this* defendant unreliable. Thus police conduct which would have had no effect on a man of experience, especially one with a criminal record, may well be deemed to render a confession by a more vulnerable suspect unreliable.

17.1.5.3   Miscellaneous points on s. 76

(a) Section 76(4) preserves the existing law. Thus if, say, a suspect gives an inadmissible confession but while confessing says where stolen goods are to be found, and these are found where he said, and are, e.g., covered in his fingerprints, the finding of the goods and the fingerprints can be referred to in evidence although no mention of the confession can be made unless the accused himself refers to it (s. 76(5)).

(b) If there is something relevant in the confession to show that the accused *speaks, writes, or expresses himself* in a particular way then even though the confession is ruled inadmissible the part of it which shows that the accused does speak, write, etc. in that way may be admissible for that purpose. An example would be, say, a kidnapping case where the ransom note contains a strikingly mistaken spelling and the confession has the same mistake thus showing that the accused is likely to be the kidnapper.

(c) There is a special provision in s. 77 of the 1984 Act whereby, in addition to the matters arising under s. 76, in the case of a confession made by a mentally handicapped person (as defined), if the confession was not made in the presence of an 'independent person' (i.e. a person other than a policeman or police employee), the judge must warn the jury of the special need for caution before convicting the accused on any confession made by the mentally handicapped person.

(d) Case law under the 1984 Act as a whole had led to a largely unexpected development. Before the 1984 Act the law on confessions was reasonably clear and was separate from a different body of law which relates to the exclusion of other evidence (that is apart from confessions) which had been obtained in some way unfairly, e.g., where police trick a suspect into revealing the whereabouts of stolen goods, or act as agents provocateurs by pretending to be members of a criminal gang and thus actually procure the commission of the crime. The separate body of case law on that kind of situation will be considered separately at **18.1** in the chapter on improperly obtained evidence.

There is a particular provision in the 1984 Act which was widely thought to make no difference at all to the common law. This was s. 78(1) which confers a discretion on the court and provides:

In any proceedings the court may refuse to allow evidence on which the prosecution proposes to rely to be given if it appears to the court that, having regard to all the circumstances, including the circumstances in which the evidence was obtained, the admission of the evidence would have such an adverse effect on the fairness of the proceedings that the court ought not to admit it.

It was usually thought that this provision would be considered quite separately from the law on confessions but, to the great surprise of many, from the earliest cases the courts have been prepared to apply both s. 76 and s. 78 together. Some cases on this will be considered in the context of the law on the questioning of suspects below but on the obtaining of the confession pure and simple it is important to consider the case of *R v Mason* [1988] 1 WLR 139. In this case the accused had been tricked by the police who had falsely pretended that his fingerprint had been found at the scene of the crime. The police had maintained this pretence not only to the accused but to his solicitor. At the end of the prosecution case counsel for the accused objected unsuccessfully to the confession subsequently made. On appeal the conviction was quashed because of the deceit practised by the police both on the appellant and his solicitor. It seems that the reason why the police conduct was considered particularly bad on this occasion was because of the further lie told to the solicitor. If the lie had only been told to the accused, then it is perhaps more questionable whether the confession would have been disallowed.

It is actually a relatively common police interrogation technique to pretend that they have more evidence in their possession than they actually do have, even if it is not usually a claim to such a damning piece of evidence as in this case. It is somewhat difficult to see whether this is a correct application of s. 78 given that it requires the unfairness in the case to be 'in the proceedings'. It is suggested that, however laudable the outcome of this case, the court has in fact applied its mind to general considerations of unfairness in the whole criminal process rather than to the trial itself which arguably is a misinterpretation of s. 78. The court was, perhaps rather disingenuously, anxious to stress that it was not attempting to discipline the police by excluding the evidence. Whilst it did describe the police conduct as 'absolutely reprehensible' the court stressed that s. 78 did no more than restate the common law and that it was no function of the court to use the law of evidence as a way of disciplining the police.

We shall now go on to consider the related topic of the questioning of suspects and then deal with a number of cases under the 1984 Act to examine the general principles.

17.1.6 THE QUESTIONING OF SUSPECTS

Few confessions come about by the guilty person walking into a police station and handing over a previously prepared written statement confessing guilt. In the normal case, confessions come about in response to police questioning. However much additional evidence the police have against a person, they still generally prefer to see if a confession is forthcoming, believing, perhaps correctly, that it will be more difficult for a person to plead not guilty in the face of his own confession than if he had not made one.

So confessions usually come about in the course of interrogation, usually at a police station. Interrogation may end in a full written confession signed by the suspect, or there may merely be statements made admitting some fact relevant to guilt in the course of answering questions without a subsequent written statement. These 'confessions' are usually called 'verbals' and much of a trial used to be taken up with establishing whether or not the words amounting to a confession were ever said, in the common instance where the accused alleged fabrication or misunderstanding by the police who recorded his alleged answers to questions. These problems are now obviated to a large extent as tape recording of interviews is now universal, although even here there will be occasions when 'verbals' are alleged to have occurred at some stage before tape recording can start, e.g., in the police car taking the suspect to the police station or, as we shall see in one recent case, where the suspect made an alleged confession only after the tape recorder was switched off. We shall now deal with the questioning of suspects, and the effect of failure to observe proper procedures on the admissibility of confessions subsequently obtained.

17.1.7 CODES OF PRACTICE

There are two Codes of Practice issued under ss. 60 and 66 of the 1984 Act which are of importance in the context of confessions. These are the Code of Practice for the Detention, Treatment and Questioning of Persons by Police Officers; and the Code of Practice on the Tape Recording of Police Interviews. The latest version of the Codes took effect from 10 April 1995. Part of these Codes are set out at the end of **Chapter 4** (**4.9–4.14**; see also **4.5**).

The relevance of the Codes of Practice is dealt with in s. 67(11) of the 1984 Act which states:

In all criminal and civil proceedings any such Code shall be admissible in evidence, and if any provision of such a Code appears to the court or tribunal conducting the proceedings to be relevant to any question arising in the proceedings it shall be taken into account in determining that question.

Accordingly, breach of the Codes ought only in itself to be relevant to the admissibility of a confession if the breach has some factual bearing on the reliability of the confession. Breach of the Codes is a police disciplinary offence but the court will not in general use the breach as a means of punishing the police by excluding the confession. Everything will depend upon the nature and seriousness of the breach and the directness of its relevance to how the confession came about.

The same ought also to apply to the case of breach of other substantive provisions of the 1984 Act. A number of other sections relate to the conduct of interrogations, in particular s. 41 of the 1984 Act prima facie limits the police to a maximum period of 24 hours for the detention of a suspect without charge; s. 58 guarantees a suspect the right to consult privately with a solicitor (unless there are exceptional circumstances); s. 56 guarantees the right for a person to have details of his whereabouts communicated to a friend or relative. Breach of any of these ought only to matter so far as admissibility is concerned if the breach is causally related to the confession.

Reference to the Codes should be made for their precise terms. They provide for reasonable comfort, rest and refreshment during interrogation. They provide that from the moment of arrival in a police station the suspect is in the norminal custody of the custody officer who is a policeman of at least sergeant rank who has the duty of ensuring that full records are kept relating to the custody of the suspect, such as time, duration of questioning, and so on, and who has the power to control the way in which the suspect is treated by the officers actually involved in investigating the case in question. This is so even though those officers are of higher rank than the custody officer. The custody record kept by the custody officer may be called for and used at the trial and therefore it is very much in his interest to keep this meticulously and to ensure proper treatment for the suspect. See further **4.4** and **4.5**.

The Codes further provide for a suspect to be cautioned by the police in the words: 'You do not have to say anything. But it may harm your defence if you do not mention when questioned something which you later rely on in court. Anything you do say may be given in evidence.' This caution must be administered, or readministered at various times, in particular:

    (a)   when he is first suspected;

    (b)   upon arrest;

    (c)   when resuming questioning after arrest;

(d) after any break in questioning;

(e) upon charging.

Note also:

(a) After a person has been charged he should not be further questioned except for the purpose of minimising harm or loss or clearing up ambiguities.

(b) If after a person has been charged a policeman wishes to bring to his notice any written statement made by another person he should hand him a copy of that statement but not invite comment on it save to caution him.

That then is a bare outline of the main provisions of the Codes. The Court of Appeal has shown that it is prepared to scrutinise individual words and phrases within the Codes closely and to treat apparently small breaches as fatal to any confession subsequently obtained. It would be wrong however to say that the Court of Appeal's approach has been consistent throughout the cases, varying results having been obtained in different cases where the facts seem somewhat similar.

17.1.8   THE IMPORTANT CONCEPTS

As we have seen there are three concepts that need to be considered:

(a) oppression;

(b) unreliability;

(c) unfairness.

17.1.8.1   Oppression

As explained above, this is defined in s. 76(8) of the 1984 Act in such terms that very serious police misconduct is contemplated. As also noted in **17.1.5.1**, in the first important case on oppression, *R v Fulling* [1987] QB 426, the court decided to invoke the dictionary definition of the word 'oppression' and did not refer itself at all to the definition in the Act. This is a highly questionable method of statutory interpretation and the law might be thought to have taken a wrong turning from that point. In an emotive passage in the judgment the court said: 'There is not a word in our language that expresses more detestable wickedness than oppression' and 'we find it hard to envisage any circumstances in which such oppression would not entail some impropriety on the part of the interrogator'. Not surprisingly on the facts of the case the court did not find oppression in this or any other sense. The Court of Appeal expressed the view that police conduct was 'unsporting' but not 'oppressive'.

The concepts envisaged by the statute have been considerably blurred by the looseness of some of the language in decided cases. There seems in particular to be an overlap between oppression and unfairness which is unnecessary if the court approaches the sections in a logical sequence as will be suggested below.

17.1.8.2   Unreliability

Cases on unreliability tend to be rather more clear cut. Having said that, there is a number of cases where the court seems to have jumped straight from a finding of breach of the Codes of Practice into considering the confessions subsequently obtained as being of necessity 'unreliable' without much evidence that that was so. It is worth giving a factual example from a decided case though it must be reiterated that each case turns on its own facts.

R v Harvey [1988] Crim LR 241

The accused and her lesbian lover were present when the victim, a male, was stabbed to death. No one else was present. Both women had blood on their clothes and were arrested near the scene of the crime. On arrest the accused's lover confessed to the murder in her presence. The defendant was a woman of low intelligence who suffered psychopathic disorder aggravated by alcohol abuse. Shortly after the arrest she also confessed to the murder. The other woman later retracted her own confession and indicated that she would be a prosecution witness against Harvey but died before the trial. The only evidence against the accused was her confession. Two psychiatrists gave evidence to the effect that on hearing the confession of her lover the defendant might herself confess in a childlike attempt to take the blame and protect the lover. In the circumstances evidence of the confession was excluded and the jury directed to acquit.

17.1.8.3 Unfairness

This is the most difficult area. We have already considered the case of *R v Mason* (see **17.1.5.3**), where deliberate hoodwinking of the defendant's solicitor by the police led to the confession being excluded. As we have seen the court expressly said that it was not doing so in order to discipline the police but simply in application of the principle of unfairness.

Many of the cases involving s. 78 have had to do with wrongful refusal of a solicitor to a suspect in a police station. In deciding what use to make of s. 78 the court has to decide what effect, if any, the refusal might have had. Sometimes the court holds, quite understandably, that it can never know what precise effect the refusal of a solicitor may have had and therefore acts in the accused's interests by excluding the confession. On other occasions, especially with experienced criminals, the court has been able to conclude that the refusal of a solicitor would have made little difference to a suspect who was well aware of his rights.

An equally difficult question is to know how the court should respond where there is a failure by the police to keep proper custody records. If an accused is to have the chance of challenging his confession at trial it is important that there should be a custody record available for inspection. Arguably therefore an accused will be prejudiced in every case where there is a failure to keep such proper records.

There has been an increasing number of cases reported, particularly in the *Criminal Law Review*, over the last five years on the question of confessions. Many of the reports demonstrate how a single substantial error in police procedure, or a handful of more minor errors, seem to lead to confessions being excluded almost automatically.

Particular areas of difficulty for the police have included knowing when precisely an 'interview' is taking place rather than preliminary questioning; and of complying with important changes of wording in new Codes of Practice which replaced the original Codes in 1991. Purely as factual illustrations the following brief case notes will assist in seeing the general picture.

R v Absolam (1988) 88 Cr App R 332

Failure to explain right to legal advice, caution, and properly record interview — confession excluded.

R v Saunders [1988] Crim LR 523

S would only be interviewed if nothing was written down. The police wrote up their notes of the interview later. Confession excluded — the police were wrong to allow an 'off the record' interview. The making of contemporaneous notes and the submission of them to the accused for checking is mandatory.

R v Delaney (1988) 88 Cr App R 338

D was of low IQ and charged with indecent assault. He suffered emotional disturbance. The police told him that their main concern was to help him with his problems and they failed to record the interview until the next day. Conviction quashed as confession unreliable.

R v Rogah [1989] Crim LR 141

F, aged 16, was suspected of mugging. He was asked questions informally in the street some way from the scene of the crime and confessed. The confession was excluded, an 'appropriate adult' should have been allowed to be present, and the police could not allege that their informal discussion with F was not an 'interview'.

R v Trussler [1988] Crim LR 446

The accused was arrested and initially a police doctor agreed he was not fit to be interviewed because of his state (he was a drug addict). The doctor confirmed he would be fit to be interviewed six hours later. Eventually he was interviewed on a number of occasions briefly and these were properly recorded. Some hours later, however, the officer in the case decided to have 'a general chat' with the defendant during which a confession was made. The court held that there was no such thing as 'a general chat'; only formal interviews should take place and these should have been properly recorded. Confession excluded.

R v Canale [1990] 2 All ER 187

The accused was charged with conspiracy to rob. He had made a number of damning admissions in interviews with police to the effect that he was a member of a gang of professional robbers who lived in France and visited the United Kingdom to carry out robberies to finance their lifestyle. There were very serious breaches of the Codes of Practice, in particular a total lack of a contemporaneous record in the interviewing policemans' notebooks and lack of a subsequent record made on the prescribed form. The appellant testified that he had been tricked and induced to make the confessions. It was held on appeal that the lack of a contemporaneous note of the interviews meant that on the *voir dire* the judge was deprived of the very evidence which would have enabled him to decide whether the evidence of the admissions was admissible and subsequently the jury were also deprived of the evidence necessary for them to decide whether his denial of being implicated was true. The policemen had flagrantly and cynically breached the Codes of Practice. The appeal was allowed and the conviction quashed.

R v Bryce [1992] Crim LR 728

An undercover officer contacted the accused and asked him if he had stolen cars for sale. On being told that he had, an appointment was arranged. The accused and the officer met thereafter so that the officer could inspect a car. The officer asked the accused how long ago it had been stolen and received incriminating answers. He then arrested the accused. The accused was interviewed at the police station on tape but made no comments to any questions. When the tape had been switched off the accused said 'I'll tell you what happened but I don't want it recorded'. There was then a conversation during which he admitted guilt.

At trial a submission was made that evidence of both conversations before arrest and the conversation after the tape recorder was switched off should be excluded as they were in the nature of an interrogation and the Codes of Practice had not been followed. The judge refused to exclude any of them. On appeal the conviction was quashed. The officer, by assuming an undercover pose, was circumventing the Codes and each of the early conversations was clearly an interrogation. The interview after the tape was finished was a fresh interview and a fresh caution was needed. As to the relevance of this case see also *R v Christou* [1992] QB 979 and *R v Smurthwaite* (1993) 98 Cr App R 437: *R v Gill* (1993) 97 Cr App R 215 which are discussed more fully in the context of improperly obtained evidence: see **18.3**.

17.1.9   SUMMARY

The law's confusion has really been caused by the eliding and overlapping of the three categories of oppression, unreliability and unfairness. Of these three areas the most surprising problem has been created by the way in which the court has dealt with the question of oppression. Under the pre-1984 Act law, oppression was the cumulative effect of conduct, short of threats or inducements, which sapped the free will of an individual so that he spoke when otherwise he would have wished to maintain silence. Typical examples involved overlong questioning.

As we have seen, the definition in the 1984 Act contemplates extreme conduct mainly of a physical nature. To this definition the courts have tacked on the very artificial dictionary definition. The use of dictionary definitions to express the semantic content of technical legal concepts is usually considered questionable. From that error can be traced a certain amount of the confusion which has crept into the present position. The courts seem to have been prepared to treat conduct that was relatively similar (although the individual circumstances of every case obviously differ) as in some cases *oppression*, in others conduct which would render the confession *unreliable*, and in others conduct such that makes the proceedings *unfair*. It is suggested that the following should be the correct approach:

(a) It must always be remembered that if anybody suggests that a confession has been obtained by oppression or is unreliable that it is for the prosecution to prove beyond reasonable doubt that this is not so. This is why sometimes apparently technical breaches of the Codes have led to exclusion because it is then difficult for the prosecution to demonstrate (the burden being on them) that the breach has had no effect. From that point, the procedure should be as follows.

(b) Is the conduct complained of 'oppression' in the sense of serious misconduct contemplated by s. 76(8)? Although the definition given there is an *inclusive* definition, on any reasonable interpretation of the section for conduct to amount to oppression it must be equivalent to violence or inhuman treatment as the words of the section indicate.

(c) On the assumption that actual oppression is not found, the court must then examine everything said or done which might tend to make the confession unreliable. This gives the court a wide mandate to enquire into all the circumstances in which the confession was obtained from the moment when the suspect was first in contact with the police, or indeed with anyone else connected with a prosecution (e.g., a store detective). Applying a subjective test and bearing in mind that the burden of proving reliability is on the prosecution, the court ought to examine whether there seems to be any causal link between everything that has happened and the giving of a confession. It ought also to be borne in mind that there need be no police misconduct at all under this provision. Thus, to take a straightforward example, if the suspect were to enquire whether giving a confession and pleading guilty would obtain more lenient treatment from the court it would be perfectly accurate for a policeman to say that generally speaking it would indeed lead to a discount on sentence. Despite the fact that that is a perfectly accurate statement of the law it could still be contended that it had the effect of making the confession unreliable because an innocent suspect who thought that he might nonetheless be wrongly convicted might be tempted to make a false confession in order to obtain more lenient treatment.

(d) Finally, having decided whether or not the confession is unreliable, the court should then apply its mind to any representations made to it about fairness *in the proceedings*. It follows from the previous common law and from the express statements made by the court in *R v Mason* (see **17.1.5.3**) that, in deciding this, fairness is all that matters and the courts will not use s. 78 as a means of disciplining the police. Having said that it seems that, whether or not it recognised what it was doing, the court in *R v Mason* did in fact intend to discipline the police. Had the court wished to make it clear that it was not doing so it could equally well have proceeded under s. 76(2) because it could have been suggested that Mason (on being misled as to the state of the evidence against him and concluding that he was going to be wrongly convicted) might have made an untruthful confession to obtain more lenient treatment and that confession could therefore have been excluded on the grounds of reliability.

17.2 Admissions and the Reaction of the Accused to Statements made or Questions Asked in his Presence

One can envisage various situations where the prosecution may wish to prove what the accused said to show his reaction to accusations or the course of questioning, for example, where a child victim sees his attacker in the street shortly after an attack and goes up to him with his parent and says 'that's the man'. Or the more common example where the police may wish to prove answers made by the accused to interrogation, perhaps very lengthy interrogation. In neither case will the accused's replies (even if they *were* admissible) be intelligible unless the prosecution were *also* permitted to prove what was said by way of accusation or question. The exception to the hearsay rule which permits this is usually called 'statements made in the presence of the accused' or 'statements taxing the accused with incriminating facts'.

One may thus wish to prove two items of hearsay: an accusation — which may itself contain second-hand hearsay, e.g., 'The man who was robbed said he saw you run away with the bag'; and the response to the accusation — an acceptance, a denial, some ambiguous statement, or silence.

There may clearly be serious dangers in allowing evidence of the accusation to be given before the jury. If an account of a lengthy interrogation is given, often repeated accusations or accounts of circumstantial detail may influence the jury to treat facts as established which are actually in dispute or unproved. This difficult problem has been dealt with by the following rules which are not affected by the 1984 Act.

(a) Whilst an accusation when made is never evidence of the facts stated, it may become so to the extent that the accused makes a reply which shows he *accepted* the truth of the accusation.

Example The victim of an assault sees the perpetrator in the street some time later and tells a policeman. Together they go up to the criminal and the policeman says 'You are the man who attacked this lady'. The criminal says 'Yes I am'. In such cases it is proper to let the whole evidence go before the jury because the accused's simple reply 'Yes I am' in this example amounts to his 'adopting' the accusation. In this case the full rules as to confessions apply, i.e. the confession must be shown to be *reliable*.

(b) If the accused makes an *ambiguous* reply to the accusation the judge must decide as a preliminary issue whether to let the jury hear the evidence at all. It may be necessary to send the jury out and hear arguments in their absence where it is clear from the depositions which the judge sees in advance of trial that this is the case. Where for some reason the judge does not hold a *voir dire* on the issue there is a concept which is known as 'conditional admissibility' which applies. The judge permits the jury to hear the evidence but directs them that the words of accusation are only admissible to introduce the accused's reaction to them, and that unless they find that his reaction indicates that he accepted the accusation they must ignore the accusation and not treat it as evidence of any fact stated in it.

Examples of ambiguous reactions would be some inconclusive remark, an insult, silence, violence, mere facial expression, etc.

(c) If the accused makes a *denial* then neither the accusation nor the reply should be put before the jury because nothing of any evidential value has occurred. An accusation has been made out of court which has also been made in court — by the charge being put to the accused — and he has said it is untrue, which he has also said in court by his not guilty plea. This principle is clear and the only area of difficulty occurs where a denial is made, but one which might have some evidential value because it is *not very strenuous* — or a denial is made which is in an *inconsistent form* with the defence actually adduced at the trial, e.g., an accused who denies at first ever striking the victim but whose defence at trial is that he did so in self-defence.

The rule is that if a denial does have some evidential value because of ambiguity, lack of certainty, or inconsistency, a judge may allow evidence of both accusation and denial to be put to the jury but again he must direct them that such items are only of value if they draw an inference of guilt.

Where a suspect remains silent in the face of questioning, everything will depend on the context. Until 1995, when questioned by the police, a suspect had an unequivocal 'right to silence' which the words of the traditional caution were meant to emphasise. The words of the traditional caution included the phrase, 'you are not obliged to say anything'. As has already been noted, the wording of the caution has now been changed to indicate to the suspect that inferences may be drawn from his failure to mention facts in his defence. For ease of reference the relevant provisions of the Criminal Justice and Public Order Act 1994 which have affected the 'right to silence' are discussed together below at **17.3**, both as to the right to silence during police questioning and the right to silence during trial.

17.2.1 OTHER MATTERS

Three remaining matters to note are:

(a) Despite the above rules, where an account of interrogation is tendered to the court it is usual to put the whole interrogation before the court (editing out any matter which is inadmissible under any other rules) and not merely those questions and answers which culminate in an admission/confession as such. This is no doubt to preserve coherence but it is far from clear under precisely which rule such hearsay is admitted.

(b) In the Crown Court, where a deposition makes clear to the judge in advance that the form of the admission incorporates some matter which is inadmissible under some separate principle, as we have seen the judge will require the matter to be 'edited' out of the version eventually placed before the jury. If the trial is in the magistrates' court however, where there may be prior written disclosure of evidence, this is not possible, and the admission will be repeated to the magistrates, who ought no doubt to direct themselves to ignore it although whether this is possible in reality is open to doubt.

(c) Where there is a tape recording of an alleged confession the jury may be allowed to hear the tape; this will normally only happen where it is considered important that they hear the precise words used as they were spoken, for reasons of intonation or to judge such things as threatening demeanour, pace of the questioning, etc., to assist them in deciding on the truthfulness of what is said.

17.3 The Right to Silence

As is well known, until 1995 the accused was not compelled to speak at any stage of the criminal process. Even if he refused to plead it would be interpreted as a 'not guilty' plea. The much discussed 'abolition of the right to silence' is in fact rather less dramatic than that phrase might indicate. It is obvious that nothing can physically compel an accused to speak. He may thus maintain his silence if he wishes. Neither indeed do the new provisions, effective from April 1995, have the effect of making it a separate offence, or a contempt of court, for an accused not to answer police questioning nor to testify during trial. Having said that, once an accused begins to testify he becomes for most purposes a witness like any other, and may not refuse to answer proper questions. Therefore, at that stage, failure to answer a proper question from prosecution or judge might indeed amount to a contempt as indeed it would with any other witness.

The crucial effect of the change in the law relating to the accused's silence during the criminal process has to do with the extent to which prosecution counsel, or the judge, may properly comment on it to the jury and invite them to draw adverse inferences. Formerly, prosecuting counsel could not comment at all, and the judge could only comment in a very limited way, but the changes in the law now clearly allow stronger comment by both.

It is convenient to deal first with the effect of the accused's failure to assist the police by answering questions about relevant matters after caution, and secondly with the effect of the accused's refusal to testify.

17.3.1 EFFECT OF THE ACCUSED'S FAILURE TO MENTION FACTS WHEN QUESTIONED OR CHARGED, s. 34, CRIMINAL JUSTICE AND PUBLIC ORDER ACT 1994

Section 34 of the Criminal Justice and Public Order Act 1994 provides that where evidence is given that the accused at any time before he was charged with the offence, on being questioned under caution, failed to mention any fact relied on in his defence or on being charged failed to mention any such fact, where the fact is one which in the circumstances existing at the time the accused could reasonably be expected to mention, the court may draw such inferences from the failure as appear proper.

Thus this applies where an accused eventually relies on a fact in his defence (e.g., self-defence, alibi) and the test of 'which in the circumstances existing at the time the accused could reasonably have been expected to mention' is satisfied. (Presumably, if the accused was too tired or confused or had other reasons for not mentioning it at the time, on the basis of a subjective test it would not necessarily lead to adverse comment.)

Where, however, the accused does fail to mention a relevant fact, the court may draw such inferences as appear 'proper'. It will still be possible for an accused to explain his reluctance or inability to mention any particular fact and that will affect whether or not any inference at all is proper and if so what the strength of that inference may be.

It should be noted that silence cannot assist to establish a prima facie case. Moreover, if the accused has no fact which he could have contributed, e.g., if he simply contends the prosecution have not made out their case and does not rely on a particular defence, this can have no effect.

Where an accused reserves his defence until trial and after the close of the prosecution case, the question of inferences drawn from failure to mention facts will not arise. Thus at the stage of a submission of no case to answer, such inferences will not be appropriate to assist the prosecution to compensate for deficiencies in their case as presented so far. It is only the eventual trier of fact who may draw inferences at the end of the case.

It should also be noted that the failure to respond is only relevant where the accused was being questioned *under caution* or *on being charged*, in which case a caution will be administered in any event. The previous form of caution was of course a reminder that the accused need say nothing. The new form of words, reached not long before the Codes of Practice came into force, supplemented a previously proposed 60-word caution which was withdrawn on the basis that it was too complicated to be comprehensible. The new form reads: 'You do not have to say anything. But it may harm your defence if you do not mention, when questioned, something which you later rely on in court. Anything you do say may be given in evidence.'

17.3.1.1 The practical effect; advising the suspect

The practical effect is clearly a matter of some debate. Despite almost unanimous hostility to the reduction of the 'right to silence', many experienced criminal lawyers used to advising suspects in the police station seem to doubt whether it will have much effect. This is because it will always be proper for a lawyer to advise his client to remain silent until the lawyer has sufficient details of the case against him. This is unlikely to be at the initial interview, however cooperative the police may be, and a lawyer may conclude that he does not have sufficient information until he has had advance disclosure of witness statements at a later stage.

It is suggested also that the type of 'professional' criminals at whom the 1994 Act was allegedly aimed and who allegedly were relying on the right to silence wholesale and procuring unmeritorious acquittals might well learn a form of words which substantially undermines the intended effect of the provision. For example, if a suspect says to the policeman that he is wholly innocent but wishes to consult a lawyer before dealing with the unfounded allegations against him; and if at the police station a competent defence lawyer advises the accused to say nothing and evidence is given at trial to this effect, much of the force of the change in the law may be undermined. If it becomes widely known to the lay persons who constitute juries that competent defence lawyers always advise their clients not to speak at the initial interview stage, then the existence of this as a recognised defence tactic may mean that much of the suspicion that might otherwise inevitably have attached to the accused will be dissipated.

Moreover, at trial, a suspect may paint such a picture of confusion and embarrassment that it would be difficult for the court to draw a heavy adverse inference. No doubt defence counsel in their closing speeches will become used to putting to the jury a picture of the suspect alone and frightened and not wishing to commit himself to anything until he has had competent legal advice.

It should also be remembered that this must have some interplay with the Codes of Practice which provide for a suspect to have legal advice at the earliest appropriate moment. If in the light of that advice a suspect insists on remaining silent, it will be difficult for the court to criticise, however erroneous they believe the lawyer's advice to be. It may therefore be that this will have a more limited effect than originally feared.

It is important to note that the 1994 Act could have provided that even if no response is given immediately under interview, a defendant should be obliged to disclose his defence in some form well before trial. However, that provision was not put in and thus it will be perfectly legitimate for an accused who has exercised his right to silence in interrogation to maintain it until trial and he does not run any risk of a stronger inference being drawn from that. Neither is there any provision in the 1994 Act stating that if the accused, having kept silent at interview, does choose to disclose his defence well before trial, he should in some way receive credit for it in the form of the way in which the judge directs the jury.

It would however be obvious that any fair-minded judge should give some credit for such early disclosure when commenting on the evidence to the jury. It may thus come to be a well-recognised tactic that a full account of the defendant's evidence should be supplied to the prosecution well in advance of the trial, and if possible even before the committal proceedings.

It should also be noted that s. 34 refers to questioning by persons other than constables charged with a duty of investigating offences or charging offenders and thus extends, for example, to store detectives, customs officers and the like.

17.3.2 INFERENCES FROM FAILURE OR REFUSAL TO ACCOUNT FOR OBJECTS, SUBSTANCES MARKS OR PRESENCE AT SCENE OF THE CRIME, ss. 36 AND 37

Sections 36 and 37 of the Criminal Justice and Public Order Act 1994 refer specifically to cases where there is any object, substance or mark on the person, clothing or footwear in the possession of the accused or in any place at which he is at the time of his arrest. In these cases, failure to reply by an accused who is asked to explain such matters may be relevant at trial and evidence about it may be given and an appropriate inference drawn. There is thus obviously substantial overlap between s. 34 dealing with general questioning, and ss. 36 and 37. Thus, for example, if the accused is asked about the presence of a tear in his clothing when it is alleged he has been involved in a knife fight, and fails to explain that it was torn the previous day in a work accident but puts this fact forward at trial, some inference may be drawn. The Code of Practice C at paragraph 10.5B indicates the procedure to be adopted by the police. Before any inference can be drawn, an interviewing officer must have told the suspect in ordinary language what offence he was investigating; what fact he is asking the suspect to account for; indicate that he believes that that fact may be due to the suspect taking part in the commission of the offence in question; and reminding him again that a court may draw a proper inference from failure to account from the fact; and tell him that a record is being made of the interview which may be given in evidence at trial.

17.3.2.1 Other inferences and s. 34

It should be noted that s. 34(5) makes it clear that the inferences to be drawn are in addition to, and not prejudicial to, other inferences which might have been drawn at common law. Thus all the law about evidence of reaction of a suspect to a statement made in his or her presence (see *R v Christie* [1914] AC 545) is preserved and even where an acknowledgment by silence may be deemed to be an admission.

17.3.3 FAILURE TO TESTIFY IN COURT, s. 35

The background to s. 35 of the Criminal Justice and Public Order Act 1994 is of course that an accused is permitted a right to silence in court and nothing in the statute expressly prohibits this. It would have been possible, e.g., to have expressly made it a criminal offence in itself not to testify at one's own trial, but this draconian course has not been taken. The basic position was as described in *R v Bathurst* [1968] 2 QB 99, namely that the judge in such cases is obliged to give a direction that although the jury may be disappointed that the accused has not testified and given his version, he is perfectly entitled to sit tight and make the prosecution prove their case. They are not to infer that he is guilty from his refusal to testify.

The change in the law on the right to silence at trial is arguably less contentious than that during interrogation because during interrogation a suspect may well not have full knowledge of the case against him and may be at a serious disadvantage in testifying before receiving legal advice. This does obviously not apply at the trial stage.

The most recent case of importance on judicial comment before the 1994 Act came into force was *R v Martinez-Tobon* [1994] 1 WLR 388 where the Court of Appeal laid down the following principles where an accused does not testify:

(a) The judge should give the *Bathurst* direction.

(b) Where he has done that the judge may go on, if he thinks it appropriate, to make a stronger comment if the defence case involves alleged facts which are at variance with prosecution evidence or additional to it and exculpatory and must if true be within the defendant's knowledge.

(c) The nature and strength of such comment are within the discretion of the judge but it must not be such as to contradict or nullify the essentials for the *Bathurst* direction.

There are two important evidential effects of the new 1994 Act:

(a) Section 168(3) and sch. 11 repeal s. 1(b) of the Criminal Evidence Act 1898 and thus permit the prosecution in their closing speech to comment on the failure of an accused to testify. This reverses the previous law.

(b) Section 35 provides that the court shall, at the conclusion of the prosecution evidence, satisfy itself that the accused is aware that the stage has been reached at which he may testify and if he chooses not to give evidence it will then be permissible for the court or jury to draw such inferences 'as appear proper from his failure to give evidence or his refusal without good cause to answer any question'.

It has been argued this may merely declare the common law position permitting inferences to be drawn, e.g., as in the case of *Martinez-Tobon* where the defence was that the accused thought the smuggled goods were emeralds and not drugs and the comment was 'if he thought that one might have thought he would be very anxious to say so'. That was held to be a permissible comment given the surrounding facts.

It seems however that s. 35 is actually meant to go much further. It is worth considering a Northern Ireland case on a similar provision applicable only in Northern Ireland, namely *K S Murray* v *DPP* [1994] 1 WLR 1 where the trial judge gave a very strong direction on the accused's failure to testify. In the House of Lords the judgment of Lord Mustill held that there was still a need for there to be a prima facie case to answer and failure to testify could not support that. However, he went on to say that:

(a) If a defendant does not go on oath to say that the witnesses who have spoken about his actions are untruthful or unreliable, then the fact finder may suspect that the defendant does not tell his story because he has no story to tell or one which will not stand up to scrutiny.

(b) Likewise, if the defendant seeks to outflank the prosecution case by means of a 'positive' defence, e.g., provocation on a charge of murder, if he does not give evidence in support of this allegation, there will be a legitimate inference in many cases that the defence is untrue.

(c) However, it is not in every situation that an adverse inference can be drawn from silence, the more so because in all but the simplest case permissible inferences may have to be considered separately in relation to each individual issue and everything will therefore depend upon the nature of the issue, the weight of the evidence adduced by the prosecution upon it, and the extent to which the defendant in the nature of things is able to give his own account. It is therefore impossible to generalise.

The extra inference which the judge may direct the jury to draw will depend on the view of the case as a whole. Given that the prosecution will now be able to comment on the accused's failure to testify, the prosecution will also have to be wary about making a stronger comment than permitted by the circumstances, as will the judge.

It should be noted that the new provisions refer both to an accused not testifying at all and to his failure to answer any question asked of him. The question must of course have been a proper one in the first place and therefore this does not in itself mean the prosecution may question him, e.g., about his previous character.

17.3.4   PRACTICE DIRECTION OF 12 APRIL 1995

The Lord Chief Justice has issued a Practice Direction entitled *Practice Direction (Crown Court: Evidence: Advice to Defendant)* (1995) *The Times*, 12 April 1995. It indicates that where an accused is legally represented, the judge should, in the presence of the jury, enquire of his advocate in these terms:

> Have you advised your client that the stage has now been reached at which he may give evidence and, if he chooses not to do so or, having been sworn without good cause refuses to answer any question, the jury may draw such inferences as appear proper from his failure to do so?

On the assumption that the advocate would reply that he had so advised his client, the case would proceed. Should the advocate admit that he had not, then there should be a brief adjournment so that the relevant advice could be given.

If the accused is not legally represented, then the judge must give a similar warning to the accused personally, also in the presence of the jury, indicating that the time has been reached for him to give evidence in his defence if he chooses to do so and reminding him of inferences that may be drawn if he chooses not to do so. The judge must also remind the accused that he can, whether or not he gives evidence, address the jury by arguing his case from the dock, but at that stage he must not give evidence. The warning must conclude with the question: 'Do you now intend to give evidence?'

Many judges will no doubt think it as well, if an accused is unrepresented, whilst using this form of words, to go on to explain in more detail to the accused the way in which he may present his case, since it is notorious that in such cases an accused finds great difficulty in conducting cross-examination of prosecution witnesses without mixing in evidence of his own and making comment on the evidence. Naturally, some latitude is always allowed to such an unrepresented accused, when he is cross-examining, as it will doubtless also continue to be at the stages of him giving evidence and making a closing address to the jury. The reminder to an accused that if he chooses not to testify he is limited to argument to the jury and must not add what in effect are matters of his own evidence is very important and may need to be stressed more than once.

17.3.5   JUDICIAL CONSIDERATION OF THE RIGHT TO SILENCE

The first important cases on the right to silence exercised during the trial and s. 35, Criminal Justice and Public Order Act 1994 reached the Court of Appeal in *R v Cowan; R v Gayle*; and *R v Ricciardi* [1995] 3 WLR 881. Two of the three appeals were allowed and one was dismissed. The court however, rejected an argument that s. 35 should be permitted to operate only in exceptional cases. The court held that even before the 1994 Act the accused had been in some respects inhibited from always exercising his right to silence and that the burden of proof, far from being altered in any way, remained firmly on the prosecution. The effect of s. 35 was simply to add a further evidential factor in support of the prosecution case. The court emphasised that silence cannot be the only factor on which a conviction is based, and the prosecution remain under an obligation to establish a prima facie case before any question of the defendant testifying is raised. The judge should make it clear to the jury that they must be convinced of the existence of a prima facie case before drawing any adverse inference from silence.

The court expressed its sympathy to the two judges from whose directions the appeals were allowed who had not had the benefit of the specimen direction formulated by the Judicial Studies Board which was promulgated in summer 1995. That specimen direction commenting on the appropriate inferences to be drawn from the right to silence should be used in all appropriate cases, although it is impossible to anticipate all the circumstances in which a judge might think it right to direct or advise a jury against drawing any adverse inference. The court also commented that decisions of the European Court of Human Rights were not binding on English courts, but were only of assistance to resolve any ambiguity in domestic law of which there appeared to be none in the present case.

Subsequently in *R v Condron and Condron* (1996) *The Times*, 4 November 1996, the Court of Appeal considered a case where the judge had had to direct the jury about the inferences which might be drawn where the accused had failed to answer questions at interview. The court held that the essential matters recommended in the case of *Cowan* should be included in the judge's direction to the jury even where the silence came during interview rather than at trial. thus, where the appellants had conducted a 'no comment' interview, they could both be asked at trial why they had not made any mention of facts about which they now gave evidence and the judge was entitled to invite the jury to draw adverse inferences. The court considered that it would be appropriate for a Practice Direction similar to that dealing with silence in court under s. 35 to be promulgated as soon as possible. The court went on to observe that if, in order to explain why no answer had been given during interview, an accused called his solicitor to testify, the solicitor might very well be cross-examined about the reasons for the advice he had given since the accused could be held to have waived his privilege generally. This approach was taken further in *R v Argent* (1996) *The Times*, 19 December 1996, where the Lord Chief Justice indicated that for there to be any question of an inference from silence:

(a) There must be proceedings in which the issue arises. Thus, if a solicitor is unable to be satisfied that there is sufficient evidence to bring a charge, the appropriate advice will still often legitimately be to remain silent.

(b) There must be a failure to answer questions prior to charge. This will encourage the growing practice of making a considered statement at the moment of charge which is then placed with the charge record. It must be remembered that questioning after charge is only allowed in restricted circumstances and therefore no inference from silence can be drawn if there is inappropriate questioning after charge under s. 34.

(c) There must be a failure to answer a question directed to discovering whether and by whom an offence has been committed. This is a helpful indication for solicitors whose duty to intervene in interview is now given considerable prominence. Thus solicitors attending an interview could in their turn ask investigating officers how a given question is directed to discovering whether and by whom an offence has been committed and, in the event of an unsatisfactory reply, give the client advice not to respond.

(d) There must be a fact which could reasonably be expected to be mentioned. The court must therefore examine the circumstances existing at the time of questioning to see if this defendant could reasonably have been expected to mention the relevant issues, the test being a subjective one to this defendant. The Lord Chief Justice listed factors which could be relevant, e.g., the time of day; the defendant's age; his criminal experience; his mental capacity, state of health and sobriety; tiredness; personality; and the actual legal advice given to him. To avoid any difficulties arising over the question of waiving privilege because of what was said in *Condron*, solicitors may wish to avoid giving these factors as reasons for silence, but will rather have them recorded on the custody record as 'relevant issues'. If the custody officer refuses to add them to the record, a solicitor can hand in a written document setting out the factors and under Code C, paragraph 5.8(b) the custody officer must then keep a record of that document.

17.3.6 EFFECT OF THE CRIMINAL PROCEDURE AND INVESTIGATIONS ACT 1996

As from April 1997 the Criminal Procedure and Investigations Act 1996 requires defendants who are to be tried on indictment to draft and serve a 'defence statement' indicating the nature of their defence (for full details of these important provisions, see **9.6**). There is as yet no case law or precedent to assist with regard to the drafting of such statements. The purpose is to avoid the defence 'ambushing' the prosecution at trial with a defence which comes as a complete surprise and which the prosecution have not got the evidence available to meet. Subsequent to the defence statement, there will be some form of plea and directions hearing at which further clarification of the issues may be asked for. The defence statement may not necessarily need to be long. If, e.g., the defence is alibi, then the statement need do little more than name the witnesses and indicate the times between which and places at which the accused was with the alibi witnesses. If the defence is self-defence, or provocation, it may well be shorter still. The prosecution will therefore be entitled to get some information out of an accused before trial, but this will clearly not be of anything like the length or detail that they would have sought to get by way of interrogation. Comment may well therefore continue to be appropriate as to the accused's refusal to answer questions during interrogation and indeed for those cases where the defendant refuses to give any defence statement in accordance with the Act (something which is only likely to happen where he or she is not legally represented). Case law or Practice Directions will in due course no doubt indicate the ambit of appropriate comment from the judge to the jury in respect of the absence of such a statement.

17.3.7 THE RIGHT TO SILENCE AND THE EUROPEAN CONVENTION ON HUMAN RIGHTS

Article 6 of the European Convention on Human Rights requires that in the criminal process the accused has the advantage of the presumption of innocence. Cases are coming before the Court already in respect of other aspects of the right to silence and the extent to which this infringes the presumption of innocence. A strong authority is the case of *Funke* v *France* (Case–82/1991/334/407) in which in a judgment dated 25 February 1993 the European Court of Human Rights held that it was in breach of the right to a fair trial under Article 6(1) for the government to require the accused to produce bank statements which might be used against him in criminal proceedings.

In the case of *Ernest Saunders* v *United Kingdom* (Case–43/1994/490/572) the European Court of Human Rights held that the requirement under s. 434 of the Companies Act 1985 on persons 'to attend before the Inspectors when required to do so ...' and ... otherwise give the Inspectors all assistance in connection with the investigation', and to answer questions on oath subject to criminal penalties akin to contempt of court, amounted to a requirement for Saunders to provide evidence against himself and deprived him of a fair hearing by way of infringing his rights. They thus found the United Kingdom in breach of Article 6(1) of the European Convention on Human Rights. The decision was given on 17 December 1996 and the Court rejected the UK government's argument that these powers were not such as to deprive the accused of his right to a fair trial. The outcome in that case, however, must be contrasted with that in *John Murray* v *United Kingdom* (Case–18731/91) which decides that not every infringement of the so-called 'right to silence' amounts to a breach of the Convention. These cases are more fully discussed in **13.5**.

17.3.8 MISCELLANEOUS POINTS

(a) Counsel for a co-accused is *entitled as of right* to comment on another co-accused's failure to testify since s. 1, Criminal Evidence Act 1898 is silent on this. For example, in *R* v *Wickham* (1971) 55 Cr App R 199 it was held that, where there was a conflict in the evidence of two co-defendants, counsel for one defendant has the right to comment on the failure of the co-defendant to give evidence and the judge has no discretion to prevent such comment.

(b) In addition, if the accused wishes to call expert opinion evidence, he is required, by rules of court, to disclose it in advance of trial (see **21.2.6**).

(c) A number of statutes have the effect anyway of requiring a suspect to answer questions in certain restricted circumstances. A good example was s. 6, Official Secrets Act 1920 which made it an offence to withhold information from a duly authorised policeman investigating infringements of the Official Secrets Act 1911 (now repealed). Other statutes which require persons questioned to supply information include the Road Traffic Acts and various statutes relating to taxation, rating and gaming.

EIGHTEEN

THE LAW OF EVIDENCE (5): IMPROPERLY OBTAINED EVIDENCE IN CRIMINAL CASES

18.1 Introduction

Evidence which has been obtained illegally or improperly by the prosecution provides a difficult problem of jurisprudence. In some jurisdictions, particularly the USA, the courts in the main attach a high regard to procedural propriety on the part of public officers, such as the police, and effectively use the law of evidence to discipline them. So if evidence has been obtained unfairly it will be excluded even if it is conclusive of the accused's guilt. The proposition is that the court itself is tainted if it allows illegally obtained evidence to be given before it and that the higher good of the public standing of the court requires it to use its discretion in this way.

In the main, English law has gone in quite the opposite direction and will not allow the law of evidence to be used as a means of disciplining the police. The statement of Crompton J in *R v Leatham* (1861) 8 Cox CC 498 still represents English law: 'It matters not how you get it — if you steal it even it would be admissible in evidence.'

The question of improperly obtained evidence arises in three main situations, namely:

(a) Evidence obtained as a result of a confession which has already been ruled inadmissible. For example, a confession is obtained by threats or violence and is thus inadmissible but within the confession the suspect has told the police where they can find other incriminating evidence, e.g., a body or the stolen goods. The question then is whether the finding of the body or the goods is admissible.

(b) Evidence obtained by unlawful search, entry or seizure.

(c) Evidence obtained by entrapment, e.g., by a plain clothes policeman in effect becoming one of a gang of criminals and pretending to participate in their activities.

In all three cases, English law has decided that the law of evidence is not to be used as a means of disciplining the police, so that if evidence is admissible in itself and relevant, it is not made inadmissible by virtue of having been obtained illegally or unfairly. The leading case is *Kuruma* v *R* [1955] AC 197. In this case, at a time when emergency regulations applied in Kenya, it was a capital offence for natives to possess ammunition. Powers of search were conferred by the regulations on policemen of a certain rank. The accused was unlawfully searched by two policemen of a lower rank than that stipulated in the regulations, and they found ammunition upon him. At his trial, he contended that since the search was illegal it would be improper to permit the Crown to take advantage of its own misconduct. The Privy Council held that the only test is whether evidence in such a case is relevant. If it is relevant, it is admissible.

18.1.1 EVIDENCE OBTAINED IN CONSEQUENCE OF AN INADMISSIBLE CONFESSION

In the first of the cases mentioned above, as we have already seen, s. 76(4) of the Police and Criminal Evidence Act 1984 expressly provides that the finding of a thing in consequence even of an inadmissible confession is admissible, although we must also remember s. 76(5) of the 1984 Act which provides:

> *Evidence that a fact to which this subsection applies was discovered as a result of a statement made by an accused person shall not be admissible unless evidence of how it was discovered was given by him or on his behalf.*

In other words where a confession is excluded but the accused said in it, e.g., where something was to be found, the evidence of finding the thing is admissible but no reference back to the reason why the police looked in that place may be made unless the accused himself gives evidence as to how the thing came to be discovered. Therefore if the discovery of the thing in question cannot otherwise be linked to the accused (e.g., by the fact that it has his fingerprints on it), there may be no point in the prosecution adducing the finding of the evidence.

18.1.2 EVIDENCE OBTAINED BY ILLEGAL SEARCH, SEIZURE AND ENTRY

Before the coming into force of s. 78 of the Police and Criminal Evidence Act 1984, which we shall consider below, it was quite clear that in the two other cases mentioned above, namely evidence obtained by unlawful search, seizure or entry, or by entrapment, the authorities were entirely in favour of admissibility and of the principle in *Kuruma*. *Kuruma* itself is a clear illustration of the law in relation to evidence obtained by illegal search.

18.1.3 EVIDENCE OBTAINED BY ENTRAPMENT

Cases such as *R v Birtles* (1969) 53 Cr App R 469 and *R v McCann* (1971) 56 Cr App R 359 clearly established that, even where policemen acting in plain clothes and participating in a crime go too far and incite criminals to commit offences which would otherwise not have been committed, the law of evidence will not be used to discipline the police. There is no defence of 'entrapment' known to English law and the law of evidence could not be used to create such a defence by the device of excluding otherwise admissible evidence. Where police had gone too far, the question of their misconduct would be dealt with in police disciplinary proceedings; but insofar as the accused was concerned, entrapment would only be relevant to mitigate the sentence imposed, not to the question of admissibility.

18.2 The Court's Discretion to Exclude

The law was restated in the former leading case of *R v Sang* [1980] AC 402, which confirmed that the court was only concerned with the relevance of evidence *not* the means by which it was obtained, except in the case of confessions. *Sang* confirmed nonetheless that there is an overriding discretion to exclude evidence if its prejudicial effect outweighs its probative value so as to make it unfair to the accused to admit it. Sometimes improperly obtained evidence might fall into this category but this is a rule of general application and is not only applicable to evidence allegedly obtained illegally. The question for the court is *how fair the trial* will be and not how fair were the police in obtaining the evidence in the manner which they used. This discretion, which existed at common law, is expressly preserved by the words of s. 82(3) of the Police and Criminal Evidence Act 1984. It is important in this context to consider s. 78(1) of the 1984 Act which we have already looked at in connection with its relevance to confessions. The section provides:

> ... *the court may refuse to allow evidence on which the prosecution proposes to rely to be given if it appears to the court that, having regard to all the circumstances, **including the circumstances in which the evidence was obtained**, the admission of the evidence would have such an adverse effect on the fairness of the proceedings that the court ought not to admit it.* (Emphasis added.)

18.3 Test for Admissibility

The test therefore remains 'will it have an adverse effect on the fairness of the proceedings'? It was at first considered difficult to visualise an example of how the actual method of obtaining the evidence could possibly affect the 'proceedings' (i.e. the trial itself) rather than merely demonstrating 'unfairness' in some more general sense, which would surely be irrelevant on the wording of the section. It was widely considered that the section added nothing to such discretion as there was following *R* v *Sang* and that the section would certainly not be used to discipline the police. However, surprisingly, and with one must say a good deal of rather suspect reasoning, the courts have taken a robust view of the nature of their discretion under s. 78.

The somewhat surprising line of cases which have considered s. 78 as supplementary to s. 76 so that breaches of other sections of the 1984 Act (e.g., s. 56 or s. 58) or the Codes of Practice have led to the exclusion of confessions even where the confession had initially been ruled reliable. The most important of these cases, referred to earlier, is that of *R* v *Mason* [1988] 1 WLR 139 where it will be recalled a confession was obtained from an accused after he and his solicitor were both untruthfully told by the police that the police had damning fingerprint evidence and was excluded under s. 78 notwithstanding that it had initially been held reliable under s. 76. In *Mason*'s case the court expressly stated that:

(a) The evidence *was not* excluded in order to discipline the police.

(b) Section 78 does no more than restate the power which the court had at common law.

(c) It was the deception of the solicitor by the police that was particularly offensive and fatal to the evidence.

The reasoning in *Mason*, laudable though the outcome might be felt to be, is suspect. If an innocent man might have confessed on hearing these untruthful representations by the police in the belief that they had framed him and that he might therefore just as well confess (since he would be disbelieved at trial) in order to obtain more lenient treatment, then it would seem that the confession was rendered *unreliable* by the falsehood. If it was not thought to be unreliable, then it is hard to take any other view than that s. 78 was used to discipline the police.

What is relevant to this chapter however is to consider whether the court will use s. 78 to exclude evidence which is obtained by entrapment or by illegal search and seizure. A problem is that, although there is some anecdotal evidence that Crown Court judges may be using s. 78 in that way, since the prosecution have no general right of appeal to a higher court where evidence is excluded which is vital to the prosecution's success, such instances will not be fully reported.

In *R* v *Christou* [1992] QB 979 undercover policemen set up a jeweller's shop in an attempt to recover stolen property and collect evidence against thieves and handlers. Cameras and tape recorders recorded all transactions. Most conversation involved bartering about the price, but to maintain their cover the police would also engage in banter and ask questions to be expected of shady jewellers, such as in which areas of London it would be unwise to resell the goods they were offered. The information obtained helped trace the true owners and discover the dates of thefts. Fingerprints were usually obtained from the suspects by asking them to give a written receipt.

At trial it was argued by the defence that the whole concept of the shop involved a deceit or trick designed to deprive visitors of their privilege against self-incrimination. The evidence should be excluded either under *Sang* or under s. 78. No cautions had been administered and the conversations were caught by the Codes of Practice. In dismissing the appeal, the Court of Appeal held that the judge had been right to consider s. 78 and *Sang* but the criteria of unfairness were the same on whichever basis the discretion was exercised. The court held that no trick was applied to the appellants; they had voluntarily applied themselves to the trick. It could not be the case that every trick which produced evidence against an accused meant there had been unfairness. For example, a victim might be used to help trap a blackmailer. The case of *Mason* was completely different.

The case of *R v Keenan* (1990) 90 Cr App R 1 (a case on confessions) held that it was wrong for policemen to adopt or use an undercover pose or disguise to facilitate the asking of questions about an offence uninhibited by the requirements of the Codes with the object of circumventing them. That proposition was taken further in the case of *R v Bryce* [1992] Crim LR 728 which has been considered earlier at length in the context of confessions (see **17.1.8.3**). Undercover officers in that case contacted a man suspected of theft and held conversations with him. The Court of Appeal held that the series of questions by the undercover officers offended against the principle set out in *Christou*. It was blatantly a case of interrogation with the effect of using an undercover pose to circumvent the Code. In addition, the words used were hotly disputed and there was no contemporary record, unlike the tape and video recording in *Christou*.

In the important cases of *R v Smurthwaite* (1993) 98 Cr App R 437: *R v Gill* (1993) 97 Cr App R 215 the court had to consider again the issue of entrapment. In each case the accused had separately solicited the murder of their respective spouses. In each case the person solicited to carry out the murder also proved to be an undercover policeman. The court reviewed the authorities, and in particular s. 78 of the 1984 Act, and concluded that entrapment or the use of an agent provocateur does not in itself afford a defence in law to a criminal charge. That is not to say, however, that entrapment or the use of a trick would always be irrelevant to the application of s. 78. The court said that the right approach was to consider whether, in all the circumstances, the obtaining of the evidence would have the adverse effect described in the statute. It is necessary to consider the question of fairness in its context not only of fairness to the accused, but fairness to the public. In exercising his discretion, a judge would take into account: whether the officer was enticing the defendant to commit an offence which he would otherwise not have committed; what was the nature of any entrapment; whether there were admissions of the completed offence; how active or passive was the officer's role in obtaining the evidence; was there an unassailable record of what occurred or was there strong supporting evidence of it. In each of the present cases the officer's conduct had remained, with one small exception, on the *Christou* side of the line and not crossed to the *Bryce* side and thus the evidence was admitted.

Finally, one other important case which deserves mention is *R v Khan* [1994] 4 All ER 426. In this case the appellant was convicted on the basis of listening devices planted in private property without the knowledge or consent of the owner or occupier which enabled the police to obtain a tape recording of the private conversations that took place in the house. The accused appealed contending that evidence of private conversations on private property were inadmissible and should have been excluded. The Crown accepted that the installation of the device had involved civil trespass and impropriety but contended that it had been necessary in the circumstances. The Court of Appeal held that it could apply the established rule of the test of admissibility which was relevance and, even if illegally obtained, such evidence was admissible.

The Court of Appeal's reasoning was upheld when the case came to the House of Lords ([1996] 3 WLR 162). The House of Lords affirmed:

(a) that it was an established principle of English law that the test of admissibility was relevance; that relevant evidence, even if illegally obtained, was admissible and that therefore the evidence of the tape-recorded conversation was admissible;

(b) that in the circumstances, including the facts that the trespass and damage was slight and that the criminal conduct being investigated was of great gravity, albeit that the evidence obtained constituted a breach of Article 8 of the European Convention on Human Rights in terms of its invasion of privacy, that damage was outweighed by the public interest in the detection of crime.

The House of Lords went on to observe that the courts could have regard to the European Convention on Human Rights on matters to do with 'fairness' in a trial generally. That did not however alter their conclusion in the present case.

18.4 The Importance of s. 78 of the 1984 Act

We have now considered s. 78 in its most important aspects of exclusion of confession evidence and as to whether or not it will be used in the case of illegal searches or evidence obtained by entrapment. Section 78 however is of general application. It can be used in respect of any item of prosecution evidence. It is thus the section used to reinforce the Code of Practice in relation to identification so that breach of the procedures at identification parades may lead to all the identification evidence being excluded (see **19.5.3**).

Another specific use of it does not involve any suggestion at all of misconduct by the police. It is used when the court has to consider its general discretion on the principles of unfairness to let in evidence of convictions which came about in other proceedings under s. 74 of the 1984 Act. This section does not refer to *the accused's* own previous record as to which quite other considerations apply. It is a section which permits proof of conviction to establish the facts on which prior convictions of *other people* were based. An important use of it is that, where X has been convicted of theft of certain goods, then his conviction can be used at the trial of Y on a charge of handling the same stolen goods as a way of establishing the important preliminary fact that the goods were stolen. Under the previous law this was not possible and the prosecution would, at the trial of the handler, have had to establish anew that the goods were stolen in the first place.

18.5 Sections 78 and 74 of the 1984 Act — Applicable Principles

The use of s. 74 is subject to the court's discretion under s. 78 because in some circumstances obviously great prejudice could be caused to a defendant by virtue of 'guilt by association' if the convictions of some person with whom he had recently been, or some family member, were put before the court as an alleged piece of circumstantial evidence against the defendant.

The case that sets out the principles best is *R* v *Boyson* [1991] Crim LR 274, in which B was charged with being concerned in the importation of drugs. She was charged with four others, three of whom pleaded guilty to the same counts. The fourth person was her co-habitee who had been separately convicted of conspiracy. The Crown applied for leave to adduce the evidence of the guilty pleas and convictions. B was convicted and appealed and the Court of Appeal held that the following were the applicable principles:

(a) That s. 74 should be sparingly used and evidence of other convictions should only be introduced when clearly relevant to an issue in the case and must always be followed by a clear direction as to the issues to which the conviction is or is not relevant.

(b) Although the judge had referred in his summing up to the dangers of guilt by association he did not properly deal with the issue of the co-accused's convictions on different offences.

(c) The introduction of each one of the convictions was irrelevant to any issue in B's case and was prejudicial, nor was there any proper direction.

(d) The judge had not considered his discretion under s. 78 properly. Nonetheless there was ample evidence of B's involvement and the proviso was applied. The court expressly disapproved of the apparently growing practice of allowing evidence to go before a jury which is strictly irrelevant, inadmissible, prejudicial, or unfair simply because it is convenient for the jury to 'have the whole picture'.

This case therefore is an extremely useful authority on the way in which ss. 74 and 78 should be considered together.

18.6 Practical Considerations

(a) Section 78 only applies to evidence to be adduced by the prosecution. If it is a co-defendant who wishes to adduce improperly obtained evidence then the judge has a wide discretion, not fettered by statute, to do justice between the parties.

(b) When a defence advocate is considering the prosecution evidence, whether this comes about under the advance disclosure rules in the case of summary trial, or the provisions for prosecution disclosure prior to a Crown Court trial, it is important to weigh each item of prosecution evidence to test its relevance, admissibility and weight. This is inherent in consideration of any kind of evidence.

(c) Quite apart from any questions of strict admissibility however, it is always relevant to consider whether there is any ground for applying to the court to exclude otherwise admissible evidence within its discretion. This application may be framed under the general common law discretions, the rule in *R v Sang*, under s. 82(3) of the 1984 Act, or under s. 78 of the 1984 Act. These overlap in many respects, although on the wording of s. 78 special attention has to be given to the question of *how the evidence was obtained*.

(d) It must be borne in mind that one is not, when relying on s. 78 as a ground for seeking the exclusion of evidence, necessarily relying on deliberate and callous flouting of some rule of practice or procedure. It may be, e.g., that the police or Crown Prosecutor have simply confused matters procedurally or even proceeded by honest oversight. There are instances of the use of s. 78 to which we shall turn shortly where the section has been used to exclude the whole of evidence obtained at an identification parade because of a bona fide mistake made by the police. It is therefore always as well to have in mind the court's discretions to exclude and in particular to have the Codes of Practice and the authority of *Mason* available, the latter being the highest point of the court's willingness to exclude for procedural impropriety. The effect of *Mason* is clearly at its most pointed with confession evidence but there is no reason why it cannot be prayed in aid in other situations, for example evidence obtained in disregard of powers of search, seizure or entry; misconduct in relation to the accused's legal representative; and even the residual possibility that on some particularly gross facts the court will, in effect, be prepared to recognise that entrapment might be a possible ground for exclusion.

NINETEEN

THE LAW OF EVIDENCE (6): CORROBORATION: EVIDENCE OF IDENTITY

19.1 Introduction

Corroborative evidence is that which independently tends to support or confirm other evidence.

The general rule has always been that evidence does not require corroboration and that the court may act on the uncorroborated evidence of one witness alone, however serious the charge. Until 1995, however, there were individual classes of cases where the type of evidence, or the type of witness, were deemed inherently 'suspect' in some way so as to require extra caution from a court before it considered its verdict.

The law on corroboration evolved in a haphazard and piecemeal way and was burdened with difficult technicalities. Classically, three kinds of witness were thought to be sufficiently suspect to require corroboration of their evidence before there could be a conviction, namely children, accomplices, and victims of a sexual offence.

There were, in addition, rules which indicated that corroboration should generally be looked for in any case where a witness might have some personal motive for wishing to secure the conviction of the accused, for example someone who had a grudge against the accused, or who might himself have fallen under suspicion of the crime in question.

In these cases, a judge would have to remind the jury, in very technical terms, of the risk of convicting on the evidence of the 'suspect' witness and then go on to describe what items of evidence could have the technical quality of corroboration on the particular facts of the case. Judges were notoriously prone to get aspects of corroboration wrong, either by directing the jury with insufficient force about the risks of acting without corroboration, or by misidentifying items of evidence in the case which they might say were technically capable of amounting to corroboration but which in fact lacked the necessary quality.

The difficulty, technicality and illogicality of the existing law has led to pressure for reform, particularly over the last decade. It was suggested, in particular, that the evidence of children is, within reason, no more suspect than that of any other person. Likewise, the technicalities relating to the evidence of an accomplice lacked any inherent logic because there would be many cases where the evidence of an accomplice would be of high quality whereas that of other kinds of witness might not. In particular it was also considered offensive to require corroboration of the victim of sexual offences, the way in which these victims were generally treated in court, in relation to the corroboration requirement and in other ways, was such as to deter victims from coming forward, especially in rape cases where consent was alleged.

19.1.1   THE PRESENT LAW

Eventually, s. 34, Criminal Justice Act 1988 abolished the requirement for corroboration of children's evidence and s. 32(1), Criminal Justice and Public Order Act 1994 has abolished the requirement for the judge to give a warning to the jury in the case of either accomplices or victims of sexual offences.

Quite apart from these cases where there had been a corroboration requirement at common law, the Sexual Offences Act 1956 imposed a separate requirement for corroboration in respect of certain classes of sexual offence, including procurement of a woman by threats for the purpose of intercourse; procurement of a woman by false pretences; administering drugs to facilitate intercourse; causing prostitution; and procuration of a girl under 21. The requirement for corroboration has been repealed in relation to these offences also.

Therefore there are now only a handful of statutes, of minor importance, which individually still require more than one witness in order to obtain a conviction. The only significant one is s. 89, Road Traffic Regulation Act 1984, under which a person cannot be convicted of speeding solely on the evidence of one witness to the effect that in his *opinion* the driver was exceeding the speed limit. Moreover, if two witnesses give their opinion, it must concern the speed observed over the same stretch of road. However, a person *can* be convicted on the evidence of one person where that amounts to something more than an opinion, e.g., where the speed can be checked on a speedometer or by other device: see *Nicholas v Penny* [1950] 2 KB 466.

The abolition of strict requirement to give the corroboration warning, and the many technicalities attending it, were explored soon after the 1994 Act came into effect, in *R v Makanjuola: R v Easton* (1995) *The Times*, 17 May 1995. Here the Court of Appeal, headed by the Lord Chief Justice, summarised the effect of the abolition of the requirements to give the corroboration warning as follows:

(a) There was no requirement to give a corroboration warning in respect of an alleged accomplice or complainant of a sexual offence simply because a witness fell into those categories.

(b) It was a matter for the judge's discretion what, if any, warning was considered appropriate in respect of such a witness, as indeed in respect of any other witness in whatever type of case.

(c) In some cases it might be appropriate for the judge to warn the jury to exercise caution before acting on the unsupported evidence of a witness. There would need to be an evidential basis for suggesting that the evidence of the witness in question might be unreliable.

(d) If any question arose as to whether the judge should give a special warning in respect of the witness, it was desirable that the question be resolved by discussion with counsel in the jury's absence before final speeches.

(e) Where the judge did decide to give some warning in respect of a witness, it would be appropriate to do so as part of the judge's review of the evidence, and his comments as to how the jury should evaluate it rather than as a set piece legal direction.

(f) Where some warning was required, it would be for the judge to decide the strength and terms of the warning. It did not have to be invested with 'the whole florid regime of the old corroboration rules'.

(g) Attempts to reimpose the strait-jacket of the old corroboration rules were strongly to be deprecated.

(h) Finally, the Court of Appeal would be disinclined to interfere with the trial judge's exercise of his discretion save in a case where his exercise was unreasonable in the *Wednesbury* sense, i.e., the basis considered in *Associated Provincial Picture Houses* v *Wednesbury Corporation* [1948] 1 KB 223.

This case therefore provides essential guidelines for how the judge is to consider directing the jury in a case where there is some apparently suspect evidence tendered by the prosecution, whether in terms of the nature of the evidence or the nature of the person who gives it. The case confirms that the judge in that situation will have a very wide discretion as to the way in which he directs the jury.

19.2 Evidence of Identity

Evidence of identification has always presented special problems. If the perpetrator of a crime is known to the victim or witness, or apprehended at the scene of the crime, evidence of identification is less hazardous (although not free of problems even here) but in the case of a crime committed swiftly and observed fleetingly by a bystander a number of well-publicised cases have shown the dangers of convicting on identification evidence alone.

The topic is best considered by examining:

(a) Problems of admissibility connected with identification.

(b) Problems of weight in identification evidence.

(c) Procedure at identification parades and the use of photographs and videos.

19.3 Problems of Admissibility

Obviously there is no theoretical objection to a witness testifying that the accused is the man he saw commit the crime. This is direct evidence by a first-hand observer. As will be seen in **19.4**, however, where this happens (i.e. where the witness sees the accused at the trial for the first time after the offence) it is known as a 'dock identification' and is frowned on except in exceptional circumstances.

But what if there has been, as there now usually will be, some identification procedure between crime and trial at which the witness has picked out the accused to assist the police? If the witness confirms at the trial that he has previously picked out the accused, is he not, in effect, testifying as to a prior consistent statement? Moreover the hearsay implications are compounded if some other person is called to confirm that the witness picked out the accused at the identification parade. The point is inadequately analysed and it is far from clear as to whether the courts have acknowledged the hearsay problem at all. See, e.g., *R v Osbourne and Virtue* [1973] 1 QB 678 where the witnesses in court could not remember whom they had picked out at an identification parade. A police inspector who had been present was allowed to testify about what had happened at the parade without the court acknowledging the hearsay point.

19.4 Problems of Weight in Identification Evidence

An old practice, now disapproved, is the so-called 'dock identification' (referred to above) where a witness is asked if the man seen at the scene of the crime is present in court. There will clearly be a tendency to look at the man in the dock and pick him just because he is there in that position. In a parliamentary statement on 27 May 1976 the Attorney-General said counsel should not seek a dock identification from a witness who had not previously made a successful identification unless the reasons were exceptional. There is a practice in some courts, where a dock identification is unavoidable, of letting the accused sit anywhere in court before the identifying witness is brought in.

The present law is governed by the case of *R v Turnbull* [1977] QB 224 decided by a Court of Appeal of five judges. This case followed shortly after the report of the Devlin Committee on Evidence of Identification in Criminal Cases which itself was a response to some well-publicised cases which turned on identification evidence and where it was demonstrated that serious miscarriages of justice had occurred. Although the guidelines in *R v Turnbull* were said to involve only changes of practice and not of law, the court emphasised that failure to follow them would lead to the conviction being quashed where the failure makes the verdict unsafe. The guidelines are as follows:

(a) The judge should warn the jury of the special need for caution before convicting the accused in reliance upon the correctness of identification evidence drawing their attention to possibilities of error (p. 228D) and to the fact that a witness may be honest but mistaken.

(b) The judge should invite the jury to examine closely the circumstances in which the identification was made, including conditions, length of time of observation, how soon afterwards the witness gave a description to the police, and whether the witness knew the defendant (p. 228E).

(c) The judge should specifically remind the jury of any weaknesses which have appeared in the identification evidence (p. 228G).

(d) If the prosecution have reason to believe that there is a material discrepancy between the description of the defendant given at first to the police and his actual appearance, they should supply the defence with particulars (p. 228F).

(e) Where the quality of the identification evidence is good the jury may safely be left to assess it; where it is poor the judge should withdraw the case from the jury and direct an acquittal unless there is other evidence which supports the correctness of the identification. This need not be corroborative in the technical sense, i.e. it need not come from a source independent of the witness. The judge must direct the jury in specific terms about the supporting evidence.

(f) In particular he must direct them that the fact that the accused elects not to give evidence cannot of itself support it, and also where the accused puts forward an alibi they need not treat any proven falsity of this as supporting evidence if, e.g., it was put forward out of stupidity or panic, but they may treat it as supporting evidence if they conclude that it was put forward for the sake of deceiving them (p. 230H).

Note also:

(a) The main problem with an identification witness is that there is not (usually) any suggestion that the witness is lying. The problem is one of an honest but mistaken witness who is convinced that he has got the right man.

(b) The need for a clear warning following *Turnbull* has been repeatedly stressed. Briefer forms of warning which paraphrase or elide the various parts of the *Turnbull* warning have been criticised on appeal and convictions quashed in such circumstances. It is vitally important in any case based on 'fleeting glimpse' identification that the full warning is given. See in particular *R v Tyson* [1985] Crim LR 48.

(c)   It must be borne in mind however that the *Turnbull* guidelines only provide a primary test. They do not apply by any means to every case of visual identification. So the warning will not be required, e.g., in cases where there has been a lengthy deliberate observation carried out by police who already know the suspect, and have had a tip-off about his involvement in a crime; or if the real issue is not whether the victim can identify the suspect but whether the victim is telling the truth at all. See, for example, *R v Courtnell* [1990] Crim LR 115 where the defence was that the identification witness was totally fabricating his evidence to conceal his own involvement in the crime.

(d)   It is worth stressing the last part of the *Turnbull* direction because it reflects a more general rule about how a judge should direct a jury if an accused should tell lies at any stage, whether out of court or in the course of giving evidence. The case of *R v Goodway* [1993] 4 All ER 894 confirms that wherever an accused has been found to have told lies, the judge should direct the jury that they must approach the matter cautiously and not conclude that, necessarily, the lies indicate conclusively that the accused is guilty. The judge should remind the jury that many people invent lies out of panic, fear, resentment or shame even though they are in fact innocent, for example an innocent man who was falsely accused who may, in the heat of the moment, invent an alibi which is later shown to be fabricated.

The important case of *Goodway* has been approved and had various glosses put on it in a series of recent decisions. Because the form of the caution now invites a suspect to give some version of what happened which may subsequently prove to be untrue, the judge needs to be very astute in considering how to direct the jury on the effect of lies. Recent cases show a sophisticated approach to this and the judge will always need to examine the relevance, if any, of the lies. In a number of cases the Court of Appeal has had to consider appeals based on failure to give a strong direction about the possibility of an innocent man telling lies and has ruled that it will always consider whether, in the end, what has happened at the trial is such as to make the conviction unsafe, and if it concludes that there has been no net effect, it will dismiss the appeal even where there has been an inadequate direction.

19.5   Procedure at Identification Parades and the Use of Photographs

We shall now go on to consider the use of photographs, videos and photofits together with procedure at identification parades. The guidelines are now in the Identification Code issued under s. 66 of the Police Criminal Evidence Act 1984. Part of the Code is set out for reference at **4.9**.

19.5.1   PHOTOGRAPHS

If the police already have a particular suspect in mind, or indeed have arrested anyone, there is no need for the use of photographs. Photographs should be used to enable the police to get some idea as to who might be a suspect where they have no immediate candidates. If there is a suspect then the police should go straight to the stage of identification parade because obviously there is less evidential value in such a parade where a witness has already recently identified a photograph.

In a case where photographs have been used the defence are placed in a great dilemma. The defence would normally wish to cross-examine a witness searchingly about all matters relevant to his recollection and the circumstances of identification. The danger of course is that if they do this some reference to photographs will come out and the more alert members of the jury will inevitably infer that since the police had a photograph of the accused, the accused must have a criminal record.

Some of the practical problems appear in the case of *R v Lamb* (1980) 71 Cr App R 198. The accused was charged with wounding. It was alleged that he and two other men had followed three students out of a restaurant, behaved abusively towards them and that the accused had then attacked one of the students. The accused who had a record of violence was picked out from among 900 photographs by two witnesses of the attack. He then attended an identification parade where the victim and another witness picked him out with varying degrees of confidence. The case against the accused depended entirely on visual identification made over a period of 20 minutes in good lighting conditions but without any other independent evidence. After the jury retired they returned and on request were allowed to see a 'mug' shot of the accused and permitted to have the page on which it appeared with 11 other photographs. These items had already been put in evidence by the Crown. The accused was convicted. On appeal the conviction was quashed and it was held that to put in photographs as part of the prosecution case was a serious irregularity which should not have occurred for it was the equivalent of telling the jury that the accused had a criminal record. In such a case the defence should be informed that photographs were used and it is then up to defence counsel to decide how to conduct his case and whether he wishes to bring out the matter.

None of this should be confused with the situation where police are trying to trace a *known* wanted person's whereabouts, e.g., by showing a photograph door-to-door or on television.

19.5.2 PHOTOFITS

As an alternative to the use of photographs, a method of attempting to obtain details of the appearance of a suspect, which when first introduced was expected to be more useful than it has proved, is so-called 'photofit' evidence. In this case a detailed description of the facial features of a criminal is obtained from close eye-witnesses. It was widely assumed that such photofit pictures were merely for incidental use in establishing a suspect who could then be put on an identification parade. A very strange result however occurred in the case of *R v Cook* [1987] QB 417.

In *Cook* the accused was convicted on the basis of a photofit prepared by the victim. After the photofit had been prepared the police arrested the suspect and put him in an identification parade. The victim identified him. In the course of the trial the photofit was put in evidence, the judge having ruled it admissible as 'part of the circumstances of the identification'. This was upheld on appeal. It was considered that neither the hearsay rule nor the rule against admission of a previous consistent statement applied to this situation because in preparing the photofit the officer was merely doing what a camera would have done. This result has been much criticised and it is suggested that it is wrong. A photofit is nothing like a camera because there is the interposition of human intelligence. It is suggested that a photofit is hearsay, just as a verbal description of the accused would have been and should have been ruled inadmissible. The decision however, has been upheld in another case, *R v Constantinou* (1989) 91 Cr App R 74, on somewhat similar facts.

19.5.3 IDENTIFICATION PARADES

Reference should be made to the full text of the Code of Practice (and see **4.6**) but we will summarise the most important points:

(a) A parade must contain at least eight persons similar in appearance to the suspect.

(b) The suspect may choose his own position in the line and change it after each witness has gone down the line.

(c) The suspect may have a solicitor or friend present.

(d) The parade must be organised by a uniformed officer of at least the rank of inspector who must not be involved in the case (so as to ensure his impartiality).

(e) The suspect must be given written information about his rights.

(f) A full record of everything that happens on the parade must be kept.

(g) Each witness who walks along the line must be warned that the person he saw may or may not be in the line (so that he should not feel obliged to identify somebody if in any doubt).

(h) Witnesses must be kept away from each other before and after the holding of the identification parade.

(i) An accused cannot be compelled to attend the parade. However, if he declines to attend, this fact may be given in evidence and the prosecution may make alternative arrangements which do not require the accused's consent and which are likely to be less favourable to him.

In addition:

(a) A parade *must* (usually) be held if the suspect asks for one.

(b) A group identification can be held if the suspect refuses to appear on a parade or fails to turn up to one or if it is impracticable to hold a parade.

(c) A confrontation which does not require the suspect's consent may take place only when neither a parade nor a group identification is practicable.

(d) Photographs or other pictorial aids such as photofits should not be shown to a witness where a suspect is already available to be paraded or to participate in a group identification.

It is a time-consuming business to organise a parade with persons sufficiently similar in appearance to the suspect, and all the more so if there are several suspects and witnesses. Procedure in organising parades varies greatly around the country. Some police forces appear unwilling to go to a great deal of trouble to organise the necessary number of relatively similar-looking suspects for parades; much depends on the number of suspects and the degree of difficulty which is anticipated. Increasingly, use is being made of informal methods of confrontation, e.g., street confrontations where the suspect is released into a crowd and invited to walk past the identifying witness.

Particular problems have been experienced in cases involving black suspects or, specifically, dreadlock-wearing suspects where the police have had difficulty in finding sufficient members of the public willing to stand on a parade. It is clearly established that the police must be amenable to reasonable requests, e.g., a request to delay the parade so that the suspect's solicitor can attempt to find members of the public willing to stand in the parade with him (*R v Britton and Richards* [1989] Crim LR 144). In general a suspect has a right to a parade if he wants one and reasonable efforts must be made therefore to set up a workable parade (*R v Gaynor* [1988] Crim LR 242). Even if the number of suspects make identification parades impossible, there should be group identifications rather than jumping straight to confrontation (*R v Ladlow and others* [1989] Crim LR 219, where there were 21 suspects involved).

The police must use some ingenuity in ensuring the parade is fair. Thus, for example, in *R v Gall* (1990) 90 Cr App R 64 the suspect had a large scar on his face. Other participants in the parade were made to wear sticking plaster in the position where the scar was. Clearly there will be cases where the police will find it impossible to arrange (e.g., where the suspect has a major deformity).

Before any of the procedures relating to identification parades apply, however, it must be clear that there is a 'disputed identification' issue. If there is no such issue, then a defence request for an identification parade need not be granted. For example, in *R v Montgomery* [1996] Crim LR 507 where the only eye-witness told the police that she would never be able to identify the person who had defrauded her. Accordingly when Montgomery was arrested the police did not put him on an identification parade and they proved their case by linking him to the crime by other evidence including fingerprint and handwriting evidence. The Court of Appeal dismissed his appeal against conviction which was brought on the basis that there should have been an identification parade because it was clear that as the victim had said she would never be able to identify the person concerned there was no 'disputed identification evidence'.

It has become apparent recently that the problems of identification have become almost as technical and fraught with appealable points as confession evidence. The possibilities for the police to get what seems a fairly simple procedure (but which is often not) wrong have been demonstrated to be endless on the facts of recent cases. In some of these, relatively minor technicalities have been considered to be sufficient to make the whole process unfair. In others, the police have been excused infringements and the identification procedure upheld. It is difficult to see a consistent policy emerging from the courts. So in the case of *R v Gall* mentioned above an investigating officer came into the parade having brought one of the witnesses to it. The witness then identified the accused. It was held that the judge should have excluded all the identification evidence because of the considerable suspicion that could be felt if the investigating officer came into the parade room and spoke to a witness. Similarly, in *R v Nagah* (1990) 92 Cr App R 344 where the police wrongly refused a suspect the right to a parade, and instead arranged an informal identification by the complainant sitting in a police car, the conviction was quashed. Likewise in *R v Finley* [1993] Crim LR 50 the suspect was a slim blonde skinhead and everyone else in the parade was larger and dark. The conviction was quashed for this and other irregularities. On the other hand, in *R v Ryan* [1992] Crim LR 187 a key witness was driven to the parade by one investigating officer. Although criticising the officer's conduct the Court of Appeal declined to quash the resulting conviction notwithstanding the substantial breach of the Code.

A situation sometimes encountered by the police and which causes difficulty is where there has been some incident, particularly a robbery or sexual attack, and they come to the scene quickly. If the victim is able to tour the area in a police car there is a chance of finding a suspect. If a suspect is then seen by the victim, is there any point in holding a subsequent parade since she will obviously clearly recognise the person she has just identified? The answer appears to be that a subsequent parade is otiose in those circumstances according to the authorities of *R v Brown* [1991] Crim LR 368 and *R v Oscar* [1991] Crim LR 778.

19.5.4 CHALLENGING IDENTIFICATION EVIDENCE

When identification evidence is challenged, a variety of possible situations which may occur. Instead of there being simple legal argument as to admissibility in the absence of the jury it may well be appropriate for the judge to receive factual evidence on how the identification was conducted and thus to himself perform a factfinding function. It has sometimes been urged by defence counsel that there should therefore be a *voir dire* in the absence of the jury along the lines of that pertaining to confessions. In two cases which tend to the same result, namely *R v Beveridge* (1987) 85 Cr App R 255 and *R v Flemming* (1987) 86 Cr App R 32, objection was taken to various aspects of the identification process. It seems that the judge was asked to hold a trial within a trial on the issue. In both cases on appeal it was held that whilst this was always an option open to a judge in an appropriate case, basically a judge was able to make up his own mind about the factual issues by reading the depositions and listening to submissions by counsel. It was not necessary in every case for him to go on to hear evidence about the identification even though he might be asked to apply s. 78 of the 1984 Act.

If the whole of the prosecution case depends on identification evidence however, and there are serious objections to the procedures adopted in respect of which the court will need to undertake some factfinding exercise (e.g., as to what really happened during the identification parade) then one should not hesitate to ask for a trial within a trial on that specific point. If one succeeds in establishing one's objections, the court is likely to exclude all the identification evidence because non-compliance with identification procedures means that the accused loses a crucial protection since the prosecution are left with the straight 'jump' from identification at the scene to identification in the dock which, for the reasons previously discussed, is frowned upon.

19.5.5 VIDEOS

An interesting development in recent times concerns the showing in court of video films. This has been held possible at least since *Kajala* v *Noble* (1982) 75 Cr App R 149 where a BBC news video was shown in court to allow a witness to identify an accused at a public disturbance. In the United States, filmed reconstructions of torts and crimes are often shown to assist the court in visualising how things have occurred.

This will not be permitted in the United Kingdom according to *R* v *Quinn and Bloom* [1962] 2 QB 245. The accused were charged with keeping a disorderly house by permitting indecent striptease acts to perform there. The defence had prepared a film depicting the acts as a deliberate reconstruction of what had happened on the premises. The evidence was excluded as not being the 'best evidence' in that it would be impossible to recreate accurately every movement of the original striptease in the court, especially as a snake was used.

Quite a different situation would be the showing of a film depicting something directly relevant to the issue, e.g., in a personal injuries action where the plaintiff is alleged to be totally disabled but is suspected of malingering, a film taken by private detectives showing him jogging. These are quite routinely admitted in evidence. Or as in cases where the actual commission of crimes has been filmed, such as drug dealing.

Videos which show actual crimes (whether or not supplemented by identifying witnesses) have been admitted in many cases. In such cases the jury are in effect turned into the identification witnesses themselves. Sometimes this has to do with recognising whether the people on the security video are the accused; it may even extend to the jury having to decide whether any offence occurred at all (as where security cameras in a department store appear to show shoplifting but are unclear). So in the early case of *R* v *Dodson and Williams* (1984) 79 Cr App R 220 the jury were invited to say whether the suspects were the men shown on a security camera which filmed a building society robbery; in *R* v *Fowden and White* [1982] Crim LR 588 the suspects were traced having been filmed on a security camera by a store detective who knew the two accused personally. In this case it was also left to the jury to say whether on the film the accused were committing theft at all.

19.6 Attacking Identification Evidence

One should always be aware as a defence advocate of the provisions of the Codes and carefully examine the factual situations surrounding any identification evidence. The fallibility of the police in numerous cases in organising parades has already been mentioned. If it is possible to get crucial identification evidence excluded because of breach of the relevant Code of Practice, it may well be that the whole prosecution case collapses. Accordingly, if one has succeeded in having identification evidence excluded, a submission of no case to answer may often be appropriate in such instances.

TWENTY

THE LAW OF EVIDENCE (7):
EVIDENCE OF DISPOSITION
AND CHARACTER

20.1 Introduction

The word 'disposition' is used to denote a tendency to act think or feel in a particular way. The word 'character' may include disposition, or sometimes mean 'general reputation' or merely the question of whether or not the accused has a criminal record.

20.2 Evidence of Disposition

Evidence of disposition is in general inadmissible for the prosecution both because it is not necessarily logically relevant to the issue of the accused's guilt of the offence with which he is now charged and also because it is clearly highly prejudicial to the accused for the jury to be told of his previous disposition. The risk is that the average jury will lose sight of everything else in the case apart from the striking revelation of the accused's bad character. This is exacerbated in the case of an accused who has convictions for crimes in the past which are notoriously unpopular with the public, such as rape, child abuse, or even house burglary. There is thought to be a tendency in laypersons to wish to punish the accused again for his former crimes whatever his guilt of the present offence.

20.2.1 THE GENERAL RULE

The general rule therefore is that evidence of the misconduct of the accused on another occasion *may not be given if its only relevance* is to show a general disposition towards wrongdoing or even a general disposition to commit the type of crime of which he is now accused. Usually in this context 'disposition' will mean the commission of crimes in the past but this need not be so. For example, evidence of regular drinking or a quarrelsome nature might appear to be relevant to some issue. It would be inadmissible under the rule notwithstanding that drinking and quarrelling are not *per se* crimes.

20.2.2 SIMILAR FACT EVIDENCE

The exception to the general rule is the case of so-called 'similar fact' evidence. In this case the law will permit the prosecution to adduce evidence of previous conduct where its nature, *modus operandi* or some other circumstance, shows an unmistakable similarity to the offence charged. This must be strong enough to go beyond any question of coincidence so as to lead the jury to conclude 'this is the work of the same man'.

It should be noted that many cases turn not only on whether evidence of past crime A is relevant at the trial for crime B but on whether the accused who is now charged with two or more offences has the right to have each tried separately before a different jury, so that the jury trying crime A do not hear of crime B and vice versa. Clearly this application to try each charge separately (or 'sever the indictment') may be crucial — a jury trying a man accused of ten different cases of a fairly distinctive type of crime are much less likely to accept that the police have been mistaken ten times. If the accused succeeded in his application to have ten separate trials with each jury kept in ignorance of the other nine cases, he would obviously stand a better chance in each of the ten trials. Even if the accused is tried on all ten charges together because the judge thinks at the outset that the 'similar fact' principle might apply, when the evidence comes out during the trial it is possible for the judge to change his mind. At that stage a very clear direction to the jury must be given that they must approach each crime entirely separately and not treat the fact that the accused is charged with crime A as any evidence relevant to crime B, C, etc. For the exact procedure see *R v Scarrott* (**20.2.3**).

It must be remembered that, under the indictment rules and the authorities stemming from them, there are complex rules about which charges may be tried with which other charges and in respect of which offenders (see **9.3.2**). It is *not* only when the similar fact principle applies that two charges can be heard by the same jury. Examples of the difficulty are cases such as *R v Dixon* (1991) 92 Cr App R 43 where the accused was charged together with four offences of rape, six of robbery and one of indecent assault. Some of the offences of robbery and the sexual offences concerned the same victim. Issues arose as to the propriety of trying these various charges together in respect of some of which the 'similar fact' principle could be said to apply. The case unfortunately is vague as an authority, the court concluding that most of the charges were correctly tried together whilst quashing some convictions.

A more dramatic case is *R v Cannan* (1991) 92 Cr App R 16 where the accused was charged with abduction and sexual offences in respect of victim 1; attempted abduction of victim 2; and abduction and murder of victim 3. The incidents were given wide publicity and the circumstances of the last incident where the victim had been kidnapped and later found murdered were regarded as particularly horrifying. None of the incidents properly fell within the similar fact principle and the accused contended that in the absence of that principle he should have been entitled to separate trials in respect of each victim. The court reviewed the question of whether, in the absence of the similar fact principle, it was right in every case to order severance of the indictment. It was argued strongly on behalf of the defendant that because of the appalling nature of the crimes alleged, the jury would inevitably be prejudiced against him. The Court of Appeal concluded, having reviewed some of the similar fact principles and other cases involving severance and in particular the earlier case of *Dixon*, that it was legitimate for a series of offences to be joined notwithstanding that the similar fact rule did not apply. The judge had given a careful, full and clear warning to the jury to consider each matter separately and the appeal should be dismissed.

20.2.3 ILLUSTRATIONS OF THE RULE

The leading case is *Makin v Attorney-General for New South Wales* [1894] AC 57. The accused were charged with murdering two children whose bodies were found buried under their backyard. Both babies had been received from their mothers by the accused together with a small amount of money for their maintenance on the accused having indicated to the mothers that they wished to adopt the children. There was evidence that several other children, all of whom were found buried in the gardens of houses occupied by the accused, had been 'adopted' in similar circumstances. It was held that this evidence was admissible and relevant as tending to negative any possible defence of death from natural causes or accident. Lord Herschell stated:

It is undoubtedly not competent for the prosecution to adduce evidence tending to show that the accused has been guilty of criminal acts other than those covered by the indictment for the purpose of leading to the conclusion that the accused is a person likely from his criminal conduct or character to have committed the offence for which he is being tried. On the other hand the mere fact that the evidence adduced tends to show the commission of other crimes does not render it inadmissible if it be relevant to an issue before the jury, and it may be so relevant if it bears upon the question whether the acts alleged to constitute the crime charged in the indictment were designed or accidental, or to rebut a defence which would otherwise be open to the accused.

In *R v Straffen* [1952] 2 QB 911, the accused was charged with the murder by strangling of two little girls in 1951. He was found unfit to plead and committed to Broadmoor. He escaped from Broadmoor in 1952 and was at large for 48 hours. In that time another little girl went missing and was later found strangled. There were said to be the following similarities between the first two murders and this third murder, namely:

(a) each victim was a young girl;

(b) each was strangled;

(c) there was no sexual or other apparent motive;

(d) that there was no evidence of a struggle;

(e) there was no attempt to conceal the body.

It was held that the evidence of his having committed the earlier two murders was admissible at his trial for the third murder. This case is also an illustration of the fact that the previous conduct proved under the rule need not have led to a conviction as such. It also usefully underlines the point, discussed fully in much more recent cases, that the establishing of primary admissibility of the similar fact evidence is only the first step. The judge must then go on to consider whether the *prejudicial nature* of the evidence *outweighs its probative value* before letting the jury hear it.

One of the most important uses of the similar fact principle was in the case of crimes involving homosexuality. Between the early years of the century and the mid-1970s the principle appeared to be that because homosexuality is so unusual it is admissible at the trial of a person for an offence involving homosexuality to put to him that he has a disposition to homosexual behaviour from other incidents or past convictions. The idea that homosexual offences were in a special category was laid authoritatively to rest in *DPP v Boardman* [1975] AC 421. The accused was a headmaster of a boarding school for boys. He was charged with homosexual offences in relation to S and H. At the trial the judge ruled that the evidence of S on the count concerning him was admissible as corroborative evidence in relation to the count concerning H and vice versa. The similar fact principle applied in that the accused's method of approaching each boy was similar and the manner in which he wished to perform the homosexual conduct was likewise similar and allegedly very unusual.

The Law Lords made it clear that homosexuality was not so unusual as to require such offences to be in a special category and that it was important for judges to keep abreast of current standards of sexual behaviour. Earlier cases which had given special attention to homosexual conduct were described as 'like a voice from another world'.

The test was therefore twofold:

(a) does the conduct on another occasion have 'striking similarity' to the crime presently charged and, if so,

(b) is the inevitable prejudice to the accused outweighed by the probative force of the evidence. Lord Wilberforce (p. 445) found the case of *Boardman* 'right on the borderline' so far as the 'striking similarity' was concerned, and the actual result in Boardman has been criticised as setting the standard of 'striking similarity' too low.

The great majority of the case law after *Boardman* is concerned with sexual offences. Because of the requirement for 'striking similarity' more mundane offences such as theft, burglary and the like can only rarely be brought properly within the principle. Occasionally there have been such cases, e.g., *R* v *Rance and Herron* (1975) 62 Cr App R 118 where, on charges of corruption concerning payments made by builders to local councillors, proof that the accused had on previous occasions bribed another councillor by the same method and had similarly sought to conceal the corrupt payment by a false entry in their own company's books was held properly admitted at trial as the evidence was highly probative. On the rare occasions however where the similar fact principle was applied to more run-of-the-mill crimes, e.g., shoplifting as in *R* v *Mustapha* (1976) 65 Cr App R 26 and *R* v *Seaman* (1978) 67 Cr App R 234, it is usually considered that the cases were wrongly decided and the principle misapplied becuse of the quite mundane circumstances of the incidents in each case.

An important case which demonstrates the correct procedure to be followed where the prosecution intend that the similar fact principle applies is *R* v *Scarrott* [1978] QB 1016, in which the accused was charged with 13 counts of homosexual assault in relation to eight boys over a period of four and a half years. His counsel applied to sever the indictment and have separate trials in respect of each boy. The judge ruled that the similar fact principle applied and that the evidence of each boy was admissible in relation to the charges in relation to each other boy. This view was upheld on appeal. There was sufficient similarity in method of approach and method of indecency to each of the boys to come within the similar fact principle. Scarman LJ further held:

(a) That when an application to sever an indictment is made the judge should have regard to his discretion under the Indictment Rules 1971. He should read the depositions and see whether in his view the offences appear to be of a similar character and form a series. He must ask himself whether in his judgment at that stage it would be open to a jury properly directed to treat the evidence on each count as mutually admissible in view of the striking similarity.

(b) This is not a final decision as to the admissibility of the evidence. If he allows the multi-count indictment to proceed he may still have to rule later that the similar fact principle does not apply once he has heard the evidence. At that stage, if, e.g., he is impressed with the possibility that the evidence is tainted by conspiracy he may decide that the evidence though strikingly similar is so prejudicial that its prejudicial effect outweighs its probative value. He will then have to make it very clear to the jury as to whether they may or may not treat the evidence of any given complainant as corroboration or mutually admissible in relation to the evidence of any other complainant.

(c) If he continues to hold that the similar fact principle applies he may direct the jury appropriately that each complainant's evidence is admissible in connection with, and corroborative of, the evidence of the other complainants.

20.2.4 DEVELOPMENTS AND APPLICATIONS OF THE SIMILAR FACT PRINCIPLE

The case law up to 1991 established the following basic principles:

(a) Evidence of previous criminal conduct, whether leading to conviction or not, is not admissible to show a general propensity towards crime or even towards the particular type of crime charged.

(b) Exceptionally it may be admissible if:

(i) It has some feature which so takes it out of the everyday type of crime as to be 'striking', i.e. sufficiently unusual to have a positive probative value in relation to its similarity with the crime charged.

(ii) Its positive probative value outweighs the inevitable prejudice to the accused which will ensue from the jury coming to hear of the accused's previous conduct.

(c) It is a matter of degree as to whether there is sufficient nexus between the present offence and past conduct.

(d) The nature of the defence is not in itself relevant to the preliminary decision on 'striking similarity' but it is a factor which may influence the judge when deciding in any case where the probative value is less than extremely cogent. There is obviously a great risk of prejudice in the case of an outright denial of involvement.

(e) Homosexual offences are not in a special category. The prosecution should not be allowed to ask the accused whether he is a homosexual nor it is submitted to achieve the same effect by proof of finding articles commonly used by homosexuals at his residence.

(f) The issue may arise either at the stage of an application to sever the indictment or in the trial proper.

20.2.5   RESTATEMENT OF PRINCIPLES

In 1991 there were two cases in quick succession which led to a restatement of the similar fact principle by the House of Lords. The first of these cases was very similar to several older cases and at the time appeared to be an orthodox statement of the law. The first case is *R v Brooks* (1990) 92 Cr App R 36 which was shortly after held to have been wrongly decided in the new leading case of *DPP v P* [1991] 2 AC 447.

In *R v Brooks* the accused was charged with numerous counts of incest and indecency relating to his three daughters. It was alleged that from an early age he had forced each daughter in turn to engage in sexual intercourse and other sexual acts with him and that as each daughter grew to a certain age she replaced her predecessor. The youngest of the daughters refused to give evidence against her father and a formal verdict of not guilty was entered on the charge relating to her. The accused's defence was that the allegations were entirely false and concocted, being actuated by jealousy and spite. It was argued that as an element of collusion might have been present, the trial judge should have ordered separate trials of the charges in respect of each of the daughters. The judge refused to sever the indictment on the grounds that justice required the jury to hear the whole of the case. The jury convicted the accused unanimously on all the remaining counts.

The accused appealed on the basis that, although the allegations were sufficiently similar in themselves to be within the similar fact rule, the judge should have used his discretion to order separate trials because of the inevitable prejudice to the accused. The convictions were quashed. It was not enough for facts to be similar; they must tell the court something useful. The court must enquire what the evidence set out to prove and whether there were any features of the evidence which made it probative of the facts in a permissible way. In the present case the similarity alleged was the 'stock-in-trade' in the case of father-daughter incest and there was a very real risk here that the two girls had colluded so that particular caution was required. The proper course would have been to treat the evidence of each daughter as inadmissible in the case of the other and to have tried the charges separately.

This case demonstrates the vital importance of the similar fact principle in cases of child abuse. There is of course the risk of collusion between different children, especially if there are matrimonial difficulties between the spouses where the children may take sides and in some cases regrettably be coached by their mother to invent false accusations. Corroboration is required in such cases so that, if the prosecution do not succeed in satisfying the court that the similar fact principle applies and that all charges should be heard by the same jury, there is a strong likelihood of the accused being acquitted by the separate juries who hear each charge or group of charges becuse of the lack of corroboration.

Shortly after the case of *Brooks*, the similar fact principle reached the House of Lords for the first time since *Boardman* in 1975. The case is *DPP* v *P* [1991] 2 AC 447.

The accused was charged with the rape of and incest with his two daughters over a long period. It was suggested that he had used force and threatened both girls and that he had paid for abortions for both of them. He applied for the counts relating to each daughter to be tried separately; the trial judge refused and he was convicted of all charges. He appealed to the Court of Appeal which allowed his appeal on the ground that there were no such striking similarities between the girls' accounts of their father's behaviour to permit the evidence of one girl properly to be admitted on the trial of the counts relating to the other; the Crown appealed to the House of Lords. It was held that evidence of an offence against one victim could be admitted at the trial of an allegation in relation to another victim if the essential feature of the evidence was that its probative force in support of the allegations was sufficiently great to make it just to admit the evidence, notwithstanding that it was prejudicial to the accused as tending to show that he was guilty of another crime.

Such probative force could be derived from striking similarities in the evidence about the manner in which the crime had been committed but there was no justification in restricting the circumstances in which similar fact evidence could be admitted to cases where there was 'striking similarity' since what had to be assessed was the probative force of the evidence. In the present case no injustice had been shown to the accused and the conviction should be restored. Cases like *R* v *Brooks* should be overruled.

This then is a quite remarkable case which appears to extend the circumstances in which evidence of conduct on other occasions can be advanced and replaces the former test of 'striking similarity' with the vaguer test of 'real probative value'. Unlike the former leading case, *DPP* v *Boardman*, where there were five speeches, there was only one in the present case by Lord Mackay and it is a very brief one indeed to effect, if it does, a change in the similar fact principle. It must be remembered however that the question certified for the House of Lords was restricted to cases involving sexual offences against children or young persons. To that extent the observations in the case could be restricted to those offences although clearly they would have powerful persuasive force in respect of other kinds of crimes.

20.2.6 ADVOCACY AND TACTICS IN SIMILAR FACT CASES

A defence lawyer will not commonly be presented with a case involving similar fact evidence in the magistrates' court, despite the arguable weakening of the requirements by the case of *DPP* v *P* [1991] 2 AC 447. In magistrates' courts the use of previous character tends to be restricted to where it arises under the Criminal Evidence Act 1898 which we will discuss below. In the Crown Court one's first attack on the prosecution case will inevitably be by way of an application to sever the indictment, that is to have each charge, or each group of charges, or the charges relating to each separate victim, tried separately. Because of the weakening of the similar fact principle in *DPP* v *P* and because of the inevitable consequences in terms of court time and costs, which are to be taken into account in deciding on 'the interests of justice', it may increasingly be the case that applications to sever the indictment are refused where the prosecution depositions show some prima facie case that the similar fact principle applies. Where one is hoping to sever the indictment one must closely analyse each of the factual elements of the *modus operandi* to see whether it can properly be argued that the kind of offence, incident or method used is too mundane to be within the principle so that the prejudicial effect of the evidence outweighs its probative value. It is a useful exercise to attempt to list every element of the *modus operandi* and then to discuss with the prosecution, or to have counsel approach prosecuting counsel, to see whether the principles said to bring the case within the similar fact rule can be isolated, and any key differences identified for an effective submission. Whilst the use of previous authorities, now more than ever, will be of limited value because of the vast range of factual possibilities, it may sometimes be possible to bring the case within the scope of past decided cases.

20.3 Evidence of Character

The general rule was that the character of any party in a civil case, or any witness in any case, is open to attack. The purpose of such attack is of course to show that the party or witness should not be believed. Answers as to credit in cross-examination are final, as has been indicated earlier, to avoid a multiplicity of side issues. Exceptionally, by s. 6 of the Criminal Procedure Act 1865, where the form of the attack on a witness's character is to allege previous convictions, they may be proved if not admitted.

The fundamental rule, as we have seen earlier, is that the prosecution may not for the purpose of proving an accused's guilt adduce evidence of the character of the defendant whether of previous behaviour, previous convictions, or general reputation. The reason is obviously the extreme prejudice to the accused in the eyes of the jury. The main exception to this is the use of the 'similar fact' principle.

The issues to discuss are:

(a) The good character of the accused and the evidential value of this.

(b) The bad character of the accused and the exceptional circumstances where this may be proved.

20.3.1 THE GOOD CHARACTER OF THE ACCUSED

It has been recognised from the 18th century that an accused could call witnesses to speak to his good character, or cross-examine prosecution witnesses in an attempt to get them to do so. This was exceptional and was intended as an additional protection for an accused, who could not testify before 1898.

The important point to note however is that *character is indivisible*. One cannot assert a good character for one type of behaviour without the prosecution having the right to cross-examine or call evidence about other aspects of one's character. See, e.g., *R v Winfield* [1939] 4 All ER 164 where the accused was charged with indecent assault upon a woman and called evidence as to his previous good behaviour in relation to women. It was held that in the circumstances the prosecution were entitled to prove the accused's convictions for offences of dishonesty. It was not open to an accused to put only half of his character in issue.

The common law rule is therefore that where an accused calls witnesses or testifies himself as to his good character, the prosecution may cross-examine the witnesses or the accused about their own credibility, the accused's character, and their knowledge of it. They may, moreover, call evidence in rebuttal of the defence evidence. This common law right to rebut an assertion of good character has survived the Criminal Evidence Act 1898 and now overlaps with it.

20.3.2   THE EVIDENTIAL VALUE OF GOOD CHARACTER

There were two possible views:

(a) that a previous good character makes it less likely that the accused committed the offence;

(b) that previous good character is only relevant to the accused's credibility as a witness.

The issue arises in a clear form where the accused elects not to testify, because then if his character were only relevant to his credit it would be of no relevance and the jury should be directed to ignore it. A case which settles the issue in favour of the wider view is *R v Bryant and Oxley* [1979] QB 108. The accused were charged with robbery and decided not to testify. One of the accused had good character and the judge directed the jury to the effect that the evidence of his good character went only to his credibility and hence where he had not testified was of no use. On appeal it was held that although evidence of good character did go primarily to the issue of credibility it was also capable of being evidence relevant to innocence.

There were numerous cases in the period 1990–93 which left unclear what direction the judge should give in respect of a defendant with good character who chooses not to testify. The Court of Appeal has now given comprehensive guidelines in the case of *R v Vye* [1993] 1 WLR 471. In this case the Court of Appeal held:

(a) Where a defendant had not given evidence at trial but relied on exculpatory statements made to the police or others the judge should direct the jury to have regard to the defendant's good character when considering the credibility of those statements though he might draw to their attention that none of them were made on oath. Clearly if a defendant of good character did not give evidence and had made no statements before trial, no issue as to his credibility arose.

(b) With regard to the 'second limb' direction as to good character making it less likely that the accused committed the crime, there was no distinction between cases where the defendant had testified and cases where he had not. A direction as to the relevance of good character should be given in all such cases although how the judge tailors the direction to the particular circumstances might vary.

(c) Where defendant A had a good character he was entitled to have the judge direct the jury as to its relevance in his case even if he was jointly tried with defendant B of bad character. That left the question what, if anything, the judge should say about defendant B. In some cases the judge might think it best to grasp the nettle in his summing up and tell the jury that they had heard no evidence about B's character and should not speculate. In other cases the judge might think it best to say nothing about the absence of evidence or comment on B's character. Nothing in this principle affected the question of the possibility of separate trials and there was certainly no rule in favour of separate trials for defendants of good and bad character.

This last point clarifies a difficult issue which has recently been before the Court of Appeal in *R v Gibson* (1991) 93 Cr App R 9 where one accused had a good character and the other had not. Because of his fear of overstressing the good character of one, the judge simply said 'G is a musician who has not been in trouble before'. On appeal the court quashed the conviction holding that this was inadequate because G's own counsel had dealt with character very briefly expecting the judge to deal with it fully.

The correctness of the case of *Vye* has now been confirmed by the House of Lords in *R v Aziz* [1995] 3 WLR 53 where the House said that as the defence case must be put before the jury in a fair and balanced way, and as evidence of good character is evidence of probative significance, the judge must always direct upon it whether the defendant testifies or not. Moreover, it is suggested that if there is some difficulty as to whether or not the judge should give a direction in relation to good character the matter must be canvassed with counsel who should be invited to make appropriate submissions in the absence of the jury. The House of Lords went on to consider other exceptional situations including that where the defendant's claim to a good character was 'spurious' in the sense that although there may not have been a criminal record, there was other clear evidence of criminal behaviour.

20.3.3 THE BAD CHARACTER OF THE ACCUSED

Apart from the general rule mentioned above as to rebuttal of evidence of good character at common law, the law on character is now contained in the Criminal Evidence Act 1898, s. 1(e) and (f):

> (e) *A person charged and being a witness in pursuance of this Act may be asked any question in cross-examination notwithstanding that it would tend to criminate him as to the offence charged:*
>
> (f) *A person charged and called as a witness in pursuance of this Act shall not be asked, and if asked shall not be required to answer, any question tending to show that he has committed or been convicted of or been charged with any offence other than that wherewith he is then charged, or is of bad character, unless—*
>> (i) *the proof that he has committed or been convicted of such other offence is admissible evidence to show that he is guilty of the offence wherewith he is then charged; or*
>> (ii) *he has personally or by his advocate asked questions of the witness for the prosecution with a view to establish his own good character, or has given evidence of his good character, or the nature or conduct of the defence is such as to involve imputations on the character of the prosecutor or the witnesses for the prosecution or the deceased victim of the alleged crime; or*
>> (iii) *he has given evidence against any other person charged in the same proceedings.*

The statute was enacted to make special provision for the accused when he became a competent witness. Parliament had to decide how far he could be cross-examined as to his character and there were two distinct possibilities:

(a) The accused could have been given *complete immunity*, which would have meant that he was in a better position than other witnesses as he would have been able to attack the character of all prosecution witnesses without fear of repercussions.

(b) He could have been treated as an *ordinary witness* so that he would have been liable to cross-examination as to his previous convictions to show lack of credibility. The obvious risk of this is that the jury will make what has been called the 'forbidden connection' and use their knowledge of his bad character as a matter *not relevant* to *credibility* but to *guilt*.

In fact the 1898 Act adopts a compromise of those two possibilities. The accused is provided with a shield from the disclosure of his record until he acts in such a way as to 'throw away his shield'. This can be done in one of three ways:

(a) By raising his own good character.

(b) By casting imputations on the character of the prosecution or its witnesses.

(c) By giving evidence against a co-accused.

Proviso (f) in general prohibits four types of questions:

(a) Those tending to show that an accused has been charged with other offences.

(b) Those tending to show that an accused has committed other offences.

(c) Those tending to show that an accused is of bad character.

(d) Those tending to show that an accused has previous convictions.

Under s. 1(f)(ii) and (iii) some action by the accused is necessary before the exceptions are brought into play but the operation of s. 1(f)(i) is not (unlike (ii) and (iii)) dependent on the way in which the accused conducts his defence.

We shall now consider the three exceptions to proviso (f) in turn.

20.3.3.1   Section 1(f)(i)

This subsection covers cases where evidence of previous character would anyway be admissible in itself. It must be remembered that the whole text of s. 1(f) deals only with cross-examination of an accused by prosecuting counsel or counsel for co-defendants. The situation envisaged in s. 1(f)(i) is the exceptions case where the prosecution will already have had the right to adduce evidence of other offences as part of their own case; in such cases where the accused gives evidence he may then be cross-examined about the previous offences if necessary. The use of this subsection does not depend upon the way in which the accused conducts his case. It follows on from whatever rights the prosecution may have had to adduce evidence of his previous character in evidence-in-chief. The subsection applies in two instances:

(a) Where the prosecution are entitled to prove other offences under the similar fact principle discussed earlier.

(b) Where evidence of previous crimes is specifically admissible under a particular statute. There are numerous such statutes and they are basically of two kinds:

(i) Where the *definition of the offence* is such that it can *only be committed by a previously convicted person*, e.g., s. 21 of the Firearms Act 1968, which makes it an offence for certain convicted persons to possess firearms, or the offence of driving while disqualified where the prosecution must prove the previous disqualification. In these instances, proof of the previous conviction is essential to the offence.

(ii) The second class of statute is where a previous conviction can be used to show *some mental element* in the crime, e.g., s. 27(3) of the Theft Act 1968, which may be summarised as providing that on a charge of handling stolen goods evidence of a conviction for theft or handling within the last five years is admissible to prove that the accused knew or believed that the goods were stolen.

20.3.3.2   Section 1(f)(ii)

This subsection can be conveniently divided into two parts:

(a) Where the accused puts his character in issue.

(b) Where the nature or conduct of the defence is such as to involve imputations on the character of the prosecution or a prosecution witness.

Where the accused puts his character in issue

Generally, the accused's own evidence of his character will take the form of some allusion to his innocent or praiseworthy past. Decided cases show that the courts are certainly not reluctant to hold that he has put his character in issue on what might seem relatively innocuous assertions falling far short of a claim to absence of a criminal record. It seems that asserting any fact not directly relevant to guilt whose purpose may lead the jury to infer that one is not the sort of person likely to commit a crime is sufficient to put character in issue, e.g., in *R v Ferguson* (1909) 2 Cr App R 250 where the accused claimed to be 'a regular attender at Mass' it was held that he had put character in issue. The result was the same in *R v Coulman* (1927) 20 Cr App R 106 where the accused claimed to be 'a family man in regular work'. In each case the accused, whilst no doubt having the good qualities referred to in his claim, had several convictions for dishonesty and thus it was appropriate for the prosecution to cross-examine on the whole character.

It will be remembered that the Rehabilitation of Offenders Act 1974, which forbids mention of 'spent' convictions, has no relevance in criminal cases, but *Practice Direction (Crime: Spent Convictions)* [1975] 1 WLR 1065 requires that the leave of the judge should be obtained before using such convictions so that the spirit of the 1974 Act should be honoured.

In all of these cases the effect of s. 1(f)(ii) is to permit the prosecution to cross-examine the accused if he gives evidence. They also have the right at *common law* to *call witnesses* of their own *in rebuttal* of the assertion of good character, and these witnesses may of course give evidence of previous convictions of the accused. One should not lose sight of the fact that s. 1(f)(ii) therefore deals with *cross-examination* of the accused; it has no relevance if the accused declines to testify, though the common law rule would still allow the prosecution to call evidence in rebuttal.

A case which demonstrates two important aspects of s. 1(f)(ii) and in which there was considerable confusion in the judge's mind is *R v Butterwasser* [1948] KB 4. The accused was charged with wounding and his evidence was that the alleged victim had been the aggressor. The accused did not give evidence. The trial judge held that by virtue of s. 1(f)(ii) of the 1898 Act the police were entitled to read out a record of the accused's previous convictions. The appeal was allowed. The 1898 Act referred only to cross-examination. An accused did not put his own character in issue by attacking the character of the prosecution witnesses through his counsel in cross-examination, nor does the Act have any application unless the accused testifies.

Asserting *good character* does not mean only lack of previous convictions. Clearly it would be foolish for an accused who has previous convictions to do that. It covers reputation and disposition even down to the marginal matters referred to in *R v Ferguson* and *R v Coulman* above. (Conversely cross-examination as to, or evidence of, *bad character* in a criminal trial is almost entirely limited to previous convictions.)

Imputations on the character of the prosecutor or his witnesses or on the deceased victim of the alleged crime

The leading case on this part of s. 1(f)(ii) is now *Selvey v DPP* [1970] AC 304. Before this case there was a problem as to whether the accused lost his shield by making imputations on prosecution witnesses which were necessary to *develop his defence*, or whether he only lost it if the imputations were *merely to attack* their credibility. Clearly in some cases the whole defence will hinge upon attacking the character of prosecution witnesses, e.g., any defence of self-defence; or that it was a prosecution witness who actually committed the offence; or that the complainant consented in a rape case; or simply that a prosecution witness is lying on oath. The problem is answered by *Selvey v DPP*.

The accused had convictions for homosexual and dishonesty offences. He was charged with buggery. He denied the charge and when testifying alleged, in effect, that the complainant was a male prostitute who had fabricated the complaint. The trial judge then permitted the prosecution to cross-examine the accused concerning his homosexual convictions. In explaining the meaning of s. 1(f)(ii), the House of Lords held:

(a) The words of the statute must be given their ordinary and natural meaning.

(b) Subsection (ii) permits cross-examination of the accused as to character where he casts imputations on prosecution witnesses either in order to show their unreliablity or where he does so in order to establish his defence.

(c) In a rape case the accused can allege consent without losing his shield.

(d) If what is said amounts in reality to no more than a denial of the charge then an accused does not lose his shield.

(e) There is an unfettered judicial discretion to exclude cross-examination as to character even if strictly permissible but there is no general rule that this discretion should be exercised in favour of the accused even where the nature of his defence necessarily involves his attacking prosecution witnesses.

What is an imputation?

The difficult question which is for the judge to decide is: 'What is an imputation?' The courts have tried, not always with great success, to draw a distinction between what is merely a *denial* of the charge by the accused in forceful language and what amounts to an imputation. This has led to some illogical consequences. It has for example been held that where the accused describes a prosecution witness as 'a liar', that even though this may in effect be an allegation of perjury it should be treated as just a denial of the charge in forceful language.

Imputations and the police

In the 1970s a practice arose of cross-examining police witnesses, carefully alleging that their version of events was 'wrong' or 'mistaken' rather than fabricated and at that time putting an allegation in that way did not generally involve losing the shield. This practice was brought to an abrupt halt by the case of *R v Tanner* (1978) 66 Cr App R 56 where the judge asked the accused to say positively whether he was accusing a policeman of complete invention. When the accused agreed that that was the position the trial judge then allowed cross-examination of the accused on his record under s. 1(f)(ii). The case of *Tanner* was approved in the leading case *R v Britzman and Hall* [1983] 1 All ER 369 where the Court of Appeal laid down guidelines for consideration of the discretion under s. 1(f)(ii):

(a) Where there is merely a denial, however emphatic or offensively made, of an act or even a short series of acts amounting to one incident or one interview, the judge's discretion should be used in favour of the defendant. The position would be different however if there was a denial of evidence of a long period of detailed observation or of long conversations.

(b) Cross-examination should only be allowed if the judge is sure there is no possibility of mistake, misunderstanding or confusion and the jury will inevitably have to decide whether prosecution witnesses have fabricated evidence. Defendants sometimes make wild allegations when giving evidence and allowance should be made for the strain of being in the witness box and the exaggerated use of language which sometimes results from strain or lack of education or mental instability. Particular care should be taken when a defendant is led into making allegations during cross-examination. A defendant who is driven to explaining away the evidence by saying it was made up or planted on him usually convicts himself without having his previous convictions brought out.

(c)   There is no need for the prosecution to rely on s. 1(f)(ii) if the evidence against the defendant is already overwhelming.

20.3.3.3   The purpose of the cross-examination under s. 1(f)(ii)

The purpose is to undermine the accused's *credit as a witness* and *not* to show that he committed the crime charged. The judge must direct the jury carefully on this. The difference is of course fairly elusive to most juries. His record is relevant as to whether his imputation is believable and thereafter as to his credibility generally. No specific way of putting matters to the jury so that they will clearly grasp this seems to have been found. Whatever the rationale is supposed to be, it is really a case of 'tit for tat'. Even if the imputation is incontrovertibly true (e.g., that a prosecution witness has, in fact, a conviction for perjury) the shield is lost.

A case which clearly illustrates the correct direction is *R* v *Prince* [1990] Crim LR 49. P was tried for robbery. His counsel led evidence that he had previous convictions for numerous other offences but that in this instance his defence was a complete denial. In summing up, the trial judge directed the jury that a previous conviction even for other offences of robbery did not signify guilt as such but that the jury should put that in the balance and give whatever weight it thought to those convictions. Defence counsel asked the judge to reconsider this direction but he refused. The accused was convicted but his appeal was allowed. The omission of the crucial matter of a direction as to the criminal record affecting only P's credibility as a witness was a misdirection. The judge should always direct the jury that offences of previous convictions for dishonesty or other offences are relevant only to credit and not to guilt.

20.3.3.4   Miscellaneous matters

Before leaving s. 1(f)(ii) it is appropriate to consider three miscellaneous matters namely:

(a)   Against whom must the imputation be made to bring in s. 1(f)(ii)?

(b)   May anything about early offences other than the fact of conviction be proved?

(c)   Judicial discretion.

Against whom must the imputation be made to bring in s. 1(f)(ii)?

According to the section, the imputation must be made on the character of the 'prosecutor or the witnesses for the prosecution or the deceased victim of the alleged crime'. It is not entirely clear at present who the 'prosecutor' is. At the time of the 1898 Act the prosecutor was the victim and the section would probably now be interpreted so that a gratuitous attack on a victim who was not called as a witness would bring the accused within the section.

The words 'or the deceased victim of the alleged crime' were added by s. 31 of the Criminal Justice and Public Order Act 1994.

In an old case, *R* v *Biggin* [1920] 1 KB 213, the accused alleged that the murder victim provoked him by making improper advances and it was held at the time that this did not invoke s. 1(f)(ii). This was because the deceased was not the 'prosecutor' nor a witness.

The 1994 Act remedied this situation so that if an accused makes what amounts to imputations against the deceased victim of the alleged crime, who obviously is not there to give evidence himself or to have his own credibility judged by the jury, it will allow the prosecution on the 'tit for tat' principle to bring out the accused's record, subject to the discretion of the judge. It is notable that although the new words appear to indicate homicide offences, they are surely wider than that so that, e.g., the victim of any crime who before trial has died, even from unrelated causes, comes within the category subject to the discretion of the trial judge.

It should be noted that attacks on other persons who are not called as witnesses do not fall foul of this section, for example see *R v Lee* (1975) 62 Cr App R 33 where allegations by the defence that two other men who were not called as witnesses actually committed the crime, did not invoke the section. A more contemporary problem would arise if the accused should make an attack on the character of absent witnesses whose evidence is tendered under one of the exceptions to the hearsay rule, e.g., ss. 23 and 24, Criminal Justice Act 1978. There is no clear authority as to whether this would in fact bring the section into operation.

May anything about earlier offences other than the fact of conviction be proved?

The authority on this is slightly unclear due to a conflict in the case law, but the better view is established by the case of *R v France and France* [1979] Crim LR 48. In this case the three accused went into a jeweller's shop. Two of the accused distracted the shopkeeper's attention whilst another stole items from a window display. The defence case involved making imputations upon the character of police witnesses. Leave was therefore given to the prosecution to cross-examine the accused on their criminal record, but the cross-examination went beyond mere details of the offences for which they had been convicted and into questions of how they had committed the previous crime. Their previous *modus operandi* had in fact been identical to the present crime although the case did not really fall within the similar fact principle. It was held on appeal that as cross-examination under s. 1(f)(ii) is admitted as relevant to the credibility of the witness, it was irrelevant to show that the method of the previous crimes was similar to the present one.

Although an accused may not therefore be questioned about how he committed previous offences under the section, it has long been accepted that, in using s. 1(f)(ii) where the accused has lost his shield, the prosecution may ask the accused not just about his past convictions, but about *how he pleaded* at his former trials. It seems acceptable on the issue of credit to show that an accused has been convicted despite a not guilty plea and thus, presumably, has been disbelieved by a jury.

Judicial discretion

Even though an accused may have made sufficient imputations to permit s. 1(f)(ii) to be invoked, the judge has a discretion to disallow cross-examination in a given case where 'it may be fraught with results which immeasurably outweigh the result of the question put by the defence and make a fair trial impossible': see *R v Jenkins* (1945) 31 Cr App R 1 (at p. 15). Thus a judge should take into account the gravity of any imputations made compared with the prejudicial results to the accused of his character being disclosed. For example, if the present charge is relatively trivial and the accused makes some imputation in conducting his defence (e.g., says that a store detective has fabricated evidence of shoplifting) but the accused's record is for very bad previous offences such that a jury would inevitably become prejudiced against him when hearing of them, a judge may well prevent the prosecution relying on s. 1(f)(ii) notwithstanding that technically it is applicable to the case.

No doubt, despite *Selvey v DPP*, a judge will usually wish to bear in mind the issue of how essential to the defence the imputation was and be the more favourably inclined to use his discretion to disallow cross-examination in a case where it was *essential to attack the prosecution witnesses*, rather than one of *gratuitous imputation*.

20.3.3.5   Section 1(f)(iii)

This provides that where one or more co-accused has 'given evidence against any other person charged in the same proceedings', the shield may be lost.

The reason for the rule is that where one co-accused gives evidence against another he has become, *in effect*, a prosecution witness (albeit not competent to be called by them), and nothing should be done to inhibit an accused from discrediting his accusers. It has accordingly been held that a judge has *no discretion* to refuse a co-accused his right to cross-examine under s. 1(f)(iii) although he does of course, as we have seen, have a discretion under s. 1(f)(ii). It is for the judge to decide whether what the co-accused has said amounts to 'giving evidence against'.

What is meant by 'has given evidence against'?

These words involve a consideration *not* of a co-accused's intention and certainly not of any requirement for actual malice against a co-accused. All one needs to consider is the objective tendency of his evidence — *its likely effect on his co-accused's case.*

In *Murdoch* v *Taylor* [1965] AC 574 the accused M and another man L were charged with receiving stolen cameras. The accused gave evidence to the effect that he had not known what the contents of a certain box were because it was entirely L's responsibility. The judge held that L's counsel was entitled to take advantage of s. 1(f)(iii) and cross-examine M as to his previous convictions. The conviction was upheld on appeal. The accused had given 'evidence against' L. There was no requirement for hostile intent.

Guidance for a judge called upon to decide whether one accused has 'given evidence against' another is contained in the leading case of *R* v *Varley* [1982] 2 All ER 519. The co-accused, A and B, were jointly charged with robbery. At trial, A admitted that he and B had participated in the robbery but stated that he had been forced to do so by threats on his life made by B. B gave evidence that he had taken no part in the robbery and that A's evidence was untrue. The trial judge permitted counsel for A to cross-examine B on his previous record under s. 1(f)(iii). On dismissing the appeal, the Court of Appeal laid down the following guidelines:

(a) If it is established that a person jointly charged has given evidence against a co-defendant that defendant has a right to cross-examine the other on his record and the trial judge has no discretion to refuse an application.

(b) Such evidence may be given either in chief or during cross-examination.

(c) It has to be objectively decided whether the evidence either supports the prosecution case in a material respect or undermines the defence of the co-accused. Hostile intent is irrelevant.

(d) If consideration has to be given to the undermining of the other's defence, care must be taken to see that the evidence clearly does have that effect. Inconvenience to or inconsistency with the other's defence is not of itself sufficient.

(e) Mere denial of participation in a joint venture is not of itself sufficient to rank as evidence against a co-accused. Such denial must lead to the conclusion that if the witness did not participate, then it must have been the other accused who did.

(f) Where one defendant asserts a view of a joint venture which is directly contradicted by the other, such contradiction may be evidence against the co-accused.

There has been a flurry of recent cases considering the effect of *Varley* in its application to individual facts. The outcome of these cases depends on the facts and in particular on the extent to which defences adduced by co-defendants are mutually inconsistent. The Court of Appeal stressed in *R v Crawford* (1997) *The Times*, 10 June 1997 that the case of *Varley* should not lead to over-complicating a straightforward and easily applicable test.

20.3.3.6 Character arising in other circumstances between co-accused

Character can often arise in difficult circumstances without the 1898 Act being necessarily involved. See the difficult case of *R v Miller* [1952] 2 All ER 667. A, B and C were charged with conspiracy to evade customs duties. The defence of B was that he was not concerned in the conspiracy but that C had masqueraded as him (B) and used his (B's) office to commit the offences. To further that defence B's counsel asked a prosecution witness whether at a time when there were no illegal importations C had not been in prison throughout the period on other matters. In the circumstances the question was relevant. The application for a new trial was refused.

On a strict interpretation of the section these facts would not amount to 'giving evidence' although the tendency would obviously be the same (*R v Miller* itself did not involve s. 1(f)). Clearly if the co-accused *repeats* the suggestion made to the prosecution witness in *his own evidence*, s. 1(f)(iii) would apply. Where the 1898 Act does not apply, as in *R v Miller*, a judge has a duty to balance the interests of the co-accused and ought not to permit evidence of character to be introduced unless it is clearly relevant to guilt.

20.3.3.7 The meaning of 'in the same proceedings'

These words were substituted by the Criminal Evidence Act 1979 for the original words 'with the same offence' which had led to obvious problems since it by no means follows that co-accused are always charged with the same offence. It must be remembered that the mere fact that one accused is likely to give evidence against a co-accused is not by itself a ground for ordering separate trials: see *R v Hoggins* [1967] 3 All ER 334.

20.3.3.8 Who may cross-examine under s. 1(f)(iii)?

Where there are two or more co-accused in a criminal trial, it is far from unknown that they may reach relatively complex agreements on procedure and tactics. Suppose, e.g., that a certain crime must have been committed by one, or other, or both of two men each of whom has a long criminal record and have been colleagues in crime on many occasions. They might agree that each will be separately represented at trial and that each will totally blame the other for the crime. They will thus hope that when the judge directs the jury, as he must, to consider each of them separately if there is insufficient evidence of joint enterprise, and to be sure in each individual case that first A is guilty beyond reasonable doubt and then alternatively that B is guilty beyond reasonable doubt, there is some possibility that the jury, taking careful note of the burden and standard of proof, will have to acquit both because they cannot be sure which of them is guilty. By this tactic each ensures that the jury is left under the impression that the two men both have good character. Had each availed himself of his right to cross-examine under s. 1(f)(iii), obviously the jury would have been highly likely to draw the conclusion (especially if some of the offences are revealed to have been committed jointly by the men on other occasions) that they both committed the crime and both would have been convicted. The issue is whether in that situation the Crown are permitted to cross-examine under s. 1(f)(iii). There seems to be no reason why not, because nothing in the section stipulates who can make use of the right to cross-examine where it arises. See, for example, *R v Seigley* (1911) 6 Cr App R 106 where the accused together with K was charged with theft. The accused gave evidence hostile to K. K's counsel did not cross-examine the accused on his character but the prosecution were permitted to do so under s. 1(f)(iii).

The rule is thus that the prosecution may, subject to the judge's discretion to prohibit it, cross-examine under s. 1(f)(iii) but *only exceptionally*. See *R v Lovett* [1973] 1 WLR 241 where L was charged with theft of a television set and G his co-accused with handling it. L cast serious imputations on a prosecution witness and gave evidence against G. G's counsel immediately cross-examined him on his previous convictions. He was convicted and G was acquitted. On L's appeal the Court of Appeal held that cross-examination under s. 1(f)(iii) as it then was worded was improper because the two co-accused were not charged with the same offence (see now Criminal Evidence Act 1979 referred to above). But as counsel for the prosecution had intended to seek leave to cross-examine under s. 1(f)(iii) the Court of Appeal exercised discretion and dismissed the appeal.

20.3.4 INADVERTENT REFERENCES TO CHARACTER

Finally, one should note that if some *inadvertent* reference to an accused's character is made in the case (e.g., as by a witness in *R v Smith* (1915) 11 Cr App R 229 who unexpectedly referred to the accused as having been in prison) the judge has three options:

(a) To stop the trial and discharge the jury. This is a matter within his discretion and he will bear in mind the inconvenience and expense of a new trial, the nature of the reference to character, and the prejudice to any co-accused.

(b) To ignore the matter if it is likely to be overlooked or forgotten by the jury. One must doubt whether this will often be proper, except perhaps if the reference was very oblique (e.g., if a witness says 'I knew the accused in Barlinnie' — it would perhaps not be obvious that he meant Barlinnie Prison — at least to an English jury).

(c) To let the trial proceed and give a very clear direction to the jury on the irrelevance of character to guilt.

It is suggested that in order that justice may be seen to be done it will usually be best to discharge the jury, in principle, although considerations of convenience and cost must also play a part, e.g., if the revelation comes near the end of a lengthy multi-defendant trial.

20.3.5 THE ACCUSED'S RECORD: TACTICS TO ADOPT

One must remain clearly aware of the overall picture. If an accused has a criminal record but also has other creditable aspects of his past, then one must weigh the effect on the jury of the two. If, e.g., there are some trivial thefts committed 20 years ago and the accused has led an admirable lifestyle since, it may be worth bringing out evidence of character. His total reform, quite independently of any good works he has latterly done, will be an extra feature after a bad start in life and may help to persuade the jury. More normally however one will wish to keep bad character from the jury. The following points should be borne in mind:

(a) That if one has to strongly attack prosecution witnesses, it may still be possible to do so without the judge or magistrates finding that there has been an 'imputation'. For example, to suggest that identification witnesses are completely wrong and are being stubborn in their persistence in wrongly identifying the accused would probably not fall foul of s. 1(f)(ii).

(b) Similarly, it may be possible to suggest that policemen have got some aspects of the Codes of Practice wrong and have, say, carried out an identification parade in breach of the Code of Practice, albeit in good faith, without falling foul of the section.

(c) It may be possible to make very forceful denials of the charge and put it to prosecution witnesses that they are lying in such a way as not to fall foul of the section. Everything will depend upon the latitude given to the accused by the court under the principles in *R v Britzman and Hall* [1983] 1 All ER 369. (See **20.3.3.2** above.)

(d) To go anywhere beyond this however and to make positive allegations of fabrication of evidence, perjury or flouting of the Codes of Practice, or to suggest improper motives in bringing the prosecution such as personal malice or grudges, will inevitably fall foul of the section and the accused's character will be brought out if he testifies.

(e) It must always be borne in mind that it is a perfectly viable tactical option for the accused to have all the imputations he wishes made on his behalf, but not to testify. If he does that then he cannot be cross-examined about his record nor can the prosecution bring it out by any other means so long as there is no positive assertion of good character.

(f) Nonetheless it is often seen as a bad tactic to fail to give evidence, quite apart from the enhanced powers of the prosecution and the judge to comment. Magistrates will be even more prone than formerly to draw adverse inferences in the case of a defendant who declines to testify and it will be even more risky for an accused now to fail to testify in view of the possible comment from prosecutor and judge. In any event, jurors naturally speculate and may well feel disappointed that an accused has not given his version. Nonetheless this is a tactic which must be carefully considered along with other matters when the decision is made as to whether an accused should testify.

(g) Sometimes it will be decided that there is no option but for an accused to testify and that imputations must be made against prosecution witnesses. If the accused's only defence is that evidence was planted on him or that admissions have been totally fabricated by the police, then there is really no alternative but to say these things if one wishes to have any hope of an acquittal. In such a case where the character is bound to come out there are some well recognised techniques for mitigating the damage namely:

  (i) If character is inevitably going to come out, then it is much better for the accused to appear to volunteer it in his evidence-in-chief. He can do this with the appearance of candour and this takes away the possibility of the prosecution triumphantly rising to cross-examine on his lengthy criminal record.

  (ii) Where bad character must inevitably come out, there is absolutely no harm in trying to make the best of things and to point to things which demonstrate good character as well. It may, e.g., be possible to indicate that although there was a bad run of burglaries in the accused's record ten years ago, all of these were at a time when he was suffering from heroin addiction and were undertaken in a desperate effort to finance this habit. One can then go on to show that remedial treatment has worked and that there have been no convictions in the last ten years, during which time the accused has acquired a wife, home, family and regular employment and thus one can paint a picture for the jury of an accused who is, virtually, a man of good character.

(h) It must always be borne in mind that if one says anything which makes a co-accused's conviction more likely, under the principles in *Varley*, that, unless there is some agreement with the co-accused about the matter, he will be entitled to cross-examine. There are usually few problems with the subtleties of this rule since in most such cases it is a clear case of one co-accused blaming another. If the case becomes more subtle, regard will have to be had to the principles in *Varley* and the corresponding risks. (See **20.3.3.5** above.)

(i) In the magistrates' court, if character has come out, then powerful stress should be given in the closing speech to the magistrates about the evidential uses of their knowledge of bad character which are entirely for assessing the credibility of the accused. In the Crown Court the judge's direction to the jury on this point should be particularly carefully noted.

(j) If the accused in fact has a good character, this may be stressed in any convenient way and it may be in some kinds of case that a great deal should be made of it by not only asserting absence of criminal record and describing positive creditable acts, but by the calling of witnesses. A particularly effective witness, e.g., in alleged dishonesty cases, would be an employer or past employer for whom the accused has worked, especially in a job involving handling money, where there have been no discrepancies or shortages over a long period.

TWENTY ONE

THE LAW OF EVIDENCE (8):
EVIDENCE OF OPINION: PRIVILEGE

21.1   Introduction

The general rule is that a witness may only testify as to matters *actually observed* by him and he may not give his *opinion* on those matters. The drawing of inference from observed facts is the whole function of the trier of facts, i.e., in a criminal case the jury.

The distinction between fact and opinion is easy enough to see in cases at either end of the spectrum — thus a statement that A was driving on the wrong side of the road is clearly fact; that he was driving negligently is opinion; but statements of how fast someone was driving or as to identity of handwriting are clearly both. Where it is impossible to separate facts from inferences based on them the law usually permits the witness to narrate both.

> **Example**   A witness wishes to say 'X was drunk'. Whilst this is a matter of opinion the witness would certainly be permitted to say it since, if asked, he could narrate the matters of *fact* on which his opinion was based, e.g., he could say 'X staggered'; 'his breath smelt of drink'; 'his speech was slurred'; 'his eyes were glazed', etc.

21.2   Expert Witnesses

To the general rule prohibiting evidence of opinion there is one exception, namely the case of expert witnesses. Expert opinion evidence is in principle admissible as to matters upon which the judge or jury may legitimately require assistance. The most common modern use of experts is that of a medical witness in personal injury litigation. Other frequent instances are the evidence of consultant engineers, handwriting experts and valuers, evidence of current commercial practices, and so on.

21.2.1   WHO IS AN EXPERT?

It is for the judge to decide whether a witness is an expert, that is whether he has undergone sufficient course of study to be an expert. Such evidence is always introduced by a statement of qualifications etc., although no *formal* qualifications are required unless the nature of the activity about which expert evidence is to be given demands them. Thus, e.g., in the old case of *R* v *Silverlock* [1894] 2 QB 766 the expert evidence of a solicitor who had acquired expertise in handwriting identification was admitted even though he was an amateur. It should be noted that, in the modern era, forensic document examination is acknowledged as a proper scientific discipline and the evidence of an enthusiastic amateur would be unlikely to be accepted now. Nonetheless the possession of diplomas and degrees is not a necessary requirement so that, e.g., evidence of an experienced car mechanic would undoubtedly be acceptable about some matters to do with motor vehicles notwithstanding absence of formal qualifications.

21.2.2   THE SCOPE OF EXPERT EVIDENCE: THE 'ULTIMATE ISSUE' RULE

There was a rule to the effect that expert evidence was *not admissible* on the *very question* which the jury had to decide. The reason was said to be that this would usurp the function of the jury and that the accused (or parties in a civil case) was entitled to be tried by jury (or judge) and not by experts. Thus, e.g., it was held proper to ask a medical expert to comment on the mental state of the accused but not proper to ask the direct question as to whether he was sane. It is now generally considered that, in cases involving, in particular, the mental state of the accused, expert evidence may be admissible even if it is on the 'ultimate issue' so that a consultant psychiatrist may be asked about the sanity of the accused.

21.2.3   THE SCOPE OF EXPERT EVIDENCE: WHEN IS AN EXPERT REQUIRED?

In criminal cases, expert evidence is admissible to furnish a court with a scientific explanation of matters outside the experience and knowledge of the jury. But the fact that an expert has impressive scientific qualifications does not of itself make his opinion on matters of human nature and behaviour any more helpful than that of the jurors themselves.

The rule is thus that expert evidence is inadmissible as being superfluous where the subject matter in the trial does not call for expertise. See, e.g., *R v Chard* (1971) 56 Cr App R 268 where the accused was charged with murder. Counsel desired to question a medical witness on the supposed inability of the accused to form any intent to kill or do grievous bodily harm. It was held that the question was rightly ruled improper by the trial judge. Where no issue of insanity, diminished responsibility or mental illness has arisen and it is conceded that the accused is entirely normal, it is not permissible to call a medical witness to give his opinion about how the defendant's mind might have operated at the material time.

See also *R v Turner* [1975] QB 834 where the accused was charged with murder of his girlfriend by hitting her several times with a hammer. His defence was provocation in that she had just told him of her infidelity with other men and that he was not the father of her expected child. The accused wished to call a psychiatrist to give his opinion based on information from medical records and interviews that the defendant was not suffering from a mental illness and not violent by nature but that his personality was such that he could have been provoked in the circumstances and thus was likely to be telling the truth. The judge ruled the psychiatric evidence inadmissible. It was held on appeal that the question of whether the defendant was suffering from mental illness was not in issue and the psychiatric evidence, although arguably admissible, was irrelevant and had been rightly excluded. The defendant's veracity and the likelihood of his having been provoked were matters within the competence and experience of the jury and the psychiatric evidence was superfluous.

In connection specifically with defences applicable to a murder charge therefore, it could be said that *automatism, insanity and unfitness to plead* will be appropriate for expert evidence but *duress, provocation*, etc. will not.

21.2.4   HOW MUCH MUST AN EXPERT KNOW?

An expert need not have personal knowledge of every relevant matter within the field of his expertise. Once someone qualifies as an expert he is entitled to base his testimony on academic or learned articles, professional publications, research data from the experiments of others, etc.: see *R v Abadom* [1983] 1 WLR 126. The accused was charged with robbery and much of the Crown's case rested on evidence that fragments of glass found embedded in his shoes had come from a window broken in the course of the robbery. An expert witness for the Crown gave forensic evidence that the glass from the window and the fragments found in the shoes had an identical refractive index which was very rare. The witness gave evidence that he had in fact consulted statistics compiled by the Home Office and had found that this index occurred in only 4 per cent of all glass samples. This clearly implied a very strong probability that the glass had come from this window. The accused appealed against his conviction contending that the expert's evidence was hearsay and inadmissible because it was based on statistics of which he had no personal knowledge. It was held that where an expert witness was asked to express his opinion on a question, his opinion must be based on primary facts of which he had personal knowledge. However once such facts were provided the expert witness was then entitled to draw on the work of others in his field of expertise as part of the process of arriving at his conclusion. He must, however, refer to that material in his evidence so that the cogency and probative value of his conclusions could be tested by reference to the material.

21.2.5 THE RESPONSIBILITIES OF EXPERT WITNESSES

In *National Justice Compania Naviera SA* v *Prudential Assurance Co. Ltd* [1993] 2 Lloyd's Rep 68 the court explained the duties of an expert witness in *civil* cases. In particular:

(a) Expert evidence should be the independent product of the expert uninfluenced as to form or content by the exigencies of litigation.

(b) Independent assistance should be provided by way of objective, unbiased opinion. An expert witness should never assume the role of advocate.

(c) Facts or assumptions upon which the opinion was based should be stated, together with material facts which could detract from the conclusion in the opinion.

(d) An expert witness should make it clear when a question or issue fell outside his expertise.

(e) If the opinion was not properly researched because it was considered that insufficient data was available the expert should say so. If the witness could not assert that the report contained the truth, the whole truth and nothing but the truth, then that qualification should be stated on the report.

(f) If after exchange of reports an expert witness changed his mind on a material matter, that change of view should be communicated to the other side and to the court.

(g) Photographs, plans, survey reports and other documents referred to in the expert evidence had to be provided to the other side at the same time as the exchange of reports.

Although this case is specifically referable to civil proceedings, the principles, being eminently sensible, would seem to be equally applicable in criminal cases.

21.2.6 PROCEDURAL RULES GOVERNING EXPERT EVIDENCE

(a) In civil cases there is now a general requirement for prior disclosure of expert evidence in advance of trial. This requirement is said to assist with efficiency and fairness in that each side is well aware of what the other side's experts will say and each can in turn obtain their own expert witnesses' comments upon the findings of the opposing experts. Thus counsel is fully armed at trial with the material on which to cross-examine opposing expert witnesses.

(b) In criminal cases there was no such requirement of disclosure until s. 81(1) of the Police and Criminal Evidence Act 1984. By that section:

Crown Court rules may make provision for—

(a) *requiring any party to proceedings before the court to disclose to the other party or parties any expert evidence which he proposes to adduce in the proceedings; and*

(b) *prohibiting a party who fails to comply ... from adducing that evidence without leave of the court.*

Rules of court have now been made implementing the section which are broadly similar to those applicable in civil proceedings so that for the first time the defence must disclose their expert evidence to the prosecution. Similar rules now apply in the magistrates' court.

(c) There is a particular provision relating to expert evidence in s. 30 of the Criminal Justice Act 1988, which provides:

(1) An expert report shall be admissible as evidence in criminal proceedings, whether or not the person making it attends to give oral evidence in those proceedings.

(2) If it is proposed that the person making the report shall not give oral evidence, the report shall only be admissible with the leave of the court.

(3) For the purpose of determining whether to give leave the court shall have regard—
    (a) to the contents of the report;
    (b) to the reasons why it is proposed that the person making the report shall not give oral evidence;
    (c) to any risk, having regard in particular to whether it is likely to be possible to controvert statements in the report if the person making it does not attend to give oral evidence in the proceedings, that its admission or exclusion will result in unfairness to the accused or, if there is more than one, to any of them; and
    (d) to any other circumstances that appear to the court to be relevant.

(4) An expert report, when admitted, shall be evidence of any fact or opinion of which the person making it could have given oral evidence.

(5) In this section 'expert report' means a written report by a person dealing wholly or mainly with matters of which he is (or would if living be) qualified to give expert evidence.

The section thus recites criteria for admission of a report in the absence of the expert witness concerned which are substantially the same as the criteria in s. 25 of the 1988 Act for the adducing of documentary evidence generally. A special section was required to deal with the position of expert evidence because ss. 23 and 24 only deal with witnesses giving evidence of any *fact*. As we have seen, expert evidence is concerned with both facts and *opinion*. The term 'expert report' is defined by s. 30(5).

(d) Despite the fact that expert evidence may be admissible in the absence of the expert, in the normal course of things if it becomes known that the expert evidence is to be contested, then clearly the court will want to be satisfied that there is a good reason why the expert is unavailable to testify and be cross-examined. The court will look particularly to the protection of the accused and thus will presumably be more assiduous in requiring that the prosecution's experts attend than those of the defence.

21.2.7 USING AN EXPERT IN CRIMINAL PROCEEDINGS

(a) Where one wishes to use medical evidence in criminal proceedings, very much the same considerations apply as in civil cases. An appropriate expert with a medico-legal practice should be consulted. Inevitably this is likely to be a psychiatrist in cases where the mental state of the accused is in issue. All necessary instructions should be sent to the expert. Special consideration needs to be given to the question of his fees. In the case of a psychiatrist it may well be that he needs to see the accused on more than one occasion to form any view; and if the accused is remanded in custody these interviews will of necessity take place at the remand centre, and thus one may well be paying for a great deal more of the expert's time than say in the case of an orthopaedic specialist in a personal injury case.

(b) In such cases a detailed conference with counsel before trial with the expert present is also undoubtedly going to be of major assistance. With prior disclosure of expert evidence it may of course be possible to obtain agreement with the prosecution, but if it is not possible then the whole case is likely to turn on the conflict between the experts. It should be borne in mind that this may arise not only on questions of guilt or innocence but on questions of disposal of the accused whether by prison or by some form of treatment. Radically different views between medical men as to the proper method of treatment of persons, even persons accused of the most serious of all crimes, is well known. Care should be taken when choosing an expert to ensure that he will be taken seriously by the judge. Some psychiatrists contend that even the most violent offenders can be treated as out-patients and such evidence is looked on with great scepticism by the judge. As in all cases of expert evidence, counsel should be approached for his suggestions as to which witness to employ in such cases.

(c) With regard to the more esoteric disciplines of forensic science, until very recently there was a huge imbalance in the resources available to defence and prosecution. There are however now a number of independent forensic science laboratories capable of carrying out much the same kind of tests which the prosecution will carry out. Often these are staffed by former Home Office scientific officers who are therefore well versed in the criminal process. A key difficulty is likely to be that the prosecution have a great deal more manpower to bring to bear on the problems, and that they will get in earlier and obtain samples, specimens, etc., and test them in a much fresher state. For this reason consideration needs to be given to expert evidence as soon as one is consulted in an appropriate case.

(d) Again careful attention must be paid to the legal aid or fee situation and the necessary authorities to employ potentially expensive experts obtained. At the time of writing it is suggested that the Home Office's own forensic science laboratories may become open to private work and thus supply evidence for both defence and prosecution. If difficulty is encountered in finding the right kind of expert the Law Society provides a register of experts; and again an approach to the counsel that one intends to use at trial for his recommendation may be worthwhile.

21.3   Privilege

In general, public policy favours the open and frank conduct of legal proceedings. This means that any question ought to be able to be asked at trial, and an answer insisted upon, and that any material document should be made available to all parties, and to the court, for inspection. However this cannot be an absolute rule. There are conflicting interests and in some circumstances facts or documents whose relevance may appear vital to the fair conduct of litigation can be withheld, either in the public interest or in exercise of private privilege, that is a rule which protects certain kinds of private communications from disclosure. It is now appropriate to consider the doctrine of privilege under its two main heads: private privilege and public interest privilege.

21.3.1 PRIVATE PRIVILEGE

21.3.1.1 Self-incrimination

In a criminal case no witness can be compelled to answer any question which would, in the opinion of the judge, have a tendency to expose the witness to any criminal charge. In the case of an *accused*, by s. 1(e) of the Criminal Evidence Act 1898 he may not be asked questions which tend to show that he may be guilty of any other offence than that with which he is presently charged. The effect of s. 1(e) is of course to be read subject to s. 1(f) so that if his 'shield' is lost then such questions can be asked, not merely about previous convictions, but in certain circumstances, about offences for which he has not been tried.

21.3.1.2 Legal professional privilege

In both civil and criminal proceedings, comunications, oral or written, can be withheld from evidence (and inspection before trial) by both the client and the legal adviser with the client's consent if *either* the communication:

(a) was to enable the client to obtain legal advice; or

(b) was with reference to litigation.

Lawyer–client communications

The privilege applies whether the communication relates to litigation or not — the important point is said to be that anyone taking legal advice is asking about legal rights which may have to be enforced by litigation, however unlikely it may seem. The communication must be with reference to the lawyer-client relationship in some way, so that casual conversations between friends who also happen to be solicitor and client are not within the privilege. The privilege extends to all forms of communication, written, verbal, telex, etc.

Where this privilege applies it is virtually absolute and can only be overridden, so that the court may call for the documents or compel answers, where there has been some criminal element in the giving or obtaining of the advice (see **21.3.1.3** below), on the authority of *R v Derby Magistrates' Court ex parte B* [1996] AC 487.

Communications with third parties for the purpose of actual or pending litigation

For this privilege to apply there must be a definite prospect of litigation but it is not necessary that the accused should have been charged, or even arrested. The communication must have been made, or the document brought into existence, for the purpose of enabling the legal adviser to act or advise with regard to litigation. So the following are obvious examples of privilege applying: advice from counsel to solicitor on conduct of the action (this is also privileged as a lawyer-client communication); statements taken from witnesses by the solicitor; medical reports or other expert witnesses reports obtained for litigation.

There is now a statutory definition of 'items subject to legal privilege' in s. 10 of the Police and Criminal Evidence Act 1984. This section gives protection to such items against seizure pursuant to a search warrant. Although enacted for that limited purpose it has been said in the House of Lords in *R v Central Criminal Court ex parte Francis and Francis* [1989] AC 346 that it is a statutory enactment of the common law. Section 10 provides:

> (1) Subject to subsection (2) below, in this Act items subject to legal privilege means—
>   (a) communications between a professional legal adviser and his client or any person representing his client made in connection with the giving of legal advice to the client;

(b) *communications between a professional legal adviser and his client or any person representing his client or between such an adviser or his client or any such representative and any other person made in connection with or in contemplation of legal proceedings and for the purposes of such proceedings; and*

(c) *items enclosed with or referred to in such communications and made—*

(i) *in connection with the giving of legal advice; or*

(ii) *in connection with or in contemplation of legal proceedings and for the purposes of such proceedings,*

when they are in the possession of a person who is entitled to possession of them.

(2) *Items held with the intention of furthering a criminal purpose are not items subject to legal privilege.*

In the context purely of search warrants, therefore, a client who had material subject to legal professional privilege is placed in something of a quandary because if he refuses physically to hand it over to police executing a search warrant in reliance on his privilege he may be charged with obstruction if his interpretation of what is subject to the privilege is wrong. On the other hand, if he does hand it over, even under protest, he may be held to have waived his privilege. For this reason, full and accurate legal advice to a client faced with a search warrant is often required. Search warrants are rarely executed at solicitor's premises unless the solicitor is himself alleged to be involved in the crimes concerned. We turn now to the exceptions to the rule.

21.3.1.3 Exceptions to the rule

Even though legal professional privilege prima facie applies, the general principle may be affected by the following exceptions:

(a) *Waiver by the client*

It must be remembered that the privilege belongs to the client not the solicitor and the client may always waive it and direct the solicitor to disclose the relevant material.

(b) *Communications to facilitate crime or fraud*

In *R v Cox and Railton* (1884) 14 QBD 153 a fraudulent document was executed and backdated to defeat the effects of a judgment. At the trial of Cox and Railton, the prosecution called a solicitor to say that the accused had consulted him as to how to defeat the judgment and he had told them it could not lawfully be done. It was held that communications to facilitate crime or fraud are not privileged. If the lawyer participates in the fraud he ceases to act as a lawyer; if he is himself innocent of any fraud, as in this case, the privilege is still lost if the clients have a criminal purpose.

21.3.1.4 Inadvertent disclosure of privileged documents

One difficult question is: Is the privilege lost if the privileged document falls into the hands of someone else, e.g., one's opponent? The rule is that where this happens in criminal proceedings the privilege is usually lost.

In *R v Tompkins* (1977) 67 Cr App R 181 the defendant had given certain evidence in examination-in-chief. A note which he had earlier written to his counsel and which had apparently been found on the courtroom floor and given by mistake to prosecuting counsel was put to him in cross-examination. The note in effect contradicted his earlier evidence. The contents of the note were not read out but upon seeing it the defendant admitted that he had not told the truth earlier. It was held that the prosecution had been entitled to make use of the note although originally privileged. Its actual loss entitled the prosecution to make use of it once it was in their hands.

There is clearly some overlap here with the question of improperly obtained evidence. Thus if, say, vital solicitor client communications were obtained by the police burgling a solicitor's offices, there would be nothing in the law of *privilege* which would exclude the evidence so obtained. The court would then have to consider the ambit of s. 78 of the Police and Criminal Evidence Act 1984 and in particular cases such as *R* v *Mason* which we have discussed earlier, 18.3.

21.3.1.5 Other professions

There is no general professional privilege for other professions, even those such as accountants who may give quasi-legal advice. However, in *British Steel Corporation* v *Granada Television Ltd* [1982] AC 1096 two judges in the Court of Appeal appeared to hold that whilst denying that any special privilege existed, the press and broadcasting companies would not generally be compelled by the courts to disclose their confidential sources of information, on the general grounds of public policy. These views were expressly rejected by all but Lord Salmon in the House of Lords. However, now by s. 10 of the Contempt of Court Act 1981:

> No court may require a person to disclose, nor is any person guilty of contempt of court for refusing to disclose, the source of information contained in a publication for which he is responsible, unless it be established to the satisfaction of the court that disclosure is necessary in the interests of justice or national security or for the prevention of disorder or crime.

In essence therefore a new type of partial privilege is created by the section. One should note that:

(a) The words 'interests of justice' in s. 10 refer to the administration of justice, that is legal proceedings in court rather than any abstract concept of the phrase — see *X Ltd* v *Morgan-Grampian (Publishers) Ltd* [1991] 1 AC 1.

(b) The words 'is necessary for the prevention of disorder or crime' do not have to refer to any particular crime but may refer to crime in general. See *Re an Inquiry under the Company Securities (Insider Dealing) Act 1985* [1988] AC 660.

21.3.2 PUBLIC INTEREST PRIVILEGE

Where evidence is excluded because of some public interest in withholding it which outweighs the usual public interest in open litigation, it is usually now called 'public interest privilege', or 'public interest immunity'. In older cases the term 'Crown privilege' appears but this is no longer apposite. Many of the bodies who have been able to claim the privilege have not been in any sense the Crown, indeed in some cases there has been no connection between the body and government at all.

Although most of the important cases have arisen in a civil context, the principles of public interest immunity are exactly the same in criminal proceedings. In civil cases, of course, the principle is likely to be called into question at the stage of discovery of documents rather than the trial itself. As there is no corresponding stage in criminal proceedings the matter arises rather differently. An important case demonstrating the principle is *Burmah Oil Co. Ltd* v *Bank of England* [1980] AC 1090. Discovery was sought of various memoranda of meetings attended by government ministers and other documents which would have revealed the inner workings of high-level government. It was held that it would be going too far to lay down that no document in any particular category should ever in any circumstances be produced, even when they were high-level documents to do with government. The nature of the litigation and the apparent importance to it of the documents in question might in an extreme case demand production even of the most sensitive communications at the highest level. The courts are concerned with the consideration that it is in the public interest that justice should be done and should be publicly recognised as having been done. This might lead, though only in a very limited number of cases, to the inner workings of government being exposed to the public gaze (Lord Keith of Kinkel).

Lord Wilberforce (dissenting) however said:

> with regard to the suggestion that persons preparing minutes, writing memoranda etc. might make them less candid if they thought they might one day be exposed to public gaze, it now seems rather fashionable to decry this (alleged possible loss of candour) but if as a ground it may at one time have been exaggerated it has now in my opinion received an excessive dose of cold water. I am certainly not prepared, against the view of the minister to discount the need in the formation of such very controversial policy as that with which we are here involved, for frank and uninhibited advice from the bank to the government and from and between civil servants and ministers.

The court is essentially engaged in a balancing exercise. It must weigh the conflicting principles of public interest giving due weight to the minister's views and eventually deciding whether confidentiality or candour is the more important in each case. In *Air Canada* v *Secretary of State for Trade (No. 2)* [1983] 2 AC 394 the House of Lords held that even Cabinet documents might in certain circumstances have to be disclosed, e.g., if serious misconduct is alleged against a Cabinet Minister. Conversely, relatively low-level documents may be withheld if they are not of significant relevance to a case. It must also be remembered that in connection with actions involving departments of state that many public bodies are involved in areas with little true 'political content' and much of their activity and the documents it generates are of purely commercial importance. In such cases it would be more difficult to sustain a claim to public interest privilege.

It should be noted that the matter of public interest is a matter for the court. Accordingly, in some recent cases, the courts have held that they should consider the matter even where the Crown has not raised the issue.

21.3.2.1 Confidentiality and privilege

As we have seen above, only the legal profession usually has its communications protected by privilege as such. There is however a lesser legal concept, that of 'confidentiality' which may exist in all manner of professional-client relationships. The court will often give weight to this principle and attempt to protect it unless disclosure of the document is truly vital for the doing of justice in the litigation. Thus in civil cases, doctor-patient communications and confidential business communications to which no genuine *privilege* can be said to attach have sometimes been protected.

Such a point arose in a criminal context, albeit not a criminal case, in *W* v *Egdell* [1990] Ch 359. A consultant psychiatrist who had become aware of certain matters, in the course of a confidential relationship with a patient whom he was treating for serious mental illness and who had committed multiple killings, was afraid that a decision might be made which might lead to the release of the patient from a secure mental hospital. Accordingly he disclosed to the Home Office certain confidential information which he had obtained from the patient whilst treating him. He was afraid that, unless the responsible authority was able to make an informed judgment that the risk of repetition of murder was small, that there was a risk of the patient being released. The patient on finding that the doctor had passed on a copy of his report to the mental hospital commenced proceedings against the doctor alleging breach of the duty of confidence. It was held that the court must balance the public interest in confidentiality and the greater public interest. In the present case the court held that, since there was no professional privilege involved, the doctor was justified in taking the course he did in the wider public interest.

21.3.2.2 Information given for the purpose of criminal investigation

Finally, one originally separate basis of public privilege which has merged somewhat into the mainstream is the rule that no question may be asked in proceedings which would tend to lead to the identification of any person who has given information leading to the institution of a prosecution. There is said to be an overriding public interest in protecting the anonymity of such informants. The principle has been extended to cover bodies other than the police who need to rely on a supply of confidential information, e.g., in *Alfred Crompton Amusement Machines Ltd* v *Commissioners of Customs and Excise (No. 2)* [1974] AC 405. In this case Commissioners of Customs and Excise received information from customers of a company relating to the company's liability to purchase tax. The circumstances were such that the customers' information was obviously intended to be confidential. It was held that although the 'confidentiality' was not in itself absolutely decisive as a ground of privilege in the present case, disclosure would be likely to result not only in a breach of confidence but in information not being given so candidly in future.

The main use of the principle however is in respect of police informants. The rule derives from the case of *Marks* v *Beyfus* (1890) 25 QBD 494 which established both the principle, that a policeman was entitled to refuse to answer a question which would have revealed his informant, and the exception, namely that there was also a public policy which might sometimes allow for the need to answer the question about the name of the informant where there was good reason to think it would help establish the innocence of the accused.

The principle was upheld in *R* v *Hallett* [1986] Crim LR 462 where the accused was charged with conspiracy to import cocaine. The police had relied on information given to them by informers. The trial judge refused an application that the informants' identities should be disclosed to the defence. The accused appealed against conviction. It was held, dismissing the appeal, that evidence as to the identity of informants is excluded unless the judge concludes it is necessary to override that rule and admit the evidence in order to prevent a miscarriage of justice and in order to prevent the possibility that a man may, by reason of the exclusion of that evidence, be deprived of the opportunity of casting doubt upon the case against him.

The principle was extended to withholding details of the location of police observation posts in *R* v *Rankine* [1986] QB 861. The accused was charged with drug offences. Police gave evidence of observing him committing the offences. Prosecuting counsel asked that the location of the police observation post should not be identified other than to say that it was some 65 yards away from the accused at the time of the crime and that the officers had used image intensifiers. The accused appealed against the refusal to give further details of the observation post. It was held, dismissing the appeal, that it is in the public interest that nothing should be done to discourage members of the public from providing information to the police and likewise these rules apply with equal force to the identification of the owner or occupier of premises which the police have been allowed to use for surveillance.

This was confirmed more recently in *Blake and Austin* v *DPP* [1993] Crim LR 283 in which the court observed that the guidelines set out in another case, *R* v *Johnson* [1988] 1 WLR 1377, should be observed. These principles required the policeman in the case to give positive evidence as to the attitude of the occupiers of the house used as an observation post to the disclosure of its location. If those householders objected then their objections should be upheld.

The police have sometimes tried to extend this principle to enable them to refuse to answer all manner of questions about the surrounding circumstances of an investigation. See, e.g., *R* v *Brown* (1987) 87 Cr App R 52 where on charges of theft, policemen who were carrying out a surveillance operation in the East End of London claimed to have seen the two accused committing the crime. The defence was that the police evidence was a total fabrication and that when their surveillance had proved abortive they had made up the evidence. Officers refused to answer questions about the surveillance including a question about the colour, make and model of the police vehicle used on the day in question. The police would not even tell prosecuting counsel about the vehicles. The judge allowed the prosecution to withhold the information on public interest grounds. The accused successfully appealed against conviction. This was not a case like that of *Rankine* where identification of premises should be withheld because that would have tended to identify the owner of those premises. Here what was sought was relatively low-level information in order to enable the appellants to challenge the prosecution case factually. The trial judge was not entitled to fetter counsel for the defence in the way he had done and to exclude the evidence. It was a material irregularity.

Examples of the main exception to the rule are contained in cases such as *R v Agar* (1989) 90 Cr App R 318. In this case the defendant alleged that the police had induced an informer to go to a house at which the police had themselves planted drugs and which the accused was to visit. Defence counsel wished to cross-examine with a view to revealing the plot between the informer and the police. The judge prevented this and on appeal the conviction was quashed on the basis that:

(a) It was a well-established rule of public policy to protect disclosure of the identity of informers but an exception had to be made where it was necessary to make such disclosure for the purpose of defence to a criminal charge.

(b) Distinctions would sometimes have to be drawn between professional informers who supply information regularly for reward and a case such as the present where it was alleged that the informer in a single instance had given information to the police to get himself out of difficulties or to get favours from the police in relation to that offence.

21.4 Practicalities of Privilege in Criminal Proceedings

The case law demonstrates that privilege is of far more importance as a concept in civil cases. In criminal proceedings it is rare that the defence will need to concern themselves with privilege in respect of their own documents but there are two possible situations where this may arise:

(a) Where there has been unlawful search and seizure by the police or prosecuting authorities either at the client's premises or more rarely at the solicitor's offices. Arguments demanding the return of the material based on privilege may then need to be mounted either in the course of proceedings or by civil proceedings for an injunction requiring their return.

(b) It may sometimes be that prosecution authorities suggest to a solicitor that they should be permitted to inspect his files or other documents because the solicitor has unwittingly been used as a dupe in a fraud by the client and thus comes within the principle of *R v Cox and Railton* above. This may for example happen where it is alleged that the client has been involved in mortgage fraud by making false applications for mortgage finance, perhaps in different identities using different solicitors, and the police wish to interview the solicitor as a witness and obtain copies of documents. At this time the solicitor will need to give very careful consideration to the legal and professional position. It may in a difficult case be necessary to take advice from the Law Society or from counsel. Prosecuting authorities who habitually meet this situation often supply copies of relevant Practice Rules or case law to demonstrate to anxious solicitors the exception to the usual rules of client privilege. Care must always be taken to ensure that the course of action suggested by the prosecution does indeed fall within such a principle.

21.4.1 PROSECUTION DOCUMENTS AND THE BACKGROUND TO THE CRIMINAL PROCEDURE AND INVESTIGATIONS ACT 1996

(a) It may be suggested by the defence that some document in the prosecution's possession should be disclosed. There is of course no formal stage of discovery in criminal cases, but there is a clear principle that, if the prosecution have evidence which favours the defence, they are obliged to give the defence at least that witness's name and address if not his statement (*R v Bryant* (1946) 31 Cr App R 146, approved more recently in *R v Lawson* (1989) 90 Cr App R 107). That duty of disclosure relates to witnesses of fact and also to expert evidence, see *R v Maguire* [1992] QB 936.

(b) The Attorney-General issued guidelines in 1982 about disclosure which in fact went far beyond what was strictly required in the case law. Those guidelines are set out at [1982] 1 All ER 734. The Crown Prosecution Service is in principle obliged to follow those guidelines and to disclose to the defence all 'unused material' including statements from potential witnesses whose evidence the prosecution do not intend to use and which might assist the defence. Depending on the bulk of the material, the defence may either be given copies of it all or be allowed to inspect the originals. It should be noted that this principle does not apply to *every* item of evidence in the case. The prosecution need not disclose the statements of witnesses which help them and do not assist the defence, but where they do not intend to call those witnesses (because they feel they may be unreliable). Likewise unused material which is sensitive and includes details, e.g., of a police informant, need not be disclosed. It forms part of the Bar Code of Conduct that prosecuting counsel must consider whether all witness statements have been properly served in accordance with the guidelines.

(c) New principles were clearly expressed in the very important case of *R v Keane* [1994] 1 WLR 746. In this case, which considered the earlier case of *R v Ward* [1993] 1 WLR 619, the court had to consider what duty of disclosure there was on the prosecution in respect of material which they did not wish to use. The court held that it was generally for the prosecution, not the court, to identify the documents and information which were material according to the appropriate criteria. These criteria were that documents or material, if they can be seen on a sensible appraisal by the prosecution, are:

  (i) to be relevant or possibly relevant to an issue in the case;

  (ii) to raise or possibly raise a new issue whose existence is not apparent from the evidence that the prosecution proposes to use;

  (iii) to hold a real as opposed to fanciful prospect of providing a lead on evidence which goes to either (i) or (ii).

That case and another similar case *R v Brown* [1995] 1 Cr App R 191, therefore, held that the prosecution were to determine what was 'material' as defined. In exceptional cases where the prosecution had doubts about materiality, the court could be asked to rule on that issue. In this respect it was noted in the case of *Keane* that 'the more full and specific the indication the defendant's lawyers give of the defence or issues they are likely to raise, the more accurately both the prosecution and the judge will be able to assess the value to the defence of the material'. This led to the development of the so-called 'Keane letter' which the prosecution would often send to the defence, together with the disclosed material, identifying what the prosecution has taken to be the issues in the case and inviting the defence to respond if that was not accepted.

The above however, must now be considered simply as background to the Criminal Procedure and Investigations Act 1996. This legislation will be read in conjunction with Codes of Practices under s. 23 of the Act issued by the Secretary of State and removes the common law rules regarding disclosure. It provides a simple three-stage procedure whereby, after an offence has been committed to the Crown Court, the prosecution must undertake disclosure in the following way:

(i)   'Primary disclosure' must be made first in which the prosecution disclose any material which in their opinion might undermine the prosecution case against the accused, or alternatively give a written statement that there is no such material. At the same time a schedule under the Codes of Practice which has been prepared by the 'disclosure officer', i.e., the officer who has been responsible for handling the administration of the criminal investigation, must be given to the defence. The schedule lists material retained by the investigator which does not form part of the case against the accused. Although items which in the investigator's opinion might undermine the prosecution case are to be disclosed, there may be a separate schedule of 'sensitive' material which need not be disclosed, and what is to go in this is a matter entirely for the decision of the prosecution.

(ii)   'Compulsory disclosure' is then required by the accused who must give the prosecution a defence statement which, in general terms, sets out the nature of the defence, indicates the matters on which issue is taken with the prosecution, and sets out in each matter the reason why issue is taken. It can readily be seen therefore that the defence must now disclose at least an outline of the matters they propose to rely on and this probably goes a little further than the current requirement to be open about such matters during the plea and directions hearing.

It should be noted however that if the defence statement sets out any inconsistent defences or is different from the defence put forward at trial or is given late, then the court or the prosecution (with the judge's leave) may comment, and the jury may draw proper inferences.

(iii)   Upon receiving the defendant's statement the prosecution should undertake 'secondary disclosure', that is, of any material not previously disclosed which might reasonably be expected to assist the accused's defence as disclosed by the defence statement or give a written statement that there is no such material.

A formalised procedure will therefore be necessary instead of the previous requirement on the prosecution to disclose unused material.

It should be noted that the prosecution have a continuing duty to keep under review the question of what ought to be disclosed which might either undermine their case or assist the defence right throughout the procedure until the jury return their verdict.

Public interest immunity

At each stage in the proposed procedure the prosecution should not disclose material which the court, on an application by the prosecution, concludes is not in the public interest to disclose, and orders accordingly. Such material will obviously include documents which would reveal the identity of informers, documents which would involve the workings of the security forces, and the like.

The provisions as to disclosure under the 1996 Act are discussed more fully at **9.6**.

(d) If the material is not served then it may either give rise to the possibility of a successful appeal or, if it comes to light considerably later, may lead to a successful application for judicial review as in the case of *R v Leyland Justices ex parte Hawthorn* [1979] QB 283, where the statement of a witness favourable to the defence was not disclosed, or even as in a case like *R v Bolton Justices ex parte Scally* [1991] 1 QB 537, where through an honest mistake a conviction had been obtained on a potentially unsafe basis without any police impropriety.

(e) If some essential part of the defence case will involve an attack on the prosecution for which the identity of a police informant or details of police procedures, e.g., the location of observation posts, are thought essential, the case law will have to be carefully considered to see whether it may be possible to suggest that the information sought by cross-examination falls into the category of low-level facts as in *R v Brown* above (**21.3.2.2**). Or even that, although the prosecution contend that they ought not to be obliged to disclose the identity of their informant, the informant falls into the category of 'one-off' suppliers of information to escape his own difficulties, as in the case of *R v Agar* above (**21.3.2.2**), rather than being a professional police informant.

(f) Much more rarely in criminal cases it may be contended, on ministerial certificate, that there is some public interest immunity of a more significant kind, that is that evidence prejudicial to the public interest should be withheld. A certificate signed by the minister must deal with all relevant matters setting out the identity and nature of the documentary evidence with sufficient particularity and the grounds of the objection. It will then be for the court to decide, in accordance with the established case law, on which side of the dividing line the relevant document falls.

INDEX